THE VEGETABLE BOOK

COLIN SPENCER

THE VEGETABLE BOOK

PHOTOGRAPHY BY LINDA BURGESS

RIZZOLI
NEW YORK

In memory of Conal Walsh

Throughout the book recipes are for four people unless
otherwise stated.

Project Management: Lewis Esson Publishing
Editors: Lewis Esson and Penny David
American Editor: Norma MacMillan
American Gardening Consultant: Leslie Land
Art Direction: Mary Evans
Design: Meryl Lloyd
Design Assistant: Ian Muggeridge
Picture Researcher: Clare Limpus
Food Styling: Jane Suthering assisted by Emma Patmore
Production: Jill Beed
Typesetting: Ian Muggeridge

First published in the United States of America in 1996 by
Rizzoli International Publications, Inc.
300 Park Avenue South, New York, NY 10010

First published in Great Britain in 1995 by
Conran Octopus Limited
37 Shelton Street, London WC2H 9HN

Text copyright © 1995 Colin Spencer
Photography copyright © 1995 Linda Burgess
Design & Layout copyright © 1995 Conran Octopus

Library of Congress Cataloging-in-Publication Data
Spencer, Colin.
    The vegetable book/Colin Spencer; photography by Linda Burgess.
    p.   cm.
    Includes biographical references and index.
    ISBN 0-8478-1871-X (hc)
    1. Cookery (Vegetables) 2. Vegetables. I. Title.
TX801.S678 1996
641.6'5--dc20   96-6998
                                                        CIP

Printed and bound in Hong Kong

CONTENTS

INTRODUCTION

Over the last fifteen years or so we have learned to value vegetables more highly, not only for their singular flavors but also for their nutritional value as an essential part of a healthy diet. At the same time, more and more new and unexpected vegetables have appeared in the market. Some look and sound bizarre; others look appealing, but both caution and orthodoxy are strong inhibitors to kitchen experiments. So these pages contain old standbys and newer vegetables as well as all those vegetables that one has seen around for years, yet never got around to trying. As our horizons grow ever-further distant, as we hear and see other cultures eating their way enthusiastically through their own cuisines, the challenge to try new foods and recipes is ever-more compulsive. Let us then be adventurous. Do, I implore you, experiment with the strange and unfamiliar, because your mind, palate, and cuisine will all be enriched.

Because of air-freight and the demands of ethnic groups within our societies, the vegetable market now reflects world trade. Upon a display shelf or market stall, one can now travel from Paris to Tokyo, from California to Israel, from Madrid to Sydney. Such a polyglot display can even be off-putting in its richness. What is a yam? In some parts of the U.S., sweet potatoes are called yams, but surely they are different families altogether. The same vegetable is called an "eddo" on one stall and "dasheen" on another. And what on earth is "elephant's ear"? The answers are all in these pages.

You will find here all the vegetables that we now commonly eat and which are regularly sold in our markets. You will also find wild vegetables—like purslane and dandelion—that were once popular but which we now tend to neglect.

LEFT Swiss chard

The vegetables in this book have been grouped broadly into their botanical families, eight of them in all, but with six smaller families grouped under the heading A Miscellany of Vegetables, and a further chapter on Mushrooms and Truffles—making ten chapters in all. To find a particular vegetable, consult the index. If you know its family, you can go straight to the relevant chapter. A short history of each vegetable is given, followed by notes on its nutritional value, some information on the varieties, advice on buying and storage, guidance on its preparation, a summary of its general cooking qualities, and, finally, some particular recipes.

Every vegetable has a history. Some, like taro, are so ancient that no wild variety exists today; others date from just before cultivation began; others are astonishingly recent—the rutabaga or the orange carrot, for example. All have a tale to tell; all have incidents in their lives that reflect on humankind, on what we thought and felt, exposing our vanity and aspirations, our most intimate personal habits and beliefs—as revealing as any archeological remains. Why, for example, should we always think the consumption of garlic and onions is so vulgar? Why have so many vegetables been considered aphrodisiac—especially arugula, the only vegetable the seeds of which were strewn around statues consecrated to Priapus. Did the Ancient World know something we don't? They certainly valued the medicinal qualities of vegetables and herbs in a way that we have almost lost. How interesting, too, to discover so many of their techniques forgotten in the West but still carried on in the East. The Greeks used to wind-dry cabbage leaves, and this practice is still continued in China today. Cabbage was greatly valued for many qualities, not least that it was said to protect against drunkenness.

ABOVE Vegetables on sale in Madeira, Portugal

Our relationship with the plants that we have used for our survival is close and complicated and dates from the earliest beginnings of our evolution.

IN THE BEGINNING

There are few places on the Earth where plant life is impossible—deserts of extreme aridity, mountainous peaks, regions of permanent ice—and these are the same regions where humans can barely exist. Even so, for a short period each year the desert flowers after rainfall and plants race through their life-cycle in that abrupt interval. Humankind, if passing, would harvest what plant food it could gather.

We could not have survived without plants, because, most of all, they sheltered us from the elements. The tropical rain forests, the temperate deciduous forests, the grasslands, all act as blankets of vegetation that soften the impact of wind, of heat, of frost, and of rain. Forest was shelter for humankind:

it was dry, shady, and cool. In colder climes, the forest was warmer—the forest was home. It was also the pantry: so much of what we still eat now was eaten then. Mushrooms we still pick from the wild, but berries also—not just blackberries, but blueberries, wild strawberries, and cranberries. However, I suspect nowadays we would be at a loss to feed ourselves outside the harvest season, because we do not recognize many of our cultivated vegetables in the wild, and we neglect many greatly sustaining wild foods since there is no necessity for us to forage.

In the early spring, foods are limited. There is, however, a range of plants that store their nutrients over the winter for their coming growing season. For example, the onion family, plants of their close cousins the lily family, and the rhizomes of Solomon's Seal (*Polygonatum multiflorum*), which lie near the surface. In antiquity the rhizomes of bracken were dried and ground into a flour. Water plants were also once

ABOVE *The vegetable market in Bali, Indonesia*

a rich source of flour: the tubers of the yellow water-lily (*Nuphar*), arrowhead (*Saggitaria*), and bulrush (*Schoenoplectus*) were the three species of lotus (*Nymphaea*) dried and ground in Ancient Egypt.

In early spring, as soon as the frost fades, the roots of the trees begin to take up water and then the sap starts to flow up the trunks. Sap is rich in sugars from the starch that has been stored over winter, and this is a valuable food source. We are familiar with maple syrup, but other species of trees, such as birches, lime, and aspen, all produce abundant sap.

A week or so later in spring, plants start to send up their shoots. These are all highly nutritious (as we know when we sprout seeds or beans), because they contain the growing energy of the plant. Asparagus is one of the few plants we still eat at this vital stage. However, in the forest many shoots would be blanched naturally beneath the thick covering of leaves on the forest floor. Bellwort, common poke-weed, sea holly, bracken, seminole asparagus, and the asparagus bush are but a few whose growing shoots can be eaten. Also, baby pine cones and buds of trees such as lime are a rich source of protein.

At this time of year deciduous forests contain an important source of food that we know now as slippery elm, a highly nutritious and digestible diet for invalids and people with gastric disorders—the source is cambium. In the spring, the trunks of trees begin to widen, due to a single layer of cells (the cambium) which sheaths the trunk. These young cells are rich in protein and carbohydrates. The exterior bark of the tree would have been cut away and the new moist cambium scraped off. Such removal of living tissue would have certainly reduced the vigor of a tree, if not killed it, if the cambium was scraped away in a ring around the tree. Slippery elm comes from one particular species—*Ulmus rubra*—but poplar, ash, lime, and even pine, as well as elms, could have been used. Until recent times a bark bread was made in Scandinavia from cambium from an elm (*Ulmus glabra*).

In late spring and early summer, all kinds of new green leaves could be eaten—a huge range, when you consider there are 3,000 species of food plants from which humankind could forage. We know that the pounding of roots and leaves occurred before the discovery of fire. We might conjecture, then, that the mucilaginous plants—the leaves of mallow (*Malva*) being but one—would have been useful in holding disparate ingredients together. Certainly the mucilaginous plants (okra is one we still eat) were widely used, just as seaweed was foraged by peoples who lived near river estuaries and the sea.

Particular families of plants have always been favored. The Umbelliferae or parsley family, which includes the wild carrot and parsnip, samphire or salicornia, and fennel, is one. Another member never eaten now, the earthnut or pignut (*Conopodium denudatum*), is a small edible tuber that has never been cultivated but always known to be delicious. In Europe, it can be dug up from June onward. Another family is Polygonaceae, the buckwheat family, the seeds of which are nutritious and have always been eaten by animals and ourselves. Rhubarb and dock were eaten, and sorrel—with its astringent gooseberry flavor—must have delighted early foragers, as well as the fact that it shoots out of the ground so early in spring. There was another favorite in this family—the root and leaves of bistort (*Polygonum bistorta*), used until very recently in England as the main ingredient in dock pudding—though this only uses the leaves. The root was soaked to steep out the tannin, then dried and ground into a flour, but the first young shoots were eaten as well.

Throughout spring and summer, flowerbuds were gathered, especially the largest like the water-lily (*Nymphaea*). Once flowering is over, it is the seeds that become a source of food, as in the vetches and all the grasses. Berries and soft fruits are almost too obvious to mention, but one imagines their sweetness was welcomed because we have no idea how early the gathering of wild honey began.

When winter is threatening, the problem is to find foods that store—nuts are the obvious answer. Hazelnuts, walnuts, sweet chestnuts, pine nuts (*Pinus pinea* and *P. edulis*), butternuts (*Juglans cinerea*), hickories (*Carya*), beechnuts (*Fagus grandifolia*), and acorns—for the oak was the dominant tree of all the temperate forests. Roasting or boiling acorns destroys their bitterness (caused by tannin), so acorns could only appear as a winter staple after the discovery of fire. If the ground was not frozen hard, bulbs and tubers could be dug up. There is also evidence of winter storage of seeds and the drying of fruits, currants, and wild strawberries. The fungi were also of immense value at this time, especially the large ones like *Fistulina hepatica*, a massive bracket fungus that grows on trees. And we must not forget lichens, such as the reindeer moss (*Cladonia rangiferina*) which is one of the staple foods of reindeer and caribou. There are also algae growing over ponds and lakes; the Aztecs gathered blue-green algae (*Cyanophyta*), dried it, and made it into cakes that stored well.

It has to be said, however, that gathering and foraging are haphazard. There is an enormous element of luck involved, and food sources can so easily be wiped out by floods, frosts, and earthquakes, or by herds of grazing animals. How much better it would be for humankind if they could control the food they searched for, if it could be grown near their shelter. The impulse to settle and garden must have been there among small clans and individuals worldwide, long before domestication actually began.

The other fascinating aspect of the early gatherers is how much experimentation was needed, for so many of the food families have toxic parts or members. Take the Solanaceae or potato family: how many people died from the berries of deadly nightshade? How many found out that tomato leaves and stems, potato leaves, and the green patches on the potatoes themselves are poisonous? What of cassava, a staple food over much of the tropical world? How did people find it was edible once the cyanide had been washed out? The older members of any small group must have been greatly valued, for it was they, with their experience, who could memorize the edible parts of a plant, where it was likely to grow, and at what time of year. The botanical knowledge must have been vast, passed on to each new generation: the plants that heal, the plants that refresh as drinks when steeped in water, as well as the plants that were eaten. This knowledge could not be written down; language itself must then have first come about to describe the food that lay in and around the earth, its characteristics, and how it was to be eaten.

This is a very crude summary of the potential food store in wild plants, which humankind needed to survive. It is crude because I have purposely omitted dates and places. I merely wanted to suggest to the general reader how the cultivated plants eaten now have their distant roots in the past, and that, nutritionally, humankind might even have had a better diet then than we have today. Out of those 3,000 species of plants eaten for food, only 150 of them were ever cultivated, and today the world lives off just 20 main crops. Most importantly, I want to stress how several million years of living from plants and then crustaceans and plants—long before hunting began—has a possible significant message for our present-day metabolism. Humankind has relied on wild foods for 99.8% of our time, and through these millions of years human physiology has adapted to such foods. According to *The Driving Force—Food in Evolution* by Michael Crawford and David Marsh: "There is a diet to which humans are adapted; this diet includes regular exposure to substances on which human metabolism is dependent, only some of which to date have been labeled as 'essential nutrients.'"

According to a scientific paper, "Vegetables, Fruit and Cancer" by Kristi A. Steinmetz and John D. Potter (*Cancer Causes and Control, Vol. 2* 1991): "Vegetables and fruits contain the anti-carcinogenic cocktail to which we are adapted. We abandon it at our peril."

I believe strongly that vegetables, grown organically, are vital to our health and spiritual well-being. Of course, they can be in a mixed diet of fish and meat, but the latter in my view should be an occasional garnish or flavoring.

ON NUTRITION

Understanding the chemical nature of our food is a very recent science. It began in the eighteenth and nineteenth centuries, when chemists isolated the main food components and divided them into carbohydrates, proteins, and fats. The food components that occur in very small amounts took longer to analyze— the vitamins, pigments, and flavor compounds required twentieth-century laboratory techniques before they could be isolated and characterized.

However, the greater our knowledge the greater it also clarifies how little we know. In fact, the newest research is inclined to give to the micro-nutrients— the trace minerals—and the way in which they interact with each other in a mysterious cocktail, more possible power in our metabolism than had ever seemed possible before.

So, though each of the entries in this book has some nutritional information, this cannot be absolute in any way. For example, tests on various apples for their vitamin C content found that it ranged from 3.1 mg per 100 g to 31.8 mg. This kind of range must be true of all the vegetables included in this book. Such a range cannot be otherwise, because plants are living entities as different in themselves as we are individuals. Consider, the nutrition of each fruit and vegetable is influenced by the soil and any fertilization it gets in its growth, and these factors are a moveable feast. The nutritional facts given herein, then, are merely rough guides. For greater detail and an attempt at precision by taking the mean from a range of samples, consult *Bowes and Church's Food Values of Portions Commonly Used* (16th edition, 1994) by Jean A. Pennington, published by J. B. Lippincott.

The World Health Organization Committee wrote in the *W.H.O. Report on Diet and Chronic Diseases* (1990): "Vegetables and fruits are low in energy, but high in fiber, vitamins and minerals. They play a protective role in preventing the development of cancers." It is believed that vitamins C, E, and beta-carotene are those that are involved in attacking and destroying the free radicals responsible for cancer. We should aim to eat at least 400 grams (about 14 ounces) of fresh fruit and vegetables every day— the equivalent of 4 apples. I try to eat a large mixed salad each day—simple in the summer when there is so much to choose from and such a variety of green leaves (remember that the darker the leaf, the more vitamins it contains). But winter salads of raw grated vegetables can be just as good.

Alliaceae

THE

ONION

FAMILY

ONION *Allium cepa*
GARLIC *Allium sativum*
LEEK *Allium ampeloprasum* var. *porrum*
SHALLOT *Allium cepa* var. *aggregatum*
CHIVE *Allium schoenoprasum*
WELSH ONION *Allium fistulosum*
ROCAMBOLE *Allium scorodoprasum*
CHINESE or GARLIC CHIVE *Allium tuberosum*

Liliaceae

ASPARAGUS *Asparagus officinalis*

Until quite recently the onion and its close relatives were classified as members of the Liliaceae family (the lilies), rather than constituting a family of their own. They are also considered by many to form a subdivision of the Amaryllidaceae (which comprises the amaryllis, the narcissus, and the snowdrop).

The onion family itself has about 325 members, most of which seemed to originate in Asia, but seventy of which are indigenous to the Americas. Some varieties of onion grow wild, like the wild garlic (Allium vineale) or ramps (A. tricoccum), while many others are cultivated as vegetables.

Except in the case of the leek and chive, it is generally the bulbs that are eaten. Some, like chives and Chinese chives, are popular as herbs and have been

15

used as such for centuries. Extraordinarily enough, leek and garlic are cultivars not found in the wild, which shows how very ancient their culinary use is.

For our purposes we also include in this chapter the one member of the Liliaceae family cultivated as a vegetable—the asparagus.

ONION

Allium cepa

The onion and all its nearest relatives recede far back into prehistory. As well as other roots, like the wild turnip and radish, the wild onion must have been eaten with pleasure by man throughout his evolution, even if—before the advent of fire—chewing through uncooked fibrous matter must have been at times unrewarding. All the more exciting, then, to find a root that did not need a great deal of mastication and that enflamed the mouth, thereby stimulating the gastric juices, and which was also full of its own juice. Once the first grains were cultivated, the onion also grew well in the semi-humid climate found along the banks of irrigation canals.

Though its native country is unknown (it grows in all temperate zones), the onion is thought to be indigenous to the Middle East—the cradle of civilization. It is mentioned in the Bible (*Numbers* 11:5) as one of the foods the Israelites longed for in the wilderness. Certainly it was common fare in Egypt: the Greek historian Herodotus, writing in the fifth century BC, says that an inscription on the Great Pyramid stated that 1,600 talents had been expended on onions, radishes, and garlic, which had been consumed by the laborers when building it.

Carvings of onions appear on the inner walls of the pyramids of Unas (c.2423 BC) and Pepill (c.2200 BC) in tombs of both the Old and New Kingdoms. Wooden models of onions have been found in tombs, as has evidence of the practice of placing onion bulbs in the bandages of mummies—in their armpits, eye sockets, and body cavities—in an attempt, it is thought, to stimulate the dead to breathe again. The onion was also used as a means of assessing female fertility: it was introduced into the vagina and if the smell could be perceived next day in the mouth of the female it meant she was fertile; if not, the woman was sterile.

Some Egyptian priests refused to eat onions and garlic. This could be because they were thought to incite lust, a conviction that was to continue for some time, well into the Middle Ages. Another reason given was that the onion was the only plant to thrive throughout the waning of the moon. Though the taboo existed about consuming onions, they were not excluded from the sacred altars—paintings frequently show priests holding them or depict an altar covered in the plants.

A proverb emphasized another aspect of the onion of which priests might have been wary: "If your mother is an onion and your father garlic, how could your smell be sweet, poor chap?"

Bread and onions were certainly the basic diet not only of Egypt but also of Mesopotamia. As now, onions were preserved throughout the winter by being dried, then braided into strings, which is how they were sold then and up to fairly recent times.

An ancient myth of the Turks places onion and garlic at beginning of time, when the devil was sent out of Paradise and first set foot on Earth. On the spot where he placed his right foot there grew the onion and in the place of the left grew garlic. It is interesting to note the implication that both these strong-tasting bulbs—fiery and intense in their raw state—had a certain diabolism for the peoples of the eastern Mediterranean.

Onions were also popular in Ancient Greece: the physician and "father of medicine," Hippocrates, mentions in 430 BC that onions were commonly eaten, other important vegetables being garlic, cabbage, peas, and lentils. Theophrastus (370 BC), the philosopher and pupil of Aristotle, lists a number of varieties of onions and garlic in his botanical works.

All the varieties with which we are now familiar existed in classical times. The Roman writer Pliny (AD 79) claims that the round onion is the best, but that red onions are more highly flavored than white. Palladius (AD 210) gives detailed directions for the culture of the onion. In Roman cooking, if we take the work of celebrated gourmet Apicius (AD 230) as an example, the onion was used to season dishes rather than as an ingredient. In his celebrated recipe book, *De re coquinaria*, there are thirty-three recipes in which the onion is used as a flavoring and only two dishes in which it is used for itself: a purée of lettuce with onion and roasted meat served with onions. The Romans much preferred leeks. This, however, is a class difference: the poor began the day with bread and raw onion, and this is very likely why Apicius does not include the onion as a vegetable itself (except for the two recipes mentioned above), because to do so would be to add a common, even vulgar, note to meals for the ruling élite.

However, Roman distaste had some allies in the East—much of India refused to eat either onions or garlic. The higher castes, the Brahmins, refused on the grounds perhaps that onions represented common food, or that as they were allied with the cooking of meat they were somehow tainted. There is still suspicion about the use of onion in cooking; it still has class connotations, and the raw onion is not eaten in polite society.

After the upper-class Roman aversion for the onion, it was the barbarians who brought the onion back into mainstream cooking, as they added it liberally to their roasting meats. Charlemagne ordered onions to be planted, and in centuries to come they frequently appeared in feudal tithes as one of the crops to be paid to the landowner.

Onions were indispensable in medieval cooking and were used in soups, broths, and stews because, at this time, strong, aromatic, pungent flavoring was preferred. Onions cooked for a length of time with ginger, caraway, mustard, cardamom, and coriander were favorite flavor combinations. They continued to be popular throughout the Renaissance, but the onions were diffused by cooking, their strong flavors part of the context of many a meat dish in unison with other herbs, spices, and flavorings.

Much that modern research has shown to be efficacious about the onion was somehow learned and absorbed by the ancient world, and folklore became full of the health-giving properties of both onion and garlic. In *The Four Seasons of the House of Cerruti*, a fourteenth-century Latin manuscript that is based on the wisdom of the medieval alchemists, the onion is praised as follows:

"An excellent thing, the onion, and highly suitable for old people and those with cold temperaments, owing to its nature, which is hot in the highest degree, sometimes moist, and sometimes dry. The most desirable of the many varieties are the white ones, being rich in watery juices. They generate milk in nursing mothers and fertile semen in men. They improve the eyesight, are softening, and stimulate the bladder. Headaches, which are sometimes caused by onions, can be cured with vinegar and milk. Those suffering from coughs, asthma and constrictions in the chest should eat boiled onions, or onions baked under the embers, served with sugar and a little fresh butter."

Though the Old World's onion varieties were introduced into the Americas, the inhabitants there had their own indigenous onion types. Wild leeks have always grown in the woods of the Northeast, and the Native Americans liked wild garlic and chives. Bernal Díaz, the writer who accompanied the conquistador Cortés in Mexico, remarked that the Indian arrow shafts smelled strongly of garlic. In 1674, Father Marquette, the Jesuit explorer, told of being saved from starvation by eating the American native varieties (tree onions and nodding onions) on the southern shores of Lake Michigan. Marquette camped on what was to be the site of Chicago, which in a Native American language means the odor of onions. Oddly enough, though, the varieties later grown for cultivation in North America were all brought over from Europe.

GROWING AND VARIETIES

There are more than 450 different varieties of *Allium cepa* available from seed companies. Though colors, shapes, and pungencies vary, the most important divisions are between storage onions such as Southport Yellow Globe and those for fresh use such as Walla Walla, and between the long-day and short-day varieties. (Choose the type that is right for your area: short in the South, long in the North. Growers in the temperate middle can plant long-day varieties in

---

ONION *Allium cepa*

February for late spring harvest, or short-day varieties for growth in summer and fall.)

The cheapest way to grow your own onions is to sow seed. It will germinate in two to three weeks. Once transplanted, onions will take varying times to mature, according to variety and when planted. If you live in cold climes, you need to germinate the seed in a greenhouse.

Onion seeds are vulnerable to pests, particularly the onion fly, hence the popularity of onion sets. In addition, sets are guaranteed to be virus-free, and are heat-treated so that they should not bolt. Onion or shallot sets are just the immature bulbs; once planted, they will take about twenty weeks to mature.

PICKLING ONIONS: White onions are preferred for pickling as they tend to be the most reliably solid and dense. After the harvest of white onions is graded for size, the smallest are sold to commercial picklers, who do not generally insist on any particular variety. Home picklers can be just as broad-minded, though White Pearl and White Portugal are two varieties that are particularly recommended.

RED ONIONS: These are now readily available in markets. Most are quite pungent, while some are milder and sweeter in taste and can be used raw in salads or added to the marinating liquor for a *ceviche*. There are many red varieties that you can grow: Red Torpedo is the torpedo-shaped red onion from Italy; Purplette are small onions that are good to use raw as they are so decorative—if pickled they turn pink; Rouge de Florence is from France; Burgundy, Red Bermuda, and Red Hamburger are all sweet "salad-type" onions.

SPANISH AND BERMUDA ONIONS: These are large varieties of yellow, white, or red onion, about the size of a grapefruit, that are generally globe-shaped, sweet, and mild. The white variety of Spanish onion has a flatter top and base than the original Spanish, but there is no difference in the flavor. Spanish and Bermuda onions used to be more popular than they are now—cookbooks of forty years ago abound in recipes for stuffing and baking them.

SCALLIONS OR GREEN ONIONS: On the whole these are not separate plants: they are merely young *Allium*

RIGHT Red and yellow onions

cepa grown from seed and harvested while the green shoots are sturdy and before they die off. There are now, however, several varieties that are grown specifically as salad "spring onions" or scallions (named after the ancient Palestine port of Ascalon). Most are white-skinned, and can be either highly pungent and peppery or mild. White Lisbon is the most popular of the varieties, but Ishikura, which has long, straight stems and never forms bulbs, is also becoming readily available. All scallions contain traces of protein, carbohydrate, fiber, and very little fat, and are excellent raw or briefly stir-fried.

WHITE ONIONS: These are available all year round, although they are not as common as yellow onions. They come in all shapes and sizes: round, oval, large, and small. Their flavors can vary from mild to strong, and there is no certain way of telling which will be which, except by trial and error.

YELLOW ONIONS: Old-fashioned, long-keeping Stuttgarter is widely available as sets. Ailsa Craig must be grown from seed, but is a popular choice for those who want huge, comparatively mild-flavored onions. The various Grano and Granex types produce very sweet onions that are quite large; however, these do not keep well.

SWEET ONIONS: Much sweeter than Spanish or Bermuda onions, these are Maui onions from Hawaii, Vidalia onions from Georgia, and Walla Walla onions from Washington state. All are very juicy, and excellent both raw and cooked.

NUTRITION AND MEDICINAL

Both onion and garlic are packed with therapeutic compounds. The onion contains vitamins B, C, and E, carotene, calcium, iron, phosphorous, potassium, sodium, sulfur, and traces of copper. Both onion and garlic also contain a natural antiseptic oil, allyl disulphate, and cycloallin. The latter is an anti-coagulant that helps to dissolve clots that form on the walls of blood vessels, hence onions and garlic do reduce the risk of heart disease. The really good news is that cooking—by boiling, frying, or roasting—does not destroy these therapeutic properties. What is more, very little onion (only 10 grams—about a tablespoon) eaten per day will lower blood cholesterol.

CHOOSING AND STORING

Buy onions that are hard and firm with no sign of green shoots. Buy them in strings, if you can, and hang them up somewhere dry and cool. Onions are intended to keep throughout the winter, and perhaps because we know this we tend to forget about them, finding them months later sprouted and shriveled. So try to keep onions where you will notice them every day, and test for freshness by pinching them. If there is any sign of softness, use them up as soon as possible. The golden skins are an excellent coloring for stocks and hard-boiled eggs.

PREPARING

Once an onion is cut it releases a volatile substance (a sulfur compound) that makes the eyes water and then in turn produces sulfuric acid in the tears. No wonder it stings. These odor compounds are quickly driven off by cooking, and some of them become converted to another complex molecule that can be 50–70 times sweeter than sugar. The reason for the onion having so much juice is that the many layers are all leaf bases that surround very small shoots. These store water and starch during the bulb's first year of growth, for use during the second.

The best way to prepare an onion is as follows: first slice off the top and base. The colored outer skin should then flake away readily with a little help from the knife or fingernail. As it is frequently dry or damaged, the layer beneath the skin often also needs to be removed. Occasionally you want the onion to be sliced fan-shaped but still held together by the basal stem (this can look good in dishes in which the onions are not cooked too long). To achieve this effect, cut the onions lengthwise, stopping short of the base. Otherwise, gouge out the basal core of the onion, slice the onion in half through the core, and place each half cut-side down. Holding it firmly with the fingertips of one hand, slice it across thinly for crescent parings as used raw in salads: for minced onion, slice again lengthwise.

If shedding tears while preparing onions bothers you, try wearing goggles or cutting under water. The former is a good measure if preparing onions for pickling, which can take a long time.

ABOVE The author's favorite version of onion tart, made with uncooked onions (see overleaf)

COOKING

One of the easiest methods of cooking onions is merely to throw them into a baking pan, unpeeled, and let them roast in a preheated 375°F oven for about 1½ hours (the size will dictate the exact length of time). Then take the outside skin off: the inside will be moist, sweet, and cooked through. If barbecuing, do the same: cook them unpeeled, wrapped in foil, on the coals. As the duration of time will be shorter when the fire is hot, choose small onions so that they are thoroughly cooked.

The eighteenth-century English food writer Hannah Glasse gives many recipes using onions, including one for ONION PIE. In this, onions, potatoes, apples, and eggs are all layered, with bits of butter and seasoning strewn between them, six spoonfuls of water are added, then a crust is placed over the top, and it is baked for 1½ hours. It is not clear whether the eggs are just beaten or have been hard-boiled, but I suspect the latter as she suggests adding 12 eggs to 1 pound each of onions, apples, and potatoes. She adds mace, nutmeg, salt, and pepper as her seasonings. I have made a pie inspired by this recipe that omits the eggs and changes the seasoning to sage, marjoram, and parsley. It is a good autumn or winter pie and makes an excellent supper or luncheon dish with a green salad. Apple, onion, and potato are highly satisfactory together.

One of the great classic dishes is ONION TART—*tarte à l'oignon*—which is a famous Alsatian dish. I confess I have eaten disastrous versions of it, where the onion has merged into a thick egg custard and tinged it all with an unbearable sweetness. I have also made tarts that have been unmitigated failures. I do not want my tart filling to be either bland or sweet, nor do I particularly want it to be rich in butter, egg yolk, and cream, though the tart might benefit with just one of those ingredients.

ONION *Allium cepa*

Here, then, are some recipes that strive toward keeping the onions' fieriness. Make sure the pastry base is thin—a basic pie pastry rich in butter is the best, though a puff (if rolled very thin and if made with butter) could easily be substituted. A pastry made with half wholewheat flour blends well with the onion flavor. For an 11-inch tart pan with a depth of ½ inch you will need just over 1 pound of onions (i.e., about 4 or 5 medium-sized onions), sliced across (thickly or thinly, it hardly matters). Sauté the onions very gently in 6 tablespoons of butter in a covered pan for about 30–40 minutes. Raise the heat and take the lid away, to let any liquid evaporate and to caramelize the onions slightly—this takes about 2–3 minutes. Then let the onions cool while lining the pan with the pastry. Preheat the oven to 425°F.

VARIATIONS

• If you want the classic onion tart, you now mix in 2 egg yolks and 2 tablespoons of heavy cream, a pinch each of salt and nutmeg, and plenty of black pepper. Then the tart is baked for 20 minutes.

• If you want to taste more onion in your tart, omit the yolks and cream, and simply spread the onion mixture over the bottom of the pastry shell. Bake for 15 minutes until the pastry is cooked through and the onion has caramelized more.

• A sharper, denser flavor can be achieved by adding 2 tablespoons of soy sauce to the onion mixture before raising the heat. Then, when the liquid has evaporated, add a tablespoon of flour to thicken the onions. Season with salt and pepper, then spread this in the pastry shell and sprinkle ½ cup of grated Gruyère and ¼ cup of grated Parmesan cheese over the top. Bake for 20 minutes.

• Before cooking, add 1 seeded and chopped hot red chili to the sliced onions. Then, before raising the heat, stir a tablespoon of sweet paprika into the mixture. Season with salt and pepper, then spread this in the pastry shell and bake for 20 minutes.

• To make my favorite onion tart, slice a little less onion (3 onions rather than 4) and don't cook them; toss them in a bowl with a tablespoon of good Dijon mustard and 1½ tablespoons of very good olive oil, plus salt and freshly ground black pepper. Pile these sliced onions in the uncooked pastry shell and bake for about 15 minutes, or until about one-third of the sliced onion has browned slightly. You should get not only the crunch of the almost raw onion, but also some onions that have softened in their own steam and some that have caramelized.

This recipe does not need a pie shell for its pastry base, as there is no custard or sauce for the sides to hold in. So a flat, round pastry base, like a pizza, spread on a baking sheet—with the onions piled up on it—is perfectly satisfactory.

FRENCH ONION SOUP is another classic dish that, when cooked perfectly, justifies its standing as one of the great soups of the world. Like the onions for the tart, when cooked in the classic manner they need long, slow, gentle cooking so that they caramelize. In my opinion, the best recipe for onion soup, *gratinée lyonnaise*, appears in *French Regional Cooking* by Anne Willan. In her recipe, the soup is enriched with egg yolks and port.

There are many other versions of French onion soup, for example *tourin* (sometimes *tourain*, *thourin*, or *tourrin*) of the Périgord and Bordeaux areas. This is made with goose fat, garlic, onions, egg yolks, bread, and red wine. In Quercy, they sometimes add some preserved goose or shredded kohlrabi.

The soup below is an adaptation of a recipe from *The Lady's Companion*, 1753, a cookbook that Martha Washington owned. How the recipe came to be called The King's Soup is a mystery, for onions do not figure large in royal kitchens.

THE KING'S SOUP

4 tablespoons butter
½ teaspoon ground mace
1 pound onions, thinly sliced
1½ teaspoons sea salt
5 cups milk
(use soy milk if concerned about fat intake)
2 egg yolks
a handful of chopped parsley
croûtons, for serving (optional)

Melt the butter in a large saucepan. Throw in the mace, onions, and salt. Let the onions sweat, stirring occasionally, for a few minutes.

Pour in the milk, bring to a simmer, and let cook over a low heat for 30–40 minutes.

Pour a little soup into a bowl, add the egg yolks, and mix thoroughly. Then pour the egg mixture back into the soup. Stir until slightly thickened.

Add the parsley and serve with croûtons, if using.

FRIED ONIONS

These are an unexpected treat as long as they are floured before frying. Slice the onions in fairly thick rings, then put the rings into a plastic bag with a little flour and shake it well. Fry in a light oil, like sunflower, until they are golden and crisp. Dust lightly with paprika before serving.

ONION AND CHILI SALAD

1 teaspoon garam masala
juice of 1 lemon
⅔ cup plain yogurt
sea salt
3 large onions, sliced
1 English cucumber, chopped small
1 hot red chili, seeded and minced
1 green bell pepper, seeded and minced

Mix the garam masala, lemon juice, and yogurt together with some salt. Place all the vegetables in a bowl, pour the yogurt mixture over, and toss well.

Leave for about 20 minutes and then serve.

MOROCCAN ONIONS

3 tablespoons olive oil
3 large onions, sliced
salt and freshly ground black pepper
2 tablespoons tomato paste
3 tablespoons mixed golden and dark raisins

Heat the olive oil in a heavy-based pan. Throw in the onions, sprinkle a little salt over them, and let them cook over a low heat, stirring occasionally. When they are softened, add the tomato paste and the dried fruit. Continue to cook gently, but stirring so that it does not burn. Cook for 5 minutes longer, then adjust the seasoning. Serve hot or cold.

GRATIN OF ONION AND POTATO

2 tablespoons butter
1 pound potatoes, thinly sliced
1 pound onions, thinly sliced
sea salt and freshly ground black pepper
½ cup grated Gruyère cheese
½ cup grated Parmesan cheese

Preheat the oven to 350°F. Grease a shallow baking dish lightly with a little of the butter.

Arrange layers of sliced potato and onions in the dish, dotting each layer with a little butter, some seasoning, and a sprinkle of a tiny amount of each cheese. Finish with a thicker layer of the mixed cheeses.

Bake for 40–60 minutes, until the top is bubbly and golden.

ONION-POTATO PURÉE

This is a way of serving mashed potatoes that is unexpectedly good. The onion is left raw and added, chopped small, to the potato purée after milk and butter have been mixed in. The crunch of the onion adds a wonderful texture as well as flavor. This dish is excellent as an accompaniment to game, and if there is any left over it can be made into potato cakes, dusted with bread crumbs, and fried in oil.

GARLIC

Allium sativum

This powerful little bulb is one of the most ancient of flavorings. It was one of the staple foods of the poor, the majority of the world's population, for it comprised the basic relish to be eaten with bread. Literary references to garlic in the ancient world are legion. Its beginnings in prehistory are thought to be in the area of the plains of western Tartary, and from there it was transported over the whole of Asia (except Japan), North Africa, and Europe.

The Egyptian garlic that helped sustain the laborers as they built the Great Pyramid had rather small cloves (around 45 to a head) and was of a light purplish hue, a color we can still grow. Some garlic heads have been found in tombs; clay models of garlic bulbs have also been found in Pre-dynastic burials at Naqada (3200 BC). In the *Ebers Codex*, a medical work compiled around 1550 BC, there are over 800 therapeutic formulae, and 22 of them mention garlic for various ailments, from headaches to childbirth.

Theophrastus praises Cypriot garlic to be used as a dressing for salads; he directs you to pound the garlic well because "it increases wondrously in bulk making a foaming dressing." Garlic also had magical properties for the Greeks, and was taken before battle to make warriors strong. Garlic heads were placed on piles of stones at crossroads as a supper for Hecate, the goddess of enchantment and spells. Indeed, from antiquity garlic gathered its reputation to ward off evil. Greek midwives crushed the cloves in the room in which the child would be born, and a garlic clove might well be fastened about the baby's neck.

Hippocrates (460 BC) praised the therapeutic qualities of garlic—good for wounds and toothache among many other ailments—as did Aristotle, a hundred years later. Dioscorides (AD 40) was a Greek physician who traveled as a surgeon with the Roman armies, which gave him the opportunity to study the distribution and qualities of a host of plants. He noted the effects of sleeping potions made from opium and mandragora, which is used for surgical anesthetics. His observations on garlic are particularly acute: after noticing the various types—the white, the purple, and the wild (a type that has escaped from cultivation)—he goes on to write about its efficacy: "it eliminates tapeworm, with wine it is good against snake bite, soothes coughing, clears the arteries, heals eczema and much else." He concludes by adding that a purée of crushed garlic and black olives is a diuretic.

As with onions, garlic was disapproved of by the élite of both Greece and Rome. It was common people who ate it and, therefore, smelled of it. In fact, it is surprising that those parts of the world that were still not conquered by Rome could not smell the advance of the Roman legions, who ate great quantities of garlic. Not only was garlic thought to be an aphrodisiac, but along with the Greeks the Romans believed it made men strong and powerful. Pliny includes sixty-one garlic remedies in his *Natural History*; as an aphrodisiac it should be "crushed and beaten up with fresh coriander and taken in pure wine."

But what of garlic in cooking? French gastronome Marcel Boulestin placed his finger on the pulse when he declared: "It is not an exaggeration to say that peace and happiness begin, geographically, where garlic is used in cooking." Where would the cuisines of France, Italy, Spain, Greece, the Middle East, the Slavic and Balkan countries, and much of the Orient be without it? Surely it is the most powerful ingredient in the history of cooking, used as we have seen from earliest times. The Chinese text *Shih Chins*, or *The Book of Songs* (600 BC), describes the life of the warrior farmers on the northwestern highlands of the Shensi province. At a spring initiation rite, held after the fields had been plowed, they sacrifice a lamb seasoned with garlic and comment, "What smell is this, so strong and good?" Garlic is mentioned in a verse of Ibn al-Mitazz, the tenth-century Caliph and poet: "Here pungent garlic meets the eager sight / And whets with savor sharp the appetite..."

The garlic sauce, forms of *aïoli*, whether emulsified with egg and oil or not, and garlic soup exist in all countries and cultures.

NUTRITION AND MEDICINAL

Garlic contains calcium, phosphorus, iron, and potassium, plus thiamine, riboflavin, niacin, and vitamin C.

Its two volatile oils, allin and allinase, are separate inside the bulb, but once cut and crushed the two mix and become allicin; this is the sulfur compound of the pungent odor we know so well. It is also a powerful antibiotic: seventy-two separate infection agents can be deterred by garlic. Cooking will destroy this antibacterial agent, though it leaves untouched other therapeutic qualities (see page 20).

Since 1983, over 130 scientific papers have been published giving evidence of garlic's powers to retard heart disease, strokes, cancers, and a wide range of infections. It lowers blood cholesterol levels astonishingly quickly and increases the assimilation of vitamins. Blood tests have revealed that the most ardent garlic eaters display the least clot factor, an important element in helping to prevent heart disease.

Raw garlic kills bacteria, boosts immune functioning, and probably helps to prevent cancer. One or two cloves a day is all you need. I take mine in the vinaigrette dressing with the daily salad: nothing is more delicious or more trouble-free. I gladly confess to enjoying raw garlic in sandwiches, too, seasoning combinations such as avocado and lettuce or tomato and mozzarella with very thin slices of garlic.

Cooked garlic can lower blood cholesterol, helps keep blood thin, acts as a decongestant and cough medicine, and helps prevent bronchitis. Lastly, there is no evidence to suggest that the garlic preparations sold by healthfood stores are in any way equal to the real thing, so stick to the daily use of garlic in your cooking. For the last thirty years I must have consumed about three or four heads a week.

GROWING, CHOOSING, AND STORING

Garlic can be tricky to grow. It needs lots of fertilizer, must be thinned and weeded, and rots in wet climates. But it is well worth a try. The individual cloves have to be sown about 6 inches apart at the end of October or in November. They will sprout quite soon and stay throughout the winter, through snow and frost. By March, you will have healthy young garlic, and you can use the green tops in a host of dishes. In Spain and southern France, you will find sheaves of young garlic in the market at this time. The main crop is ready in June or July.

Whenever possible try to use fresh garlic. Although the outside may look dried, the cloves will feel hard and be full of juice. Freshly harvested garlic has an excellent fiery flavor. Some of the insides of the green stem can be used, too.

How you buy your garlic depends on how frequently you use it. I can have strings of garlic hanging in the kitchen because they are not there long enough ever to dry out. If you use garlic modestly, buy a few heads and keep them in the salad drawer in the refrigerator or somewhere cool and dark.

Feel heads before purchase: if soft, they are old. Never buy heads that have started to sprout. Buy only those that are firm and fresh-colored or white; if a little dingy, they have been around too long.

PREPARING

The easiest method for taking the outside papery skin off garlic cloves is to blanch them, as one does tomatoes, in a little boiling water. The skin then slips off easily. Or, if you crush garlic cloves with the help of the flat of a knife blade and the weight of your hand, you can extract the papery covering.

Cookbooks used always to tell you to crush garlic with a little salt. How did this direction come about? It is quite unnecessary—all salt does is to activate moisture so the garlic will ooze its own juices more readily. If this happens on a chopping board it can be a nuisance. It was American food writer Richard Olney who taught his students never to use a garlic press because it alters the flavor. I have never noticed this to be true and use one all the time.

Do not worry about garlic that is shooting. Use what you can and—if you do not mind a great intensity of garlic flavor—use the chopped green shoots in a salad. There is a myth that shooting garlic tastes bitter. In fact, it merely tastes powerfully garlicky.

COOKING

If you want to roast garlic, you can simply throw some cloves in a baking dish with a little oil and leave them to cook for 30 minutes in an oven preheated to 375°F. Eat the soft, melting interior by cutting into the clove with a knife. There is an excellent recipe by Richard Olney in which you cook new potatoes with

ABOVE Garlic hanging to dry

olive oil and plenty of unpeeled garlic in a covered pan over a low flame for 40–45 minutes. The garlic is partly fried, partly steamed, and once released by your knife and fork from its papery wrapping, it makes the most delicious purée for the new potatoes.

If you are as passionate about garlic as I am, then you will not mind peeling 40–50 cloves to be baked beneath a pheasant. I have quite happily peeled 200 cloves for garlic soup, and I do believe that the more garlic you use in a dish the less pungent it ends up being. Cooked garlic in soup, for example, has a quite different flavor; it is both sweet and savory, has a depth of pungency that is immensely satisfying, and is warming to the spirit in the long winter months.

A splendid *GARLIC BUTTER* for toast as an appetizer or as a sauce for pasta can be made quite quickly by adding 10 or 12 peeled cloves to a little boiling salted water and letting them simmer for 5 minutes until soft. Then drain and mash the garlic with 6–8 tablespoons of butter and use for spreading. An alternative

is to use olive oil instead of butter and to blend the oil with the cooked garlic, adding one anchovy fillet. Again, you will find that a garlic sauce made from poached garlic has a deeper and more fulfilling flavor than the more fiery variety made with raw garlic.

A similar *GARLIC SAUCE* can be made using, say, 20 peeled garlic cloves and poaching them in 2½ cups of milk for 10 minutes, or until they are soft. Blend the milk and garlic to a smooth consistency and add 2 egg yolks to thicken the sauce. This is excellent with roast goose stuffed with apple and potato.

I am unrepentant in my love of garlic—the smell I inhale like perfume, the aroma on others' breath is a sign of life and its celebration. What angers me are directions for merely rubbing a garlic clove around a salad bowl—as if you are going to eat the utensil—and the snobbery that still links garlic odors with impolite society. In our age of deodorants and perfumes we tend to fly away from our own reality, and this limits our awareness of the true nature of life.

GARLIC *Allium sativum*

EGGPLANT WITH PARSLEY AND GARLIC

for 6

This appeared in Elizabeth David's *French Provincial Cooking*. On rereading this classic book, which helped to revolutionize British cooking, it is astonishing to see how little garlic Mrs. David used or recommended. I have thus changed the amounts.

2 large eggplants
olive oil
7 or 8 garlic cloves, chopped
a handful of parsley, chopped
1 lemon
sea salt and freshly ground black pepper

Slice the eggplants thinly across in rounds. Place in a colander and sprinkle with salt. Let drain for an hour so that they lose some of their juice. Rinse under a tap, otherwise they will be too salty, and pat dry.

Heat the olive oil in a pan and fry the eggplant slices. Take your time (Elizabeth David says, "fry them slowly"); they should be golden brown and soft. When done, keep warm, and quickly fry the garlic.

At the last moment, add the parsley and whisk it around the pan. Pour this over the eggplant, then squeeze lemon juice over everything and season.

GARLIC SOUP

for 6

There are many variations, all of which are amazingly delicious. This is the simple version to begin with. What gives the soup its velvety texture is the emulsion of the puréed garlic in the olive oil. The flavor will not be much altered by the actual amount of garlic used, but the texture will. Hence, the more garlic, the smoother and thicker the velvet.

3–4 tablespoons olive oil
3 heads of garlic, their cloves peeled
a pinch of saffron strands
7½ cups vegetable stock
(use 2 good-quality bouillon cubes)
sea salt and freshly ground black pepper
3–4 tablespoons minced parsley or chives

Heat the olive oil in a saucepan. Throw in the garlic and saffron. Lower the heat, put a lid on the pan, and let the garlic sweat for 3–4 minutes.

Pour in the stock, bring to a boil, and simmer for 15 minutes. Let cool, then blend to a thin purée.

Reheat, adjust the seasoning, and add the parsley or chives before serving.

VARIATIONS
• Add 2 egg yolks (as described for The King's Soup, page 22) to thicken and enrich the soup.
• Add garlic croûtons on serving.
• Add 1 cup ground almonds with the stock.
• Add 1 cup mashed potato before blending.
• Add several softened bread crusts before blending.

SKORDALIA

There are almost as many versions of this garlic sauce or appetizer as there are Greek islands, because almost every island has its own method of making it. The basic ingredient after the garlic can be potato, almonds, walnuts, or bread; or you can have a mixture of garlic, nuts, and bread. It is eaten with fish or on its own as a mezze or part of a first course.

Greek restaurants here often feature it, but I have never tasted a good one. So it is worth making.

1 head of garlic, cloves peeled
3 or 4 thick slices of wholewheat bread,
soaked in water then well squeezed
juice from 1 lemon
⅔ cup ground almonds
sea salt and freshly ground black pepper
¼ cup olive oil

Place the garlic cloves in a blender and crush them to a pulp. Add the bread, lemon juice, and almonds, season generously, and blend again.

Then add the olive oil slowly, until the mixture is the consistency of molasses—thick but a little runny.

RIGHT Garlic soup and roasted garlic

LEEK

Allium ampeloprasum var. *porrum*

This third vegetable of the onion family also goes back far into antiquity, gathering an enthusiastic following. Our modern leek has a resemblance to the wild leek (*Allium ampeloprasum*) which is a native of the Mediterranean region and the Atlantic islands of the Azores, Canaries, Cape Verde Islands, and Madeira. It is this leek that was found in the remains of Jericho as early as 7000 BC. Other names for the wild leek are "great-headed garlic" and "Levant garlic." It is a hardy perennial, remarkable for the size of its bulbs. For thousands of years it has been eaten raw by the peoples of the Mediterranean and the Middle East.

The earliest written records of leek cultivation are Egyptian and date from 3200 BC: "Fix his allowance at a thousand loaves of bread, a hundred jars of beer, one ox and a hundred bunches of leeks." It was thought, then and later, that the leek originated in the Middle East. As we have noticed, however, this area was the first to domesticate plants, and the leek was one of the favored vegetables of summer. Pliny thought the best leeks came from Egypt, and also from Aricia in Italy. They had a great vogue in Rome, because the emperor Nero ate them for several days once a month in the belief that they cleared and strengthened his voice, so that he could more effectively sing and declaim his works—thus earning leeks the nickname "porrophagus."

Leeks remained popular throughout the Dark Ages. Charlemagne's list of foods to be cultivated in his domains includes them, and their success did not decline in the Middle Ages. The classic herbal of the fourteenth century (*The Four Seasons of the House of Cerruti*) tells its readers to choose pungent-smelling leeks to be cooked and mixed with honey and then swallowed slowly. This is not only an aphrodisiac, it declares, but also a diuretic that helps chest problems, gets rid of catarrh, and cleanses the lungs. Nero's example has obviously been remembered, if not mentioned.

Leeks have become the national emblem of Wales, recalled by Shakespeare in *Henry V* when Fluellen wears his leek in his hat. Pistol announces, "tell him I'll knock his leek about his pate upon Saint Davy's day." The origin of wearing a leek on St. David's Day, March 1st, is in memory of an ancient victory when the Welsh identified themselves with the vegetable, wearing it like a feather in the cap.

Thomas Tusser, English farmer and poet, wrote in 1557: "Now leeks are in season, for pottage full good, / And spareth the milch-cow, and purgeth the blood, / These having with peason, for pottage in Lent, / Thou spareth both oatmeal and bread to be spent."

People feel slightly equivocal about leeks. On the one hand they have been praised as being a great delicacy, having a far subtler flavor than the rest of the family: useful as a purée and mixed with egg yolks in a classic *flamiche aux poireaux* or the leek tart of Florence, *porrata*, the pastry of which is made with yeast and eggs. Or, people disparage leeks as being tainted by their close relationship with garlic. They are, in fact, "a poor man's asparagus."

Jane Grigson notes that leeks fell from grace for all of three centuries. They began to disappear in the sixteenth century and they were not much applauded when they crept back in the nineteenth. Mrs. Beeton's classic nineteenth-century cookbook gives only two recipes, and admonishes the cook to boil the leeks well or they will "taint the breath."

NUTRITION

Nutritionally, leeks have many of the properties of onion and garlic, are even richer in nutrients, and have a higher protein content; hence, they are good to eat as a staple ingredient in everyday cooking.

VARIETIES

Leeks are useful vegetables because they have a long growing season, and are at their best in cooler months. King Richard (an early variety with a long stem) and Musselburgh (a Scottish variety with thick stems) are both tasty and mild. The old standards are Large American Flag and Broad American Flag. Winter Giant is the hardiest variety of all. There is little difference in flavor among the varieties, but some have darker green leaves than others and are excellent for coloring soups and purées.

CHOOSING AND PREPARING

Choose firm leeks whose green ends are not discolored or fading. Small leeks are useful for dishes where they will be served whole; but for soups, purées, and tarts, where the leeks will be sliced, large leeks are less trouble to prepare. Clean them by cutting off the coarser green leaves, then splitting the leek down the middle so that any soil and grit can be washed away. If you wish to keep the leeks whole, simply split through the green to where the dirt is and soak or rinse. When rinsing leeks, hold them green ends down to prevent grit being driven deeper into them.

COOKING

For soups *et al*, just slice as thinly as you want, diagonally across the leek, place in a pan with a tiny amount of olive oil, butter, or both, and place over a low flame. Leave to steam in their own moisture for 5 minutes or until soft, until the next stage.

Dorothy Hartley, in her seminal *Food in England* (1954), claims that leeks braise better than they boil, and suggests you cook them whole in a closed well-buttered dish with the addition of a little milk or stock. "It is a mistake," she says, "to serve these delicate vegetables with thick sauce; the liquor and butter together in the dish should be sufficient."

What would she have made, I wonder, of this centuries-old Roman recipe? Chop 1 pound of leeks and sauté in 2 tablespoons each of olive oil and white wine, then add ⅓ cup of chopped green olives and 1 tablespoon of *nam pla* (Indonesian fish sauce), which is our substitute for the Roman *liquamen* (see page 143). Simmer for 5 minutes more, then the leeks should be ready to serve.

Here is an excellent medieval leek recipe that also uses wine. Wash and trim the leeks, then slice in half lengthwise. Cook in 2 tablespoons of olive oil and a glass of white wine and season. The leeks will cook in

BELOW **Leeks on their way to market**

LEEK *Allium ampeloprasum* var. *porrum*

about 5 minutes. Have some fresh crusty toast ready and pour the leeks with the sauce over it.

Italian food writer Anna del Conte tell us that when leeks are very young they can be served raw, but she suggests first soaking them in cold water to get rid of their strong flavor. Then she cuts them into thin rounds and dresses them with olive oil, vinegar, a little mustard, salt, and pepper. I use them raw, without the soaking, cut paper-thin and often mixed with other raw winter vegetables—such as grated carrot, beets, or celeriac—particularly the last, as leeks add a great deal of zip to a celeriac *rémoulade* (see page 221).

Anna del Conte also gives a marvelous leek dish from northern Italy that she says is an old favorite: *PORRI ALLA MILANESE*. This would make an excellent luncheon or supper dish for two. She says this is the poor man's version of *asparagi alla milanese*. I have changed the method slightly: in the original version the leeks are boiled first.

Wash and trim 6 leeks, slice them in half lengthwise, and place them in a buttered baking dish. Dot the leeks with a little more butter, season, and cover the dish. Bake in an oven preheated to 375°F for 20 minutes. Uncover the dish and sprinkle ½ cup of grated Parmesan cheese over the leeks. Bake for 5 minutes more, while you fry 4 eggs in a little more butter, being careful to cook the white but leave the yolks runny. Then slide the eggs over the leeks. Eat with good crusty white bread to soak up all the delicious juices.

The Welsh dish *cawl* (pronounced cowl) is a national leek dish. It is made with meat and any amount of vegetables, though leeks must always feature. It lies somewhere between a soup or broth and a stew. In fact, it can be eaten in two stages—the broth first and the meat and vegetables second. In Wales, they have many variations of leek soup; it is indeed almost the same as the French *potage à la bonne femme* or, if cooled and with some added cream, *vichyssoise*. Leek soup, I believe, is one of the great soups of the world. It can hardly fail: the fusion of that stringent aspect that all in the onion family have with the bland earthiness of the potato is always immensely satisfying.

SIMPLE LEEK AND POTATO SOUP

1 pound leeks
1 pound potatoes
2 tablespoons butter
7½ cups vegetable stock (see note below)
sea salt and freshly ground black pepper

Chop the leeks across into chunks, and peel and dice the potatoes.

Melt the butter in a pan and throw in the vegetables. Let them sweat for a minute or two, stirring with a wooden spoon.

Pour in the stock and simmer for 15 minutes. Leave to cool, then blend until smooth. Return to the pan and reheat. Taste and adjust the seasoning.
Note: The success of this soup hinges on the stock you use. It must not be too strong: the leek and the potato must be the most prominent flavors. You can use just water, but I believe the soup benefits from a slight sub-text of savoriness from the stock. There are now many excellent vegetable bouillon cubes; experiment and find one you like.

VARIATIONS
• For a more interesting texture, blend just half the soup and return it to the pan.
• Add 1¼ cups of light cream after blending, and reheat carefully without letting the soup boil.
• Add a spoonful of sour cream and croûtons or a sprinkling of freshly grated Parmesan to each portion when serving the soup.
• Add a glass of dry sherry before serving.

In the spring and summer months the soup, in the *vichyssoise* tradition, can be served chilled.

STIR-FRIED LEEKS

I use this method of cooking leeks more than any other, because I like to eat leeks when they are young and fairly slender.

1 pound young leeks, trimmed and cleaned,
but left whole
1 tablespoon sesame oil
1½ tablespoons grated fresh gingerroot

1 hot red chili, seeded and chopped
3 garlic cloves, chopped
a pinch of sea salt
a pinch of sugar
a few drops of light soy sauce or
dry sherry (optional)

Chop the leeks into 3-inch lengths.

Heat the sesame oil in a wok or a frying pan. Throw in the gingerroot, chili, and garlic, followed by the pieces of leek. Stir-fry vigorously for about 3 minutes, or until the leeks have softened on the outside but are still *al dente* inside.

Add the salt and sugar at the end. Also, if you wish, you can add a few drops of light soy sauce or dry sherry at the last minute.

GRATIN OF LEEK AND POTATO

I like the flavor of leeks and green peppercorns together. I have used this mixture in a tart and a roulade, but one of the simplest of dishes consists of leeks served with a white sauce studded with green peppercorns. The following recipe, however, is another variation—a gratin.

1½ pounds leeks
1 pound potatoes
2 tablespoons dried green peppercorns
½ cup grated Gruyère cheese
½ cup grated Parmesan cheese
sea salt
2½ cups light cream

Preheat the oven to 300°F. Chop the leeks diagonally, and slice the potatoes thinly.

In a shallow earthenware or other baking dish, arrange layers of the vegetables, starting with the leeks. Sprinkle each layer with a few green peppercorns, a little of each cheese, and some salt. Continue layering, finishing with potato.

Pour the cream over the top and conclude with a final dusting of cheese. Bake in the preheated oven for 2 hours. The slow cooking allows the potatoes to soak up the cream and flavoring.

SHALLOT

Allium cepa var. *aggregatum*

Named after the ancient Palestine port of Ascalon (now modern Ashqueion, in southwest Israel), where it was thought to originate, the shallot differs from the common onion in that it bunches up with bulbs that multiply freely. Shallots make a separate group with the "potato onion" or the "multiplier onion." Both Theophrastus and Pliny mention the Ascalon onion with a degree of admiration, noting how good it was in sauces.

John Mortimer, the English agricultural writer, in *The Whole Art Of Husbandry* (1707), says of shallots, "They give a fine relish to most sauces and the breath of those that eat them is not offensive to others..." Mortimer is quite right. Shallots have a delicate flavor and a less stringent smell than most other members of the onion family. They also have the capacity to dissolve easily into a liquid when they are cooked. Hence, they are of immeasurable use in the creation of a variety of sauces.

Shallots are a vital component of many of the most noted classic sauces of French haute cuisine: namely Bercy, béarnaise, bordelaise, chivry, and duxelles. These onions are also a classic accompaniment to grilled or pan-fried steak or chops. Shallots are best, in my view, if they are added to a little red wine, mustard, and salt and then just barely cooked so that the finely chopped pieces of shallot still have plenty of bite and texture to them.

VARIETIES

Shallots are most easily grown from sets—one shallot will expand into a cluster of 6 or more over the course of the growing season—but they may also be grown from seed and will, if planted early, make good-sized clusters in a single season.

French Red is a reliable set, widely available in North America. Breeders in Holland are responsible for the newer varieties of shallots from sets, Atlantic and Pikant. The earliest seed type is Atlas, a French-style, red-skinned variety that will produce clusters in as little as 90 days.

SHALLOT *Allium cepa* var. *aggregatum*

SWEET AND SOUR SHALLOTS

for 6

I am fond of shallots, eaten either hot or cold as in the following recipe. This makes an excellent first course on a bed of salad leaves.

1 pound shallots
2 tablespoons butter
2 tablespoons red wine vinegar
1 tablespoon Barbados or brown sugar
a pinch of sea salt

Peel the shallots and throw them into some salted boiling water. Simmer for 3–4 minutes, until they are just soft on the outside. Drain.

To the same pan, add the remaining ingredients. Stir until the sugar has dissolved and the shallots are glossy. Leave to cool.

These are delicious warm or cold. To serve, simply pour a little sauce and a few of the shallots over some salad leaves arranged on individual plates.

CHIVE

Allium schoenoprasum

These green tufts of aromatic grass are perennial and indigenous to the whole of the northern hemisphere, from Arctic Europe to Japan. They may be found from the Mediterranean shores to Sweden and across North America. The bulbs are tiny, and it is the spear-like leaf that has always been used for flavoring. The American botanist Sturtevant noted, in the nineteenth century, that chives were much used in Scotch families and are considered "next to indispensable in omelettes." The English herbalist Gerard thought they "made a pleasant sauce and a good pot-herb."

Certainly we do not make sauces using chives, as the fugitive flavor does not really survive lengthy cooking, but chives appear with unceasing regularity in herb mixtures and are particularly useful mixed with soft cheeses. Commercial herbed cheeses might look attractively speckled in green, but the delicate chive flavor rarely comes through. It does, however, when you use chives in home cooking, such as in omelets and roulades, or mixed with mashed potato, and in vinaigrette used to dress fish or vegetable molds. The whole leaf can be used to garnish a dish so that it appears like green stripes.

The chive flower has also been pressed into service. It is indeed edible, but few people enjoy consuming flowers as much as I do. Try picking the flowerbuds and using them in a salad.

WELSH ONION

Allium fistulosum

You will not normally find Welsh onions in markets, but they are quite popular with gardeners. Other names are Oriental or Japanese bunching or everlasting onion. In fact, they have nothing at all to do with Wales, and probably originated in Eastern Asia or Siberia. This is the favorite onion of China and Japan, and is perfect for flavoring because the green leaves can be cut off and the bulb then simply grows more.

For centuries this onion has been a staple in the cuisine of the East. Joy Larkcom calls it, "the most ubiquitous of Chinese vegetables. In Taiwan I drove through a famous onion village, where long onions were hanging to dry from every window and roof." The advantage of the bunching onion is that different parts of it can be harvested at different times—the small leafy shoots first for flavoring and salads, the small scallion next, and then the long, mature blanched stem last. The Latin *fistulosum* in the botanical name refers to the hollow stems.

ROCAMBOLE

Allium scorodoprasum

Rocambole was once thought to be a form of garlic and it certainly has the garlic flavor, though on a more delicate scale. It is also called sand leek and Spanish garlic. It grows wild in southern Europe and on the Mediterranean coast, especially in the Greek Islands. Rocambole can be identified by a stem that coils in the upper part, and by the fact that its seedhead is a cluster of bulblets.

There is no record of the plant ever being cultivated in antiquity, though the herbalist Gerard mentions it as a cultivated plant in 1597. The seventeenth-century English diarist John Evelyn prefers it to garlic, which "is not for ladies palettes, nor those that court them, rather...a light touch on the dish with a clove thereof, much better supplied by the gentler Roccombo."

By 1718, Richard Bradley, the English botanist, laments, "The Rocambole, for its high Relish in Sauces, has been greatly esteem'd formerly, but now a-days is hardly to be met with," adding that "considering how small a Quantity of it is sufficient to give us that Relish which many onions can hardly give, it ought to be preferred." Only the bulblets in the head of the rocambole were added to the sauce.

Soon after this, rocambole disappeared from kitchen gardens completely. Now, sadly, it is virtually unknown, unless you happen to find it in some unspoiled part of the Mediterranean.

ROCAMBOLE *Allium scorodoprasum*

ABOVE Bundles of unopened flower-stalks of Chinese chives

CHINESE or GARLIC CHIVE

Allium tuberosum

These have been used for centuries throughout the East. They are easily grown, but take time to get established. They are worth the wait because they have a most attractive but delicate garlic flavor. Use them like chives. All the parts can be used, both the white and green of the stem and the bulbs, as well as the pretty flowers.

They are also a decorative asset to the garden because they remain green throughout the spring and summer without the unattractive yellowing or browning that ordinary chives soon develop. Ethnic markets usually stock Chinese chives.

Liliaceae

ASPARAGUS

Asparagus officinalis

Asparagus is a member of the lily family (Liliaceae), which is allied to the onion family. In its wild state asparagus grew around the seashores and the river banks of southern Europe and the Caucasus. It was the wild plant (*Asparagus aphyllus*) that was known and loved in ancient Greece. The Romans cultivated it—though, following Cato's instructions, it would have been grown from the wild seed. The growing of asparagus was obviously an act of love. Pliny says, "of all the plants of the garden it receives the most praise-worthy care." Yet he adds, "nature has made the asparagus wild, so that anyone may gather as found." Then he tells us of a much-manured asparagus at Ravenna, three spears of which weighed a pound. The Roman pound weighed 0.721 of our pound, so I estimate that each spear would have weighed about 3½ ounces, which is very impressive but no bigger than some giant spears you might find now. The Latin poet Martial also praises Ravenna asparagus, saying it was the best in the world.

There is no doubt that the Romans loved the vegetable and also knew how best to cook it. The Emperor Augustus coined a phrase, *velocius quam asparagi conquantur*, meaning to do something faster than you can cook asparagus. Julius Caesar first ate it in Lombardy, and wanted it served with melted butter. Though the ancient world recorded its love affair with this plant, asparagus then strangely vanished entirely from history. However, much later, in the seventeenth century, John Evelyn waxes enthusiastically over English asparagus being "sweet and agreeable though of moderate size"—better by far than the Dutch kind, which had large spears due to "the rankness of the beds."

Another species (*Asparagus prostratus*) grows wild around the grassy sea cliffs and dunes of northern Europe. This was almost certainly eaten from the earliest times, the first moment being in March when the edible shoots showed their tips above the surface. It is one of those plants that likes salt, so it will feel at home close to the sea. The flavor is strong and rather bitter, which is why it is often boiled and chopped, then mixed with eggs. The flavor is then highly satisfactory, because the bland creaminess of the eggs offsets the salty tang of the wild plant.

There are three types of cultivated asparagus: white, purple, and green. All three are grown and enjoyed in France. Other countries tend to have their particular favorite; for instance, Spain mostly cultivates the white, and much of the harvest is canned. White asparagus never sees the light; the furrows in the fields are piled up (like potato cultivation) in rows and there is not a plant to be seen. I asked a Spanish farmer how on earth anyone finds the asparagus to harvest it. With great pleasure he showed me the hair cracks along the mound, evidence of that thrusting spear below. When the crack was seen, the knife went in, following the spear down and slicing it 6 inches below. The purple variety is allowed to grow 1–2 inches above ground before it is cut, and I think it has more flavor than the white. It is, however, green asparagus that we go for in North America, Britain, Italy, and France, and to my mind it is unquestionably the finest.

When the asparagus is thin and pencil-like it is called sprue. As such, it is frequently used in Italy, often with the addition of grated Parmesan, the flavor of which blends so well with that of the asparagus.

Because of its shape and its method of consumption, asparagus has always been considered an aphrodisiac. However, the Emperor Augustus would hardly have approved of the method of cooking recommended in an Arab love manual, in which the asparagus is first boiled, then fried in fat, and then covered in egg yolk. A daily portion of this dish, it was said, would keep the virile member alert night and day. Both Gerard and Culpeper wrote of the vegetable "increasing seed and stirring up lust."

Louis XV's mistress, Madame de Pompadour, in her eagerness for aphrodisiac foods, lived off asparagus tips and egg yolks, with an occasional dish of truffles, celery leaves, and vanilla. Her name is given to a recipe—*asperges à la Pompadour*—which includes egg yolks, but unfortunately it uses cornmeal to thicken the sauce, an ingredient she was unlikely to have had at her disposal.

The most striking characteristic noticed by people who have consumed asparagus is the strong, unusual odor of their urine. It was noted by Dr. Louis Lemery, in his *Treatise Of All Sorts Of Foods* in 1702, that "asparagus causes a filthy and disagreeable smell in the urine as everybody knows." The phenomenon is caused by the excretion of methyl mercaptan, triggered by the sulfur-containing amino acid methionine in the asparagus. There are some who claim they have never noticed the exotic smell, but the ability to detect the odor differs from person to person.

NUTRITION

Asparagus contains vitamins A, B2, C, and E, plus calcium, copper, magnesium, iron, and phosphorus. It is also an excellent diuretic, and is said to break up oxalic acid and crystals in the kidney; hence, it is good for relieving rheumatism and arthritis.

VARIETIES

Asparagus plants may be either male or female. The male plants, being fruitless, tend to be more vigorous, producing thicker-stalked spears. They have the added virtue of being non-invasive (asparagus berries are much loved by birds, and stray seedlings in the asparagus patch can become pesky weeds). Until recently, growers had to rogue out females after plants matured, but there are now all-male hybrids available in both seed and crown forms. Jersey Giant is the most widely adapted, Jersey Prince the earliest. Growers were once advised to wait two years after planting crowns, three years after planting seeds, before cutting the first spears. Current wisdom permits a small harvest in as little as 12 months from crowns if the young plants are sufficiently vigorous.

CHOOSING AND STORING

Buy and enjoy asparagus in season, from February through to the middle of June in a good summer. The plant needs both plenty of rain and sun for a good growing season.

Fresh white asparagus can be bought in specialist markets. You can also find fresh asparagus, both purple and green, in the winter months, although I must say I am a great enthusiast for eating foods when they are in season. I would not bother at all with canned green asparagus.

Fresh asparagus will keep well for some days (if you must, up to a week) in the salad drawer of the refrigerator. If you intend to keep it, untie the bundle so that the spears are not pressed against each other and each is given room to breathe.

PREPARING

Most recipes direct you to peel the asparagus, from the tips down to the woody stems. I do not agree that this is at all necessary. The spears need only be rinsed briefly under a running tap, as everything is edible down to the fibrous, woody end, which may be simply cut off.

COOKING

Freshly picked asparagus is very good raw. Evelyn notes that the spears were sometimes "but very seldom eaten raw with oil and vinegar."

What is the perfect way to cook asparagus? There is little doubt that an asparagus steamer is by far the most foolproof method. Drop the spears, tips upward, into the wire basket. Bring a few inches of water to the boil in the steamer and drop the basket in. Place the lid on and leave for 5 minutes. The exact cooking time does depend upon the thickness of the spears, but it is far better to have a spear with a little crunch to it than one overcooked and flabby.

If you don't have a steamer, stand the bundle upright in a large saucepan and wedge it with new potatoes, which you boil in the water. Cover the top with a dome of foil. There is no need to eat the potatoes at the same time, though their flavor is superb; they will make an excellent salad.

What to dip these spears into should not tax the connoisseur too hard. I agree with Julius Caesar: there is little doubt that melted butter is the most delicious, though I would add the juice of half a lemon to sharpen it. Both hollandaise and *aïoli* are excellent, but the simplicity of the dish is now

RIGHT Green, white and wild asparagus and sprue

blurred and the calories are mounting up. A vinaigrette made from sherry or balsamic vinegar is as delicious as anything else and is perhaps the simplest. Sauces can also be made from sour cream flavored with herb vinegar and nut oils, plus, perhaps, chopped herbs or spices. Thick plain yogurt with a few similar additions is a slightly healthier alternative.

Quite another method of cooking that has lately found favor—ensuring an *al dente* spear with quite a bit of crunch—is grilling. Melt some butter in a ridged grill pan and lay the spears on it, turning them so that they are well covered. Then grill for up to 5 minutes, turning the spears so that they are briefly seared on all sides. Alternatively, make up a mixture of olive oil and soy sauce and paint each spear with this before grilling them.

QUICK ASPARAGUS RISOTTO

1 vegetable bouillon cube
1 pound asparagus, trimmed and chopped
2 tablespoons butter
2 tablespoons olive oil
3 shallots, sliced
6 scallions, diced
⅔ cup basmati rice
sea salt and freshly ground black pepper
½ cup grated Parmesan cheese

Bring 1 cup of water to a boil, add a vegetable bouillon cube, and throw in the chopped asparagus. Simmer for 3 minutes.

Meanwhile, in another pan, melt the butter in the oil. Throw in the shallots and scallions, let them sweat for a moment, and then add the rice. Stir so that the rice is coated with the oil and the onions are softened. Now add the asparagus and almost all its vegetable stock—about ½–¾ cup. Stir the risotto, then cover and let cook for 8 minutes.

Take a peep: if it looks too dry, add the rest of the stock; if it looks done, taste and see. Add a little seasoning and stir in half the Parmesan. Put the lid back on and leave for another minute.

Then turn onto a serving dish and sprinkle with the rest of the Parmesan.

ASPARAGUS SOUP

for 6

1 pound asparagus
1 vegetable bouillon cube
sea salt and white pepper
1¼ cups heavy cream

Cut off the woody ends from the asparagus spears and discard. Cut off the tips of the asparagus and drop them into 1½ quarts water with the bouillon cube. Bring to a boil and poach for 5 minutes. Take out the tips with a slotted spoon and reserve.

Now boil the asparagus stalks for up to 15 minutes. Allow to cool and then blend until smooth. Taste and adjust the seasoning. Make sure there are no fibers; if so, press the soup through a strainer.

Mix in the cream, add the asparagus tips, and chill for an hour. Alternatively, you can reheat the soup to serve hot, taking care it does not boil.

ASPARAGUS SAUCE

This is good with egg or fish dishes or with crudités.

12 asparagus spears
1 vegetable bouillon cube
1 teaspoon celery salt
⅔ cup heavy cream

Cut off the woody ends from the spears and discard. Chop the spears into small dice.

Heat 2 cups water with the bouillon cube and throw in the asparagus. Boil for 3 minutes. Leave to cool and then blend until smooth. Press through a strainer to ensure there are no fibers. Mix in the celery salt and cream.

Note: This sauce can be turned into a mold by adding some unflavored gelatin. Alternatively, add one beaten egg, place in a ramekin, and bake in an oven preheated to 375°F for 20 minutes. Leave to cool and then unmold.

RIGHT Grilled asparagus sprinkled with
Parmesan cheese

Chenopodiaceae

THE

BEET

FAMILY

SPINACH *Spinacea oleracea*
SWISS CHARD *Beta vulgaris* subsp. *cicla*
BEET *Beta vulgaris* subsp. *vulgaris*
ORACH *Atriplex hortensis*
GOOD KING HENRY *Chenopodium bonus-henricus*
GLASSWORT, SAMPHIRE or SALICORNIA
Salicornia europaea
QUINOA *Chenopodium quinoa*

Aizoaceae

NEW ZEALAND SPINACH *Tetragonia expansa*

This family includes, among other edible plants, spinach and beets. The tribe derives its botanical name, meaning "goose foot," from the Greek chen *(goose) and* pous *(foot)—an allusion to the characteristic design of the leaves, which is supposed to resemble the webbed feet of geese.*

They grow in temperate climes, often near the seashore, on salt marshes and waste ground. It is interesting to note that so many food plants grow near the seashore, underlying the fact that the earliest settlements were by estuaries and river deltas—regions enriched by the minerals continually being washed down from the mountains and absorbed by living organisms. The plants within the beet family contain large quantities of iron and many other minerals.

In all, spread across the world, there are about 600 members of the family. Quinoa was eaten in South America at the same time as spinach beet was eaten by the Romans.

Also in this section is New Zealand spinach, the one edible plant of the carpet-weed family (Aizoaceae), which includes iceplant and living stones. The former are Mesembryanthemum crystallinum, a familiar sight in California, where the plant clothes many embankments with a thick, fleshy, green carpet dotted with purple daisy-like flowers.

SPINACH

Spinacea oleracea

"Spinach is not worth much essentially," writes the eighteenth-century French gourmet Grimod de la Reynière, adding, "it is susceptible of receiving all imprints: it is the virgin wax of the kitchen." One wonders what had occurred to Reynière's taste-buds that he could claim such nonsense. Spinach obviously is one of those flavors that has its fervent disciples as well as its detractors. For example, Louis XIV, forbidden spinach by his doctor, was supposed to have sent for it, saying, "What! I am King of France and I cannot eat spinach?"

This vegetable, loathed by many young children, was made famous as a health food earlier this century by the cartoon character Popeye, who is given mythic strength through eating it. Alas, the strip cartoons and animated films never achieved their aim of boosting the consumption of the vegetable (or the consumption of green vegetables in general by children). I am, however, a fervent disciple and love it for its powerful flavor.

Spinach is not mentioned in antiquity, but Swiss chard—a very similar leafy vegetable—was noticed by Aristotle and many others, so it is odd that spinach was neglected. It is, after all, too individual and too powerful in flavor to have been overlooked if it had been grown either in its wild or cultivated state. If it had been growing, the Greeks surely would have discovered it when Alexander conquered Persia, for it was certainly growing wild there, and I suspect would have been used in Persian cooking with other wild leaves and herbs.

The first mention of spinach plants was 800 years later, as a present from the King of Nepal to the Chinese Emperor in AD 647. It was obviously a success because, by the ninth century, it is recorded in a work on Chinese agriculture, and we know it was continually grown in the Imperial gardens and parks. It had come to Nepal from Persia, where it was regularly cultivated. I imagine its cultivation there must have been recent, for the Greeks—and certainly the Romans—would have begun using it if the plant had been growing any earlier.

The name derives, via the Arabs, from the Persian word *espenaj*. From Persia, it was accepted by the Arabs in their cooking and was introduced to Europe through the Moorish occupation of Spain. Spinach is much richer in protein than other leaf vegetables, with a high vitamin A content. It was valued by Arab physicians, and its first appearance in a cuisine must have been in those highly spiced dishes of the Middle East, where its strong mineral flavors would have stood up well to the addition of many spices—totally unlike the "virgin wax" of Reynière's statement.

Albertus Magnus (1200–80), the teacher of St. Thomas Aquinas and disciple of Aristotle, knew the prickly-seeded form of spinach, so the vegetable had moved north from Spain into Germany by that time. It came to be associated with Lent, because if the seeds were sown in winter they would leaf in time to be used for Lenten dishes. It appears in a list of vegetables recommended for monks on fast days in 1351.

Spinach appears as "spynoches" in the earliest English cookbook, *The Forme of Cury* (compiled 1390), in which the most popular vegetables are cabbage, leeks, and radishes. Catherine de' Medici, the daughter of Lorenzo, who married Henri II of France in 1533, was said to be very fond of spinach, so much so that in French cooking the description *à la florentine* indicates that the dish contains spinach.

It is the prickly-seeded form that is the original plant. We in Britain now call it winter spinach, though with modern improvements both the prickly seeds and the round seeds can be sown in autumn, for late winter harvesting. Smooth-seeded spinach made its first appearance in the sixteenth century; it is lighter green in color and not quite so intense in flavor.

Spinach was popular as much for its coloring as its taste. Spinach water was used to color cakes and desserts. It was also used to make touch-paper for fireworks, because paper that had been soaked in it and then dried out would smolder well.

By 1536, spinach had become thoroughly acceptable, known in both England and France. Elinor Fettiplace, in her *Receipt Book,* uses spinach as a sauce with chicken, either as a purée or cooked with parsley, mace, currants, raisins, dates, and prunes and diluted with half a pint of sack. Murrel's *Two Bookes of Cookerie* (1638) gives a recipe for French Puffs with Green Herbs. These were sweet; the use of spinach in tarts had become popular.

The Tudors inherited the medieval love of coloring; the dark green spinach studded with dried fruits looked as splendid as it must have tasted. (It is interesting to see how ideas survive. Mrs. Leyel, the English herbalist, food writer, and founder of Culpeper House, in 1925 published a recipe for spinach purée studded with candied cherries, to be served on ice with cold tongue.)

By 1747, Hannah Glasse, in her *The Art of Cookery Made Plain and Simple*—the only really important English cookbook of that century—tells her readers how to cook spinach without water in a tightly closed tin box over a fire. She also explains how to dress spinach by first stewing it, then draining and chopping it, and adding half a pint of cream, salt, pepper, grated nutmeg, and a quarter pound of butter. This is simmered over the fire for a quarter of an hour, stirring often. A long French roll, sliced and fried in butter, and any number of poached eggs are served with the spinach. Serve it for supper, Hannah Glasse suggests, or as a side dish at the second course.

Adam's Luxury and Eve's Cookery, in 1764, still includes a recipe for a sweet spinach tart flavored with dried fruits and candied peel, plus two other sweet recipes, but creeping in (influenced no doubt by Hannah Glasse) is a savory—a spinach purée with cream and pepper topped with poached eggs, which could well be served now.

Spinach had reached North America by the 1800s. Thomas Jefferson grew it in his garden.

NUTRITION AND MEDICINAL

Spinach and its relatives have a long history of medicinal use. The darker green the vegetable or leaf, the richer in minerals and vitamins it is; so spinach is one of the very best vegetables in nutritional terms. It contains plenty of vitamins C, A, and B and some vitamin K, as well as potassium, calcium, magnesium, iron, iodine, and phosphorus.

Cooked spinach yields up oxalic acid, however, which forms insoluble compounds with the calcium and iron and therefore halts the absorption of these minerals by the body. So if you wish to gain all the nutrition from the dark green leaves, it is far better to eat them raw.

Recent studies have suggested that spinach might be a help as an antidote to lung cancer, because of its high concentration of carotenoids, including beta carotene. Raw spinach has more carotenoids (36 mg) than raw carrots (14 mg). It is also reputed to lower blood pressure.

VARIETIES

Spinach can be grown in the cool, short days of spring and fall, and through the winter in milder climates. (It is daylight-sensitive and starts to bolt when days are longer than 12½ – 15 hours.) Some varieties do better than others as days lengthen and warm. Spinach is always at its best when it is in its infancy and the leaves are small.

Of the summer varieties, an old favorite is Bloomsdale Long Standing, which has good heat tolerance. Giant Nobel is similar in habit. Viking has large leaves and is also resistant to bolting.

Giant Winter and King of Denmark both stand cold weather well, and can be planted in late summer for abundant fall crops. Monnopa has less oxalic acid content than most (see above), so is recommended if you have young children to feed.

SPINACH *Spinacea oleracea*

CHOOSING AND PREPARING

Be sure to buy spinach that has firm stems and springy leaves; these will show that the spinach has been picked very recently. Discard all the limp and discolored leaves; really old spinach goes not only limp but yellow. You will need to buy about a pound to get enough for two people. Store spinach in the salad drawer of the refrigerator, and don't keep it longer than about two days.

To prepare: cut off the stems. If the central ribs are thick, tear the leaf part away and discard the ribs. Wash the leaves well in cold running water, then drain and shake them dry.

Old cookbooks are keen on washing spinach leaves with care several times. Industry was, of course, a lot dirtier than it is today, and where market gardens were near big cities, as they often were, the leaf vegetables accumulated soot and grime on the leaves.

COOKING

There are two schools of thought on how to cook spinach: first, with no water at all, and second, with lots. I am against the gallon of water approach and prefer to cook my leaves without any added water.

After washing and draining the leaves, place them in a covered saucepan with a little salt and leave over a low heat. The leaves will simply sweat and steam, cooking in their own moisture. About 1 pound of spinach should be cooked through within 5 minutes, but the exact time depends on the amount of leaves. Double that quantity will take another 2–3 minutes.

When the spinach leaves are reduced to a soft mound at the bottom of the pan, take the lid off, raise the heat, and evaporate the rest of the moisture. Now the spinach, termed *en branche* by the French, is ready for serving. All it needs is a little chopping and squeezing to extract the last of the liquid.

The mistake people often make is to continue to cook the leaves, which will obligingly exude more and more moisture, shrinking all the time as they do so. You can stop this by various methods. One is to cook the spinach as above, take it off the flame, and serve. Another is to add some butter, cream, or oil to coat the leaves. A third method is to add flour and make the spinach into a roux, preparatory to adding milk or cream for a spinach sauce. Sometimes spinach also needs to be coated in this way as a preliminary stage in a particular recipe.

Large spinach leaves, once blanched, are useful for wrapping mousses and molds. They can be used like grapevine leaves in *dolmades*. In fact, as a change from salad, the next best way of consuming raw spinach leaves is wrapped around other vegetable mixtures. These wrapped mousses and molds can also be cooked. The spinach that is at the top of the mold must be protected by paper and foil; even so it will dry out and darken. But once unmolded, the base will be the top, so it will not show. Cut these molds like a cake, if large. They can also be made in individual-portion sizes, and these are excellent first courses.

SPINACH SOUP is one of the best of soups and it is the easiest to make. For six people you will need 2 pounds of spinach and 5 pints of liquid, made up of half vegetable stock and half milk. The latter can be soy milk for a soup that is healthful and slimming (I enjoy the nutty taste of soy milk), or cows' milk (or even a mixture of that and cream for added richness).

Simply cook the spinach leaves in the stock for about 4 minutes. Leave to cool, then season and blend until smooth. Add the milk, soy milk, or cream and milk and reheat gently. Garnish with yogurt and chopped chives, or a few crushed green and pink peppercorns, or geranium petals. Spinach soup is perfectly delicious eaten cold as well.

Because of its intensity of flavor, spinach is often teamed with cream, cheese, and eggs because these tone it down and make a flavor that is rich but acceptable. One of the most famous dishes with spinach is *oeufs à la florentine*, or *EGGS FLORENTINE*. This dish, in which the spinach leaves or purée are mixed with a cheese sauce and poured over poached eggs, used to be a popular beginning to a meal in Italy or in Italian restaurants elsewhere. Most of us would now be content to enjoy it as a main course or as a supper dish.

The success of the dish is the fusion of the soft-cooked yolk with the cheese sauce and the fragments of spinach beneath. If the yolk is cooked through, the dish fails. Thus, the dish becomes a good test for the quality of a restaurant kitchen. Even if the egg is poached perfectly—the white set, the yolk still runny—the next stage, of placing the spinach and cheese sauce over the eggs to brown in the oven or under the broiler, will usually cook the yolk completely. The trick is to allow the poached eggs to get cold; then you can safely cover them with the topping and broil. The eggs will warm sufficiently to be eaten, but will not start cooking again.

There is another method that I sometimes follow. This is to serve the poached eggs on top of the spinach mixture, garnished with fresh sage and grated Parmesan. It is not the classic dish, but it works well and it ensures that perfect combination on the palate of runny yolk and cheesy spinach.

For this dish, as well as for a spinach soufflé or *timbale,* there are again two methods of treating the spinach—leaving it *en branche* (see above) and just chopping it or turning it into a purée. It depends on your personal tastes. For myself, I would always leave it *en branche* because I like texture and variety in food.

Lastly, there is a famous recipe for *BUTTERED SPINACH* quoted by Elizabeth David in *French Country Cooking.* It was originally given in a weekly magazine published in Paris in August, 1905. The story concerned the Abbé Chevrier and his best friend, the celebrated gastronome Brillat-Savarin; the latter was intrigued by the spinach cooked in butter at the Abbé's table. "Nowhere does one eat spinach, simple spinach cooked in butter, to compare with his." Brillat-Savarin discovered the recipe: the dish is cooked over the course of five days.

The spinach is cooked in the normal way, and afterward, for each 1 pound of spinach, ½ cup (1 stick) of butter is added over a low flame. Stir the spinach into the butter so that the spinach absorbs the butter. Put aside in a cool place. The next day, add 3 tablespoons of butter to the spinach over a low flame until the spinach has absorbed it, working the spinach with a wooden spoon into the melted butter. Repeat this procedure for the next two days. Finally, on the day you are going to serve it, add 4 tablespoons of butter. Each pound of spinach will absorb 10½ oz of butter, and the spinach will dissolve into a velvety purée. Mrs. David adds that in her opinion it is preferable to cook 2 or 3 pounds of spinach with this amount of butter.

I cooked this recipe once with about 2 pounds of spinach to 10 ounces of butter. It was astonishing, one of the most blissful few mouthfuls I have ever enjoyed. One feels, though, that heart-attack is imminent, yet for a special dinner party it is very well worth trying.

SPINACH ROLLS

These are perfect appetizers or party snacks.

12 spinach leaves, blanched
for the filling:
1 cup ricotta cheese
a generous handful of chopped herbs
(parsley, chives, dill, basil, cilantro)
bunch of scallions, chopped
1 teaspoon paprika
2 garlic cloves, minced

Mix the filling ingredients together well. Place about 2 teaspoons of the filling on the corner of each blanched spinach leaf and roll it up, tucking the ends in carefully as you go.

SPINACH CROQUETTES

2 pounds spinach, cooked en branche *(see page 46)*
2 tablespoons gram flour (ground chickpeas), plus more
for dusting
1 tablespoon garam masala
1 egg, beaten
sea salt and freshly ground black pepper

Mix the cooked spinach with the gram flour, garam masala, beaten egg, and seasoning. Leave in the refrigerator to firm up a little.

Form the firm mixture into cakes or croquettes, roll these in flour to coat, and fry briefly in hot oil until uniformly golden.

SPINACH *Spinacea oleracea*

PURÉE OF SPINACH AND POTATO

This is superb with roast game or meat.

1 pound spinach, cooked and puréed in a blender
2 pounds mealy potatoes, cooked and mashed
2 tablespoons butter
⅓ cup milk or cream
sea salt and freshly ground black pepper

Combine the potato and spinach purées and mix thoroughly by hand. (Do not use the blender as it turns the potato into glue.)

Add the butter, milk or cream, and seasoning to make a smooth green purée.

SPINACH ROULADE

This makes an excellent first course, and you have a choice of fillings.

1 pound spinach
4 eggs, beaten
½ cup grated Gruyère cheese
sea salt and freshly ground black pepper
½ cup grated Parmesan cheese
for the Taramasalata filling:
6 ounces smoked cod roe
juice from 1 lemon
1 garlic clove, minced
⅓ cup olive oil, approximately
for the Red Pepper-Cream filling:
1 cup mascarpone cheese
1 red bell pepper, seeded and diced small
1 red onion, diced small
1 teaspoon paprika

First, make the roulade: cook the spinach, then chop it small. Add the beaten eggs, Gruyère, and seasoning.

Preheat the oven to 425°F. Line a 13- x 9-inch baking pan with parchment paper. Butter or oil it well.

Pour the spinach and egg mixture into the lined pan and spread it out evenly. Bake in the oven for 15–20 minutes, until it is crisp at the edges and spongy in the center. Leave to cool a little.

Have ready another sheet of parchment paper sprinkled with the grated Parmesan. Turn the roulade onto this and peel away the parchment paper lining the bottom. Once completely cool, the roulade is ready to be filled and rolled.

To make the Taramasalata filling: cut up the roe with a knife, skin and all, place in a powerful blender, and add the lemon juice and garlic. Blend well, then add the olive oil in a steady stream—the result should be thick, creamy, and smooth.

It is impossible to give exact quantities for the amount of oil because it depends on the quality of the roe. Some will absorb much more oil than others. Sometimes the roe will curdle, in which case a dash of whiskey or brandy will help; otherwise you have to start again.

If you choose the Red Pepper-Cream filling, simply mix the cheese with the diced vegetables and season with paprika.

Smooth either the taramasalata or the red pepper cream over the roulade, leaving a ½-inch border clear around the edges. Roll up the roulade gently from one short end to the other, using the piece of parchment paper under it to help you get started. Place the roll on a platter, seam-side down, and chill for an hour or two.

Serve cut across into ½-inch slices.

THE BEET FAMILY *Chenopodiaceae*

ABOVE Spinach, pine nut, papaya, and avocado salad, and spinach roulade

SPINACH, PINE NUT, PAPAYA, AND
AVOCADO SALAD

This simple and refreshing dish makes a terrific colorful first course, or it can be served for lunch with some good crusty bread.

1½ pounds fresh spinach leaves
¼ cup olive oil
1 tablespoon wine vinegar
a pinch of sugar
sea salt and freshly ground black pepper
1 ripe avocado
1 ripe papaya
3 garlic cloves, sliced
⅓ cup pine nuts
1 tablespoon chopped tarragon

Wash, trim, and drain the spinach leaves, then pat them dry in a clean dish towel.

Make a dressing with 3 tablespoons of the olive oil, the vinegar, sugar, and seasoning.

Peel and slice the avocado into a large salad bowl. Pour the dressing over it. Toss so that the avocado slices are well covered. Peel and slice the papaya, adding it to the bowl.

Pour the last tablespoon of oil into a pan. Add the sliced garlic and the pine nuts. Fry for a minute or two so they turn golden brown. Leave to cool.

Add the spinach leaves to the salad bowl and toss thoroughly. Pour over the pine nuts and garlic with their oil. Serve garnished with the chopped tarragon.

SPINACH *Spinacea oleracea*

49

SWISS CHARD

Beta vulgaris subsp. *cicla*

Chard is very like spinach in flavor, but the stems are eaten as well. Some people prefer it to spinach, and pies made from it using the stems as well as the leaves have a pleasant, silky richness. Also called leaf beet and spinach beet, chard is a form of beet grown for its leaves rather than its root. How it came to be called Swiss is somewhat of a mystery. The word chard comes from the Latin and French words for thistle. The French word for cardoon—which is a type of thistle—is *chardon*, and a seed merchant may well have given chard the extra title of "Swiss" to distinguish it from the cardoon.

The ancients had no such problems; they valued the beet for its leaves and spoke of white, red, and black varieties. If the root of the beet was used it was for medicinal purposes. The wild form is found in the Canary Islands, in the whole of the Mediterranean region as far as the Caspian, in Persia and Babylon, as well as around the coasts of Britain.

In 1597, the herbalist Gerard notes, "the common white Beet hath great broad leaves, smooth and plain: from which rose thicke crested or chamfered stalks..." He had also heard of another sort, "red in color, both in root and stalk, full of a perfect, purple juice." He recommends using the leaves in winter as a salad, dressed with vinegar, oil, and salt. He expresses doubt about the red and beautiful root, but has been assured that it is good and wholesome.

We, of course, now eat the root from one plant and the leaves from another, but we do tend to lead wasteful lives. When I lived on the Greek island of Lesbos in the 1960s, beets were one of the few fresh vegetables to buy in the early spring. We boiled the beets and ate the leaves, first simmered briefly then dressed with Greek olive oil, vinegar, and salt. Excellent they were, too.

NUTRITION AND MEDICINAL

Swiss chard contains less oxalic acid than spinach, so its nutrient content—roughly similar to spinach—is probably more easily absorbed by the body.

VARIETIES, CHOOSING, AND STORING

Swiss chard now comes in both white and red varieties. The latter looks sensational growing in the herb or flower border, as the stems are a bright military scarlet. Alas, this color disappears on cooking and the leaves turn a darkish green (see cabbage on page 91 for the reason for such pigmentation loss). This may well be what the Greek philosopher and botanist Theophrastus (370 BC) meant when he named a black or dark green variety. Red chard is called either ruby chard or rhubarb chard. There is even a rainbow chard that produces red, yellow, purple, and white stems. All chards tend to be hardy and prolific. Leaves can be cut repeatedly, and the plant continues to send up healthy new growth. It will stand considerable frost, only dying when the roots freeze.

Chard keeps better than spinach, but it is best to cook it within two days. Wrap it in paper and store in the salad drawer of the refrigerator. Of course, the stems keep better than the leaves.

PREPARING AND COOKING

The south of France, around Nice, is where they most value chard. Richard Olney tells us, in *Simple French Food,* that the white stems are enjoyed, while the green leaves are given to the rabbits or ducks. Once cooked, the leaves are indistinguishable in flavor from spinach. The stems, however, are another experience altogether. Trim and cook them in a little stock, simmering for about 5 minutes. Then serve them with lemon alone, as one might eat asparagus. They can also be served as a vegetable accompaniment.

There is a Provençal recipe that is the main specialty of Nice, which is served traditionally as the grand dessert on Christmas Eve: *tourte de blettes.* In a manner reminiscent of medieval spinach tarts, the Swiss chard leaves are mixed with raisins, apples, pine nuts, lemon, and cheese. An Auvergne recipe, *le pounti,* is a chard and ham quiche that may also be flavored with prunes and raisins. Strangely, Elizabeth David dismisses chard as having little flavor, and in her *French Provincial Cooking* gives only one recipe.

RIGHT White and ruby chard

THE BEET FAMILY *Chenopodiaceae*

SWISS CHARD PIE

My version of the Niçoise *tourte* omits the fruit and sugar, so is not in the least traditional, but the advantage is that it uses the whole plant. I cannot imagine why stem and leaf are not more often eaten together.

2 pounds Swiss chard
½ cup grated Gruyère cheese
½ cup grated Parmesan cheese
½ cup grated sage-flavored cheese
1¼ cups light cream
2 eggs, beaten, plus 1 extra yolk
sea salt and freshly ground black pepper
for the pastry:
2 cups all-purpose flour
10 tablespoons butter
a pinch of sea salt
2 – 3 tablespoons ice-water
a little milk, for glazing

First make the pastry (make sure you have both the flour and butter very cold). Sift the flour and salt into a mixing bowl and grate the butter into that. Rub in the butter until you have a mixture with the texture of fine bread crumbs. Add just enough ice-water to bring together into a ball. Wrap in wax paper and chill for 30 minutes.

Preheat the oven to 375°F. Allow the pastry to come to room temperature (about 10 minutes out of the refrigerator) before rolling.

Chop the chard, both stems and leaves. Throw into a heavy-based pan, cover, and cook over a low heat for 6 – 10 minutes, until both leaf and stem are tender, then drain thoroughly. When cool enough to handle, squeeze out all moisture.

While the chard is cooking, prepare the pastry shell: saving about one-fourth of the pastry for the top crust, roll out the rest of the pastry and use to line a springform pan with a diameter of about 11 inches and a depth of 2 inches. Prick the bottom of

THE BEET FAMILY *Chenopodiaceae*

52

the shell with a fork, line with wax paper, and weight with dried beans. Bake for about 5 minutes. Remove the paper and beans.

Place the drained chard in a bowl and mix in the cheeses, cream, the 2 whole eggs, and seasoning. Stir, mixing thoroughly. Pour into the pastry shell. Roll out the remaining pastry and put it in place over the top, moistening the edges with a little milk.

Glaze with the remaining egg yolk beaten with a little milk. Protect the top crust with parchment paper or foil and bake for 45 minutes or so, taking off the paper or foil for the last 5 minutes to brown the crust. Serve the pie cold or warm.

ON PASTRY

We all want to achieve crumbly, buttery pastry that melts in the mouth. When you want the pastry to make sides for a tart, however, that kind of pastry tends to collapse, so it must be prebaked with plenty of dried beans in a foil lining to hold the sides up.

It is the ratio of fat to flour, with the addition of the minimum of ice-water, that gives the crumbly texture. It is the quality of the fat and flour that gives the flavor. The best pastry I ever made used unpasteurized butter, stoneground flour, and well water. How's that for purity? Food can only be as good as its ingredients. You can dispense with the butter and substitute crème fraîche or fromage blanc, but if you use lowfat kinds of either, the pastry will be brittle and tasteless. Rich pastry needs a high amount of fat.

Also, for the best taste, it is advisable to use bottled water for your pastry.

CHARD DHAL

This is another recipe that uses both leaf and stem, and which is unexpectedly creamy.

¼ cup brown lentils
1 tablespoon turmeric
1 pound chard leaves and stems, chopped small
½ cup orange lentils
sea salt and freshly ground black pepper

Lentils do not have to be soaked. Into 7½ cups of boiling water, throw the brown lentils with the turmeric. Let simmer for 20 minutes.

Now add the Swiss chard and bring back to a boil. Simmer for 10 minutes more. Now add the orange lentils and simmer for another 10 minutes.

Season with salt and pepper. The lentils should have soaked up all the water and can be served at once, though it will do no harm to let them rest in the warm. The dhal should have an amazingly buttery texture and creamy flavor.

WILTED CHARD SALAD

Young Swiss chard leaves can be used uncooked, as a salad vegetable. Like young spinach, however, they are also excellent in a wilted salad. The term "wilted" is somewhat off-putting, but all it means is that the leaves are briefly stir-fried with a flavored oil, spices, and other ingredients for a second or two so that the leaves just reduce, or grow a little limp, and get coated with flavorings. These salads are supposed to be served warm, and jolly good they are, too.

2 tablespoons mustard or sesame oil
3 tablespoons grated fresh gingerroot
3 garlic cloves, sliced
1 hot red chili, seeded and sliced
(or broken up if dried)
1 tablespoon each of crushed cumin, cardamom,
and coriander seeds
1 pound Swiss chard, leaves torn
and stems chopped (keep separate)
¼ teaspoon sea salt
¼ teaspoon sugar
1 tablespoon amchoor (dried mango powder), or to taste

Heat the oil in the pan and throw in the ginger, garlic, chili, spices, and chopped chard stems. Stir-fry until the spices darken and the garlic browns; by then the chard stems should just be beginning to soften.

Now add the torn leaves and stir-fry rapidly for about 30 seconds. Add the salt and sugar, stirring again, then tip the pan contents into a salad bowl, sprinkle with the amchoor, and serve immediately.

SWISS CHARD *Beta vulgaris* subsp. *cicla*

BEET

Beta vulgaris subsp. *vulgaris*

We tend not to value this vegetable, relegating it to cold salad or pickles. I wonder why, for its flavor is delicious and its color remarkable. It makes the most stunning soup—*bortsch*—and when eaten small, as a hot vegetable, is an excellent foil to game. I suspect that the beet's habit of oozing its cardinal red dye over everything may be a deterrent to its popularity. There are, however, ways and means of guarding against this, and they should be taken so that we can enjoy the vegetable more.

We know that the Greeks merely ate the leaves, but they treasured the bulbous root for its medicinal qualities. The Romans cultivated the root and began eating it at table. Apicius gives a recipe for a beet salad to be dressed with mustard, oil, and vinegar.

Beet plants will stand salty soil, so they are a useful crop for growing on reclaimed land near the sea. The beet is important economically, because its siblings, the sugar beet and the mangel-wurzel, both played dramatic parts in recent history. Ever since the sixteenth century it was known that some roots contained sugar, but the human appetite for the sweet stuff used to be minuscule compared to nowadays. In 1788, the French were consuming only two pounds of sugar per person per year, while in the U.S. today the consumption is two pounds per person per week.

In 1747, a German chemist, A. S. Margraaf, isolated sugar from beets. The sugar beet looks like a large white parsnip; each one can be 2 pounds in weight and a foot in length. In 1776, the first factory to process sugar from beets began working, and twenty years later another factory in Austria was opened by a pupil of Margraaf's. The process was not particularly efficient, however: only 2 to 3 percent of the sugar was extracted from the beets. It took war and a naval blockade for the sugar beet industry to take off in a big way. The English blockaded Napoleonic France, cutting the country off from its sugar cane supplies. Napoleon ordered 70,000 acres to be planted with sugar beet. In 1812, Benjamin Delessert, a French financier, opened a refinery in Paris to process the beets. The development of the sugar beet used the white variety and, by 1880, beet sugar was more widely consumed than cane sugar in Europe, except for Britain. Production of beet sugar in Britain only began seriously in 1924, when the Treasury granted a huge subsidy to its manufacture.

The mangel-wurzel—for long a subject of schoolboy jokes in Britain—is a reddish-orange in color, not unlike rutabaga, and is grown as winter fodder for cattle. Its name is merely German for beet; it had been grown in Germany and Holland ever since the 1650s, and from there it spread to northern France where, in times of famine, it was eaten by people as well as cattle. Confusion between the German *mangold* (beet) and *mangel* (dearth) led the French to call it *racine de disette* (root of scarcity/dearth).

In the latter part of the eighteenth century, during periods of hardship in rural England, the mangel-wurzel was planted to provide cheap food. Its name and reputation were against it, however, and people were convinced that it did not save them from famine but brought it and the stigma of it to their land. It was, they thought, a food for cattle and would remain so. Already cattle were being fed through the winter with turnips and rapeseed cakes (after the oil had been pressed out of the crop), but it was not until the next century that mangel-wurzels were grown for cattle—and they still are, around me in East Anglia. In the autumn months, great piles of mangel-wurzels lie in the fields waiting to be carried to the farms. Cattle love them as they, too, like sweetness.

NUTRITION

The green leaves of the beet are very high in vitamin A and, therefore, make a good substitute for spinach. In fact, they have more iron, calcium, trace minerals, and vitamin C than spinach itself. The roots, or beets themselves, are rich in potassium and fiber, but also contain oxalic acid (see page 45).

VARIETIES

Beets come in all shapes: round, ovoid, or long and tapering like a carrot. The taste is the same whatever the shape. There is also a white beet that tastes exactly the same as the red.

THE BEET FAMILY *Chenopodiaceae*

Round red varieties—by far the most popular—include Boltardy, Detroit, Dark Red, and Monopoly, all of which are bolt-resistant. Monopoly is unique in that one seed makes one plant (ordinary beet seeds are clusters, so you must thin the plants no matter how carefully you have spaced the seed). For a small beet, plant Little Ball, which is used for commercial pickling. Of the yellow varieties, the best is considered to be Burpee's Golden; its yellow flesh does not bleed when cut. A good white variety is Albina Vereduna. A good storage beet is Lutz Winter Keeper, which can grow very large without becoming woody. Cylindrical varieties include Formanova and Cylindra.

CHOOSING, PREPARING, AND STORING

Buy your beets small if possible. Also buy them as fresh as you can and with their leaves attached, so you can see how fresh they are. The leaves will wilt after the first day.

Beets store well—up to a few weeks if necessary. After that they will certainly start to get soft and will not be worth cooking.

To prepare beets: wash the earth off them without breaking the skin, then twist or cut the leaves off, leaving about 4 inches of stem (otherwise the color will run); don't cut off the tapering root.

COOKING

Boil beets for about 30–40 minutes. Larger and older beets can take 60 minutes or more to cook through. Drain, let cool a little, then rub off the skin. If you want your baby beets very hot you will have to impale them on a fork (when they will bleed a little) and peel them that way. Older, larger beets can be baked in the oven, either just placed in a covered baking dish or wrapped in foil. They will cook in a moderate oven (375°F) and take one or two hours, depending on their size.

One of my most favorite meals is a collection of young, new-season's vegetables—beets, tiny potatoes and carrots, turnips, beans, and onions—all just simply boiled or steamed and then served on a great platter with a large accompanying bowl of glistening aïoli mayonnaise. It is one of the really great treats of early summer.

My mother used to serve a white sauce with hot beets. This was satisfactory except that the sauce slowly turned pink in splotches, which can be unsightly. Butter or a garlicky vinaigrette can also be served with hot beets, as can a sweet-and-sour sauce made with brown sugar, hot chili, vinegar, and oil.

This is a recipe from the classic French work *Le Cuisinier Royal* (1682), which shows how imaginative they were with beets then: "First rost your Beet Roots in the Embers and peel them very well. Cut them into pieces and give them a boil with a piece of sugar, a little salt and cinnamon and make them like marmelade, and put them into a fine paste with some green Citron rasp'd and a piece of butter and do not cover it but when it is baked, serve it away with perfumed sugar and Orange Flowers."

Raw grated beet makes a marvelous salad, and I can't understand why it is not eaten more often. Consuming beets will, of course, turn your urine pink or red: it is quite harmless, so do not worry.

Grated raw beet can be dressed with oil and vinegar and have other raw vegetables mixed in with it: diced tomato and onion, or finely sliced leek and grated cabbage. It is particularly good with chopped dried fruits: apricots, prunes, and raisins. I cannot recommend these salads highly enough.

One of the great Eastern European taste combinations is horseradish and beet. Ideally, you should use fresh horseradish, but if you cannot find any you can use bottled prepared horseradish: add a spoonful of horseradish to any beet salad (beets dressed with sweet-and-sour sauce certainly could also benefit from this addition).

The flavor of beets—that sweet earthiness—needs very little to accentuate it. This flavor is experienced most powerfully in soups made from beets; with their colors of deep garnet and amethyst, they belong to soup royalty. Jane Grigson makes the point most forcefully: "I do not understand why the English and Italians, and even more the French who understand such things so well, have not developed some striking beetroot soup of their own."

BEET *Beta vulgaris* subsp. *vulgaris*

ABOVE Grated beet salad with dried fruits, roasted beet wedges, and beet aspics

BORTSCH

for 6

1 pound small beets
5 pints vegetable stock (see note below)
sea salt and freshly ground black pepper
sour cream or plain yogurt, for serving

Peel the beets and slice or dice them into chunks. Add these to the stock and bring to a boil. Simmer for about 45 minutes. Allow to cool, the blend to a purée. Season and chill until needed. Serve chilled or hot, with the sour cream or yogurt in a bowl.

VARIATIONS

• Add a couple of onions and some minced garlic.
• Instead of blending, crush the cooked beets with a potato masher. Leave to get cold, then strain. You will have a lighter soup, more akin to a beet drink.

BEET ASPICS

This is a favorite summer first course, as their taste and visual charm are so enticing. To the strained beet stock of Bortsch (variation 2), add 2 tablespoons of unflavored gelatin and heat until thoroughly dissolved. Pour into molds. Chill until set.

Dilute some light fromage blanc, sour cream, or crème fraîche with a little white wine or dry sherry and flood some chilled plates with this. Unmold the aspics on the plates so that they sit in the center.

Garnish with a little chopped chive, salad burnet, chopped lovage, or petals of viola, geranium, or nasturtium—anything with flavor that also looks striking.

For a darker version flavored with ginger, cook the beets as for Bortsch, but add 3 tablespoons of grated fresh gingerroot. Blend together in the stock, let cool a little, and then add the gelatin.

THE BEET FAMILY *Chenopodiaceae*

ORACH

Atriplex hortensis

This beautiful plant, also called mountain spinach, is either red- or golden-leaved. It seeds itself each year in my own garden and flourishes. It is tall—up to seven feet—and has small, triangular, pointed leaves. When young these can be eaten in a mixed salad; the larger leaves can be treated like spinach. The plant is so beautiful, however, I can never bear to harvest it.

The name orach is a corruption of *aurum* (gold), because the seeds mixed with wine were supposed to cure yellow jaundice. Also, the seeds heated with vinegar, honey, and salt and then applied in a poultice were once used as a cure for gout.

Orach's history as a kitchen vegetable is a long one. Its cousin sea orach (*Atriplex halimus*) is one of the few plants indigenous to Egypt that can sustain man. Dioscorides, the first-century Greek physician, mentions it being cooked and eaten. It grows on the shores of the Mediterranean and northern Europe.

Orach was known by the Greeks, who boiled the leaves; the Romans knew it as *atriplex*. The wild form of orach (*Atriplex patula*) was loathed by the sixteenth-century herbalist Gerard: "It groweth in the most filthy places that may be found." He goes on to say that its smell is like stinking fish or the ruttish male goat; the common term for it was "stinking motherwort." The seventeenth-century herbalist Culpeper is in agreement, but describes its use in curing all manner of women's diseases. Perhaps this twinning of the female with a repugnant herb reflects more on then-prevalent male attitudes to women than anything else.

The common orach is called "fat hen" in some parts of Britain and, indeed, it belongs to a species that grows in farmyards and fields on muck heaps. The *Reader's Digest Field Guide to the Wild Flowers of Britain* entirely ignores what Gerard and Culpeper said of the common orach, and comments: "The garden form of orache (or orach) was served until quite recently as a table vegetable resembling spinach." Its entry under *Atriplex patula*, however, seems to confuse the common and garden varieties, and claims that we treat them both as a weed.

Garden orach was eaten in the Ancient World much as other leaves such as mustard, dock, nettle, and mallow were—the young leaves raw, the larger, older leaves boiled. Apicius gives a recipe in which he purées nettle leaves and then adds eggs. At the same time, in Britain, they were eating much the same mixture; mustard and orach seeds were found in the intestinal areas of the skeletons unearthed at ancient Glastonbury. Orach has always been an important food plant for man. The seeds contain fat and albumen, and they formed part of the last meal of the preserved Iron Age Tollund Man.

As the plant is easy to grow in temperate climes, one can assume that throughout the dark and medieval ages it remained part of the fare of the majority of people. Later, it was much used in seventeenth-century soups and stuffings, because once cooked it reduces itself to a purée. John Evelyn comments: "Being set over a fire, neither this nor the lettuce needs any other water than their own moisture to boil them in." One can imagine orach as part of the range of herbs and vegetables used at medieval banquets, as well as being an ingredient for the soup of the poor. We next hear of it in 1538, when William Turner, the physician, botanist, and Dean of Wells Cathedral, refers to orach in his *Herbal*. From then on it is continually mentioned by herbalists. By 1806, three different kinds of orach are listed in the *American Gardener's Calendar* by Bernard McMahon.

Sadly, orach disappeared from our gardens this century. However, the seeds of both the red orach (*A. hortensis rubra*) and the gold orach (*A. hortensis*) can be obtained from specialist suppliers (see page 279).

GOOD KING HENRY

Chenopodium bonus-henricus

This is another plant that has disappeared from our gardens, but which was much valued in the past. Modern writers disagree as to its culinary charms. Geoffrey Grigson, in *The Englishman's Flora* (1975), writes: "Since the young shoots and flowering tops boiled and eaten with butter are neither very pleasant nor unpleasant, this plant hardly lives up to its name as an old pot-herb." English food and garden writer of the 1940s and '50s, T. A. Layton has a quite different view: "Here is a vegetable which is quite extraordinarily easy to grow and tastes every bit as good as spinach. When the shoots are young and are earthed up in the early spring, it is as good as asparagus…" I have grown it for many years, and the trick is to do as Layton says. Do not bother with the flowering tops or the leaves, though they taste much like spinach.

The name Good King Henry is only vaguely to do with King Hal; in fact, the original German had nothing to do with a monarch at all. The plant got its name from Tudor herbalists who translated the German *Güter Heinrich* (good Henry) to distinguish it from *Boser Heinrich* (bad Henry), a poisonous plant (*Mercurialis perennis*) that it resembles. The Germans did not call it "King," and the Heinrich was probably an elf in the same way that the British give many plants the title Robin, after Puck or Robin Goodfellow, the malicious fairy of medieval folklore. Tudor herbalists, delighted with the title "good Henry," decided that a little royal flattery might not be a bad thing.

The plant was certainly cultivated with much enthusiasm in the sixteenth century, and it remained popular in some parts of England, though it seemed to have died out elsewhere. In 1783, Henry Bryant, the botanist, writes: "Formerly cultivated in English gardens but of late neglected, although certainly of sufficient merit."

H. G. Glasspoole, in his history of common cultivated vegetables, written for the Ohio State Board of Agriculture in 1875, commented that in Lincolnshire, England, Good King Henry "was preferred to garden spinach and the young shoots used to be peeled and eaten as asparagus."

GLASSWORT, SAMPHIRE or SALICORNIA

Salicornia europaea

This sea plant comes into season in summer and lasts through the fall. It can be foraged all summer, and you may see it—very rarely—in a chic market.

Glasswort grows in estuaries and salt marshes all around the European coastline, as well as along the Atlantic and Pacific coasts of North America. A walk at low tide will show the bright green spears rising about 3 inches above the mud. You can start picking them then, snapping them off above the root, or wait until August when most of the plant shows.

In the sixteenth century, Gerard describes "Glasse Saltwort" thus: "Glassewort hath many grosse thicke and round stalks a foot high, full of fat and thicke sprigs, set with many knots or joints, without any leaves at all, of a reddish greene color: the whole plant resembles a branch of Corall: the root is very small and single."

Glasswort belongs to the branch of the Chenopodiaceae that contains plants that are particularly rich in soda, such as *Salsola kali* and Spanish *Salsola sativa* among others; hence, they were used in the process of making both soap and glass. There was a thriving trade from the Mediterranean, sending the ashes of these plants, called "barilla," to northern Europe for the production of glass.

Cattle love the salty flavor of glasswort and will devour it greedily. Sir Thomas More (1478) names it in a list of plants that would improve "many a poor knave's pottage…glasswort might afford him a pickle for his mouthful of salt meat."

Glasswort needs very little cooking. First, wash it well by rinsing under a cold tap, then blanch by putting it in a shallow dish and pouring boiling water over it. Let it sit in the water for a few minutes, then drain and serve. Most writers recommend boiling glasswort for much longer: my much-respected friend and expert on wild food, Richard Mabey, actually says 10 minutes. I have tried steaming it for 5 minutes, and found it slightly overcooked, and boiling it for 3—still overcooked. So I tend now to stick to my blanching method.

How to eat glasswort: pick the pieces up by the root, place the stem in the mouth, and, with the teeth, pull off the green flesh from the rather wiry interior stem. Young glasswort picked before August has no wiry center. It is particularly good served with fish, and a whole bass surrounded by a bed of glasswort is a sight to inspire rapture.

QUINOA

Chenopodium quinoa

This is a very high-protein grain, packages of which you can buy in healthfood stores and some supermarkets. You can also grow it and harvest it in your own garden if you wish. It is a half-hardy annual and it will need a rich, well-manured soil. It grows to seven or eight feet, and its heads of seeds are a variety of colors: purple, pink, green, cream, gold, and ocher (although the plant in its wild state has only dark seeds). Quinoa is a spectacular addition to the garden even if you don't harvest it. Like all this family, the leaves will cook and taste like spinach.

Quinoa is indigenous to the Pacific slopes of the Andes, and was a staple food for the people of Peru and Chile. Garcilaso de la Vega, one of the great Spanish chroniclers of the sixteenth century (he was the illegitimate son of a Spanish knight and an Inca princess), records in the 1560s that the grain was called quinoa by the natives of Peru but *mujo* by the Spaniards. He writes: "Both the Indians and the Spanish eat the tender leaf in their dishes because they are savory and very wholesome. They also eat the grain in the soups, prepared in various ways."

Other explorers noticed how savory the seeds were when boiled in milk and then made into a type of gruel seasoned with hot chili pepper and salt. At other times the grains were toasted, then boiled in water and strained; the resulting brown-colored broth was seasoned and drunk as a favorite refreshment of the ladies of Lima. The seeds were also roasted and ground to be made into bread or mixed with fat and flavorings, rolled into balls, and steamed.

Aizoaceae

NEW ZEALAND SPINACH

Tetragonia expansa

This plant was first recorded by Sir Joseph Banks in 1770, at Queen Charlotte's Sound, New Zealand. Two years later it reached Kew gardens in England. It thrives in dry, hot regions and tends to be destroyed by a hard frost, but I grow it each year successfully.

It was not until Captain Cook's second voyage around the world that, back in Queen Charlotte's Sound, the botanist Foster noticed that the leaves of the plant much resembled orach and wondered whether it, too, might be an antidote to scurvy. The sailors ate it and found that it did give protection against the illness caused by a deficiency of vitamin C.

The plant was slow to catch on in Europe: in England it began to be cultivated in 1821, and a little later in France. It appeared in seed catalogues in the U.S. in 1828. Few people grow it now, however, though it is an attractive plant, with its creeping tendrils, spear-shaped leaves, and large seed pods. The leaves must be picked young. These are the only edible part; the stalks are fibrous and the seed pods hard.

The flavor is very similar to spinach. If the leaves are picked very young they have a creamy consistency that is particularly delicious and, like sorrel, they almost purée themselves.

BELOW New Zealand spinach

NEW ZEALAND SPINACH *Tetragonia expansa*

Compositae

THE
LETTUCE
FAMILY

LETTUCE *Lactuca sativa*
BELGIAN ENDIVE, RADICCHIO
and CHICORY *Cichorium intybus*
CURLY ENDIVE and ESCAROLE *Cichorium endivia*
DANDELION *Taraxacum officinale*
GLOBE ARTICHOKE *Cynara scolymus*
CARDOON *Cynara cardunculus*
JERUSALEM ARTICHOKE *Helianthus tuberosus*
SALSIFY and SCORZONERA
Tragopogon porrifolius and *Scorzonera hispanica*

Polygonaceae

RHUBARB *Rheum rhaponticum*
SORREL *Rumex acetosa*

Portulacaceae

PURSLANE *Portulaca oleracea*

The lettuce family is one of the largest in the plant kingdom, with many flowers that are familiar to us — asters, dahlias, marigolds, zinnias — and the weeds, dandelions and thistles. It numbers many food plants, including sunflowers and artichokes, as well as all those green leaves we love to eat as salads and one of the most pungent herbs, artemisia or wormwood, which is used as a flavoring in absinthe and vermouth.

61

A characteristic of the family is that its members tend to produce a bitterish milky sap, which, in many cases, seems to have soporific powers.

Included in this chapter is the related knotweed family, Polygonaceae, which contains over 800 species, many with astringent flavors and even blistering properties. Yet among them are valuable food plants, including herbs, shrubs, and trees, several of which used to be cultivated and have now gone wild. Also included here is the Portulacaceae family, which contains 500 species of herbs and small shrubs, native primarily to the Pacific coast of North America and southern South America.

LETTUCE

Lactuca sativa

The lettuce is a most astonishing plant. Not only must it be the most popular vegetable today—eaten all over the world, even by people who have little liking for it but who believe it to be the token "green leaves" to balance the protein in a meal—but in the Ancient World it was considered both an aphrodisiac and its opposite—an anaphrodisiac.

Contradictions dog the history of lettuce. It was eaten either before the meal to awaken the appetite, or at the end of the meal because it was believed to be soporific.

Herodotus notes that lettuce appeared on the royal tables of the Persian kings around 550 BC. It is also listed among the 250 plants growing in the hanging gardens of Merodach-Baladan, King of Babylonia from 721 to 710 BC, who died in 694 BC. The earliest mention of the lettuce, however, is the giant romaine lettuce—some nearly a yard tall—of the Egyptians, which appeared on many of their reliefs and which was sacred to the god Min.

The Egyptians believed lettuce was an aphrodisiac, suitable for the god of procreation and vegetation, because the milky sap from thick-stemmed lettuce seemed similar to semen. On the reliefs, the lettuce offerings that Rameses II gives to Min are phallic-shaped; Min himself sports an erect penis and appears to caress the huge lettuces behind him. Lettuce oil was used by the Egyptians to soothe the skin and to relieve headaches, and much of the lettuce crop was grown to harvest the seed for this oil. The oil was also used to anoint the salad itself.

In the rest of the Mediterranean, however, the lettuce was thought to be an anaphrodisiac, especially by the Pythagoreans, who meditated upon the spirit and valued the plant as a sedative on the flesh. After all, when Adonis died, Venus threw herself upon a lettuce bed to lull her grief and cool her desires.

It is certainly true that lettuce has a somewhat soporific effect—one that children's author Beatrix Potter was familiar with when she told the tale of Peter Rabbit. The Greeks and Romans liked to add other leaves to their salads, such as arugula, which would have had a stimulating effect, and would thus counter the effect of lettuce.

The only lettuce with which the Ancient World was familiar was romaine, but there seem to have been many varieties: from the giant Egyptian types of romaine to others with so broad a stem that wicker gates of kitchen gardens were made from them; there was even a squat-growing plant called a Spartan lettuce. There were also black lettuces, as well as red, purple, crinkly, Cappadocian, and Greek. One particular lettuce was named the "eunuch" (because of its "potent check to amorous propensities," Pliny tells us), while another called the "poppy lettuce" had abundant juice and was particularly soporific.

It is Pliny who tells us of the Emperor Augustus being cured of an illness by his doctor, Musa, who gave him lettuce. So grateful was the Emperor that he had lettuce pickled in honey vinegar, thus ensuring that he could eat it throughout the year.

Augustus ate his lettuce at the beginning of the meal, but by the time of Domitian the trend had reversed and lettuce was eaten at the end. Gerard quotes Martial as asking "Telle me why lettuce, which our Grandsires last did eate/Is now of late become, to be the first of meat?" Gerard goes on to say that now lettuce is eaten at both times, "before the meal it stirreth up the appetite and afterwards it keepeth away drunkenness."

Romaine lettuce is so-called because it was thought to have been brought to France by the Papal court's move to Avignon; it is also known as cos lettuce because it is said to have originated on the Greek island, Cos. The round-hearted lettuce was bred in monastery gardens some time in the early Middle Ages. Certainly the Goodman of Paris had much to say to his young wife on cultivating it: "note that they do not linger in the ground, but come up very thickly, wherefore you must root them up here and there, to give space to the rest that they crowd not."

In 1597, Gerard describes only eight different types of lettuce, and by 1822 there were only thirty. Lettuce was almost invariably eaten raw, though from Apicius onward there are also some recipes.

VARIETIES

There are now hundreds of different varieties of lettuce. We have added to the romaine and butterhead types the crisphead and looseleaf types. The latter has the advantage for the gardener of allowing the leaves to be picked without uprooting the plant.

Of the romaine types, the most popular is probably Parris Island Cos. Next in taste and form must come Winter Density. Other varieties are Plato, Kinemontpas (bolt-resistant), Little Gem, and the red-tinged Rouge d'Hiver. The best of the butterhead (Boston/Bibb) types are Buttercrunch and Tom Thumb, and the crisphead or iceberg types are Webb's Wonderful, Victoria, Centennial, Summertime, and Rougette du Midi. Looseleaf lettuces are Red and Green Lollo, Red and Green Salad Bowl, and Black Seeded Simpson.

NUTRITION

Lettuce is high in iron, calcium, phosphorus, and potassium, and it contains vitamins A, C, and E. It is, therefore, high in antioxidants, so it is true that a fresh green salad every day is a necessary part of the diet. Also, as vitamin B12 is created by bacteria acting on algae, it is a good thing to eat plenty of green leaves from the garden which have not been too scrupulously washed. It is, in my opinion, a myth that vegetarians and vegans will suffer from any B12 deficiencies when they consume so much greenery. However, sterilized plastic-wrapped leaves from the supermarket will not give B12.

BUYING, STORING, AND PREPARING

If at all possible, buy all your lettuce and salad greens from local farmers or a farmers' market, or from a wholefood market, so you know the origin of the produce. In this way you can check whether the farmer uses pesticides or nitrate fertilizers. There is no doubt that organically grown vegetables have more flavor than any others, and your own vegetables grown in your own garden are far and away the best. The fresher the vegetable and the shorter the time since it has left the earth, the greater the nutritional content and flavor.

The freshness of a lettuce is easy enough to see. It should be vibrant in color and erect in leaf. Lettuce with yellowy leaves should not be for sale. If picked fresh, all salad leaves should be eaten that day or the following. If they must be stored, take them out of their plastic bag and keep in the salad drawer of the refrigerator or somewhere equally cool and dark.

On the whole, I am against washing vegetables, and certainly the washing of salad leaves seems to be overdone; it is so difficult to dry them adequately even though salad spinners have now become a vital part of kitchen life. I would prefer to inspect the leaves and if dirt is found, remove it by discarding the leaf or wiping it clean.

Never cut a lettuce leaf—simply pull it apart—and never shred it as some cookbooks tell you. The Greek salad (and in Malta, too) is built up on sliced lettuce, but it is eaten seconds after being prepared and this alleviates the harm. Exposing cut surfaces of the leaves breaks down the cellular structure, so that the lettuce grows limp quickly, loses nutrients, and oxidizes quicker—it will then darken and bruise.

MAKING SALADS

You will need a large salad bowl, so the lettuce leaves can be gently tossed without falling out. Estimate with care the amount of dressing needed for the amount of salad. Each leaf should be finely coated, but there should be no excess dressing left at the bottom of the bowl.

LETTUCE *Lactuca sativa*

Make the dressing in a small bowl or jar, or even in the salad bowl itself where it can be mixed or beaten strenuously, then poured out into a pitcher so that it can be added to the leaves after they are in the bowl. Use one part of vinegar or lemon juice to five parts of oil, and add sea salt, a pinch of sugar, and a good turn of the pepper mill, before adding anything else. There is a variety of possible additions to this basic dressing, beginning with a minced garlic clove, to soy sauce, Worcestershire sauce, Tabasco, grated lemon or orange zest, minced onion or shallot, raw or pounded boiled egg yolk, and many others—be adventurous and experiment.

The classic addition to the green salad in nineteenth-century France was the *ravigote*, literally meaning the "pick-me-up" (from *ravigoter*, to cheer or strengthen). This is an assemblage of four herbs—tarragon, chervil, chives, and burnet. These were minced and placed in four separate saucers for the chef to create his particular mixture for that night.

COOKED LETTUCE

Lettuce needs very little cooking, but it is well worth doing occasionally, because the flavor is different and very pronounced. In my opinion, one of the greatest lettuce dishes is the French recipe for cooking green peas, Lettuce Clamart, given by Jane Grigson in her *Vegetable Book*.

In another quick recipe halved romaine lettuce hearts are smeared with a sauce and broiled. For the sauce, try mixing about one ounce of blue cheese with a couple of spoonfuls of fromage blanc or sour cream. This is smeared over the inner hearts, which are then placed in a pan and broiled for about 2 minutes. Alternatively, mix a finely diced small green bell pepper with a teaspoon of fromage blanc and use that instead of the blue cheese sauce to coat the lettuce.

Romaine lettuce is often used for cooking, because it has enough vigor to be cooked and not wilt entirely. Butterhead lettuce would decline rapidly into soft rags, but crisphead lettuce such as Iceberg and Webb's Wonderful is excellent for an instant's stir-frying to make a wilted salad. Older recipes for braising lettuce in butter for 45 minutes, as an accompaniment to roasted meat, seem to me not

worth doing. The flavor of the cooked lettuce is bitter, and the texture limp and slimy.

Large romaine lettuce leaves can replace grapevine leaves, to make a *LETTUCE DOLMADES*. For this, the central spines of the leaves are cut out and the leaves are blanched for 10 seconds, then drained thoroughly. A mixture of ricotta cheese, chopped onion, soy sauce, and chopped fresh herbs is used as the stuffing, though it could be highly seasoned cooked fish or ground game mixed with rice or bulghur wheat, moistened perhaps with a tiny amount of fromage blanc. A heaped teaspoon of the mixture is placed at the end of each leaf and the leaf is rolled up, tucking in the sides as you go. These refreshing *dolmades* make excellent canapés or first courses.

LETTUCE CLAMART

Clamart is the district in Paris where the best peas were once grown. Every summer this recipe becomes one of our most favorite luncheon dishes. No water is needed, and, though it might look like a soup, you need to eat it with a knife, fork, and spoon. It is a perfect recipe for summer vegetables. If you are lucky enough to have some baby artichoke hearts, they can be added, too.

> *2 tablespoons butter*
> *1 tablespoon olive oil*
> *1 onion or 3 shallots, minced*
> *2 or 3 large heads of romaine lettuce*
> *1½ pounds fresh green peas, shelled*
> *4 or 5 baby carrots, diced*
> *4 or 5 baby zucchini, thinly sliced*
> *a large sprig of mint*
> *a large pinch of sea salt*
> *a pinch of sugar*

Melt the butter with the oil in a large saucepan. Throw in the onion or shallots, followed by the leaves from the lettuce. Lay them across the bottom of the saucepan to provide a nest for the vegetables.

Add the peas, carrots, and zucchini. Then bury the mint among them, sprinkle salt and sugar over the top, and fit a lid tightly on the pan. Simmer over a low heat for about 15 minutes, when all the vegetables should have steamed tender in their own juices.

You will need soup bowls for serving and a large pepper mill on the table, plus possibly some more butter and olive oil.

ICED LETTUCE SOUP

2 tablespoons butter
1 onion or 3 shallots, minced
2 or 3 large heads of romaine lettuce
sea salt and freshly ground black pepper
5 cups vegetable stock
1¼ cups dry white wine
1¼ cups buttermilk or sour cream
chopped chives, for garnish

Melt the butter in a large saucepan and throw in the onion or shallots, followed by the leaves torn from the heads of lettuce. Season lightly and place a tightly fitting lid on the pan.

Let cook over a low heat for about 10 minutes, then add the vegetable stock, cover the pan again, and cook for a further 10 minutes.

Let the pan cool, then pour the contents into a blender and blend until smooth, adding the wine and buttermilk or sour cream.

Taste and adjust the seasoning, if necessary. Chill for 2–3 hours before serving, sprinkled with some chopped chives.

LETTUCE WRAPS

Crisphead lettuce such as Iceberg and Webb's Wonderful makes an excellent receptacle for other foods, especially in Asian cooking. Ground roast quail, pigeon, or duck is mixed with herbs and spices and served with a pile of crisp lettuce leaves and a separate bowl of dipping sauce. The diner places some of the mixture on a leaf, sprinkles a little sauce over it, and rolls it up, ready to eat. I find the crunch of the raw lettuce around a highly seasoned filling particularly agreeable. It is a dish worth trying at home. The following recipe is my vegetable alternative.

2 heads of Iceberg or Webb's Wonderful lettuce
for the filling:
1 cup rice cooked with a pinch of saffron
1 cup tabbouleh
2 onions or shallots, minced
1 red bell pepper, diced small
2 fresh hot green chilies, diced small
a generous handful each of chopped parsley,
chives, and basil
1 tablespoon fromage blanc
1 tablespoon soy sauce
sea salt and freshly ground black pepper
for the dipping sauce:
1 hot red chili, diced small
1½ tablespoons grated fresh gingerroot
1 teaspoon sugar
1 tablespoon Dijon mustard
¼ cup light soy sauce
1 tablespoon dry sherry
1 tablespoon sesame oil

First make the sauce: place the diced chili and grated ginger in a bowl, add the sugar and mustard, and then add the remaining ingredients. Stir well and let stand for several hours.

Make the filling by mixing the ingredients together thoroughly, then chill and place in a large bowl.

Separate the lettuce into individual leaves. Pile them on a plate.

A spoonful of the filling is placed on a lettuce leaf and the dipping sauce is sprinkled over, then the leaf is rolled up and eaten.

VARIATIONS

You can add any of the following to the filling mixture: shrimp or scallops that have been grilled or broiled and diced small; flaked cooked fish (but not an oily fish); chopped cooked mushrooms or other fungi; chopped tomato flesh; cooked artichoke bottoms or ears of baby corn; roasted game that has been ground and moistened with stock (in this case the rice and tabbouleh amounts should be halved).

LETTUCE *Lactuca sativa*

BELGIAN ENDIVE, RADICCHIO and CHICORY

Cichorium intybus

The shoot or closed white bud (or *chicon*) is called endive by the French and Americans, but chicory by the British, and the French *chicorée frisée* is curly endive. This has always been confusing to travelers—French, British, and American—but both these vegetables, however different in appearance, were developed from *Cichorium endivia* (see page 69).

The white bud kind, which was rediscovered by accident in the middle of the nineteenth century by a M. Brezier, is also referred to as Brussels chicory, Belgian endive, or witloof, which is Flemish for "white leaf." M. Brezier was growing chicory roots for coffee and found some that had sprouted white leaves. He liked the taste and so did his family, and all his life he kept the cultivation method secret. When he died, his widow told the secret to M. Brezier's successor at the Brussels Botanical Gardens so that she could keep a little interest in the vegetable, which was becoming popular. After 1872, it was cultivated commercially. Belgian endive was, and is, an easy vegetable to grow because it occupies little space and only needs warmth, water, and complete darkness to flourish.

M. Brezier rediscovered these growing buds, for they had been cultivated in gardens in Germany in the sixteenth century. Before then, the Ancients certainly gathered green chicory from wild plants. In thick undergrowth, blanching can be a natural process.

It was not until the second half of the eighteenth century that the chicory root began to be used as an additive to coffee. The root was roasted and ground before being added. As food manufacturers adulterated coffee with an overabundance of chicory, cheating was common. The addition of chicory to coffee was banned in Britain in 1832, but surprisingly the practice had collected its adherents who liked the taste and they protested. Thus, it was allowed as long as the labeling was clear as to the contents. Coffee with chicory is still very popular in New Orleans.

To get the characteristic tight sheath of white leaves, the chicory (Belgian endive) is forced by burying the roots in warm, moist peat. If it is sold cosily nested in blue paper you can be certain it has been protected from light and will be less bitter.

VARIETIES

Both white and red varieties are available in the winter months. One red variety, Rossa de Verona, with leaves attractively tinged red, can be grown in the same way as Belgian endive.

NUTRITION

This is one of those plants, like Jerusalem artichokes, in which inulin comprises the major part of their carbohydrate. It is inulin that produces flatulence (see page 76). Belgian endive also contains vitamins A, C, and K, calcium, phosphorus, and potassium.

STORING AND PREPARING

Belgian endive keeps well, for up to a week in the salad drawer of the refrigerator or in a suitable cool and dark place. It is also easy to prepare: simply slice the root end away and discard any brown or damaged leaves. Some cooks claim that cutting endive with a knife increases the bitterness (Elizabeth David recommends a silver or stainless-steel knife for cutting them), but I have never noticed any difference.

To eat them raw, the leaves need merely to be tossed in a vinaigrette, either on their own or with other leaves. A classic mixture is Belgian endive and orange. Indeed, because of the leaf's slight bitterness, the sweetness of various fruits is a natural complement. Endive with pink grapefruit, olives, and toasted pine nuts is a good combination.

COOKING

Belgian endive is often baked, but it can be stir-fried or poached. Some people dislike the slipperiness of the cooked vegetable and this, it must be admitted, is a matter of taste. To prevent the droop of the cooked vegetable, do not slice the *chicons*, but cook them whole. If serving the endive as an accompanying vegetable, allow one for each person; for a supper or lunch dish, allow two or three.

ABOVE Baked Belgian endive (overleaf) and broiled lettuce with blue cheese (see page 64)

POACHED BELGIAN ENDIVE

6 or 8 heads of Belgian endive, trimmed
1¼ cups vegetable stock
⅔ cup sweet white wine
sea salt and freshly ground black pepper
2 tablespoons grated Parmesan cheese

Pack the endive, head-to-tail sardine-fashion, into a large saucepan and pour the stock and wine over; there should be just enough liquid to cover. Bring to a boil and simmer for 30 minutes.

Take out the endive, draining well. Place in a baking dish and keep warm.

Preheat the broiler. Reduce the cooking liquid to about ⅔ cup, and season carefully. Pour this over the endive and sprinkle with the Parmesan. Broil for a few seconds to brown the surface lightly.

STIR-FRIED BELGIAN ENDIVE

1 tablespoon sesame oil
2 – 3 garlic cloves, sliced
1½ tablespoons grated fresh gingerroot
1 dried hot red chili, broken up
3 heads of Belgian endive, separated into their leaves
1 tablespoon peanut butter
a pinch of sugar
a pinch of sea salt

Heat the oil in a wok and throw in the garlic, ginger, and chili. Stir-fry for a minute.

Add the endive leaves and stir-fry for another minute. The leaves should still be crisp.

Mix the peanut butter with 2 – 3 tablespoons of water to make a thick paste. Add this to the wok with the salt and sugar. Toss in the pan and serve.

BELGIAN ENDIVE, RADICCHIO and CHICORY *Cichorium intybus*

BAKED BELGIAN ENDIVE

Salting the vegetable before cooking makes it exude more liquid, so season only after baking.

4 or 5 heads of Belgian endive, trimmed
2 tablespoons butter
sea salt and freshly ground black pepper

Preheat the oven to 375°F.

Pack the endive into a buttered baking dish. Dot the rest of the butter over, then cover the dish with foil and bake for 45 minutes. Season and serve.

BELGIAN ENDIVE IN A FRUIT GLAZE

2 tablespoons strong fruit jelly (quince, damson, blackberry, black currant, or apricot)
2 tablespoons butter
sea salt and freshly ground black pepper
4 or 5 heads of Belgian endive

Melt the jelly in ⅓ cup of water by simmering together in a small pan. Add the butter and season.

Lay the endive in a pan and pour over the liquid. Simmer for 30 minutes or until the endive is cooked.

Remove the endive. Increase the heat and boil to reduce the liquid to a few tablespoons. Serve the endive at once with this glaze poured over.

NON-FORCED CHICORIES

All such varieties stem from the wild chicory that was blanched and eaten by the Egyptians, Greeks, and Romans, all of whom enjoyed the leaves in salads as well as cooked. There are now numerous varieties of green- and red-leaved chicories: radicchio, with its cardinal-purple leaves, is perhaps the most striking. With their color and sharp taste, these make a welcome addition to winter salads.

VARIETIES In Italy all chicories are known as *radicchio*. They are often as beautiful in their coloring and shape as ornamental cabbage.

Rossa di Treviso has long pointed leaves. Its foliage is green in summer, turning red once the cold sets in. This variety is often sold young, when the root resembles a brownish radish, with the leaves like a small mop of carmine red. If you can buy it with its roots intact, you can cut off the top and eat it as salad while burying the root in warm, damp peat. Keep the container in the dark and in six weeks you should have your own red *chicons*.

Rossa di Verona forms a tight ball of leaves, thus protecting itself in the winter. Variegata di Castelfranco has green leaves blotched with red and forms a loose head of red and white leaves at its center. Variegata di Chioggia has green leaves in the summer, but goes red and white in the winter months.

All chicories are slightly bitter in taste, but in some this is far more pronounced; they get less bitter the later in the season they are picked.

COOKING All the chicories above can be cooked as well as eaten raw. Simply treat them as you would lettuce, tearing off the leaves and cooking in butter and/or olive oil, or a little stock, or adding to soups and stews. However, cooking turns the red shades into green and I cannot see much point in it, although the color is retained if the chicory is only warm.

LEFT Rossa di Treviso

CURLY ENDIVE
and ESCAROLE

Cichorium endivia

This group of salad plants is often confused with the chicories—understandably as they are close cousins, and they were considered the same family in the Ancient World. Like the chicories, they have always been used in salads and sometimes cooked. They can be divided up into curly- and broad-leaved types. We also know the broad-leaved kind as escarole, sometimes Batavia or Batavian endive.

Fine Curled is the frilly-leaved, small-headed type known as frisée, and Green Curled Ruffec is a classic large, frilly-headed type, resistant to cold and rot.

Broad-leaved varieties include Sugar Loaf, which forms a large, compact head with very tender leaves; Full Heart, which makes a large head with well-blanched interior; and Broad Leaved Batavian, a widely available producer of large heads.

WARM SALAD OF RADICCHIO, FRISÉE, AND GLAZED SQUASH

2 – 3 tablespoons olive oil
2 – 5 garlic cloves, minced
1½ tablespoons grated fresh gingerroot
1 small butternut squash, peeled, seeded, and cubed
2 tablespoons white wine vinegar
1 tablespoon sugar
1 teaspoon sea salt
1 tablespoon sesame oil
*1 head of radicchio, torn into pieces if
the leaves are large*
½ head of curly endive, torn into pieces
½ head of escarole, torn into pieces
few cilantro leaves, chopped

Heat the olive oil in a frying pan and add the garlic, ginger, and cubed squash. Fry for about 5 minutes, turning the pieces so that they brown and are crisp on the outside.

Add the wine vinegar, sugar, and salt, raise the heat, and cook for another minute.

Meanwhile, heat the sesame oil in a pan and throw in the radicchio, endive, and escarole leaves. Stir-fry for a minute or until the leaves just begin to wilt. Remove from the heat and transfer the leaves to a large serving platter.

Pour the squash over and sprinkle the bed of leaves with chopped cilantro. Serve immediately.

DANDELION

Taraxacum officinale

Our name for this plant is a corruption of the French *dent de lion*, from the medieval Latin *dens leonis*. The leaves, upright and pointed, are cut into jagged teeth and it is these that were thought, rather fancifully, to resemble the teeth of the lion. The Latin horticultural name is derived from the Greek *taraxos* (disorder) and *akos* (remedy), which are evidence of the ancient curative and medicinal uses of the plant.

The first mention of dandelion as a medicine is in the works of the Arab physicians of the tenth and eleventh centuries. It is the milky white juice contained in the root that was valued as a stimulant and diuretic—it did not get its French name *pissenlit* for nothing. A brew of the roots has also been prescribed in cases of hepatitis. Mrs. Greaves tells us that: "A broth of Dandelion roots, sliced and stewed in boiling water with some leaves of Sorrel and the yolk of an egg, taken daily for some months, has been known to cure seemingly intractable cases of chronic liver congestion." As the roots are high in inulin (see page 76) one wonders whether the patient suffered torments of flatulence under this cure.

The dandelion is an important plant for bees and the production of honey, because the flowers open early in the year, even in a cool spring, and furnish considerable quantities of nectar and pollen, while successive blooms continue throughout the year until the late autumn. The plant is highly sensitive: in fine weather the flowers follow the sun, turning toward the warmth, but long before dusk the flowers close up against the dew of the night; they will also close up at the threat of rain in the day.

DANDELION *Taraxacum officinale*

NUTRITION

The leaves are high in vitamins A and C and contain more iron than spinach, as well as potassium. They thus form a very valuable salad food, especially early in the spring when there are few fresh greens around.

PREPARING AND COOKING

Pick the leaves when they first appear, when the buds are still very tightly buried in the heart of the plant (older leaves are inedibly bitter). Use the leaves in mixed salads or on their own. Sandwiches of dandelion leaves, dressed in a little oil, lemon, sea salt, and pepper with perhaps the addition of avocado or onion, are excellent.

The leaves can also be cooked, and what better way to use the dandelions in your garden than to pick all the leaves and sauté them in a little butter and oil over a gentle heat for about 10 minutes?

GLOBE ARTICHOKE

Cynara scolymus

Both the Greeks and the Romans were very fond of artichokes, or was it the cardoon? We are uncertain, for the globe artichoke is the cultivated form of cardoon. It is thought that these handsome plants were discovered in North Africa, and then cultivated in southern Europe.

However, it was not until the middle of the fifteenth century that the artichoke was cultivated for its huge unopened flower bud. In Venice, in 1493, the chronicler and historian Ermolao Barbaro wrote of a single plant being grown as a novelty in a private garden. Soon, though, the artichoke became a staple and popular food all over Italy. Not for Goethe, however: in the eighteenth century, in his *Travels Through Italy,* he comments that the peasants ate thistles and that he found them not to his liking. (These could have been actual thistles, for the Romans ate them, and it is reasonable to suppose that Italian peasants continued to eat thistles when fashionable society had long forgotten about them.) The artichoke did not reach England until the middle of the fifteenth

century, but then quickly became popular in the kitchen garden. The plant grows well in a cool, damp, temperate climate, and by 1687 it was thought by John Worlidge—who wrote the first systematic treatise (*Systema Agriculturae*) on agricultural husbandry on a comprehensive scale—to be "one of the most excellent fruits."

Artichokes have a long history of medicinal use; indeed, the Romans thought the juice was a cure for baldness. Dodoens' *Herbal* of 1578 suggests that the root is good against the rank smell of armpits. It notes also "that it sendeth forth plentie of stinking urine," but added that this has the positive effect of amending the "ranke and rammish savour of the body."

John Evelyn tells us that in Italy artichokes were eaten with orange juice and sugar. He himself, surprisingly, cuts the small buds into four and eats them raw with vinegar, salt, and pepper, washed down with a glass of wine—following Dr. Muffet's advice—at the end of the meal. Evelyn also cooks young artichokes in butter until crisp and serves them with parsley, while he bakes the bottoms, or *fonds* in French, in pies with beef marrow and dates.

I grow more and more artichoke plants every year, and harvest the flower buds when they are small. These only need to have their pointed leaves cut away, to have the outside of the bottom peeled, and the merest few outside leaves discarded. The hairy choke has not yet formed in the young buds, so those inner yellow leaves can just be gouged out with a knife. Everyone now tells you to place the bud in acidulated water until ready for cooking, to stop discoloration, but it is only a matter of minutes before a dozen or so small artichokes can be trimmed and prepared. Once quartered, these can be fried in olive oil with some garlic and served with a sprinkling of sea salt and lemon juice. Prepared this way, they are the most delicious of all foods. Baby artichokes can also be trimmed and peeled, then sliced thinly downward, dipped in a light batter, and fried until crisp.

Interestingly, for many people eating the artichoke has a curious effect on their taste buds. American food writer James Beard commented in 1971 that wine drinkers felt that the taste of artichokes ruined the flavor of fine wines. Research conducted in the

1930s found that for two-thirds of people, eating artichokes made a drink of water seem sweet. In 1954, it
was discovered that the source of this phenomenon
was an organic acid called cynarin, unique to artichokes. This substance can stimulate the sweetness
receptors, but only in those who are susceptible to it.

VARIETIES

There are two main varieties of artichoke, the green
and the purple. The latter has rather spiky leaves and
can be more awkward to prepare, but there is no difference in flavor. Artichokes also come in round
globes or egg shapes; again there is no noticeable difference in flavor. There are dozens of different types,
and each country seems to have a preference.

BUYING AND STORING

Globe artichokes turn brown and dry out on the outside very quickly (inside a week), so pick your buds
when the exterior leaves are green and juicy. If you

are not going to eat them at once, keep them in the
salad drawer of the refrigerator for not longer than
three days. They can also be cooked and then refrig-
erated for two days. All vegetables, of course, taste
best if cooked and eaten as soon as possible after
being bought.

PREPARING AND COOKING

The habit of eating artichokes young is common all
over southern Europe, in Italy, Spain, and Greece.
On rare occasions you can find them that way in the
U.S., too, where artichokes are grown in California
for year-round consumption. In Britain, most artichokes come from Brittany, where they do not harvest them until they are as plump and large as a small
cantaloupe. I once asked that they export the artichokes to us when small, starting in March and continuing through until July, but my request fell on deaf
ears. Brittany artichokes had to be huge and plump,
and that was the way the ignorant British would

GLOBE ARTICHOKE *Cynara scolymus*

continue to get them. That, at least, seemed to be the sub-text of their indifference.

If you are serving them whole, these large artichokes need to be boiled for anything from 30 to 45 minutes. Pull a leaf out after half an hour to see how tender its base is. Large globe artichokes need to have their bases trimmed so that they sit steadily on the plate; they can also have their tops severed. Restaurants often serve them this way, but you will need a sharp, heavy knife for this operation. When you need the flavor of artichoke in the stock for a stew, you need to perform this rather radical trimming and preparation on the raw vegetable. I use a cleaver, which cuts the top half of the leaves away. Now, before it is cooked, the hairy choke can be scooped out with a sharp knife and then just the bottom, ringed with leaves, can be boiled, ready to be used as a receptacle for any flavorings.

For certain of the recipes below I think this kind of surgery is worth doing on the large artichokes. This raw receptacle or cup can then be quartered and used in various stews. For other recipes, however, this process can be done later, after the artichoke is cooked. These recipes are first courses, when the artichoke is eaten just with a dressing or served with a simple stuffing. If you decide to keep the leaves on, the most attractive way of presenting the artichoke is to fan out the exterior leaves so that it looks like a water lily, then pluck out the purplish core of inner leaves, cut out the choke beneath that, and serve on individual plates. On the other hand, you can choose to serve the artichokes as they are after being cooked, and let the individual diners perform the surgery. Do then provide a large platter in the center of the table for all the discarded leaves. Small individual ramekins filled with sauce can be supplied in which each diner can dip their leaves. The next question is, what sauce to serve with the cooked artichokes?

If the artichokes are served cold, a garlicky vinaigrette is the most common sauce; if warm, then lemon drawn butter is probably the most satisfactory. Enormous pleasure can be achieved by experimenting with other sauces for the artichokes, whether they are served hot, warm, or cold. Try buttermilk, sour cream, or yogurt flavored with lemon, garlic, chili, honey, or soy sauce and celery salt perhaps, even mustard, oil, and basil. You could go to town with Hollandaise or aïoli mayonnaise, or a mixture of a not-too-hot rouille whipped into yogurt and olive oil.

If you choose to present the artichoke stuffed, then the choke and inner leaves have to be plucked and cut out, so that the delicious bottom is exposed. All manner of flavorsome fillings can then go into the center, but they must be fairly moist because the outer leaves need to be dipped into the filling instead of a sauce. At the same time, the filling must be stiff enough to stay where it is. Purées of various kinds are the answer. A classic is Fava Bean Purée (see page 154), flavored faintly with savory; a purée of fresh green peas is also marvelous, as is a purée made from leek, mushroom, and zucchini. A rather popular first course in restaurants is artichokes filled with shrimp in a mayonnaise dressing. This seems to me to be gilding the lily. If desired, shrimp in a dressing can be eaten separately on a bed of leaves.

A favorite Victorian recipe, which needed a mountain of labor for what one imagines was a mere mouse of result, was ARTICHAUTS À LA BARIGOULE. This consisted of "parboiling them, taking away the choke, stuffing them with a mixture of onion, mushroom and parsley and adding a little chopped bacon. Then you tie the artichoke up with a cotton, wrap fat bacon around it and braise it. When done, take away the bacon and serve."

You can now buy frozen artichoke hearts and canned hearts and bottoms. The bottoms make an excellent first course used in the way that the kohlrabi base is in the recipe on page 105. Or, if you are feeling reckless, canned artichoke bottoms can be employed in other ways. For example, they are delicious in pies and vegetable stews. An eighteenth-century recipe from Hannah Glasse layers artichoke bottoms with butter, egg yolks, mace, morels and truffles, moistens with a little stock and white wine, and then bakes with a crust of puff pastry.

A simpler recipe is one of Mrs. Leyel's, where the artichoke bottom is topped with a poached egg, which is covered with artichoke paste from the leaves and sprinkled with Parmesan. If you are able to find artichoke paste in jars this is a fairly trouble-free recipe.

ARTICHAUTS À LA PROVENÇALE

This recipe for small artichokes, another of Mrs. Leyel's, is a complete winner.

Take young, tender artichokes, remove the outside leaves, trim the others with scissors, and rub each artichoke with lemon to prevent it blackening. Sprinkle them one by one with good olive oil and put sea salt and pepper between their leaves.

Put them into a saucepan with some olive oil (enough to moisten the artichokes) and then pour in enough cold water to cover. Put the saucepan on a very high heat so that the oil and water will boil quickly. After just 20 minutes of simmering the artichokes will be cooked.

Serve the artichokes on a very hot dish, pouring over the boiling oil mixture that is left. They should be eaten off very hot plates. The whole of the little artichokes is edible when they are cooked in this way. Fresh water should be drunk after eating them—wine will seem unpleasantly acid, while water will have a delicate, sweet taste.

POACHED ARTICHOKES
IN WHITE WINE

4 globe artichokes (with stems if possible)
3 tablespoons olive oil
3–4 garlic cloves, sliced
1 cup dry white wine
sea salt and freshly ground black pepper
julienne strips of carrot for garnish (optional)

First prepare the artichokes: take off the outside leaves to expose the lighter green interior leaves, then cut the top two-thirds of the artichoke away. Slice the bottom third in half and, with a sharp knife, cut out the choke and the middle cluster of leaves.

Now, heat the olive oil in a pan and add the garlic. Place the artichoke halves in the oil, cut-side down. Fry for a minute or two, then add the wine and seasoning. Cover the pan tightly and poach for about 10 minutes.

This can be eaten hot or cold, garnished with carrot if you wish. Mop up the juices with bread.

Note: If the artichokes have stems, these can be peeled and chopped into 1-inch lengths, then cooked with the rest of the artichoke. They taste like the artichoke bottoms, but perhaps a little sweeter.

GRATIN OF ARTICHOKE
AND ASPARAGUS

4–6 globe artichokes, prepared, trimmed, and quartered
1 pound asparagus, trimmed
2–3 tablespoons olive oil
3–4 garlic cloves, thinly sliced
3 slices of wholewheat bread, cubed
4–6 small shallots, whole
2–3 zucchini, sliced thinly lengthwise
sea salt and freshly ground black pepper
a little chopped parsley or lovage

Throw the pieces of artichoke into a pan of boiling salted water and simmer for 20 minutes. Steam the asparagus for 10 minutes. Drain both vegetables well and slice the asparagus into 2-inch lengths.

Heat the olive oil in a large pan and throw in the garlic, cubed bread, shallots, and zucchini. Stir-fry for as long as it takes to crisp the bread.

Add the artichokes and asparagus. Stir-fry for another 10 seconds, then season, and sprinkle with the chopped herbs. Serve hot.

SPRING ARTICHOKE CASSEROLE
WITH POTATOES AND BEANS

3 tablespoons olive oil
6 garlic cloves, sliced
4 or 6 large globe artichokes, trimmed down to
their bottoms
1 pound small new potatoes, scrubbed
1 pound young fava beans, shelled
1 pound green beans, trimmed
1¼ cups vegetable stock
1¼ cups dry white wine
1 heaped teaspoon beurre manié (mixture of equal
parts flour and softened butter)
sea salt and freshly ground black pepper
a handful of minced parsley, for garnish

GLOBE ARTICHOKE *Cynara scolymus*

Heat the olive oil in a large saucepan and throw in the garlic and trimmed artichokes. Let cook a little and then add the rest of the vegetables, together with the stock and white wine. Simmer for 20 minutes. If it gets too dry at any point, add a little more of the stock or the white wine.

Increase the heat and thicken with the *beurre manié*. Season, then serve sprinkled with the parsley.

VARIATIONS

This recipe works well because the artichoke gives something of itself to all the other vegetables, but variations can also be devised a little later in the season. For example, you can use green peas, leeks, and zucchini instead of the two kinds of beans. I have also used white kidney beans and, best of all, flageolets with fresh green peas, but replacing half the oil with 2 tablespoons butter and halving the garlic.

HOT STUFFED ARTICHOKES

4 large globe artichokes, trimmed
for the stuffing:
1 small can of anchovies
½ cup canned tomatoes
a handful of minced parsley
1 tablespoon bread crumbs
1 tablespoon capers
sea salt and freshly ground black pepper

Boil the trimmed artichokes for 30 minutes. Take them out of the pan and open out the leaves. Extract the central cone of leaves and dig out the choke beneath to expose the bottom. Arrange the prepared artichokes in a baking pan and keep hot.

Preheat the oven to 375°F and make the stuffing: cook the anchovies and tomatoes with their liquid, stirring so that it becomes a thickish purée. Add the parsley, bread crumbs, and capers to thicken and flavor the purée. Season, and spoon this into the center of the artichokes.

Warm the artichokes through in the preheated oven for 10 minutes, then serve at once.

CARDOON

Cynara cardunculus

You may be fortunate enough to eat this vegetable in Europe, and would be most likely to find it in the restaurants of southern Spain and Italy. It is in season throughout the winter months. The stalks are blanched like white celery, and they are cooked by being poached in stock. They are highly delicious, having a flavor somewhere between asparagus and artichoke. No wonder the Ancient World was so enthusiastic: Pliny said cardoon was so esteemed in Rome that it fetched a higher price than any other garden herb.

Once you have eaten cardoon you may, like me, be unable to control the desire to have a steady supply and so decide to grow the vegetable in your own garden. The cardoon is a handsome plant—tall, stately, and silver, with rather smaller thistle heads than the globe artichoke. Like artichokes, the flowers of cardoon have been used throughout history as a source of vegetable rennet.

There are two methods used for blanching (whitening) the plant, and they are done at different times of the year. As cardoons are ruined by frost and an early hard winter will destroy them, for one method the stalks are wrapped in brown paper in August and blanched for several months before being lifted in October. (The whole plant in its first year would be dug up by Victorian gardeners and the bulb eaten as well as the stalks.) The other method, which I adopt, is to blanch the new shoots as they appear in January, and to keep them warm by covering the cloches with sacking. Both methods have been used from ancient times. Cardoon can be perennial where temperatures do not fall below freezing for long periods, however, so a long-lived plant will not be the best to blanch with brown paper in the autumn, because the stems will have become too fibrous.

Cardoon has never been grown with much enthusiasm outside of the Mediterranean region, except as an unusual plant for the herbaceous border. Yet John Tradescant, the English traveler, naturalist, and gardener, saw several acres being cultivated in Brussels in 1629. He admitted that he had no idea how the vegetable was harvested or cooked.

Some authorities suggest the flower heads be eaten in the same way as globe artichokes, but in my view they are not worth the trouble. The base of the flower (the equivalent of the artichoke *fond*) has neither the flavor nor the tenderness of the artichoke.

PREPARING AND COOKING

Hannah Glasse sums it all up succinctly: "You must cut them about 10 inches, and string them, and tye them up in Bundles like Asparagus, or cut them in small Dice, and boil them like Peas, and toss them up with Pepper, Salt and melted Butter."

Young small plants can be eaten raw. In the markets of southern Spain, Italy, and France, you may well see tied cardoon hearts laid out on the stalls. Discard the outer stalks, which are too fibrous, and trim the rest, putting the pieces into acidulated water so that they do not discolor. Cut into bite-size pieces and dress with vinaigrette or a light *aïoli* mayonnaise.

The same stalks can be cut to the length of asparagus and poached in stock for 10 minutes. In Italy, they are often eaten raw with *bagna cauda* ("hot bath"), that delicious sauce of anchovy and garlic. The cooked cardoon is also traditionally served with ANCHOVY SAUCE. Heat ⅔ cup of olive oil with the contents of a small can of anchovies and 2 or 3 minced garlic cloves for a few minutes, until both the garlic and anchovies have dissolved.

As cardoon is eaten in southern Europe in late autumn, it is often teamed with nuts. Cardoon can be poached in stock with a few walnuts (and a little chopped bacon, if desired) and then served simply dressed with walnut oil and lemon. Alternatively, poach them with chestnuts in stock, plus a little white wine. The sauce is then blended to make a purée and poured over the cardoon.

CARDOON *Cynara cardunculus*

JERUSALEM ARTICHOKE

Helianthus tuberosus

This vegetable's name is said to stem from the Italian *girasol articocco*, or sunflower artichoke (you will sometimes see it sold as sunchoke). Soon after it was taken to Europe from the New World, it was called the "Canada potato" and "French potato," for it flourishes in the central United States and Canada, and, being somewhat of a pest in its spreading habits, had easily reached the Atlantic coast long before the white man did. Discussing its countries of origin in 1633, the revised edition of Gerard's *Herball* was right in mentioning Canada, but wrong when he added Peru and Brazil. Gerard also notes "that this plant hath no similarity in leafe, stalke, root, or manner of growing, with an Artichoke, but only a little likenesse of taste in the dressed root." Another early observer, Marc Les Carbot, said, "Most excellent to eat, tasting like chards or cardoons, but more pleasant..."

An English gardener, John Goodyer, was given some tubers by a Flemish merchant in 1617, and first grew the Jerusalem artichoke in Britain. It was also he who first noted the vegetable's tendency to bequeath flatulence. Goodyer writes, "...they stir up and cause a filthie loathesome stinking winde within the bodie, thereby causing the belly to bee much pained and tormented, and are a meat more fit for swine, than men." Harold McGee, in *The Curious Cook*, writes amusingly and authoritatively on the reasons for this vegetable's flatulent ability in a chapter called "Taking the Wind out of the Sunroot."

The Jerusalem artichoke contains no starch or oil and little protein; 50 percent of it is carbohydrate which is indigestible. McGee says, "the troublesome molecules have never been a sufficiently important part of our diet for us to have evolved enzymes to digest them." The artichoke lays down its reserves of energy for next season's sprouts in fructose chains named inulin, and it is this chemical that gives trouble. The curious fact is that these tubers do not affect everybody in the same way. Some fortunate people can tolerate the vegetable "by virtue of native intestinal flora and digestive physiology."

Unfortunately I am no longer one of them, and I am saddened by the effect of this phenomenon, for I used to find the flavor delicate and delicious, while a soup made from the tubers was always warmly received at dinner parties. McGee suggests methods that go some way to tame the vegetable (see below).

VARIETIES AND GROWING

Twenty years ago Jerusalem artichokes were beige-colored and very knobbly and a great deal of bother to clean. Since then varieties have become smoother, and tend now to look very much like small, irregular potatoes. Boston Red has an attractive rose-red skin and a few knobs on it. Stampede is large, white, and earlier-maturing than most.

If you want to grow Jerusalem artichokes, tubers can be sown from the ones available at the market. Only grow them if you have plenty of land, though: they will grow 6 feet high and spread alarmingly. Like the potato, they do have the advantage that they can be left in the ground until you need to dig them up. However, the smallest sliver of tuber left in the ground will send out shoots in the spring, and once planted they are difficult to eradicate.

STORING, PREPARING, AND COOKING

The tubers store well in a dark, cool place. They need to be washed under cold running water, and perhaps scrubbed if the dirt is obstinate—do not peel them.

Harold McGee tells us that the flatulent effect can be controlled by the length of time the artichokes are cooked. Even a modest 10–15 minutes' boiling in copious amounts of water will extract some of the inulin. To maximize this effect, the artichokes can be cut into slices, which increases the surface area that is exposed. McGee estimated that 15 minutes' cooking drew out almost half of the inulin. He also discovered that temperatures just above freezing affect the vegetable so that it pre-digests its own carbohydrates, thus breaking down the inulin. So artichokes bought in March and April will be more digestible than those bought before Christmas.

Like parsnips or potatoes, artichokes will roast happily after an initial boiling, but artichokes can be boiled longer than the requisite 15 minutes before being drained and added to the roasting pan. After boiling, they may also be sliced and fried in oil with garlic, or dipped into a light batter and fried.

I now view Jerusalem artichoke soup as a rather dangerous choice, because the inulin that is leached out of the vegetable is the rather cloudy, slightly sweet precipitate in the liquid that the cook needs to make a flavorful soup. For those readers who are lucky enough to be untouched by the explosive charge of this vegetable, I give the recipe.

JERUSALEM (or PALESTINE) SOUP

for 6

For years, throughout the eighteenth and nineteenth centuries, the soup was commonly referred to as Palestine or Jerusalem soup and only lost these names in this century.

Mrs. Beeton's recipe begins with 3 slices of lean bacon or ham, half a head of celery, and both a turnip and an onion before adding 4 pounds of artichokes.

She also suggests that a pretty way of serving Jerusalem artichokes is to shape them like pears, then cover these in white sauce and finish with a garnish of Brussels sprouts.

2 tablespoons butter
2 tablespoons olive oil
1 onion, chopped
1½ pounds Jerusalem artichokes, cleaned
and chopped into dice
1½ quarts vegetable stock
sea salt and freshly ground black pepper
2½ cups milk
a little chopped parsley or cilantro, for garnish

Melt the butter with the olive oil in a large saucepan. Add the onion and the artichokes. Cook for a moment, stirring the vegetables, then add the stock and seasoning.

Let the soup simmer for 30–40 minutes, then add the milk and leave to cool.

Blend until smooth and then reheat carefully. Before serving, sprinkle a little chopped parsley or cilantro over the surface.

ABOVE Salsify

SALSIFY and SCORZONERA

Tragopogon porrifolius and *Scorzonera hispanica*

These two long, thin roots belong to the same family and taste very similar. Both are white-fleshed, but scorzonera has a black skin. When young, their leaves can be eaten in salads, but they are both grown for their roots. These are high in inulin, but their flavors are so delicious that they are well worth eating.

Salsify is also called the "oyster plant" because its taste was thought to resemble oysters—with a stretch of the imagination, perhaps. Others disagree: Dorothy Hartley comments, "and so like oyster that it takes in the cat!" The taste of both is really like that of a subtly flavored globe artichoke with a hint of asparagus.

The Latin term *tragopogon* stems from two Greek words meaning "goat's beard," thought to describe the

---

SALSIFY and SCORZONERA *Tragopogon porrifolius* and *Scorzonera hispanica* fluffy character of the seed ball. The fact that the flower head closes at noon, not opening until the following morning, gave it its other popular name, "Jack-go-to-bed-at-noon." Salsify is often called purple goat's beard, its flowers being purple rather than the yellow of *Tragopogon pratensis,* a type eaten in the seventeenth century but now forgotten. The name salsify is a corruption of the old Latin *solsequium,* meaning "sun" and "following."

The whole plant was used medicinally: Culpeper advises using roots, flowers, leaves, and all, bruised and boiled and then strained, as a remedy for heartburn, loss of appetite, and disorders of the breast and liver. Salsify was not cultivated much before the seventeenth century. One of the first to mention it is John Evelyn, who refers to it as "viper-grass" because a soup made from it was considered an antidote to the poison of the viper. After pointing out its medicinal virtues, Evelyn goes on to say how good it is stewed with beef marrow, spice, and wine. He also says how pleasant it can be raw in a salad.

Scorzonera, also called black salsify, black oyster plant, and even black radish, is a member of a different genus altogether. It came from Spain and crept into the rest of Europe, especially France, Belgium, and England, whose herbalists and gardeners all took an interest in it at the end of the sixteenth century. The astonishing fact is that its flavor is hardly distinguishable from that of salsify and, once peeled and cooked, I would defy anyone to tell the difference.

PREPARING

Wash the roots under cold running water, without peeling, and boil for 10 minutes. When cool, the skin will come off like a glove, especially if held under cold running water. The roots tend to be thin, and it is easy to waste the vegetable if you attempt to peel them beforehand. Besides that, there is then all the chore of plunging the peeled roots into acidulated water to prevent discoloration.

COOKING

After peeling the cooled boiled roots, the easiest and nicest way to eat them is as a salad, tossed in a garlicky vinaigrette and served with other salads. If the vegetable is to be eaten hot, however, there are numerous methods: toss in butter and sprinkle with parsley or chives; dip the sliced roots in a light batter and fry; or stir-fry with ginger, garlic, and chili.

Polygonaceae

RHUBARB

Rheum rhaponticum

I am including rhubarb in this book because I tend to use it as a vegetable. Though it is famous as the ingredient in sweet tarts and pies, I believe its use and enjoyment should be widened far away from the dessert course. It makes excellent soups, pickles, and sauces for fish. Besides, I am fond of its bright astringency and my childhood spirits were never clouded by a dish of stewed rhubarb and custard sauce.

The first mention of rhubarb was for its medicinal use, in China. This was *Rheum officinale,* which flourished in northwest China and was favored in the Pen-King herbal from 2700 BC. It is believed originally to have grown somewhere in northern Asia—Mongolia, Tartary, or perhaps Siberia.

It reached the Mediterranean in the early Common Era, for both Pliny and Dioscorides mention it, though both rather dismissively. China began exporting rhubarb—the dried roots, that is—to the West very early on, and it began to collect various synonyms. There was Russian rhubarb, Turkish, and Chinese, all named after the various trade routes. Prior to 1842, Canton was the only port through which the Chinese empire traded, so rhubarb had to travel overland to Russia via the frontier town of Kiachta, to Turkey through the Levant. It got its name *Rha* from the ancient name of the Volga, on whose banks the plant grew. The Volga flows into the Black Sea—"the wine dark sea" of Homer. *Pontus* is Greek for sea, so *rhaponticum* indicates its trade source.

The root was used in the West as a curative potion throughout the Middle Ages. It was also grown in monastery gardens to stock abbey pharmacies. But it does not seem to have occurred to anyone to eat it. When they did, they began by eating either the root

or the leaves, and might have felt unwell enough not to try it again. The leaves were thought to be toxic, containing oxalates of both potassium and calcium. It is, then, somewhat surprising that Green says in his *Universal Herbal* (1832): "The leaves are also used by the French in their soups, to which they impart an agreeable acidity like that of Sorrel." He was not alone in this view; the gardener of the Earl of Shrewsbury at Alton Towers said he used rhubarb flowers before they opened in the same way as broccoli, cooked *au gratin* with white sauce; the cheese, it was thought, might have obscured any bitterness.

However, rhubarb stalks, which we eat happily, also contain some degree of these oxalates. And when poisoning occurred, it affected some but not others. Could it be that some people are more susceptible to oxalate poisoning? It is doubtful. Harold McGee tells us that rhubarb has had a somewhat shady reputation in the U.S. since World War I, when Americans were encouraged to eat the leaves as a vegetable supplement and many were poisoned as a result. Now it seems that the toxins present in rhubarb leaves are not the oxalates, but something else still to be identified.

In western Europe, by the sixteenth century, rhubarb was thought to be a cure for venereal disease. Two ounces of dried root and half an ounce of parsley were boiled in two quarts of water, then reduced by two-thirds. This was drunk several times a day and must have been punishment enough, without being saddled with the affliction.

As a vegetable/fruit, it was one of the last to be cultivated in Britain. It flourished in Tudor herb gardens. The apothecary to King James I, John Parkinson (1567–1650), planted rhubarb from Italy in his own garden. As late as the 1770s, the Duke of Atholl had a plantation of rhubarb on his estate at Blair Castle in Perthshire, which was all sold to an Edinburgh druggist. By that time it was beginning to creep into English cooking, but it took about 150 years before it was accepted as a fruit for tarts. A recipe of 1790 gave directions for slicing the stalks and then treating them like gooseberries. By the time of Mrs. Beeton there are recipes for tarts and boiled puddings with rhubarb, as well as some others for wine and jam.

There, in these dishes, rhubarb found its niche. No kitchen garden was without its clump, often forced in early spring by digging out some of the roots and leaving them for the "frost to get at them." The roots were then placed in the dark, and in a few weeks the shoots began to grow. For their color alone—a lively nacreous pink—they were worthy of any table, but as their acid content was high they were cooked with an excess of sugar. Because of this, such dishes have been unpopular lately. Yet rhubarb still grows in country gardens, and it still features in jams and pies, and was once famous for making wine. Indeed, Mrs. Leyel gives a recipe that uses 5 pounds of rhubarb to 3 pounds of sugar and a gallon of water.

Rhubarb also makes an unusual but excellent soup. However, it only works if the stock used has a strong savory flavor, for this must offset the acid in the rhubarb; otherwise it needs a quantity of sugar, and you will have a cordial for dessert and not a savory soup. I made the most successful version of this soup using the carcass bones from smoked quail for the stock. However, any smoked game would do: pheasant, mallard, or guinea fowl. I imagine, though I have not tried it, that the carcass of a smoked chicken or a ham bone would also be excellent. The method is simplicity itself, and the soup can be served either hot or cold. Its flavor is often difficult for guests to pin down, while the color is jewel-like.

RHUBARB SOUP

2 pounds rhubarb, trimmed and chopped
9 cups strong savory stock, strained
1 or 2 tablespoons sugar
Tabasco
sea salt and freshly ground black pepper
2–3 tablespoons sour cream or plain yogurt
a few geranium petals for garnish

Cook the rhubarb in the stock for 10 minutes or so, cool, and blend to a thin purée. Make sure it is blended thoroughly, because strands of rhubarb floating in the soup will give the game away.

Taste with care: depending on how strong the stock is and how salty, it may need a spoonful of

ABOVE *Pickled rhubarb*

sugar, or even a few drops of Tabasco: the soup has to be balanced between saltiness and astringency.

Spoon on some sour cream or yogurt and float a few geranium petals on top before serving.

RHUBARB SAUCE FOR FISH

2 tablespoons butter
1 pound rhubarb, trimmed and chopped
½ teaspoon sea salt
½ teaspoon sugar
¼ teaspoon Tabasco

Melt the butter in a saucepan and add the remaining ingredients. Simmer for 10 minutes over a low heat, then let the mixture cool.

Blend until smooth. Taste and adjust the seasonings, then refrigerate until needed (an ice-cold sauce tastes particularly good with grilled white fish).

PICKLED RHUBARB

This makes an excellent relish for game, meat, or cheese. It also looks charming on the plate. The rhubarb is "cold cooked" in the *ceviche* method that the South Americans use for fish.

2–3 pounds rhubarb, trimmed and chopped
1 ounce fresh gingerroot, peeled and thinly sliced
1 tablespoon whole cloves
2½ cups or more cider vinegar
1 tablespoon sea salt
2 tablespoons sugar

Pack the rhubarb into a sterilized canning jar, interspersed with a few slices of ginger and a few cloves.

Heat the vinegar and add the salt and sugar. Pour over the rhubarb and place an airtight lid on the jar.

The pickle is ready in three weeks.

RHUBARB *Rheum rhaponticum*

SORREL

Rumex acetosa

This is a beautiful vegetable, with a flavor of gooseberry unique among green vegetables, that is invaluable in the kitchen. It is astonishing that it is not commercially grown and readily available, but we can easily grow the plants in our own kitchen gardens. Even if you have a very small plot, a root of sorrel will be worth growing. The leaves spring up early in the year and can be picked for salads when there is little else that is green around. Later, soups and sauces can be made from the leaves. The plant will also continue to flourish late into the season and through the first frosts.

Sorrel was used and prized in antiquity. Of all vegetables, sorrel has one of the largest roots—Pliny thought, "...going as far as a yard and a half into the ground and its root is full of sap and lives a long time, even after being dug up." This is quite true: some sorrel roots I found mistakenly discarded on a compost heap, two weeks after being thrown out, were dug back into the soil and were found to be astonishingly healthy the following spring.

In ancient Rome, the acidity of sorrel led cooks to consider that it might break down the tough tissues of meat or the bones in fish. A classic dish today is *alose à l'oseille* (shad with sorrel), where the fish is cooked on a bed of sorrel in the belief that the small bones in the fish will melt. A myth, of course—they have to be filleted out, as is the case with all fish. But shad is one of the great fish of the world, with a delicately meaty flavor that only needs brief cooking, and a sorrel purée is indeed a perfect complement.

The whole of the Polygonaceae family is known for its astringency, which is caused by the presence of tannins found mainly in the roots. The leaves of another member, bistort (*Polygonum bistorta*), were used in the spring in the north of England as an ingredient in herb pudding. Its root, after having been steeped in water so that the tannin leaches out, can provide a flour. In hard times in Russia, Iceland, and Siberia, such a flour was used to make bread. Bistort used to be widely cultivated, and that which grows wild in Britain now is the progeny of those plants that escaped from gardens long past. In medieval times bistort's uses were legion, for bowel complaints and hemorrhages of lungs and stomach, and as a remedy for nose-bleeding—it is one of the most astringent medicines in the vegetable kingdom and is highly styptic. A distilled water of the leaves and root was used to soothe stings and bites, and as a throat gargle.

Culpeper thought a syrup made from sorrel itself, if gargled in the mouth, would cure sores. Gerard says that the root of bistort is good for looseness of teeth and hardening of gums, "being holden in the mouth for a certain space and at sundry times." He also goes on to say of sorrel: "The juice hereof in summer time is a profitable sauce in many meates and pleasant to the taste. It cooleth a hot stomacke; mooveth appetite to meate; tempereth the heat of the liver, and openeth the stoppings thereof."

In the time of Henry VIII, sorrel had an important place in all the kitchen gardens. William Turner referred to it in 1538 as both "sorell" and "sourdoc." Yet about 150 years later, in 1699, the zoologist Dr. Lister was surprised to discover how much sorrel was being cultivated around Paris. "There is so much taste for sorrel here that I have seen whole acres devoted to it ... nothing is healthier ... it could be a substitute for the lemon in the treatment of scurvy and its related afflictions."

From the earliest times, sorrel was cooked with cream, butter, and eggs. Indeed, this fusion is highly satisfying; the richness of the cream is refreshing, spiced with a sharp, acidic, fruity, gooseberry flavor. A sauce was also made by cooking the leaves and mixing them with sugar and vinegar, to accompany roast pork or goose. Hannah Glasse gives a recipe for poached eggs served on a bed of sorrel, with plenty of three-cornered toast stuck around the plate, and a quartered orange. Sorrel juice was even used for taking rust marks out of linen.

On the whole, however, the English tended to disapprove of sorrel: a vegetable so acid surely could not be good for you? Besides, it contained oxalic acid and too much of that was poisonous. Disbelievingly, E. S. Dallas comments: "But the French will eat it as a dish by itself; taking a whole peck of leaves to make a purée to go with a fricandeau of veal or with poached eggs. We all like some acid to go with our veal, and sorrel is a favorite accompaniment of certain fish; but after all there is no acid comparable to lemon juice for delicacy of flavor and for wholesomeness. Let us reserve sorrel for Bonne Femme Soup and wood-sorrel for Julienne."

We now, of course, think of *potage à la bonne femme* being made with leeks, though André Simon gives a recipe for it with onion, lettuce, and sorrel. The recipe's name paints a picture of a good woman, and more or less means now a soup in the simple or rustic manner. Possibly the goodness comes from the industry and skill of a good cook who can contrive a soup from whatever few vegetables are at hand. But what is the term *julienne* doing here? We think of it as being a description of vegetables cut into tiny straws. Dallas gives a fascinating interpretation of how matchstick vegetables came to be called thus, and it all rests on a tiny wild herb.

Wood sorrel (*Oxalis acetosella*) is not part of the Polygonaceae at all, but in flavor the leaf is a delicate version of *Rumex acetosa,* and since antiquity it has been used to flavor soups and salads. Do grow a plant in your own garden; it is not only delightful in its flowers, with their five purple-veined white petals, but the trefoil leaves are also charming.

The plant has a host of common names, including alleluiah and hallelujah. In different parts of England, it is called "bread-and-cheese-and-cider," "cuckoo's bread," and "sleeping clover" because the leaves fold back. Why on earth "hallelujah"? Turner, in his *Herbal* of 1568, explains that it "appeareth about Easter when Alleluja is song agayn, it is an expression of Christian celebration, an image of Christ risen." Another Christian explanation is that the wood sorrel is the true shamrock, and that when St. Patrick beheld this emblem of the Trinity he praised God.

But might it also have been a pagan cry of delight for the return of spring? The name hallelujah for wood sorrel appears in French, Spanish, and Italian, too. Dallas suggests that allelujah among peasants was corrupted into "Lujula," and in Italy this became "*Jul-ida*"—or "little Julia." In France, in turn, this became "*Julienne.*" (My French dictionary, Harrap, dated 1957,

says of Julienne, "(a) Bot: Rocket (b) julienne soup," thus implying that the soup would be made from rocket or arugula.)

But back to Dallas and his ingenious explanation. Wood sorrel is a small, low-lying plant in which the trefoil leaves grow at the end of slender, thread-like stems. To make a soup from wood sorrel, a bunch of leaves would be poached in stock, the leaves disappearing (as is the wont of all types of sorrel leaves) while the fine straws of the stems remain. What we then have is a tasty stock with slender stems floating in it. So when cooks made the soup from common sorrel, the leaves flavored the stock, but there were no stems, so cooks put threads of carrot, turnip, and celery into the julienne to simulate them.

Now, of course, nobody makes julienne soup. The end result would hardly equal the labor involved—all that detailed chopping of vegetables. *Larousse*, it is interesting to note, gives a recipe for julienne soup, but without sorrel—wood or otherwise.

There have always been varieties of sorrel other than *Rumex acetosa*; sometimes one is not certain

BELOW Sorrel growing

SORREL *Rumex acetosa*

which variety past herbals are referring to. The main ones are French sorrel (*R. scutatus*) and sheep's sorrel (*R. acetosella*). The first, as you would expect, is the type favored by the French. There is, in my opinion, no difference in flavor once cooked, though the plant's leaves are much larger and longer and almost brittle. Sheep's sorrel is a much smaller plant, and its leaves are tinged red at the end of summer. Sorrel grows wild throughout North America, and plants and seeds of *R. scutatus* are widely available.

Another member of the Polygonaceae family was used as a staple food plant by Native Americans. Solomon's seal (*Polygonatum biflorum*), which we grow in the herbaceous border for its elegant arching stems and bell-like pendulous flowers, has its tubers and roots near the surface. These were eaten for their starch. They were first soaked in water to leach out the tannins, then dried and pounded. The young shoots of Solomon's seal were also used in Turkey, where they were boiled and eaten like asparagus.

PREPARING AND COOKING

Writing in the seventeenth century, John Evelyn sums up the pleasure of sorrel when it "...first springs forth in March: in the making of sallets [it] imparts a grateful quickness to the rest as supplying the want of oranges and lemons. Together with salt, it gives both the name and the relish to sallets from the sapidity; which renders not plants and herbs only, but men themselves pleasant and agreeable."

If the leaves are very small, no longer than 3 inches, then throw them whole into the salad; if any larger, I would strip the leaf from the stem. This has to be done if cooking the leaves, because the leaf effortlessly makes its own purée in a few minutes.

Melt butter in a pan and throw in the washed and dried sorrel. Do not add any water or seasoning. Place over a low heat and within a minute, or at the most two, the leaves turn a rather unpleasant hue of army-issue brownish-green. This is the only unattractive part of sorrel. However, the taste is stunning. For *SORREL SAUCE*, simply add to this purée some crème fraîche or fromage blanc, which will lighten and improve the color. For a theatrical improvement of color, place some raw watercress leaves in a blender with the purée and liquidize. This sharpens the greenness and adds another dimension to the taste. It is a perfect sauce for fish of any kind, though for the more oily fish, such as mackerel, an acid sauce like sorrel (without added watercress) is best.

For *SORREL SOUP*, reduce the sorrel leaves to a purée, then add raw watercress leaves and liquidize, before adding stock and cream. This makes a wonderful chilled soup for spring.

POTAGE À LA BONNE FEMME

This is my own version of the classic creamy soup.

2 tablespoons butter
1 pound mealy potatoes, peeled and diced
1 large onion, diced
a handful of sorrel leaves (about 6 ounces)
7½ cups vegetable stock
1¼ cups light cream
2 tablespoons chopped chervil
2 – 3 tablespoons crème fraîche
a handful of croûtons (optional)

Melt the butter in a saucepan and add the potatoes and onion. Let them sweat a little.

Tear the sorrel leaves from their stems and add the leaves with the stock. Simmer for 20 minutes.

Leave to cool, then blend half of the soup, so that it is both smooth and textured.

Reheat and add the cream. Serve with chopped chervil sprinkled on top and the crème fraîche and croûtons, if using.

THE ORIGINAL JULIENNE SOUP

As wood sorrel is widespread, this soup could be made in early spring and summer. You will find the plant growing in woods, under hedgerows, and in shady spots. Pick a generous handful of the leaves complete with their stems. Chop the stems into 1-inch lengths. Melt some butter and sweat some chopped onion, then add the stems and leaves of the sorrel. Add a few cups of good vegetable stock and simmer for 10 minutes. Season to taste.

LAYERED FISH TERRINE WITH SORREL

2½ pounds mixed white fish high in gelatin,
such as sole, monkfish, or flounder
1 carrot
1 onion
2 celery stalks
1 bay leaf
2 garlic cloves
pared zest and juice of 1 lemon
1½ pounds sorrel leaves
2 tablespoons butter, plus more for greasing
2 egg yolks
sea salt and freshly ground black pepper
a generous handful of chopped parsley
2 tablespoons chopped chervil or tarragon
sprigs of chervil, dill, or fennel for garnish

Have the fish merchant fillet the fish, but ensure that you keep all the heads and bones. Place these in a saucepan with the carrot, onion, celery, bay leaf, garlic cloves, and lemon zest. Bring to a boil and simmer for 20 minutes. Strain and leave this stock to cool, then add the lemon juice.

Meanwhile, preheat the oven to 400°F. Tear the sorrel leaves from their stems and cook in the butter for a few minutes or until puréed. Set aside to cool. Mix in the egg yolks and season.

Chop the white fish into chunks and mix in the chopped parsley and chervil or tarragon. Prepare a terrine mold by buttering the bottom and sides, then place a strip of buttered foil on the bottom and up both long sides of the mold so that the finished fish terrine can be lifted out easily.

On the foil, place a sprig of chervil, dill, or fennel, then pack a layer of white fish down to cover the bottom. Pour in a little of the fish stock so that it just covers, then add a layer of the sorrel purée, followed by another layer of fish moistened with the stock. Continue until the mold is full.

Cover with buttered paper, place in a bain-marie half full of boiling water, and cook in the oven for 30 minutes. Take out and leave to cool, then refrigerate for 4 hours before unmolding.

Moisten a knife with boiling water and slide it around the sides, then gently pull up the foil handles. Serve with a cucumber salad (see page 145).

Portulacaceae

PURSLANE

Portulaca oleracea

Members of this family often have fleshy leaves. Wild purslane (*Portulaca oleracea*) we treat as a common weed, though the best way to get rid of it from the garden is to eat it.

You may see purslane in bunches in ethnic markets in the spring and early summer, from specialist growers. It is yet another plant that used to be widely eaten—commonly grown during the Middle Ages and often pickled—which has now fallen into neglect. This is quite unfair, because it is succulent and very slightly peppery, and the fleshy leaves lend textural interest in a salad.

Gerard says, "raw purslane is much used in salads, with oil, salt and vinegar." John Evelyn also praises it in salads, "for it is eminently moist and cooling, especially the golden." The golden variety with yellow leaves is less hardy than the green. I have failed to grow it, but green purslane I do grow in my garden, though it is best to start it off in a greenhouse. In the seventeenth and eighteenth centuries it was grown in hot beds, and used young in salads, while the older plants were pickled.

Purslane has had its critics, too. William Cobbett writes in his *The English Gardener* (1833): "a mischievous weed, eaten by French men and pigs when they can get nothing else. Both use it in salad, that is to say, raw." Earlier, however, the poet Robert Herrick (1591–1674) had written a charming verse:

Lord, I confess too when I dine
The pulse is thine,
And all those other bits that be
There placed by thee,
The worts, the purselain, and the mess
Of Water Cress.

Cruciferae

THE
CABBAGE
FAMILY

CABBAGE *Brassica oleracea* Capitata Group

BRUSSELS SPROUT
Brassica oleracea Gemmifera Group

KALE or CURLY KALE
Brassica oleracea Acephala Group

CAULIFLOWER *Brassica oleracea* Botrytis Group

SPROUTING BROCCOLI
Brassica oleracea Italica Group

BROCCOLI *Brassica oleracea* Botrytis Group

KOHLRABI *Brassica oleracea* Gongylodes Group

TURNIP *Brassica rapa* Rapifera Group

RUTABAGA or SWEDE *Brassica napus*
Napobrassica Group

CHINESE or NAPA CABBAGE
Brassica rapa Pekinensis Group

MUSTARD GREENS *Brassica juncea*

BOK CHOY or PAK-CHOI *Brassica rapa*
Chinensis Group

MIZUNA *Brassica rapa* Japonica Group

WATERCRESS *Nasturtium officinale*

UPLAND CRESS *Barbarea verna*

GARDEN or BROADLEAF CRESS *Lepidium sativum*

RADISH *Raphanus sativus*

LARGE WHITE RADISH or DAIKON
Raphanus sativus spp.

BLACK RADISH *Raphanus nigra*

HORSERADISH *Armoracia rusticana*

JAPANESE HORSERADISH or WASABI
Wasabia japonica

ARUGULA or ROCKET *Eruca sativa*

SWEET ROCKET *Hesperis matronalis*

WINTER CRESS *Barbarea vulgaris*

SEAKALE *Crambe maritima*

87

This is a large family, containing arguably the largest number of edible varieties and characterized by a general ability to withstand a rather cold climate. It also contains a number of well-known ornamental flowering plants (the cross shape formed by the four-petaled flowers gives the family its name), like scented stock and the wallflower, as well as the plant from which the Ancient Britons made the woad with which they painted themselves, and, according to Caesar, gave them "a more terrible aspect in battle."

The principal genus within the family is Brassica, *which numbers among its extensive ranks all the cabbages and their close relatives. Other important plants include the mustards, radishes, arugula, watercress, and seakale, all noted for their pungent flavors.*

CABBAGE

Brassica oleracea Capitata Group

We do not seem to be great enthusiasts for the cabbage today, though we feel more warmly about other members of the family. Yet writers in antiquity spoke highly of cabbage and its many medicinal qualities.

It was firmly believed that cabbage was a protection against drunkenness. Cato, in *On Agriculture,* sums it up: "If you wish to drink deep at a banquet and to enjoy your dinner, eat as much raw cabbage as you wish, seasoned with vinegar, before dinner." Athenaeus tells us that the Egyptians always began their meals with it. Furthermore, the seeds, if eaten with the meal, would keep one sober. Cabbage would banish headaches and, if the leaves had not been efficacious the night before, they would surely remove a hangover the day after. Cato also comments that the medicinal value of cabbage surpasses all other vegetables, and devotes five pages to its many cures.

Pythagoras loved cabbage, and Pliny comments that it would be a long task to list all the praises of cabbage. One might surmise that the Ancients did not over-cook the vegetable and experience its rank smell, but that would be incorrect, because there are constant references to "boiled cabbage glistening in

oil" and some to the unpleasant smell of cooking cabbage. It was also believed that if cabbages were grown in a vineyard it made the wine dark. Athenaeus, quoting from a fragment by Nicander, tells us that they used to dry cabbage leaves (they still do in China today). "You wash and dry them in the north wind and they are welcome in winter even to the idle...for cooked in warm water they come to life again."

All cabbages stem from the wild variety, *Brassica erratica,* which still grows on the coasts of Britain, France, Spain, and Italy. The wild cabbage is the father of all kales, Brussels sprouts, cauliflower, broccoli, and probably kohlrabi, too. Both Pliny and Cato talk of three varieties: the curly, its leaves resembling parsley; another with a large stem and open leaves; and a third with very small stems, a smooth and tender cabbage. Visitors to Egypt from Greece complained that the cabbage grown there was inferior and demanded that seed be brought from Rhodes. Even so, the seed produced a bitter plant in the second year. There is some dispute as to whether this vegetable, which was so sought after, could really be the cabbage with which we are familiar today. The cabbage was one with a thick stem—similar to the wild cabbage—and not the round-headed type.

By Roman times we have another clue as to the nature of the plant, for two types are mentioned: one, called *cymae* or *cauliculi* and sold in bundles, is expensive; while another, which sounds more like a type of kale growing near the sea, is a poor man's dish. Athenaeus writes, "They will boil sleek cabbages and serve pea soup with them." Apicius mentions the bundles, and Pliny tells us that the vegetables are tender young shoots that spring from the main stem. This sounds more like the Chinese family of brassicas, where the "cut-and-come-again" type of culture brings a steady supply of young, fresh shoots to the table. The gastronomic sensitivity that was so pronounced in the Ancient World, the Mediterranean climate, and the short cooking times likely for summer fare imply that the much-loved cabbage was nearer the Oriental brassica than the cabbage we know today.

The headed varieties with which we are familiar were very likely to have been cultivated in Northern Europe by the Celts, who were passionate and efficient farmers. By 200 BC there were no wild woods left in Europe or in Britain: every available piece of fertile land was tilled and great quantities of grain were exported from Britain to continental Europe. Scholars usually so keen to praise the sophistication of the Classical World have tended to ignore the great achievements of the Celts.

With the Roman occupation of Britain and Gaul, both types of cabbage were brought to Northern Europe, where the kale-type—very similar to the wild cabbage—was taken up as a staple food. Historians tend to be disparaging about the "ubiquitous cabbage," yet its highly healthy content—a concentrated package of several known therapeutic compounds—must have made it a valuable food in the Dark and Middle Ages. Pliny was right, after all, for there is little he claimed that cabbage does not cure.

Cabbages were chopped and added to marrowbone stews with leeks and onions and whatever herbs or spices were available, but saffron if possible. The first English recipe is from *The Forme of Cury*, where the cabbages are quartered and cooked in broth with onions and leeks, flavored with saffron and salt. Much clarified butter also went into their cooking, and this probably helps to explain how cabbage has always been over-boiled and served with butter. Traditions take a long time to die, even when the reasons for doing them have been forgotton. Peasant medieval cooking was one-pot slow cooking, simmering all day over the embers of a fire.

Sauerkraut is thought to have been discovered by the Celts of Middle Europe. Harold McGee thinks that because it stems from the principle of pickled cabbage, it was brought to Europe from China by the Tartars, for they loved to salt foods to preserve them throughout the winter. Sauerkraut was certainly in use in the Middle Ages. "He who sows cabbages and fattens a pig will get through the winter," is a proverb that crops up throughout Europe. Sauerkraut preserves the cabbage's vitamin C, so for many centuries it would have been the only source of this nutrient in the winter months until the widespread use of the potato, which was not accepted until the nineteenth century. Sauerkraut, as a fermented product, is also rich in the benign bacteria that protect the colon.

After Pliny, however, cabbage did not have a good press. Richard Burton (1577–1640), author of *The Anatomy of Melancholy*, was extremely sour. "Amongst herbs to be eaten I find gourds, cucumbers, coleworts, melons, disallowed, but especially cabbage. It causeth trouble-some dreams and sends up black vapours to the brain..."

Ever since, cabbage has sunk into the slough of diners' gloom, associated with poverty, over-boiling, and "a nasty history of being good for you," as Jane Grigson puts it. Well, here are some details of its recent beneficial history.

NUTRITION

In 1931, it was found that rabbits would survive a lethal dose of radiation if they ate cabbage leaves prior to exposure. Further tests in France, in 1950, and in the U.S. in 1959, had similar results in experiments with guinea pigs.

Furthermore, population surveys in Greece, Japan, and the U.S. have linked cabbage with protection against colon cancer. "One year-long survey in five areas of Japan published in 1986 concluded that those who ate the most cabbage had the lowest death rates from all causes..." It goes on to explain why, quoting work done by Dr. Lee Wattenberg in the 1970s. Wattenberg isolated chemicals from the cabbage family, called indoles, that blocked cancer formation in animals. Cabbage and its whole family of brassicas guard cells against the first onslaughts of cancer.

However, an unbalanced diet based on great daily amounts of cabbage would not be wise, because cabbage in excess can aggravate thyroid problems and possibly cause goiters. Thiocyanate compounds peculiar to the cabbage family interfere with the body's uptake of iodine and possibly cause goiter, although this is only likely to happen in areas where the drinking water is also low in iodine.

Cabbage is an excellent source of vitamins A, C, B1, B2, B3, and D. It is high in iron, potassium, and calcium. When cooked, however, it tends to lose about half its nutrients, particularly if cooked for a lengthy time. Pickling does not destroy its vitamin C content; in fact, Captain Cook credited the good health of his crews to daily rations of sauerkraut.

CABBAGE *Brassica oleracea* Capitata Group

VARIETIES

Apart from the red cabbage, which is dealt with later, growers divide cabbage into two categories—green and savoy. The savoy cabbage, with its crimped and colorful leaves, is the one much loved by painters for its striking aesthetic quality, rather like a prize bloom from a flower show. It is also, in my view, quite the tastiest of the cabbage varieties, having a delicate flavor that—if it is cooked briefly—is never ever sulfurous. It is a hardy winter plant and frost-resistant, so it is an important source of vitamins B and C throughout the winter season. The green cabbage may be pale green or white. These smooth and glossy globes have their leaves packed closely together. They keep particularly well.

COOKING

Cabbage is excellent raw, but if it is to be cooked let it be for the briefest time possible. For young cabbage, simply strip off the coarse outer leaves and either cook the center in a little salted water for 3 minutes, or slice and stir-fry in oil or butter.

Both the smooth green cabbage and the curly savoy can be treated in a similar fashion. Especially in the winter, both can be grated for salads and tossed (or, better still, marinated for about an hour) in a strong mustardy vinaigrette—with or without the addition of garlic, chopped scallions, sliced apple, celery, or nuts. This kind of salad is very near to the commercial and much-despised coleslaw—not that it deserves such denigration. It is, after all, a classic American salad, in which the cabbage is mixed with apple, carrot, and a pinch of paprika. Bought coleslaw has added sour cream. The name coleslaw is normally thought to stem from the Dutch *kool* (cabbage) and *sla* (salad), though others suspect that it stems from the medieval word for cabbage (coleworts).

As the savoy cabbage looks so attractive, the leaves can be blanched and used to wrap food in the manner of *dolmades* (see page 64). The savoy is the classic cabbage for stuffing and cooking whole. I am not a fan of this dish, because it involves up to an hour's cooking and that old rank smell of boiled cabbage. The smell is caused by volatile sulfur-containing compounds, released when cooking begins to break down the cell structure. Once you begin to smell the brassicas, they have begun to cook too long. The amount of hydrogen sulfide produced from boiling cabbage doubles between the fifth and the seventh minute.

It is much better to stick to brief cooking times and the preservation of the nutrients. Because of its history in stews and winter soups, there are hundreds of recipes that use cabbage in this way, but the cooking time in nearly all of them can generally be cut down to a few minutes—the leaves just need to be softened but not limp. One of my favorite ways with savoy cabbage is to slice it across thinly and then stir-fry it with ginger, garlic, and chili.

Steaming cabbage is one method of ensuring that most of the nutrients and the flavor stay in the leaves. Quarter a savoy, or if it is very large cut it into eighths, and steam for about 6-8 minutes. If in a hurry, pour ¼ inch of salted water into a pan, bring to a boil, drop in the quartered cabbage, and leave for 3 minutes. Then drain and serve.

CABBAGE AND GINGER SOUP

for 6

2 tablespoons olive oil
1 teaspoon coriander seeds, crushed
3 tablespoons grated fresh gingerroot
1 head of green cabbage, shredded
7½ cups vegetable stock
sea salt and freshly ground black pepper
2 – 3 tablespoons sour cream or plain yogurt
a few fresh chives or cilantro leaves

Heat the olive oil in a large pan and throw in the crushed coriander seeds and grated ginger. Sweat the spices for a moment.

Add the shredded cabbage and stir so that is coated and begins to shrink a little. Then add the stock, bring to a boil, and simmer for 5 minutes.

Leave to cool, then blend to a smooth, light purée. Taste and season.

This soup can be eaten cold or hot. Serve with some sour cream or plain yogurt spooned on top and sprinkled with a few chopped fresh green chives or cilantro leaves.

SAUERKRAUT

Shred several heads of green cabbage fairly thinly in a food processor, with a mandoline, or (taking rather longer) with a knife.

Pack layers of cabbage into a plastic bucket and season each layer with a few juniper berries, caraway or coriander seeds, and sea salt. Pack it tightly and place a weighted lid directly on the cabbage. It is best then to leave it in a cool garage or cellar because it tends to smell a bit.

Leave for 3 weeks while fermentation takes place. The sugars in the cabbage turn to lactic acid. The surface will become covered with a scum of yeasts and fungi, and this should be skimmed off. The juice it has made can be topped up with salt water or wine.

Transfer the sauerkraut to sterilized jars, cover with juice, and eliminate any air in the top of the jar. Screw down tightly, and it will keep for years.

Before use, rinse the sauerkraut thoroughly under cold running water to get rid of excess salt.

STIR-FRIED CABBAGE WITH WALNUTS

1 tablespoon sesame oil
3 garlic cloves, chopped
1 hot red chili, chopped
1 teaspoon mustard seeds
1 head of savoy cabbage, thinly sliced
1 onion, thinly sliced
1 tablespoon chopped walnuts
3 tablespoons dry sherry
1½ tablespoons soy sauce
a pinch of sugar
a pinch of sea salt

Heat the sesame oil in a wok and throw in the chopped garlic, chili, and mustard seeds. Stir-fry for a moment until the mustard seeds begin to pop.

Then throw in the cabbage, onion, and walnuts. Stir-fry vigorously for a minute or two, until the cabbage has shrunk by a third.

Throw in the rest of the ingredients, stir well, and serve the dish immediately, piping hot.

RED CABBAGE

All red, purple, and blue plants—which include berries, currants, grapes, radishes, beets, eggplants, and the red cabbage—acquire their pigmentation from anthocyanins. These are soluble in water, which is why all of these fruits and vegetables change color when cooked and leak their pigmentation wherever they may be. Once water touches it, the red color changes to purple or blue; the cabbage is, in fact, called *Blaukraut* in German.

Red cabbage, like all other brassicas, was developed by simply encouraging one element (in this case the pigmentation anthocyanin) over others in the original plant. It was grown in the Middle Ages. For years it was used in Britain for pickling in malt vinegar, a sad waste of a beautiful vegetable. Shredded, it makes a particularly good salad, dressed with a strong garlicky vinaigrette. Other raw vegetables can be added, carrot for example, but you must be prepared for the cabbage color to run.

Red cabbage is rich in vitamin C. As a general rule, the darker the color of the leaves the more vitamins it will contain. Thus, outside leaves of plants have more nutrients than the center. Red cabbage is an exception, as it is dark in color all the way through.

It is also an exception, I fear, to my rule above about cooking cabbages briefly. Raw red cabbage is excellent, but briefly cooked red cabbage does not have the flavor achieved by long, slow cooking.

As a general rule, this flavor is brought out best by a sweet-sour addition, that is sugar or honey with wine, vinegar, or lemon juice. The cabbage is braised for two to three hours over a gentle heat. Cooked like this it has long been a winter accompaniment to game; indeed, roast pheasant and red cabbage is a classic combination.

CABBAGE *Brassica oleracea* Capitata Group

SWEET-AND-SOUR RED CABBAGE

for 6

1 tablespoon olive oil
5 garlic cloves, sliced
1 dried hot red chili, broken up (optional)
1 onion, sliced
1 head of red cabbage, thinly sliced
⅓ cup red wine vinegar
2 tablespoons dark brown sugar
1 teaspoon sea salt
freshly ground black pepper

Heat the oil in a large casserole dish and fry the gar-lic, chili, and onion for a moment.

Add the sliced cabbage and stir to coat it with the oil. Add the wine vinegar, sugar, and seasoning. Stir again, then place a tight-fitting lid on the casserole, and let it cook over a very low heat for 2–3 hours.

I must say I prefer the cabbage when all the liquid is absorbed and it becomes a little sticky, so that some of it has caramelized. This is a matter of personal choice, but only this sort of long, slow cooking will produce such a result.

BRUSSELS SPROUT

Brassica oleracea
Gemmifera Group

Though the Romans valued cabbage sprouts as a great delicacy, this is now thought to be the new shoots sprouting from the central stem on the leaf axis, which was sold rather like asparagus, in bundles. The sprouts with which we are familiar were created by selectively breeding the stem cabbage for the ten-dency that it has to make budding heads at the junc-tion of stem and leaves.

Its history, sadly, is rather obscure. Sprouts first appear growing around the area of Brussels in the Middle Ages, long before Brussels or Belgium actually existed. Then they seem to vanish entirely until a writer—Balehin, in 1623—talks of a plant bearing some fifty heads the size of an egg. Later, in 1699, we find a cooking instruction. "Sprouts are very deli-cate, so boiled as to retain their verdure and green color…" The gardening manual quoted by Dorothy Hartley goes on to add: "The best seed of this plant comes from Denmark and Russia."

Perhaps in those intervening centuries there are Russian or Scandinavian observations in a cookbook or gardening book that could tell us more about this mysterious vegetable. For there is something odd about the plant, as if the cabbage has been tightly permed or over-wound up, so that its leaves are closely coiled, then shrunk and cloned. The Germans alone have brought a touch of poetry to the Brussels sprout; they call it *rosenkohl*—rose cabbage.

CHOOSING

Do buy Brussels sprouts with care, avoiding any with yellowing exterior leaves because they almost cer-tainly have been lying around for a week or more. Buy only tight small buds and never any loose-leaved ones. From late fall to Christmas, you can sometimes buy them still attached to their stem, and these will stay marginally fresher than the loose ones.

PREPARING AND COOKING

Constance Spry, agreeing with the gardening manual mentioned above, sums up the cooking of Brussels sprouts. "They should be regarded, I think, as minute and delicate little cabbages, mostly heart." Indeed, as for cabbages, sprouts need very little cooking and I, for one, even enjoy them raw.

Though sprouts are still classed as *Brassica oleracea* (meaning a leafy garden vegetable used in cooking), their flavor is quite different from the parent plant. They are worth using raw in a variety of ways. Serve them as a salad with a vinaigrette. Slice them thinly and mix with sliced onion or leek, or simply quarter the small ones and enjoy them in a plate of crudités.

If you choose to eat them cooked, they can be shredded, stir-fried for a minute in olive oil or but-ter, then quickly seasoned, and served. But the small green buds are, after all, appealing to look at in them-selves, so why destroy their shape? To cook Brussels sprouts in the traditional manner, throw them, whole,

ABOVE Sweet-and-sour red cabbage served with roast pheasant

into a small amount of boiling salted water and let them cook for 3 minutes—no longer. They should still have plenty of crunch to them and have retained all their flavor. If the sprouts are too firm for your taste, leave them in for at most another 2 minutes; but once you detect a whiff of sulfur, they are, in my opinion, beyond repair.

I am astonished at how cooks of the past, distinguished for their taste in so many things, treated the poor Brussels sprout. Mrs. Leyel, for example, in *The Gentle Art of Cookery*, insists that sprouts should boil for no less than 15 minutes. There are far worse stories than that: an aunt of a young friend of mine still puts the sprouts on to simmer before she goes to church on Christmas morning.

Lady Sysonby, in 1935, in a collection of recipes used by her grandmother and mother, has this to say: "Brussels sprouts—small ones—after they are boiled and well drained, tossed up in butter in the frying

pan with little bits of bacon or fried onion, make a dish everybody wishes to have more of."

Let us play with variations on Lady Sysonby's idea. Allow only 2 minutes for the boiling of a pound of small sprouts. Drain them well and toss in a frying pan coated with walnut oil, together with the addition of 2 teaspoons of mustard seeds and ½ cup of chopped walnuts; or toss the sprouts in sesame oil with chopped garlic and hot chili to taste.

Constance Spry gives a recipe for a Brussels sprout purée that uses two parts sprout to one of potato purée, while Dorothy Hartley mentions that the very small sprouts are delicious "scattered in broth." So why not add these to a clear soup, or make them part of a miscellany of winter vegetables for a hearty minestrone type of soup, remembering to put them in only for the last 2 minutes of simmering.

The English food writer Josceline Dimbleby made famous a purée of Brussels sprouts (without any

---

BRUSSELS SPROUT *Brassica oleracea* Gemmifera Group

potato), emphasizing the bright green color by serving it alongside a carrot purée.

One of the flavorings most complementary to the brassicas is orange, as well as other citrus fruit, and citrus jams and jellies. The recipes below explore this happy conjunction.

STIR-FRIED SPROUTS WITH GINGER AND ORANGE

1 tablespoon sesame oil
1½ tablepoons grated fresh gingerroot
grated zest and juice from 1 large orange (about
3 tablespoons juice)
1 pound Brussels sprouts, trimmed and halved
½ teaspoon Tabasco
½ teaspoon sugar
a pinch of sea salt
1 tablespoon Curaçao or other orange liqueur
2 or 3 scallions, chopped
a little chopped cilantro, for garnish

Heat the oil in a wok or frying pan and throw in the ginger and orange zest, followed by the sprouts. Stir-fry over a high heat for 1 minute.

Add the orange juice and Tabasco, continuing to move the sprouts around in the pan for another minute or until the juice has almost evaporated.

Add the sugar, salt, and liqueur. Give a final stir, so that the sprouts are covered with the juices. Add the chopped scallions and fry for another 5 seconds.

Serve sprinkle with the chopped cilantro.

SPROUTS POACHED IN LIME JUICE WITH WHISKY

3 limes
a large pinch of sea salt
1 teaspoon sugar
1 pound Brussels sprouts, peeled and trimmed
1 tablespoon Scotch malt whisky

Take the zest from the limes, squeeze the juice from them, and place both in a saucepan. Add the salt and sugar and bring to a boil.

Throw the Brussels sprouts into the pan and bring to a simmer. Place a lid on the pan and leave to simmer gently for 2 minutes.

Remove the lid from the pan and raise the heat. Shaking the pan so that the sprouts do not stick, boil rapidly until the liquid has evaporated to only a tablespoon or a little more.

Pour the malt whisky over and serve.

SPROUT AND NUT LETTUCE ROLLS

These tasty little rolls are excellent as appetizers or as a simple first course.

1 pound Brussels sprouts, shredded
¼ cup pine nuts, toasted
5 scallions, minced
grated zest and juice from 1 lemon
1 teaspoon Tabasco
1 tablespoon walnut oil
1 teaspoon sugar
a pinch of celery salt
10 or 12 lettuce leaves, blanched

Place the shredded sprouts in a mixing bowl. Add the pine nuts, scallions, the zest and juice from the lemon, the Tabasco, walnut oil, sugar, and celery salt. Mix thoroughly and leave to marinate for an hour.

Drain carefully, then squeeze the mixture to remove any remaining moisture.

Smooth out the blanched lettuce leaves, place a tablespoon of the filling in one corner, and roll up, tucking in the sides.

KALE or CURLY KALE

Brassica oleracea Acephala Group

The kale family comprises hardy, thick-stemmed winter plants with leaves of various shapes and types coming from the central stem (the Latin variation *acephala* means headless). Most people know curly kale with its leaves quite finely crimped like parsley. There are also silver and purple variegated leaves, some of which are used for floral arrangements. The large plain-leaved kales are used to feed livestock, because many people find the flavor of the leaves too strong for their palates.

Kale is common in supermarkets all through the cold months. Ornamental kale, with its curly heads colored white and purple as well as green, is also more and more common—it doesn't taste that good but is very pretty in salads and as a garnish.

If you grow kale yourself you have the opportunity to pick the tender new shoots; these are well worth eating, just steamed or lightly boiled for a moment but no longer.

Great quantities of kale were eaten in the Middle Ages, when it was cooked with oats, barley, and onions to make a gruel, as the main meal of the day. A similar recipe still appears in Mrs. Beeton as kale brose—a Scotch recipe, in which the ingredients make enough for ten persons: half an ox head or cow heel, a teacupful of toasted oatmeal, salt to taste, two handfuls of greens, three quarts of water. One can imagine this hearty broth being left to simmer all day, to provide the main meal for an agricultural laborer's family in the evening. Mrs. Beeton says kale needs four hours of cooking and is seasonable all the year round, but especially suitable in the winter.

GROWING AND VARIETIES

If you are a gardener, it is not difficult to have a vigorous supply of kale from early fall until hard frost, or all winter in mild climates. It will grow in early spring, too, but does not stand heat well. Seed catalogues list many different varieties, from Dwarf Green Curled to Winterbor. A word of warning, though: the young plants are especially delightful to caterpillars and if you don't take precautions a whole planting can be well-nigh wiped out overnight.

CHOOSING, PREPARING, AND COOKING

Kale is one of the strongest-tasting of all the brassicas and is excellent when mixed with mashed potato and legumes, but it is also enormously delicious as a vegetable in its own right.

First, tear the kale leaves from the stems and discard the stems, then boil the leaves in a little salted water for 3–5 minutes and drain them well. We frequently eat kale cooked in this simple manner in the winter to accompany game. The cooked leaves can also be mixed with equal amounts of mashed potato and a diced onion, then seasoned with lots of black pepper and formed into small cakes; these are then breaded and shallow-fried. Traditionally these kale and potato cakes are served with ham, though they are also excellent with cold game.

Kale can be added to soups and winter stews in a rather more sophisticated version than Mrs. Beeton's Scotch recipe above. Being of fairly strong flavor, kale goes well with dried beans and root vegetables. Because of its strength, it will stand up to strong and pungent spices, so it will happily feature even in an Indian curry, such as the one below.

KALE DHAL

If you can't find kale, collards or other greens will do just as well in this recipe.

1 tablespoon mustard oil
1 tablespoon mustard seeds
2 dried hot red chilies, crushed
5 garlic cloves, chopped
2 teaspoons ground cumin
2 teaspoons ground coriander
2 teaspoons turmeric
grated zest and juice of 1 lemon
1 pound kale, chopped small
1 pound potatoes, peeled and chopped (about 3 cups)
3½ cups vegetable stock
⅔ cup brown lentils
1 teaspoon sea salt

Heat the oil in a large saucepan and add the mustard seeds, chilies, and garlic. Fry until the seeds pop.

Add the cumin, coriander, and turmeric, together with the zest and juice of the lemon. Quickly add the kale and potatoes and move the vegetables around in the spices, then pour the stock over, bring to a boil, and let simmer for 15 minutes.

Add the lentils and cook for 20 minutes more.

Add the salt just before serving.

KALE or CURLY KALE *Brassica oleracea* Acephala Group

KALE AND POTATO PIE

This dish might seem excessively simple, but such a recipe allows the clear, uncluttered flavor of kale to come through.

2 tablespoons butter, plus more for greasing
1½ pounds kale
2 tablespoons flour
1¼ cups milk
sea salt and freshly ground black pepper
1 pound potatoes, boiled and mashed (about 2 cups)

Preheat the oven to 450°F or preheat the broiler. Butter a heatproof dish.

Cook the kale in a pan of boiling salted water for 3 – 5 minutes, then drain well. Spread out the kale in the buttered dish.

Melt the butter in a pan over a low heat, add the flour, and stir in. Cook gently for a few minutes to make a roux, then stir in the milk to make a smooth white sauce. Season and pour this over the kale, then smooth over a topping of mashed potato.

Place in the oven or under the broiler just long enough to brown the top.

CAULIFLOWER

Brassica oleracea Botrytis Group

It is perhaps difficult to imagine the cauliflower as part of the cabbage family, but it is still *B. oleracea*, with the addition of the tag *botrytis*. This means "clusters" or "grape-like," which is an apt enough description of the large white curd. The cauliflower is, in fact, a cabbage that was bred for its flowers—a process that must have taken some time, because it made a late entry into Europe.

Originally it is thought to have come from China via the Middle East. It was brought to Spain by the Moors in the twelfth century, but arrived much later in Italy—not until the fourteenth century. The seventeenth-century writer and gardener Castelvetro took pleasure in cauliflower, and recommends a simple salad of the briefly cooked florets dressed with olive oil and salt. He also recommends that they be cooked in broth and served on slices of bread with more broth poured over, seasoned with grated sharp cheese—the first mention of cheese with cauliflower. It took another two hundred years before this became a popular dish in eighteenth-century England.

In earlier recipes cauliflower tended to be cooked in milk, as in this recipe from John Murrell's *Delightful Daily Exercises for Ladies and Gentlemen* (1621): "How to butter a collflowre. Take a ripe collflowre and cut off the buddes. Boyle them in milk with a little mace and then pour them into a cullender and let the milke run cleane from them, then take a ladle full of creame being boiled with a little whole mace, putting to it a ladle full of thick butter, mingle them together with a little sugar, dish up your flowers upon suppets, pour your butter and creame hot upon it, strowing on a little slicst nutmeg and salt and serve it to the table hot."

The idea of cooking cauliflower in milk died out slowly. Hannah Glasse was still recommending it in 1747, but by Mrs. Beeton's day it is not mentioned.

NUTRITION

Cauliflower is particularly rich in vitamins and minerals. Like the rest of its family, it is also thought to be associated with lowering cancer rates. It contains phosphorus, sulfur, calcium, and sodium, plus vitamins A and C—an average helping of cauliflower would supply half the daily recommended vitamin C requirements. It also contains considerable amounts of folic acid, particularly vital for pregnant women because a deficiency of folic acid is the source of spina bifida in babies.

PREPARING AND COOKING

There has always been some dispute as to whether to cook cauliflower whole or broken up into its florets. Victorian recipes state that the whole cauliflower should be boiled for 20 minutes. I am not really an enthusiast for serving cauliflowers whole, as they are then either over- or under-cooked, while their beauty is destroyed at once at the table when the vegetable is broken up in order to be served. I do make an exception, however, when it is sometimes possible to buy very small baby cauliflowers, just the right size for an individual serving. These could not look more appealing when cooked for a dinner party.

The method I use is to arrange them in a baking pan containing ½ inch of salted boiling water and to cook in a preheated hot oven for 5 – 8 minutes, where they will both bake and steam. Drain them well and serve sprinkled with a mixture of equal parts of ground almonds and brown bread crumbs that have been fried in olive oil and garlic, then seasoned and mixed with chopped parsley.

Because of its pleasant blandness, cauliflower has classically been teamed with a cheese sauce, possibly spiced with a little mustard or, as in Welsh rarebit, made with ale. Italian recipes suggest frying the florets in oil with garlic and chilies, then sprinkling with bread crumbs and briefly broiling. Another Italian recipe adds anchovies and capers—an attractive dish for lunch accompanied by a green salad.

The creamy blandness of the cauliflower also makes it an excellent and versatile foil for many stronger-flavored vegetables, as in the selection of recipes that follows.

CAULIFLOWER SOUP WITH RED PEPPER AND GINGER SAUCE

This soup can be served cold as below, or both soup and sauce can be reheated and served hot.

7½ cups vegetable stock
a pinch of grated nutmeg
a pinch of ground coriander
sea salt and freshly ground black pepper
1 head of cauliflower, coarsely chopped
1½ cups light cream
for the red pepper and ginger sauce:
2 tablespoons olive oil
3 red bell peppers, seeded, trimmed, and chopped
1 hot red chili, chopped
3 tablespoons grated fresh gingerroot

Bring the stock to a simmer in a large pan. Add the nutmeg, coriander, and seasoning.

Add the chopped cauliflower and simmer for 20 minutes. Leave to cool, then blend to a smooth purée and add the cream.

While the cauliflower is cooling, make the red pepper and ginger sauce: heat the oil in a pan and throw in the bell peppers, chili, gingerroot, and some salt. Put the lid on the pan and leave to cook over a very low heat for 20 minutes.

Let cool and blend to a thin sauce that will emulsify a little.

To serve, pour the soup into individual soup bowls. Put the pepper sauce in a pitcher and pour it carefully into the soup, starting in the center and making a thin spiral. Serve at once.

CAULIFLOWER AND MUSHROOM PIE

baked pastry shell plus pastry for the top crust
(see Swiss Chard Pie, pages 52–3)
1 head of cauliflower, broken up into florets
2 tablespoons butter
2 tablespoons oil
2 garlic cloves, sliced
1 cup sliced mushrooms
1 tablespoon flour
2 ounces dried porcini, rinsed and soaked in just enough
water to cover
1¼ cups vegetable stock
⅓ cup vermouth or dry sherry
⅓ cup light soy sauce
sea salt and freshly ground black pepper

Preheat the oven to 400°F.

Bring about 2 inches of salted water to a boil in a pan. Throw in the cauliflower florets, bring back to a boil, and cook for 2 minutes—no more. Drain immediately in a colander and reserve.

Melt the butter with the oil in another pan. Add the garlic and sliced fresh mushrooms, and fry for a few moments. Then add the flour and stir over a gentle heat to make a roux.

Add the porcini with their soaking water, together with the vegetable stock. Bring just to a simmer and cook for a few moments, then add the vermouth or sherry, soy sauce, and seasoning (with this quantity of soy sauce you may need little or no salt).

Pour some of this mushroom sauce over the bottom of the pastry shell. Arrange the cauliflower florets in the shell, packing them tightly. Then pour the rest of the sauce into the shell. Roll out the pastry for the top crust and put it in place. Cut a small vent in the center of the top crust so that steam can escape during baking.

Bake in the preheated oven for 30–40 minutes.

SPICY CAULIFLOWER ROULADE

This makes a perfect first course or an excellent supper dish with a green salad.

> *1 head of cauliflower, chopped very small*
> *a handful of minced parsley*
> *⅔ cup fromage blanc*
> *½ pound frozen puff pastry, thawed*
> *1 large onion, minced*
> *1 egg, beaten*
> *2 tablespoons sesame seeds, toasted*
> *for the hot sauce:*
> *¼ cup olive oil*
> *2 hot red or green chilies, minced*
> *1 red bell pepper, cored, seeded, and sliced*
> *4 garlic cloves, peeled and sliced*
> *1 teaspoon ground coriander*
> *1 teaspoon ground cumin*
> *a pinch of sea salt*
> *juice from 1 lemon*
> *3 tablespoons bread crumbs, toasted*

Preheat the oven to 425°F.

Add the cauliflower to a little boiling salted water and boil vigorously for about 3 minutes, then drain and reserve. (The cauliflower should never be mushy, nor should it be only one remove from raw for this recipe. Remember that the cauliflower pieces must be small and just soft enough to be rolled in the pastry.)

When the cauliflower is cool, mix in the parsley and fromage blanc and reserve.

To make the hot sauce: Heat the olive oil in a pan and throw in the chilies, bell pepper, and garlic. Cook for 2–3 minutes, then add the coriander, cumin, and salt. Leave to cool. Add the lemon juice, then blend to a purée. Pour into a bowl and add the bread crumbs to make a thick, chunky sauce.

Roll out the pastry to a 12-inch square. Spread the hot sauce over it to about ½ inch from the edge. Sprinkle the minced onion evenly on top of the sauce and then spread the cauliflower over that.

Roll up the pastry carefully and press down the ends to seal. Brush the ends of the roll with a little of the beaten egg to seal them properly. Brush the roulade with more beaten egg to glaze and sprinkle with the sesame seeds.

Bake in the oven for 25 minutes, or until the roulade is puffed up and golden. Leave to settle for 2 minutes before slicing.

CAULIFLOWER AND QUINCE GRATIN

> *grated zest and juice of 2 oranges*
> *2 quinces, sliced*
> *1 head of cauliflower, cut into florets*
> *a pinch of sea salt*
> *2 tablespoons good marmalade*

Put the orange zest and juice into a saucepan and add the sliced quinces and then the cauliflower with the salt. Bring to a boil and simmer for 5 minutes.

Take out the cauliflower, draining well. Arrange in a warm heatproof dish.

Preheat the broiler. Stir the marmalade into the quince and what is left of the orange juice, bring to a boil, and pour over the cauliflower.

Place under the broiler for a moment, just to brown slightly.

RIGHT Cauliflower and mushroom pie (see page 97)

SPROUTING BROCCOLI

Brassica oleracea Italica Group

This vegetable gets its name from the Italian plural diminutive of *brocco*, meaning a sprout or shoot. It is a near cousin to the cauliflower and, instead of producing a single flowerhead, produces a cluster of loose flowers on several branches at the top of the stem, while below a large number of smaller heads grow in the axils of the leaves. There are two types of sprouting broccoli, one annual and the other perennial, which is discussed here. Both white and purple varieties are grown, although there is no difference in the flavor and the purple variety turns green when cooked (see page 91).

The Romans were exceedingly fond of sprouting broccoli. It was sold in bundles and was expensive: Pliny comments that they are table luxuries. Apicius gives several methods for serving the vegetable: it is to be cooked or served with cumin and salt, or with pepper, lovage, mint, rue, and cilantro leaves. The sprouting broccoli leaves themselves could be chopped and cooked with the sauce, using *liquamen* (see page 143), oil, and wine. Another method from Apicius is to mince the leaves with coriander, onion,

BELOW Sprouting broccoli

cumin, pepper, and oil, then serve them with boiled leeks, olives or pine nuts, and raisins.

Perennial sprouting broccoli takes a long time to grow. In suitable climates (where winters are damp and mild) it is planted in March and gathered the following spring. Because it has to overwinter, the species needs to be hardy, and perhaps the intensity and strength of flavor is part of this characteristic. The milder Mediterranean winter of southern Italy would have helped its survival as a garden vegetable through the Dark and Middle Ages.

Castelvetro mentions it as "the tender shoots which grow on the stalks of cabbage and cauliflower plants left in the garden over the winter." He advises that they be cooked and served cold with oil, salt, and pepper, adding that the vegetable is much improved by being cooked with a few cloves of garlic. Anna del Conte observes that all the Italian sprouting broccoli recipes come from the south, where the vegetable is blanched and then cooked with olive oil, garlic, and chili to which soft bread crumbs and cheese are added. There is no doubt that this is a most delicious recipe. She goes on to tell us that a Calabrian recipe bakes all these ingredients, in layers, in a hot oven for 30 minutes. This, for my taste, is too long; the flowerheads will have turned mushy and the strong flavor have become slightly rank.

John Randolph, who mentioned sprouting broccoli in 1775 in his *A Treatise on Gardening by a Citizen of Virginia*, summed up the essence of this delicious vegetable when he said: "The stems will eat like asparagus and the heads like cauliflower." Earlier, in 1695, the English diarist John Evelyn comments, "The broccoli from Naples...are very delicate, as are the Savoys, commended for being not so rank but agreeable to most palates."

In *Adam's Luxury and Eve's Cookery* (1764) we get very precise instructions on the cultivation but little on the cooking of sprouting broccoli. The authors first of all recommend the Roman and the Blue broccoli as being the best. They then say to sow it in May in a bed of good moist earth; after instructing the gardener throughout the year, the plants will be ready about Christmas or a little after, when the heads like small cauliflowers are cut off. These, Adam tells us, are soon succeeded by a great number of side shoots, which should be cut when about six or eight inches long. Eve suggests cooking the broccoli with a few cloves and serving it in a butter sauce.

It is these side shoots in early spring that I consider to be the most delicious. Here is the simplest method of cooking them. Take off the leaves and peel the stems, tie them in a bundle, and place them upright in some boiling water so that, like asparagus, the heads steam and the stems are boiled. Cook for only 4–5 minutes. It obviously helps greatly if you have an asparagus steamer for the job.

On the other hand, if you do not mind the stems fairly *al dente* (and I do not), steam the whole vegetable for 5 minutes. Serve with a lemon butter sauce (melted butter with the juice from half a lemon squeezed into it). Or, cook the florets briefly, and peel and eat the stems raw, dipped perhaps in some sesame salt. The whole bunch of broccoli, of course, after being prepared, can be eaten raw in a mixed platter of crudités, and it is very good dipped into an *aïoli* mayonnaise, rouille, or an herb-flavored yogurt, sour cream, or fromage blanc mixture.

Doing anything more complicated with these tender sprouting shoots seems uncalled for, but I would welcome a stir-fry.

STIR-FRIED SPROUTING BROCCOLI WITH CHILI AND PICKLED GINGER

2 tablespoons sesame oil
2 garlic cloves, thinly sliced
1 dried hot red chili, crushed
2 ounces fresh gingerroot, peeled and thinly sliced
1 pound sprouting broccoli, separated and stems
peeled and trimmed
2 ounces pickled ginger
a pinch of sea salt
a pinch of sugar
⅓ cup vermouth or dry sherry
a sprinkle of light soy sauce

Heat the oil in a wok and throw in the garlic, crushed chili, and sliced gingerroot. Stir-fry for only a second or two. Then add the broccoli and the pickled ginger.

Stir-fry for 2–3 minutes. Add the salt, sugar, and vermouth or sherry. Continue to stir-fry for half a minute, then add the soy sauce and serve.

BROCCOLI WITH A SHALLOT, ORANGE, AND YOGURT SAUCE

1 pound sprouting broccoli
for the sauce:
2 tablespoons butter
5 or 6 shallots, peeled and chopped
grated zest and juice of 1 orange
a pinch of sea salt
a pinch of sugar
¼ cup thick plain yogurt or fromage blanc

Prepare and cook the broccoli as described opposite.

Make the sauce: melt the butter in a pan and add the shallots and the orange zest. Cook over a gentle heat for 3–5 minutes. Add the orange juice and cook for 2 minutes more. Take from the heat, add the salt, sugar, and yogurt, and mix in thoroughly.

Arrange the broccoli in a warm serving dish and spoon over the sauce. Serve at once.

BROCCOLI

Brassica oleracea Botrytis Group

This is a vegetable that looks like a grander version of the sprouting broccoli. In a sense, it is the same vegetable. This is a case of commerce having "tidied up" the vegetable, so that the form and color are aesthetically highly satisfying—although the flavor is often less so. Many people say they dislike broccoli, which is a pity because it is a very healthy food, and contains potent cancer-preventive compounds.

Broccoli is grown in great quantities, and is sold loose, packaged, as whole stems with heads, as "crowns" (without stems), and, increasingly, as florets (ready to cook). Do make sure you buy it when it is at its freshest—dark green and very firm. When fresh, both sprouting broccoli and broccoli have 5 percent protein, so they are excellent vegetables to include in a vegetarian or vegan diet.

SPROUTING BROCCOLI and BROCCOLI *Brassica oleracea*

Peel the stem and follow the instructions for asparagus. Alternatively, dice the peeled stem and break up the broccoli in florets, then steam or boil them for a few minutes.

I would be tempted to cook broccoli as in the methods given below, which are also excellent for sprouting broccoli and cauliflower.

BROCCOLI POACHED IN ORANGE JUICE

1 large head of broccoli in one piece,
weighing about 1 pound
grated zest and juice of 2 oranges
1 teaspoon Tabasco sauce
½ teaspoon sea salt
½ teaspoon sugar

Slice the broccoli from the stem so that the flowerhead is kept in one piece. Peel the stem and slice it lengthwise into pieces.

Put the orange zest and juice in a saucepan and add the Tabasco, salt, and sugar. Add the slices of broccoli stem and then carefully lay the head of broccoli on the stems. Cover tightly, bring to a boil, and simmer for 5 minutes. If the juice touches the flower-

BELOW Broccoli

head it will drain the green color and bleach it beige, which is unsightly, so the flowerhead must steam. Remove the flowerhead from the pan.

Now, increase the heat and reduce the juice around the stems by half. Pour these and the juice around the broccoli head and serve.

BROCCOLI WITH ANCHOVY AND CAPERS

1½ pounds broccoli
2 tablespoons olive oil
1 dried hot red chili, broken up
3 garlic cloves, chopped
1 can of anchovies in oil
2 tablespoons capers
3 tablespoons toasted bread crumbs

Cut the florets of the broccoli into their individual pieces. Peel and dice the stems. Throw all the pieces into a pan of boiling water, cook for 2 minutes, then drain carefully.

Heat the olive oil in a pan and throw in the chili and garlic, together with the anchovies and their oil, and fry for a moment.

Then throw in the broccoli pieces and fry for several moments in the oil and flavorings. Sprinkle the capers and the toasted bread crumbs over the top and cook for a few more seconds until the bread crumbs have soaked up the oil and become crisp and slightly golden in color.

ABOVE Green kohlrabi

KOHLRABI

Brassica oleracea Gongylodes Group

Kohlrabi is not a popular vegetable in Britain and the U.S., although it deserves to be. In Europe, Israel, China, and India, it is a favorite vegetable, but we have resisted its charms. It is still in the *Brassica oleracea* category, though the kohlrabi bears the distinguishing addition of "*gongylodes*," meaning roundish or swollen. In Northern India, it is called *ganth gobhi*, meaning "knotted" or "bulbous cauliflower." The part that is eaten is the stem, which swells into a globe, rather than the root.

Kohlrabi can grow to the size of a grapefruit, but will then tend to have a woolly interior, so it is far better if harvested at half that size. There are two varieties, green or white, and purple, but both taste similar. They have a distinctive flavor: something of fresh water chestnuts with a little touch of radish and celeriac. They make a marvelous foil for other flavorings and, used in the manner below, I have fooled people into believing they were artichoke bottoms. Kohlrabi is rich in potassium, fiber, and vitamin C.

The reason for kohlrabi's dismal reputation in Britain is partly due, I suspect, to the fact that food writers have never been enthusiastic about it. Elizabeth David ignores it altogether, though *chou-rave* is prominent in French vegetable markets in the fall. Mrs. Beeton did not care for kohlrabi, damning it with faint praise: "Not generally grown as a garden vegetable," she says, "but if used when young and tender it is wholesome…" Jane Grigson thought, "there are better vegetables than kohlrabi, and worse." Constance Spry allows it four lines of tepid enthusiasm in her best-known work.

KOHLRABI *Brassica oleracea* Gongylodes Group

ABOVE Kohlrabi appetizer

So let me swim against the tide and expound on the vegetable's merits. Its flavor is quite different from, but just as good as, both parsnip and turnip. However, this flavor is utterly lost if it is overcooked. Firstly, it can be grated and eaten raw, mixed with a good garlicky vinaigrette or mayonnaise, rather like a celeriac salad. Or, the grated raw kohlrabi can be tossed thoroughly with spices that have been fried in sesame oil.

Kohlrabi is also particularly good as a salad or in a platter of crudités after parboiling. Simply slice it and simmer the pieces for a couple of minutes, then leave in cold water for a while before draining and mixing with other raw or semi-raw vegetables.

Grated, it can be lightly cooked: stir-fry like grated zucchini in a little flavored oil or butter, with some mustard seed thrown into the oil, perhaps, to give it a little spice. It can be sliced paper-thin with a mandoline and fried in hot oil like potato chips, or it can be cut into matchsticks and fried until golden brown. It can be diced and fried with garlic, ginger, chili, and onion.

Yet its bulbous shape suggested to me that it could also be cut and used as a base, or hollowed out and stuffed. Here are various recipes that show, I hope, how varied and adaptable this vegetable can be. The first can provide a base for a number of first courses.

Choose kohlrabi no bigger in diameter than 2½ inches. Peel them and slice into ½-inch disks. Drop these into boiling salted water and poach for 3 minutes. Drain and dry the slices. Dice the smaller disks but keep the larger ones whole. Fry both in olive oil and garlic until just brown. These can be used as a base like an artichoke bottom, with various additions piled upon them. The fried diced kohlrabi can be used as part of the topping mixture. I suggest mixtures of mushrooms, red and green bell peppers, corn kernels, chilies, capers, olives, and anchovies, in dressings of walnut or sesame oil.

Kohlrabi goes very well with the silky Greek sauce, *avgolemono*—a mixture of lemon and chicken stock. For this it should be peeled and sliced, boiled for 3–4 minutes, and then drained carefully. It is placed in a baking dish, the sauce is poured over, and the dish briefly browned beneath the broiler.

If you want to use the vegetable whole, it is best stuffed. Peel the kohlrabi, then cut out a good hollow in the center. Boil the kohlrabi for 8 minutes, drain with care, and fill the center with whatever stuffing you choose. Bake in a preheated hot oven for 20 minutes. All of the round root vegetables (turnips, rutabaga, sweet potatoes, yams, cassavas) can be given this treatment, and they make good winter fare.

Kohlrabi can be used instead of potato in the great gratin dishes: Dauphinois, Lyonnais, and Ardennais. In fact, the last, flavored with juniper berries, works particularly well (see below). Kohlrabi can also be used instead of the cauliflower in the Cauliflower and Mushroom Pie (page 97).

KOHLRABI WINTER SALAD

2 heads of kohlrabi, peeled and grated
3 carrots, peeled and grated
1 celery heart, chopped
a bunch of parsley, chopped
½ cup pine nuts
1 garlic clove, minced
3 tablespoons olive oil
1 teaspoon red wine vinegar
a pinch of sugar
1 teaspoon Dijon mustard
sea salt and freshly ground black pepper

Thoroughly mix all the vegetables with the parsley in a large bowl. Fry the pine nuts with the garlic in the olive oil until golden. Add these to the salad.

Add the wine vinegar, sugar, mustard, and seasoning to the olive oil remaining in the pan. Stir well and pour this dressing over the salad.

Toss, and leave to marinate for an hour.

KOHLRABI APPETIZER

1 tablespoon olive oil
2 red bell peppers, cored and sliced
1 yellow or orange bell pepper, cored and sliced
1 hot red chili
5 garlic cloves, sliced
sea salt and freshly ground black pepper
1 cup sliced mushrooms
2 ounces pickled ginger
a bunch of arugula leaves
4 slices of kohlrabi to be used like artichoke
bottoms (see left)
¼ cup tapenade
4 scallions, finely sliced, or fresh cilantro,
chopped, for garnish

Heat the olive oil in a saucepan and throw in the bell peppers, chili, garlic, and mushrooms. Season, then cover and let cook over a low heat for 20 minutes.

Add the ginger, stir, and remove from the heat.

Arrange some arugula leaves on each of four plates. Place a kohlrabi slice in the center of each arugula bed and spread the slices with the tapenade. Pile some of the bell pepper and mushroom mixture on top of the kohlrabi.

Garnish with sliced scallions or chopped cilantro and serve cool or warm.

CHOU-RAVE À L'ARDENNAISE

4 tablespoons unsalted butter, plus more for greasing
3 heads of kohlrabi, very thinly sliced
2 large onions, thinly sliced
1 tablespoon juniper berries
sea salt and freshly ground black pepper
1¼ cups vegetable stock

Preheat the oven to 400°F.

Butter a shallow earthenware baking dish and arrange in it alternate layers of kohlrabi and onion, throwing in a few juniper berries on each layer and dotting with a little butter and seasoning as you go.

Pour the stock over and bake for 40–45 minutes, or until the top is golden brown.

KOHLRABI *Brassica oleracea* Gongylodes Group

ABOVE Turnips with tomato and garlic

TURNIP

Brassica rapa Rapifera Group

I believe the popular disdain for this delicious vegetable and the inane way we cultivate it—leaving plants to grow too big and too old—stems from its use in the eighteenth century as new cattle fodder for the winter months. Defoe, during his tour of England in 1722, remarked on the extent of turnip cultivation and how fat the cattle looked. Turnips and rapeseed-oil cakes had been used thus for many years in Holland, though it was the Romans who first used turnips as winter fodder, and they may well have introduced the practice into Gaul. Turnips had the added blessing of growing well on poor soil and ignoring cold weather, so immense tracts of previously unproductive land came under cultivation.

The turnip is thought to have been indigenous to the area between the Baltic Sea and the Caucasus, where it was later cultivated, and from there it spread into Europe. Its reputation was bad, however, and it was always associated with the food of the poor. The Roman soldier, farmer, and writer, Columella, points out in the first century AD that turnips are an important food for country people as they are so filling. The leaves were certainly eaten with as much pleasure as the roots. There are early recipes for pickling the roots: even the gourmet Apicius gives one where the turnips are sliced and pickled with honey, vinegar, and myrtle berries. Pickled turnip is, in fact, delicious (see the recipe opposite). The Romans also served roasted turnips with roast duck, a dish that is still traditional in France, though it only appears in England as an Elizabethan recipe for boiling a duck with turnips. The vegetable was boiled separately, then turned in sweet butter with cinnamon, ginger, pepper, mace, and salt and served with the carved bird. The young leaves of turnips were used in salads throughout the sixteenth and seventeenth centuries. Other salads contained sliced turnip that had been boiled and then dressed with oil and vinegar.

For the last five centuries or so the turnip has endured a hard time in Britain. Everywhere, it has been largely overcooked, pulverized, mashed, pulped, and puréed. Why can't we grow those tiny, round, purplish turnips that the French so revere? The answer is that we choose still to cultivate the turnip principally for cattle fodder, and pick the same variety just a little earlier for human consumption.

The French turnip (navet) is *B. napus esculenta*; *esculenta* means edible, and it certainly is. Sturtevant, who generally restrains his lyricism, is moved to say, "it surpasses other turnips by the sweetness of its flavor and furnishes white, yellow and black varieties." These smaller turnips certainly crossed the English Channel, for they are mentioned in 1683, and appear in a garden dictionary as late as 1807, but they never caught on. British cuisine was dedicated to over-boiling root vegetables and refused to prepare them any other way. Fortunately, many greengrocers now stock the small French turnip, so we can enjoy them.

NUTRITION

If you are lucky enough to find turnip greens, cook the young leaves. They are particularly high in vitamins A, B, and C. Boil for a few minutes, drain well, and serve with a little butter or olive oil. Turnips themselves are 90 percent water, with traces of vitamins and minerals. They are very low in calories.

CHOOSING AND COOKING

Buy turnips with healthy and bright green tops; the roots should be firm with no discoloring. Turnips are excellent raw, simply grated and then dressed as for a slaw. They do not need peeling. Or, they can be sliced in fingers to be part of a platter of crudités.

Even when cooked, turnips should have some crunch. Boil them for 3 minutes, then slice them and cover with a garlicky vinaigrette or melted butter.

TURNIPS WITH TOMATO AND GARLIC

1 cup chopped canned tomatoes
2 garlic cloves, chopped
1 dried hot red chili, crushed
⅓ cup red wine
sea salt and freshly ground black pepper
1 pound turnips, trimmed and thickly sliced
2 tablespoons chopped parsley

Pour the tomatoes with their liquid into a pan and add the garlic, chili, wine, and seasoning. Bring to a simmer and cook for a moment.

Add the turnips, mix them into the sauce, and let them simmer quietly for 5 minutes.

Turn them onto a warmed serving dish and sprinkle with a little parsley.

QUICK PICKLED TURNIPS

You will find this method of pickling turnips all over North Africa and the Middle East, but this particular recipe comes from Lebanon.

The turnip turns a delicate pink and is excellent as a canapé with drinks.

1½ pounds baby turnips, trimmed
2½ cups cider vinegar
2 tablespoons sea salt
1 small beet, peeled and cut in half

Slice the turnips into disks about ⅛ inch thick.

Bring the vinegar to a boil and add the salt.

In a canning jar, arrange some layers of sliced turnip and place the raw beet halves in the center. Fill the jar with turnip slices.

Pour in the vinegar. If there is not enough, fill up the jar with water. Place a tight-fitting lid on top, then turn the jar over several times so that the contents are well mixed.

Leave for 4–5 days before eating.

TURNIP *Brassica rapa* Rapifera Group

RUTABAGA or SWEDE

Brassica napus Napobrassica Group

A very modern vegetable, the rutabaga is believed to have originated from a hybrid between the turnip (*B. rapa*) and kohlrabi (*B. oleracea*), though the latter species comprises the cabbage and all its near relatives. The root is larger than the turnip and may be white, yellow, or orange. Some varieties have a slight purpling at the neck, but once peeled the root is uniform in color. The rutabaga came from Bohemia in the seventeenth century, and was used as winter food for both cattle and man. It was introduced into England from Holland in 1755, and was called the "turnip-rooted cabbage." It quickly became popular as another easy crop to feed cattle.

There is some confusion over its name: in America it is called rutabaga, which is French for the large yellow variety—in France, the other varieties have the prettier name of *chou-navet*. The English changed from calling the vegetable "turnip-rooted cabbage" to "swede" when Sweden began to export their crop to England in the 1780s. But in Scotland, what they call a swede is in fact a turnip!

Gastronomy has avoided the rutabaga like the plague. Is this justified, I wonder? Like the turnip, it is considered to be worthy of cattle, but not of man. Yet the flavor of this vegetable is sweet, nutty, and very pleasant. It has one drawback: mashed rutabaga always seems too watery to be very enticing. It is, however, an immensely useful vegetable for winter soups. Peeled and diced, then boiled with other vegetables, such as turnip, potato, and carrot, and perhaps some bones from game birds, the resulting soup is a hearty and flavorful mixture, certainly not to be spurned on a cold winter's day.

Rutabaga needs very little cooking before it disintegrates. I suggest methods of cooking that keep the water content and most of the nutrients, for rutabaga is rich in vitamin C, calcium, and niacin.

COOKING

Peel and slice the rutabaga into ⅛-inch disks or fingers. Fry in olive oil with garlic over a high heat for about 2–3 minutes, stirring the pieces in the pan. They need to shrink a little and to brown at the edges, so that they just caramelize. This cooking method makes the rutabaga pieces crisp on the outside but keeps them juicy and tender within. Finish with a little sprinkling of salt, a pinch of sugar, and a good twist or two of the pepper-mill. A little grated Parmesan cheese sprinkled over the top before serving would also do the fried rutabaga no harm.

Alternatively, use the fried rutabaga disks, which are as large as saucers, as a base for mushrooms in tomato sauce, avocado and arugula, or any mixture you like, as a first course.

Winter vegetables are economical; they are also warming and make hearty wholesome dishes. There is huge satisfaction to be gained from simple peasant dishes, such as the one that follows.

RUTABAGA AND KALE PIE

2 tablespoons butter, plus more for greasing
1 pound kale, trimmed and chopped
2 tablespoons flour
1¼ cups milk
½ cup grated Gruyère cheese
½ cup grated Parmesan cheese
sea salt and freshly ground black pepper
2 tablespoons olive oil
3 or 4 garlic cloves, sliced
1 large head of rutabaga, peeled and sliced

Preheat the oven to 400°F and butter a baking dish.

Throw the kale into some boiling salted water and let it cook for 4–5 minutes. Drain thoroughly, pressing the vegetable to make sure all the excess water has drained away.

Make the sauce by melting the butter in a pan over a gentle heat and stirring in the flour to make a roux. Add the milk and stir until smooth and thick, then add the cheeses. Season and mix the sauce with the kale. Pour this into the baking dish.

Heat the olive oil and the garlic in a frying pan and fry the sliced rutabaga for a few minutes so that it turns golden. Arrange the slices over the kale.

Bake in the oven for 20 minutes.

CHINESE or NAPA CABBAGE

Brassica rapa Pekinensis Group

Also known as celery cabbage and pe-tsai, this variety of cabbage has become quite a familiar sight in markets. After beansprouts it is probably the best-known of the Asian vegetables in the West. It has its fans; for example, Joy Larkcom talks of its sweetness and delicacy, and Ken Hom recommends its use raw or lightly cooked, because it is "a sweet, crunchy vegetable with a mild but distinctive taste that chefs like to match with foods with richer flavors."

I fear that, unlike the other Asian brassicas, I cannot view it with great excitement unless it is cooked in a specific Asian manner. Hom is right—it is the richer flavors that it needs. To my taste, the leaves have one excellent quality: they are a good vegetable for pickling. The process of adding spices, salt, and vinegar makes them very palatable.

In Sichuan and in Tientsin, they cut the leaves and stems into small chunks. In Tientsin, they then pack the cabbage into jars with salt, garlic, and other spices. In Sichuan, they preserve the cabbage without

BELOW The harvesting of Chinese cabbage

CHINESE or NAPA CABBAGE *Brassica rapa* Pekinensis Group

garlic. Various recipes call for the use of pickled vegetables, which give a different texture and a sharp flavor to all manner of soups and stir-fried dishes.

The history of Chinese cabbage is as long as that of China itself. Cabbage is mentioned in the fifth century AD. It took over slowly from the mallow, which had been the most important leafy vegetable of ancient China. Now, alas, the venerable mallow has come to be regarded as a weed. Much later, a Nanking writer, in an essay called "Precious Things" written around 1600, describes such delicacies as lotus root, ginkgo nuts, shad, and small carp, but does not omit the daily fare of vegetables and fruits, "the turnips, onions, celery, cabbage, and pears."

John Barrow, the British traveler and civil servant, said of China in the Chia-ching reign (1796–1820) that in the "assortment of foods there was a wider disparity in China between the rich and the poor than in any other country of the world." Sadly, cabbage again was indissolubly linked with the diet of the poor—or the ascetic, as in this sad tale from *The Scholars* by Wu Ching-tzu, written at the same time:

"As they were chatting, lights were brought in, and the servants spread the desk with wine, rice, chicken, fish, duck, and pork. Wang Hui fell to, without inviting Chou Chin to join him and when Wang Hui had finished, the monk sent up the teacher's rice with one dish of cabbage and a jug of hot water. When Chou Chin had eaten they both went to bed. The next day, the weather cleared. Wang Hui got up, washed and dressed, bade Chou Chin a casual good-bye, and went away in his boat, leaving the schoolroom floor so littered with chicken, duck, and fish bones and melon-seed shells, that it took Chou Chin a whole morning to clear them all away, and the sweeping made him dizzy."

The prevalence of cabbage in China for most of this century tells us that it is still a very important staple: with mustard greens, radishes, rice, and soybeans, it is the diet of the peasant. The main meal each day is a bowl of rice, a mass of bean curd (tofu), and a dish of cabbage, fresh in season or pickled. Cabbages yield enormous harvests and are available in southern China all year round (Chinese cabbage can be grown through the winter).

The Chinese cabbage family is vast. Over a dozen varieties are grown in California for the U.S. market alone, and more are grown in Israel for the European market, while many more varieties are grown in China itself. This profusion of Chinese cabbage types can make even botanists confused. L. H. Bailey, who has written two volumes on the brassicas, has admitted to being quite perplexed.

Chinese cabbage is high in vitamin A, B1, B2, B3, C, and D, as well as having plenty of minerals, including iron, potassium, and calcium. Through cooking it will lose about half of its vitamin content, but pickling does not destroy its vitamin C. There have been various studies around the world that link regular cabbage consumption with some degree of protection against colon cancer (see page 89).

CHOOSING AND COOKING

It is a simple matter to select the least damaged Chinese cabbage, for if it has been around too long the outside leaves get tattered and torn. There should be very little wastage in Chinese cabbage: the outside leaves get thrown away and then everything else can be used. Take off what you need at the time and keep the rest in the salad drawer of the refrigerator. Either slice across the leaves and stem or cut down the leaf and slice into strips.

Stir-fry the leaves with powerful flavorings, like sesame oil, garlic, ginger, and chili. Finish by adding a little salt and sugar, and a tablespoon of Chinese rice wine or dry sherry. If you wish, you can also add a little oyster sauce or black bean sauce at the end. The cabbage needs transforming, so do not be nervous about adding strong ingredients. Some other suggestions follow.

CHINESE CABBAGE WITH GINGER AND COCONUT

1 tablespoon sesame oil
3 garlic cloves, sliced
1 teaspoon coriander seeds, crushed
3 tablespoons grated fresh gingerroot
6 cups chopped Chinese cabbage leaves
sea salt and freshly ground black pepper

⅔ cup unsweetened coconut milk

grated zest and juice of 2 limes

2 tablespoons pickled ginger slices

Heat the sesame oil and fry the sliced garlic, crushed coriander seeds, and grated ginger for a second or two. Throw in the chopped cabbage leaves and season. Stir-fry for 2 minutes.

Add the coconut milk, lime zest and juice, and the pickled ginger. Place a lid over the pan and let simmer for 2 minutes.

Pour into a dish and serve.

CHINESE CABBAGE WITH MUSHROOMS

2 tablespoons peanut oil

1 dried hot red chili, crushed or broken up

1 pound mushrooms (oyster would be best)

1 large green bell pepper, cored and sliced

6 cups chopped Chinese cabbage leaves

1 bunch of scallions, chopped

a pinch of sea salt

a pinch of sugar

2 tablespoons dark soy sauce

Heat the oil in a wok and throw in the chili, mushrooms, green bell pepper, and cabbage. Stir-fry for several minutes, until the cabbage begins to soften.

Add the scallions, salt, sugar, and soy. Stir-fry for another minute and serve immediately.

PICKLED CHINESE CABBAGE

Piled up on a small dish, this makes an excellent hors d'oeuvre—the perfect foil for dry martinis. It can also be added to stir-fried dishes.

3 pounds Chinese cabbage, chopped (about 18 cups)

1 pound coarse sea salt

3 heads of garlic, cloves peeled and sliced

2 or 3 hot red chilies, chopped

Pack the cabbage tightly into a large earthenware crock or a strong glass jar, salting and adding garlic and bits of chili to each layer. Pack down tightly and place a weighted board directly on the cabbage.

In 2–3 days a liquid will begin to ooze up around the lid indicating that the pickling has begun. The cabbage is ready to be eaten after 3 weeks. It will keep for 2–3 months or more, as long as the cabbage is submerged.

Take out what you need and rinse thoroughly to wash away excess salt, then squeeze the pieces of cabbage further to get rid of excess moisture.

MUSTARD GREENS

Brassica juncea

This is a favorite vegetable of mine. I grow it every year, and when I discovered this passage from Pliny I thought I had possibly found another enthusiast:

"…with its pungent taste and fiery effect [mustard] is extremely beneficial for the health. It grows entirely wild, though it is improved by being transplanted: but on the other hand when it has once been sown it is scarcely possible to get the place free of it, as the seed when it falls germinates at once. It is also used to make a relish, by being boiled down in saucepans till its sharp flavor ceases to be noticeable; also its leaves are boiled, like those of all other vegetables. There are three kinds of mustard plant, one of a slender shape, another with leaves like those of turnip, and the third with those of arugula. The best seed comes from Egypt."

There is, of course, no way of telling whether the vegetable that is "boiled down" is Brassica juncea or B. nigra, which gives us black mustard seeds. There are many varieties of mustard, some annuals, some biennials, all of which are thought to have originated in the central Asian Himalayas.

Selective breeding of various types of mustard over the centuries has led to an astonishing diversity. (See Joy Larkcom's fine Oriental Vegetables for a summary of many of them.) Many members of the mustard family grew wild in the Mediterranean region, but as B. nigra tends to grow to at least 6 feet in height, Pliny would surely have mentioned it.

Incidentally, it is the seed of *nigra* that is used for Dijon mustard. White mustard (*Sinapsis alba*) is the plant seedling often grown and eaten with sprouted seeds. It is milder in flavor than black, and contributes to the taste of American mustard; a little is also used in English mustard. *B. juncea* has a seed that is a lighter brown and which is also used in the manufacture of mustards worldwide, because it can be harvested mechanically.

In India, mustard greens are also grown for the extraction of mustard oil, an important ingredient in Indian cooking. The oil has long been an important export, even under the British Raj. In the year 1871–2, India exported 1,418 tons of mustard seed for the extraction of its oil. This was then used in Russia as a substitute for olive oil.

The delight of being able to grow mustard greens—they germinate quickly and easily in a cool climate—is that the seedlings and young leaves can be picked for green salads. Mixed in with much blander leaves, such as lettuce, they give great zest and interest to the salad. The larger leaves can be stir-fried in peanut, sesame, or mustard oil and then simply dressed with a little light soy sauce, sea salt, and some lemon juice. The flavor is so delicious that they need very little else.

Do not be anxious—once cooked they lose at least half of their fiery flavor. This is not a bad thing because older mustard leaves are more pungent than the young leaves picked for salad.

BOK CHOY or PAK-CHOI

Brassica rapa Chinensis Group

To confuse matters, bok choy is also called celery cabbage. It has thick white stems that fuse on the bottom half of the plant; the leaf is spoon-shaped and a glossy dark green. Bok choy looks more like Swiss chard than cabbage, and its flavor is very slightly peppery—not in the least bland like Chinese or Napa cabbage, nor fiery like mustard greens. It is, in fact,

LEFT Bok choy stir-fried with garlic, chili, and ginger

a lovely vegetable to add to the repertoire. It is easy to grow and readily obtainable from supermarkets.

Bok choy is as old as Chinese cabbage in the cuisine of ancient China, and there is a bewildering variety. Bruce Cost tells us that Hong Kong farmers alone grow over twenty kinds of bok choy, with names such as "horse's ear" and "horse's tail."

Like mustard greens, bok choy is easily grown in cool climates. The leaves can be eaten as a salad green when very small and young. The stems are juicy and sweet. Once the plant matures, use the leaves for stir-frying. If the plant begins to flower, all the better, because the flowers are delicious in salads or can be stir-fried with the leaves.

Bruce Cost recommends that Shanghai bok choy be cooked whole or cut in half lengthwise, because "the brilliant green of the cooked hearts makes an attractive adornment to a cooked meat dish." Bok choy is at its best when stir-fried fairly simply with sesame or peanut oil, garlic, chili, and ginger, and finishing with a pinch each of sea salt and sugar.

MIZUNA

Brassica rapa Japonica Group

You will find these delightful fronds in Japanese cooking rather than Chinese. Although they originally came from China, it is Japan that has cultivated them since antiquity. The aesthetics of the Japanese cuisine are more precise and detailed than those of the Chinese, and I suspect this vegetable found its place in national taste because of its intricate beauty.

It is again very easy to grow in cool climates. It forms a bushy rosette of feathery, dark green leaves, and the leaf stems are white, quite slender, and juicy. The flavor is of mild pepper and nuts. I grow mizuna every year and would never be without it. Sow in spring and again in fall. The plants bolt easily in warm weather, but are quite tolerant of cold. The young leaves are excellent in salads, and the older leaves are very good stir-fried.

MIZUNA *Brassica rapa* Japonica Group

WATERCRESS

Nasturtium officinale

There was a Greek proverb, "eat cress and learn more wit," which summed up a belief in antiquity that this vegetable was brain food. The Romans went so far as to recommend its consumption with vinegar for the insane. But which cress were they extolling? The term covers all the crucifers that have slightly pungent and peppery leaves. Cress was widely known in ancient times. "Basil, sorrel, spinach, cress, arugula, orach, coriander, and dill are plants of which there is only one kind, as they are the same in every locality and no better in one place than another," announces Pliny. Some disagreed: according to Athenaeus, Eubolus declares that Milesian cress is the best. It is likely that the mixture of mustard seedlings and cress was used in Greek times, and thus we know that here they must have been referring to upland cress (see below). When the Greeks talk of cress used as seasoning or as an ingredient in a sauce, however, it seems more likely that they are referring to the cress that grows at the edge of streams. We find them praising cress used as a seasoning with "young greens, capers, eggs, and smoked fish." And again, "the wild plants fit to cook are lettuce, cress, coriander, and mustard." It surely is watercress when Xenophon comments how "pleasant it is to eat barley cake and some cress when one is hungry by a stream."

It was noticed early on that although watercress had a peppery quality, it refreshed the palate and reinvigorated the spirits. There is a charming story of the French king, St. Louis (Louis IX), who was out hunting on a hot day and called for water. None was available but a servant brought him watercress, which so refreshed the king that he decided to honor the plant and the place where he had eaten it. The arms of the city of Vernon still today show the royal symbol, the three *fleurs-de-lis*, on one side and three bunches of watercress upon the other.

For a banquet to honor the Comte de la Marche, Charles VI's chef Taillevent wrote on the menu after the fourth course, "the watercress, served alone, to refresh the mouth." How dismal it is now to see watercress relegated to a garnish with steak, and dismissed to the edge of the plate.

The first attempt to cultivate watercress on any scale was in the sixteenth century at Erfurt in Germany, for the extraction of its blue dye. It was not until 1808 that a William Bradbury created the first watercress beds at Springhead in England.

Freshly cut watercress was sold at markets as a breakfast food, with bread, for industrial workers. A Victorian, E. S. Dallas, comments, "they are the one vegetable eaten by rich and poor in England, for health even more than for food." According to Dorothy Hartley, scientific advances in the eighteenth century made people realize the value of the "iron-rich" greenery. She goes on to say: "Very young cress is light bright green, but the knowledgeable prefer their cress 'sunburnt'—that is slightly older—when the leaves have acquired a delicate bronze."

Watercress is available year-round, with best quality in spring and fall. Hydroponically grown watercress is occasionally available. It is less peppery and often larger-leaved than conventional watercress.

BELOW Watercress

Watercress has always been valued for its color; soups and sauces made from it look good and taste wonderful. We should experiment far more with it in this way (see below). When using it for cooking do not cut all the stems off: allow a little to stay, because the most pungent flavor is there.

NUTRITION

Watercress is rich in vitamins A, B2, C, D, and E, and contains many trace minerals, including manganese, iron, phosphorus, iodine, calcium, potassium, sodium, and sulfur. It also has antibiotic properties similar to those of the onion family, so is a highly useful food to have as a staple in the diet.

WATERCRESS SOUP

Most recipes suggest cooking the cress in stock and adding cream, but cooking cress changes the color and dampens the flavor. With a blender, this soup is simplicity itself. How rich or thick you want the soup to be is up to you. You can add cream or plain yogurt to the stock and watercress mixture for a richer texture if you wish.

1 bunch of watercress, stems removed
2½ cups vegetable stock
2½ cups buttermilk, sour cream,
skim milk, or soy milk
sea salt and freshly ground black pepper
a few spoonfuls of fromage blanc or plain yogurt,
for garnish

Reserving a few whole sprigs for garnish, place the watercress in a blender with the stock and blend until you have a smooth, light green purée.

Mix whatever type of milk you choose with it and then season to taste.

If you want to serve the soup cold, leave it in the refrigerator for an hour or two to chill, then garnish each bowl with some of the fromage blanc or yogurt and a reserved watercress sprig.

If you want to serve the soup hot, heat it carefully, ensuring that it does not boil. Remove it from the heat and garnish as before.

DOROTHY HARTLEY'S WATERCRESS SALAD

Dice some cooked new potatoes and drop them into a very little salted cream. Cover the bottom of a flat dish with some sliced tomatoes. Take a small bunch of parsley and shred this finely over the tomatoes. On this green bed, make a layer of the white potatoes, and finally cover with watercress sprigs. Serve dry, and offer oil and vinegar separately. Do not use pepper with this salad.

WATERCRESS CUSTARDS

Made using individual ramekins, these are an excellent and very attractive first course.

1 bunch of watercress, stems removed
2 eggs
⅔ cup sour cream
sea salt
radicchio leaves, for garnish
for the green peppercorn sauce:
⅔ cup sour cream
2 tablespoons green peppercorns in brine

Preheat the oven to 375°F.

Reserving a few whole sprigs for garnish, place the watercress in a blender with the eggs and blend until smooth. Mix in the sour cream and salt.

Butter four ramekins and pour in the mixture. Place the ramekins in a bain-marie and bake for 15 minutes, or until risen.

While they are baking, make the green peppercorn sauce by mixing the two ingredients together.

Take the ramekins out of the oven and leave to cool slightly, then unmold onto individual plates. Garnish with radicchio and the reserved watercress.

Spoon a little of the peppercorn sauce, not more than a teaspoon or two, over the top of each custard.

WATERCRESS *Nasturtium officinale*

UPLAND CRESS

Barbarea verna

What a pity this excellent green salad plant with very pretty, edible yellow flowers is not available in farm stalls and markets. It could otherwise become a big commercial crop because it is very easy to grow and has much of the peppery delight that we find in watercress. However, those lucky people who have their own gardens can cultivate it. If sown in late summer and given the protection of a cloche or cold frame (so that severe frosts will not damage it), upland cress can be picked throughout the winter months (it will not actually grow but will remain sound if not frozen through). Its nutritional value is similar to that of watercress.

GARDEN or BROADLEAF CRESS

Lepidium sativum

This is the kind of cress that is traditionally grown with mustard sprouts in Britain, to be used in tea sandwiches. The mustard seedlings germinate 3 – 4 days earlier than cress, so you have to wait until both are ready for cutting.

Cress was originally native to Persia, and from there it spread east into the gardens of India, as well as to Syria, Greece, and Egypt. Xenophon had a theory that the Persians ate cress before they baked bread. Other than the common cress we know, there are three different kinds—curled, broad-leaved, and golden. All were familiar in the Ancient World. In fact, it is likely that they knew others. Pliny mentions a giant cress grown in Arabia. It is also interesting to discover how often bread is mentioned in connection with cress. Take Gerard, for example: "Galen saith that the Cresses may be eaten with bread and so the Ancient Spartans usually did; and the low-countries men many times do, who commonly use to feed of Cresses with bread and butter. It is eaten with other sallade herbes, as Tarragon and Rocket; and for this cause it is chiefly sown."

Indeed, cress is still marvelous in sandwiches, excellent with a smear of mayonnaise, or a little ripe avocado or tomato or cucumber. Yet I see it around infrequently and perhaps we British are not using it as we once did. It is easy to grow yourself, especially if you are into sprouting seeds and already have a sprouter. Remember, all seeds are a stored powerhouse of food and, once they start to sprout, their enzymes become active. Weight for weight, they provide more nutrients than any other natural food.

RADISH

Raphanus sativus

It is odd to think that the small radish we might crunch with an aperitif has such an ancient history that its wild ancestor has entirely disappeared. The *raphanus* refers to its redness, possibly from the Sanskrit *rudhira* meaning blood. In antiquity it was cultivated all over the civilized world, so many different varieties were established at those earlier times from the Mediterranean to the Orient. It was then grown as a staple food plant, and the leaves were almost certainly eaten as well as the root. Theophrastus lists five varieties and declares that the Boetian type was the best and the sweetest. This seems to be our salad radish: small and round, colored red and white or reddish-purple, with a leaf that can also be eaten as a salad green when young.

Prior to the introduction of the olive tree, the radish was grown in Egypt for the oil from its seeds. In Italy, Pliny tells us, "medical men recommend giving raw radishes with salt for the purpose of concentrating the crude humors of the bowels..." He goes on: "They have a remarkable power of causing flatulence and eructation; consequently they are a vulgar article of diet, at all events if cabbage is eaten immediately after them, though if the radish itself is eaten with half-ripe olives, the eructation caused is less frequent and less offensive."

The radishes of Egypt and Rome may have been of the winter radish group, which includes black radishes and the one we now know from Japanese cuisine, the daikon (see page 118). When the Greeks made their

ABOVE Varieties of small red radish with their leaves

vegetable sacrifices to Apollo at Delphi, they presented turnips on a platter of lead, beets on a silver platter, and radishes on gold plates, indicating the esteem in which they held this particular vegetable.

The Romans brought radishes to England with them. Pliny observed that they grew better in the colder climes. The larger types of radishes were very likely the ones mentioned in accounts of medieval food. Albertus Magnus, in the thirteenth century, talks of a very large root of a pyramidal shape; this was grown all over northern Europe, and was reported by the botanist Henry Lyte (1529–1607) as being the common radish of England. Gerard mentions four varieties grown in 1597, "eaten raw with bread," but, for the most part, "used as a sauce with meates to procure appetite." One supposes that the large white radishes were boiled before being puréed to make a sauce.

However, the small red variety was certainly eaten and enjoyed as a salad vegetable. Lady Fettiplace notes that "radish prove best that sowen a day after the full moon in August." Salads then, and for the next century, sound very familiar to us. The selection from a range of leaves is wide: lettuce, purslane, corn salad, sorrel, dandelion, mustard, cresses, the young leaves of radish, turnips and spinach, as well as the thinnings from rows of seedlings.

The last mention of the large white radish in English cooking appears, I believe, as late as 1845, when Eliza Acton gives one recipe for boiled turnip-radishes. She recommends leaving them whole and boiling them for up to 30 minutes, then sending them to table with melted butter or white sauce. She also adds that common radishes—when young, tied in bunches, and boiled from 18 to 25 minutes—are very good on toast like asparagus.

RADISH *Raphanus sativus*

117

Perhaps E.S. Dallas (who wrote *Kettner's Book of the Table*, 1877) should have the last word: "There are few combinations of color so beautiful and rich as the red and white of radishes against the green of the leaves. In glass dishes upon a dinner-table they are an ornament which may vie with the finest flowers."

NUTRITION

Radishes are popular with dieters as they are so low in calories and protein. They are mostly water, but have a high vitamin B and C content as well as many minerals, including calcium and sodium. The peppery flavor is caused by sulfur compounds.

Radishes have medicinal qualities: they were thought to be a remedy for stone, gravel, and scorbutic conditions. They have a mild diuretic effect, and relieve constipation and catarrh.

BUYING AND PREPARING

Choose crisp radishes with springy, bright green leaves—an excellent sign of freshness, because the leaves wilt very quickly.

The small red radish is best eaten raw, whole or sliced in salads. However, radishes tend to get lost if just added to a green salad. Try dishes in which they are diced, marinated in a vinaigrette, and mixed with dried and fresh fruit, with a sprinkling of toasted pine nuts perhaps. Explore their many possibilities by varying the salad recipe below.

RADISH, ORANGE, AND PINE NUT SALAD

½ cup sliced dried apricots
about ⅔ cup dry sherry
1 tablespoon sesame oil
2 tablespoons olive oil
1 tablespoon white wine vinegar
sea salt and freshly ground black pepper
1 bunch of radishes, trimmed and washed
2 oranges
¼ cup pine nuts
2 tablespoons hazelnut oil
1 slice of wholewheat bread, cubed
2 garlic cloves, sliced

The day before: in a small bowl, soak the slices of dried apricot overnight in just enough of the dry sherry to cover them.

Make a dressing by mixing the sesame and olive oils with the white wine vinegar and seasoning. Slice or quarter the radishes and add them with the apricots and any of their liquid. Leave them to marinate for about half an hour.

Peel and slice the oranges, catching the juice, and add both to the radishes.

Fry the pine nuts in the hazelnut oil until just brown, then fry the bread with the garlic until golden in color. Sprinkle these over the salad.

LARGE WHITE RADISH or DAIKON

Raphanus sativus spp.

"The radish occupies a far more exalted position in Oriental cultures than it does in the West, and is much larger than its Western counterpart. It is the most widely grown vegetable in Japan, where, so I've been told, gift-wrapped radishes are a token of esteem." So says Joy Larkcom, giving ten pages of detailed consideration to the various radishes used in Asian cooking. As she says, they are cooked or pickled, a few are used for salads, others are salted and dried to preserve them. "Radish leaves, stems, seed pods and seedlings are all valued as vegetables, cooked, pickled or raw."

Whenever I have bought a large white radish, it has turned out to be so mild it is almost tasteless. I suspect that, because they keep their appearance, they are stored for too long and they sadly lose their flavor. The ones I have eaten from my own garden, on the other hand, have been verging on the hot and peppery. These are a welcome addition to the stir-fry. I have also grated these and eaten them raw in a vinaigrette with the addition of grated carrot or apple.

For stir-frying white radish, the vegetable can be sliced across in disks or down in slices. It really depends on how you want the finished dish to appear.

RIGHT Black radishes, large white radishes, and assorted small red radishes

As a cooked vegetable, white radish can be trimmed and cut, then poached in vegetable or chicken stock for 5 minutes. The cooking liquid is then thickened with a little potato flour and some chopped parsley is added before serving.

BLACK RADISH

Raphanus nigra

This does not seem to have been mentioned by the writers of antiquity. It is sometimes known as the Black Spanish. There are both long and round varieties. They should be grown in fertile soil and cool temperatures so they reach full size quickly, and then be harvested promptly, for they quickly go woody and are then inedible. Boiled with their skins on for about 10 minutes, then peeled and sliced, they are excellent with an *aïoli* mayonnaise.

PICKLED SEEDPODS

There are numerous recipes throughout history for the pickling of radish seedpods. Indeed, in India and China, the green pods are pickled and are used in stir-fried dishes. Here is Dorothy Hartley's recipe: "Pick the pods when the seeds inside are like soft seed pearls, drop the pods into boiling brine, and let it grow cold—if they are now bright green you can pickle at once, but if dull, boil up the brine and pour it back over the pods once or twice till they are bright as emeralds. Drain, rinse clear of salt, pack the pods into glass bottles, with one or two scarlet peppers, cover with white clear vinegar, and cork down for winter use. They are a very pretty garnish to winter's potato salad.

"The clear green pods in a dish of pellucid pickled onions make a jade and pearl symphony that belies its potency. They are also delicious (and most decorative) with cream cheese."

HORSERADISH

Armoracia rusticana

The horseradish plant was indigenous to eastern Europe, Russia, Poland, and Finland, and is thought to have been taken down through the Caspian to Persia by the Aryans. The Egyptians used it as a medicine and a flavoring. It was popular in Rome and referred to by Dioscorides. Both the leaves and roots were eaten in Germany during the Middle Ages, but it does not appear to have reached Britain until later. Gerard mentions that the Germans use it, and the botanist and antiquary Lyte, in 1586, talks of the wild horseradish being used as a condiment.

It began to be popular in Britain in the seventeenth century, when the oilier fish such as mackerel, herring, and salmon were served with horseradish grated over them. As stronger pickles and relishes were being introduced by the East India trade, a liking for hotter sauces developed. Many pickles were now manufactured in Britain, and the pickling liquor almost inevitably included horseradish.

Horseradish sauce began to be eaten with roast beef in the nineteenth century. A recipe of the time suggests grating the root finely and mixing with a gill of cream, a dessertspoonful of sugar, a little salt, and rather more than a tablespoonful of vinegar. Another Victorian recipe, from *Kettner's Book of the Table,* suggests mixing grated horseradish with the zest and juice of an orange, three tablespoons of oil, a tablespoon of bread crumbs and one of vinegar, a teaspoon of sugar, and a pinch of salt.

Unless you grow horseradish, you may never have seen a whole root. Once grown in a garden it tends to take over and it is difficult to eradicate, because new plants will grow up from the smallest sliver of root left in the ground. If you find a root, scrub and clean it well: the skin and flesh next to it are the hottest and most aromatic parts. Grate the outside, trying to protect eyes and nostrils—the volatile oils are of the pungent mustard kind. The best method is to use a food processor, which will give some protection from the fumes. Combine it with cream, yogurt, or sour cream, and other ingredients as per the

ABOVE A Japanese horseradish farm

previous paragraph. Grated horseradish soon loses its pungency, which is why the bottled type is invariably so disappointing.

There are several other varieties of horseradish used as food in other parts of the world. In the far north and Arctic regions, the leaves of *Cochlearia danica* are eaten as a salad. In Hungary and the Balkan peninsula, they use the grated root of *C. macrocarpa*, a somewhat less acrid variety, while *C. officinalis* was once eaten as a cress in salads in Scotland and farther north. Commonly called "scurvy grass" or spoonwort, it was also used on long sea voyages as a preventative against scurvy. They even made scurvy-grass ale, which became a popular tonic drink, although the name was somewhat of a misnomer because the grass was not fermented. It was, in fact, a *tisane*: some of the leaves were infused in boiling water and it was taken in wineglassful doses throughout the day.

JAPANESE HORSERADISH
or WASABI

Wasabia japonica

Though it is not closely related to European horseradish, this is still a member of the cabbage family. It grows wild on the Japanese coast and up in the mountains, and likes wet ground beside streams. When fresh and bright green in color, it is grated to serve with *sashimi*, Japanese raw fish.

In the West, wasabi is widely sold dried and pulverized into a powder. Unlike grated European horseradish, powdered wasabi kept in its can retains almost all of its pungency. To use it, mix it with water and then leave it for 10–15 minutes, for only then will the real fiery intensity of the root be made manifest.

JAPANESE HORSERADISH or WASABI *Wasabia japonica*

121

ARUGULA or ROCKET

Eruca sativa

Of all the salad plants and their leaves, this is my own favorite by far. When small, the plant has green leaves that are slightly reminiscent of radish or dandelion leaves, or oakleaf lettuce, but the taste is singular—peppery and growing more mustard-like as the plant ages. The leaves add enormous zest to a mixed salad, though in my opinion the flavor is better without dressing. I use arugula extensively as part of the first course: its striking flavor is a marvelous foil for grilled *chèvre*, sliced avocado, or a variety of purées and salads.

Yet there is a great puzzle surrounding this edible and almost addictive plant. Why did it disappear entirely from Britain's gardens and tables for almost three hundred years? Further, one might ask, does the belief that the leaves have erotic properties have anything to do with that disappearance?

There is no doubt that the Ancient World considered arugula to possess aphrodisiac properties; it was sown around the base of statues consecrated to Priapus and believed to restore vigor to the genitalia. Ovid terms the herb "salacious," while Martial links it with scallions as "lustful." Apicius uses both the seeds and the leaves, grinding the first as an ingredient in aromatic salts to be added as flavoring (it appears in a sauce for cold boar). The leaves are used in a sauce for boiled crane, and the pounded leaves with other herbs are used as a dressing for salted gray mullet. In one recipe Apicius acknowledges arugula's salacious reputation, and teams it with bulbs "for those who seek the door of love, or as they are served with a legitimate wedding meal, but also with pine kernels or flavored with arugula and pepper."

The plant has a long history: in the Middle East, between 9,000 and 7,000 BC, arugula was one of the first plants to be cultivated. It originated as a weed with both rye and oats, infiltrating the very first cultivated plants, wheat, barley, rice, soybeans, flax, and

RIGHT Arugula and seakale

cotton. As cultivation stretched upward from the river basin to the higher regions, or traveled north to harsher climates, the so-called weeds were better adapted to these conditions and took over the fields. Thus the weeds became the crop and the crop the weed. (In the same way, the tomato plant was a weed that spread northward from Peru through the New World tropics to Mexico, as a weed of both maize and bean fields.)

Unaware that arugula was one of the first cultivated plants, the early Christian church only knew of its supposed erotic properties and frowned on its use and cultivation. Numerous writers spoke of its "hotness and lechery," and the Church, at one point, banned its cultivation in monastic gardens.

Its common name is derived from the Latin *"eruca,"* which denotes a downy stem like a caterpillar. Giacomo Castelvetro, in 1614, delights in its use as part of an early spring salad (see below). John Evelyn's arugula is derived from Spain, to be planted by his calendar in March. In the late 1690s Evelyn refers to it as both "hot and dry," but 50 years later, in 1747, Hannah Glasse omits arugula from her list of salads. Had it, by then, fallen out of favor?

Its decline is traced quite clearly in Sturtevant's *Notes on Edible Plants* (published 1919). Here he says, "in 1586 Camerarius says it is planted most abundantly in gardens. In 1726 Townsend says it is not now very common in English gardens, and in 1807 Miller's Dictionary says it has been long rejected." It is interesting to note that this decline was not paralleled elsewhere: it continued to flourish in gardens and cooking all over the Mediterranean countries, and it appeared in American gardens in 1854 or earlier.

John Evelyn shared the seventeenth-century passion for novelty in gardens; new varieties of fruit and vegetables were grown with great enthusiasm, yet were they eaten with the same enthusiasm? One doubts it. Pepys hardly mentions vegetables, except as ingredients for broths. People were suspicious of vegetables, believing them (quite rightly) to be a source of unwanted wind. Vegetables were also thought to cause melancholy. It is doubtful that arugula was ever eaten cooked in Britain (as it was and still is in the Mediterranean region), but as part of a salad it would have been well-seasoned with oil because this was thought to be an antidote to flatulence. Raw, undressed food was much frowned upon.

What could possibly be the reason, then, for the sudden disappearance of arugula from the British salad bowl, kitchen, and herb garden? After Evelyn, it stops being eaten in the British isles, until it reappears in seed catalogues around 1980. Since then, it has risen astonishingly quickly in popularity, so that every enterprising gardener and cook grows it, and supermarkets and greengrocers stock it.

It would seem that the disappearance of arugula and other salad vegetables from Britain was due to the rise in market gardens. The rapid growth and prosperity of towns favored the development of market gardens situated nearby. The vegetables and fruits grown in these gardens were chosen from the stock in the great houses, and they tended to be the most popular ones that could be sold off easily: peas, beans, potatoes, carrots, celery, cabbage, cauliflower, and the root vegetables, turnips and parsnips. Some of these vegetables became field crops; others gradually came to be grown, but not until a hundred years later, as part of the garden produce around the house to eke out the family diet. The rule of selection favored what could be cultivated and sold easily.

At first glance, this would seem to apply to arugula, because this salad plant seems too wild in appearance and habit to fit into the well-ordered market garden. Arugula can, after all, be found growing wild, and other salad leaves could certainly have been picked easily from the countryside.

Early in the nineteenth century, a countryman with a small plot of land could grow his own vegetables. Cobbett, at Singleton in Sussex, England, in 1823 notes, "the gardens are neat and full of vegetables of the best kinds. I see very few of 'Ireland's lazy root' [meaning the potato]." The vegetables tend to be the ones mentioned above, with emphasis on the brassicas. By this time, if arugula had strayed into such a garden it would have been plucked out as a weed. This conservatism is still rife today with the rural gardener,

RIGHT Arugula, mushroom, and flageolet salad
(page 128)

who looks on my own garden of salad leaves, radicchio, endive, chicory, and mustard greens as alien, and filled with plants not worth giving room to in his own plot of cabbages, beets, leeks, and onions.

The evidence for arugula's downfall and obscurity is even more striking if one consults *A Modern Herbal* by Mrs. Grieve, published in 1931 with an introduction by Mrs. Leyel, and long considered a modern classic. Here there is an entry for "Rocket, Garden," which refers to *Hesperis matronalis*, sweet rocket, but which then lists *Eruca sativa* as a synonym. It also goes on to make another profound mistake in saying that the arugula found in the wild in Britain and Russian Asia are escapes from gardens. Mrs. Grieve gives no separate entry for the great culinary arugula, *E. sativa*, an omission that is very odd in such a comprehensive work some 900 pages long. It is even more astonishing when one realizes that a small volume by Lady Rosalind Northcote, *The Book of Herbs*, published in 1912, gives a nervous appraisal of arugula, but refers back to the 1629 work of Parkinson (herbalist and apothecary to King James I), *Paradisi in Sole*, who believed arugula "causeth headache and heateth too much." Lady Northcote ends her half-page reference by commenting, "it gives little encouragement to those who would make trial of rocket."

What a pity both Mrs. Grieve and Lady Northcote did not take more notice of John Evelyn. Could it be that the ancients' admiration for arugula as an aphrodisiac made later writers nervous of it? Those who might be influenced by the severe admonitions of the medieval church, such as Edwardian gentlewomen like Mrs. Grieve, might cast it completely out of their minds and from the botanical world entirely.

CULTIVATION

Arugula is wonderfully easy to grow. Get into the habit of successive sowings from early March, depending on demand (one every two months is my own usual pattern). You can thin the seedlings and use them in a salad as soon as they have a couple of leaves, and can continue to cut leaves as they are growing. Arugula is a sturdy and flourishing plant that goes to seed easily if it is not cut back and eaten. The small white and yellow flowers can also be used in salads or as garnish. The plants will seed themselves, or the seed can be collected and ground up, to be used as flavoring. If you have a cold greenhouse you can keep arugula going throughout the winter months. Outside, the mature plants will often survive light snow and some frost.

SWEET ROCKET
Hesperis matronalis

This is a biennial that flowers early in March, in either white or lilac, and continues flowering for several months. I keep a few plants going in my herb garden, for it is not only charming but the young leaves can also be eaten in salads. They are very high in vitamin C and are valued medicinally.

WINTER CRESS
Barbarea vulgaris

This is another biennial that grows wild, not to be confused with upland cress (see page 116), though the flavor is similar. The leaves can be boiled or stir-fried. It is a sturdy plant that will flourish the more the leaves and yellow flowers are harvested.

COOKING

We tend to use arugula raw, in salads, but in Mediterranean countries it is often cooked. It is always part of the mix of wild greens called *horta,* which is gathered and cooked in Greece in the fall. The greens are simply boiled for 5 minutes, then well drained and served with oil and lemon.

Patience Gray uses arugula with pasta in *Honey from the Weed*: Orecchiette con la Rucola—'Little ears' with rocket. (Orecchiette are the traditional pasta of Apulia, shaped like little shells, particularly useful for holding the sauce.) A SALENTINE DISH. Use wild rocket, *Eruca sativa* (or broccoli heads or heads of rape). Gather the plants when small, wash them well and throw into a pan of salted boiling water. Cook the orecchiette in another pan and drain when they are al dente. Cover the bottom of a frying-pan with olive oil, add 2 hot peppers, 2 peeled cloves of garlic, sliced, and cook for a few minutes. Put the well-

ABOVE Arugula and avocado sandwich (overleaf)

drained pasta and the rocket in the pan, stir with a wooden fork, mixing all together, and serve very hot with a piquant grated cheese."

I think arugula is best when used in a salad or by itself. Perhaps Castelvetro's "excellent mixed salad" is the most beguiling of all.

"Of all the salads we eat in the spring, the mixed salad is the best and most wonderful of all. Take young leaves of mint, those of garden cress, basil, lemon balm, the tips of salad burnet, tarragon, the flowers and tenderest leaves of borage, the flowers of swine cress, the young shoots of fennel, leaves of arugula, of sorrel, rosemary flowers, some sweet violets, and the tenderest leaves or the hearts of lettuce. When these precious herbs have been picked clean and washed in several waters, and dried a little with

ARUGULA *Eruca sativa*

127

a clean linen cloth they are dressed as usual, with oil, salt and vinegar."

No writer that I have yet to discover mentions that the wonderful peppery flavor of arugula will be diminished once it is dressed with oil and vinegar. If you want to retain that crisp taste, almost of green peppercorns, keep some of the arugula undressed. This is my method: lay the arugula on a platter, mix the other salad ingredients with the dressing, and pile on top of the arugula in the center. This ensures that some leaves around the edge remain undressed.

ARUGULA, MUSHROOM, AND FLAGEOLET SALAD

a generous handful of arugula leaves
4 or 5 scallions, chopped
5 or 6 crimini mushrooms, sliced
2 or 3 tablespoons cooked flageolet beans
¼ cup walnut oil
1 tablespoon lemon juice
a pinch of sugar
sea salt
shreds of lemon zest, for garnish (optional)

Line a serving platter with the arugula leaves.

In a bowl, mix all the other ingredients with salt to taste and let them marinate for an hour.

Then pile the mixture in the center of the arugula-lined platter and serve, garnished with lemon zest.

ARUGULA AND AVOCADO SANDWICH

This is my favorite summer sandwich. Arugula and avocado go marvelously well together, but I confess I like a touch of other flavorings as well, as a kind of background track to the two stars.

This amount will make two fairly large and bulky sandwiches, which provide an excellent and satisfying lunch for two people.

2 heaped tablespoons soft goat cheese
4 slices of your favorite brown bread, buttered
a smear of Marmite, Vegemite, or Vecon
about 10 thin cucumber slices
sea salt and freshly ground black pepper
1 ripe avocado, peeled, seeded, and sliced
20 or so arugula leaves
a tiny drop of Tabasco (optional)

Spread the goat cheese on the buttered side of 2 slices of the bread and smear the Marmite, Vegemite or Vecon on the other 2 slices.

Lay the cucumber slices over the cheese, season with pepper, then lay the avocado slices on top of that, followed by the arugula leaves. Season with salt and Tabasco, if using.

Then cover with the other slices of bread. Press down the tops gently and slice the sandwiches in half with great care.

SEAKALE

Crambe maritima

This is a beautiful and mysterious plant when still in its wild state; when cultivated (I have several plants in my own garden), it looks no different from the seakale you will find on the beach in Europe. There it sits, like a great silver-green bouquet splayed over the shingle. It is astonishing to consider that the shoots have thrust their way through heavy pebbles, gravel, and sand toward the sunlight.

It is the stems of the potential leaves, the shoots, that should be blanched the minute they appear, by piling seaweed or gravel on them; or, in cultivation, by a blanching pot, which is then covered in manure so that it is warm, to hurry growth.

Seakale grows around the sandy shores of the North Sea, the Atlantic Ocean, and the Mediterranean Sea. The Romans gathered it and preserved it in barrels for eating through long sea voyages. It is recorded as being brought to English culture from Italy about 1760, and the seed then sold at a high price as a rarity. However, sea folk must have eaten the plant since time began, knowing the places along the shore where it grows and waiting to cover the growing shoots with seaweed to blanch them.

It was Louis XIV's gardener, la Quintinie, who first cultivated it in France. The people of Sussex, England, were gathering seakale in the spring and selling bundles of it at Chichester market; there is a record of this dated 1753. Thus the seed from Italy that sold at such a high price must have come to Britain through gourmet demand. So much so that by 1799, the botanist William Curtis wrote a booklet on the culture of seakale for the table, and for a time it was even cultivated commercially. It remained a popular vegetable with the elite up to about the end of the nineteenth century.

Carême discovered it, to his great delight, on sale in London: "They resemble branches of celery and are to be served like asparagus with a butter sauce, but I prefer to serve them with Espagnole [Carême's recipe for this classic sauce uses ham, veal and partridge for the stock]." He advised a lengthy 20 minutes' boiling.

If it was this popular, why has seakale all but disappeared from the table now? It must be yet another casualty of our growing urbanization—we have cut ourselves off from wild plants that still thrive in uninhabited areas and near desolate beaches. Of course, to harvest seakale in the spring, you need to know where the plants are, and for this they have to be marked the summer before. Or, like me, you can simply grow seakale in your garden.

Seeds for planting can be purchased by mail order from a few specialty houses. Alas, you cannot harvest the shoots for two years, but then, what bliss. Simply boil the shoots for 10 minutes and then eat them, like asparagus, with a little melted butter.

BELOW Seakale growing in a garden

Cucurbitaceae

THE
SQUASH
FAMILY

WINTER SQUASH
Cucurbita pepo, C. maxima, and *C. moschata*
ZUCCHINI and SUMMER SQUASH
Cucurbita pepo
SPAGHETTI SQUASH *Cucurbita pepo*
CHAYOTE *Sechium edule*
CUCUMBER *Cucumis sativus*
GHERKIN *Cucumis anguria*
CHINESE BITTER MELON *Momordica charantia*
SMOOTH and ANGLED LUFFAS
Luffa cylindrica and *L. acutangula*
BOTTLE GOURD *Lagenaria siceraria*

Most of this family's 805 species climb by tendrils or have a sprawling, prostrate habit. They are perhaps most striking for their Triffid-like, swarming growth. Nothing else in the garden, except weeds, grows at such speed. Leaves, tendrils, stems, and flowers expand rapidly, covering the soil beneath with their hairy lime-green leaves and yellow flowers the color of thick cream. They are greedy for space, and are tenacious, almost aggressive, in their expansion. Some gardeners make use of this high growth rate by growing them up arches or pergolas, using the plants decoratively.

The fruits also expand at a very fast rate. Melons at their most active put on 5 cubic inches in a day; pumpkins can average about 12 ounces, and daily gains of almost twice that have been known. This expansion is due to the accumulation of water-based sap in the cell vacuoles. *The high water content of the juicy flesh makes the fruits particularly refreshing in hot weather and tropical climes (it also makes some of them insipid when water is added during cooking). The rest is seeds, the whole protected by a more or less hard skin.*

As annuals native to temperate and tropical areas, they tend to be sensitive to temperatures near freezing, which limits where they grow and how they are cultivated. Cucumbers, melons, and gourds are Old World plants known to have been under cultivation for 4,000 years; pumpkins and the other squashes all stem from the New World, and some of the 25 species (probably the long-lasting winter squashes, with their oil-rich seeds) have been grown for 9,000 years.

SQUASH

Zucchini, and other summer squash, and the hard-shelled winter squashes are all members of the same family—the Curcurbitaceae—and are indigenous to the New World. They come in all shapes, colors, and sizes, and carry a multiplicity of names. Confusingly, the same variety may be known by different names in different countries. As a general rule, the squashes found in supermarkets bear their North American names, while the same ones in ethnic groceries bear their Asian or Caribbean names.

The whole multifarious squash family was, of course, part of the riches discovered in the Americas and described by the early explorers. They were unknown to the Old World before the time of Columbus, despite some confusion on this topic. Jane Grigson, in her marvelous *Vegetable Book,* is one of those who fall into the easy trap of believing that pumpkins were known in the Ancient World. Waverley Root, exploring this conundrum, points out that squashes are supposed to have grown in the gardens of Babylon, and that Pliny, Apicius, and Martial all mention them—in fact, the last gave a dinner composed entirely of different kinds of squash. But the Latin word could also be translated as "gourd": Albertus Magnus mentions edible gourds, and the French *citrouille* can mean either pumpkin or gourd. What

was being eaten in the Old World was fruit from the *Cucumis* section of the Cucurbitaceae (cucumbers, melons, and the edible gourds that are still preferred in both China and India today as being far more tasty than squashes). This is endorsed by the fact that there is no word for squash in Sanscrit, and none is mentioned either in the Bible or in any of the ancient Chinese writings. No trace of squash has been found in Egyptian tombs—only water flasks that were fashioned from gourds.

The confusion originated in the familiar way, when people applied an old name to a new thing. The word squash is obviously borrowed from the Native American name "*askutasquash,*" but many of the early explorers after Columbus were constantly calling the squashes "gourds." In 1672, John Josselyn, the English author of *New England Rarities discovered,* tries to describe the new fruit: "A kind of melon or rather gourd, for they sometimes degenerate into gourds. Some of them are green, some yellow, some longish, like a gourd, others round like an apple..." He adds, "all of them are pleasant food, boyled and buttered and seasoned with spice." To add to the confusion, the pattern was repeated in Spanish, and even today, in Cuba, large squashes are called *calabazas* from the Spanish for "gourd."

One useful division is into summer and winter squashes. Essentially, summer squashes are good fresh and do not keep long. Most are fairly thin-skinned. They are edible raw when young: try them grated and salted and pressed into molds (see page 138). If picked young they can be eaten unpeeled, so they retain more flavor and nutritional quality. They are excellent cut into strips and stir-fried. Their flavor is light and quite bland but always refreshing—an excellent foil for stronger-tasting vegetables and for spices. At a blind tasting, only the greatest of squash *aficionados* could detect any difference in flavor and tell which variety was which. Cooking methods are virtually interchangeable: you can substitute any summer squash in a zucchini recipe (this goes for winter squashes, too).

Winter squashes have the advantage of keeping well when allowed to ripen at a good temperature and stored in a frost-free place. Most are larger and

---

THE SQUASH FAMILY *Cucurbitaceae*

ABOVE An assortment of squashes

thicker-skinned than summer squashes, and many have hard, inedible seeds. Winter squash varieties take twice as long to grow as summer squashes—needing about 95–110 days to reach maturity. The texture of their flesh is firmer and more floury than that of summer squashes. But they do contain more protein, fat, carbohydrates, and considerably more vitamin A than summer squashes such as zucchini. They are excellent additions to winter soups, thickening and flavoring a mixed vegetable selection. They are also good for making preserves and homemade wine.

WINTER SQUASH

Cucurbita pepo, C. maxima, and C. moschata

The pumpkin is perhaps the most famous winter squash, with its deep orange flesh and its traditional role as part of Halloween and Thanksgiving, but it is only one of many winter squashes, which include acorn, butternut, buttercup, and hubbard. The pumpkin, though, has an interesting history.

Pumpkins grew in the south and in the north of the Americas. Pedro de Alvarado, reporting in 1540 on Coronado's penetration of the southwest, says that the territory grows what he calls melons. In 1584, Jacques Cartier reports from the St. Lawrence region that he has found there "*gros melons*," a phrase translated into English not as "big melons" but as "pompions." Hence the root of our word "pumpkins."

WINTER SQUASH *Cucurbita pepo, C. maxima,* and *C. moschata*

ABOVE *Ginger and squash soup and zucchini molds (see page 138) served with squash sauce*

The English translation of Estienne and Liébault's *Maison Rustique* includes the following advice: "To make pompions keep long, and not spoiled or rotted, you must sprinkle them with the juice of a houseleek..." (Houseleek or common stonecrop used to grow on walls and was thought to have considerable medicinal powers.)

Pumpkins can grow to a considerable size. Pumpkins weighing two hundredweight—224 pounds—were a common sight in London markets of the nineteenth century. No wonder they seemed like a possible starting point for Cinderella's coach. Beginning in the seventeenth century the flesh was used, mashed and puréed, to bulk out bread.

The squash's greatest quality is its color—that fiery russet, Van Gogh orange, or rich yellow sets the table aflame. The fact that its flesh melts easily into a velvet-smooth purée makes it highly suitable for soups and sauces. Its largeness also invites use as a container, hot or iced, for casseroles or salads. Try the Iced Squash Salad (see page 136), a great luncheon dish for an Indian summer day.

THE SQUASH FAMILY *Cucurbitaceae*

NUTRITION

Squash is fairly rich in vitamin A, folic acid, and potassium, with small amounts of the B vitamins, fiber, and iron.

CHOOSING AND STORING

Make sure a squash is firm, with no bruising. They come in all sizes and weights, so buy only what you need. Often a market stall or supermarket will have pre-sliced squash or will be ready to cut off the portion you need. As a general rule, the more intense in color the flesh, the more vitamins and taste it has. Also, with squashes such as pumpkin, the larger it is, the less flavor the flesh will have. So go for small squashes with a tough rind and bright flesh. Cut squash wrapped in plastic wrap will keep in the refrigerator for a week to ten days.

COOKING

Squash can be used in many ways. Cubes of flesh can be fried in oil and garlic and served with fried pine nuts and chopped fresh cilantro. Cubes can also be put in a pan with a little butter and oil and left over a low heat to steam in their own juice; they will cook in about 15 minutes. The squash can then be seasoned and puréed to use as a sauce or the basis for soup. Cubed squash can also be the beginning of a risotto, a Lombardy dish.

If you want to cook a whole pumpkin using the shell as a casserole dish (a popular recipe to serve for a Halloween party), it is best to start the day before. This gives time for all the flavors to amalgamate; the actual cooking inside the pumpkin (see recipe) can be done on the night. You will need a squash weighing about 10 pounds for this, but (as Jane Grigson points out) do measure the inside of your oven to see what size of pumpkin will fit.

Chunks of squash can also be roasted in a pan around meat or a bird. This is particularly good with game, in the fall. Cut large chunks 4 inches square, remove the peel, and simply let them brown in the fat, turning them over as you would any other roasting vegetable.

Pumpkin seeds can be hulled, dried and eaten, as they were at the table of Montezuma.

GINGER AND SQUASH SOUP

3 tablespoons grated fresh gingerroot
1 tablespoon olive oil
2 tablespoons butter
1½ pounds peeled squash, cubed (about 6 cups)
3 – 5 cups vegetable stock

This is simplicity itself. Throw the ginger into a large pan with the oil and butter, sauté for a few seconds, then add the squash. Place a close-fitting lid on the pan and leave over a low heat to cook for 15 minutes.

Leave to cool and then purée in a blender, adding enough of the stock to make the consistency of soup that you like. You will achieve a richer flavor by adding more butter, but the flavor of squash is so excellent that it needs, in my opinion, very little.

SQUASH SAUCE

Omit the ginger (if you wish) and cook as above. Leave out the stock completely, to make a thick, rich sauce; or thin down with a little stock for a runnier consistency. Wonderful to use as a pool for first courses, as an alternative to tomato coulis.

BAKED PUMPKIN CASSEROLE

¾ cup dried flageolet or other small beans, soaked for
1 hour in boiling water and drained
½ cup dried navy beans, prepared as above and drained
3 tablespoons olive oil
¼ pound fresh porcini (cèpes)
⅓ pound Portobello mushrooms
½ teaspoon asafetida (optional)
1 teaspoon turmeric
2 large onions, sliced
2 fresh hot green chilies, sliced
2 green bell peppers, cored, seeded, and sliced
1 pound tomatoes, peeled and chopped
2 pounds sweet potatoes, peeled and diced
3½ cups vegetable stock
4 ears of corn, cooked and kernels cut from the cob
3 tablespoons tomato paste
sea salt and freshly ground black pepper

WINTER SQUASH *Cucurbita pepo,* C. maxima, *and* C. moschata

Pick a large pumpkin that will fit in your oven. Cut the top off, complete with its stem, about 3 inches down, and reserve it to serve as a lid. With a knife and a spoon take out all the seeds and cottony fibers and discard. Then, very carefully, scoop out some of the flesh from the inside, leaving a layer of flesh about 1 inch thick adhering to the wall. This will be cooked and so will soften and disintegrate into the stew, but you need the outside walls to be strong enough not to collapse, so be cautious. It is best to cut away too little than too much, so go carefully to begin with; if you puncture the outside wall you will have to call it a day and start all over again with a new pumpkin.

Preheat the oven to 375°F.

With its lid back on, put the pumpkin into the oven and bake for 20–30 minutes. It will need another 10 minutes cooking with the stew inside it. This can be done immediately if you wish; otherwise, when you come to reheat the pumpkin, it will need another 15 minutes in the oven.

Cook the beans in separate saucepans; the flageolets should need only 20–30 minutes, while the navy beans could take up to 1 hour. Boil them without salt, then drain and reserve.

Heat the olive oil in a large saucepan and throw in the porcini, Portobello mushrooms, and spices, then the onions, chilies, and bell peppers. Sauté all this for 2–3 minutes, then add the tomatoes, the scooped-out pumpkin flesh, sweet potatoes, and 2½ cups stock. Simmer for about 20 minutes.

Add the cooked flageolet and navy beans, corn kernels, tomato paste, and seasoning. If the stew is too thick, add the remaining stock, but remember that the baked pumpkin shell will contain some liquid, so it is best to reserve the remaining stock until after the stew has been reheated in the pumpkin.

Spoon the stew into the pumpkin and reheat in the oven for 10–15 minutes. The pumpkin may only accommodate about half the stew—it depends on the size. Reheat the remaining stew in an ovenproof dish. Serve with good crusty bread.

Jane Grigson advises that if you have a large casserole dish into which the pumpkin can be settled, it is prudent to use this as a kind of support for the base and lower walls of the pumpkin shell.

ICED PUMPKIN SALAD

This uses the same technique of cooking the whole pumpkin described left. After baking it, let it cool, then pour off any liquid (discard it or drink it). The pumpkin flesh you have scooped out should be cubed and fried in olive oil, with a little garlic, until it is just golden brown. Reserve and cool.

Then lightly steam a collection of baby vegetables, such as small carrots, zucchini, and leeks, for about 3 minutes. They need to have plenty of crunch. Chop some parsley, chives, and basil. Mix with the baby vegetables, and add some baby mushrooms and tomatoes and a chopped yellow or red bell pepper, all raw. Make a thick *aïoli* mayonnaise and mix it with the vegetables and the cooked pumpkin. Pile into the baked pumpkin shell so that it just overflows, and decorate with any herb garnish you have, placing the lid on gently before serving.

Dorothy Hartley, in *Food in England,* gives a version of this salad, but uses a vegetable marrow (see below) instead of a pumpkin.

ZUCCHINI and SUMMER SQUASH

Cucurbita pepo

The thin-skinned squashes—zucchini, crookneck or summer squash, and pattypan—with their edible skins, soft seeds, and tender, mild flesh, are widely available in American markets. Less familiar is the vegetable marrow—really an oversize zucchini—which is cultivated in Britain. The vegetable marrow endures much disparagement from food writers in the U.K.—probably because most encounter it too late in the day, when its skin has become tough and its flesh watery and insipid, and when prepared in a way that has not done it justice. In its prime (after maturing from the zucchini stage but before going downhill into old age), the marrow is perfectly capable of playing a role in the theater of gourmet cuisine—a supporting role, perhaps—and of playing it beautifully.

Native to the Americas, with the rest of its family, the vegetable marrow was introduced to Britain in the nineteenth century. What made it popular as a cottage-garden vegetable was its ability to grow quickly and to fruit large within a very short growing season, before the early frosts. The nineteenth century, unlike the current one, romanticized the vegetable marrow, thinking it came from Persia. E. S. Dallas, in Kettner's *Book of the Table,* waxes eloquently: "Whoever brought them made a noble gift to his country. Of all the gourds in Europe the latest known, it is in England the most cultivated. It is, indeed, more prized in England than in any other European country, and can be obtained so cheaply that it is in great favor with the poor as well as with the rich. It is a watery vegetable without much nutriment, but it has a fine mellow flavor; and at the end of dinner, when we want something light to play with, its juicy slices make a delicious entremet."

Dallas even gives a recipe for vegetable marrow— a Soup for the Shah—which in appearance was "to represent the emeralds and topazes which the Persians love." This recipe was astonishingly contrived with fried crusts, green peas, and asparagus points.

A British *Encyclopaedia of Gardening* (1902) gives excellent advice on what it calls "a cottager's vegetable": "Usually the fruits are eaten whilst young and tender; if the skin is too hard to allow the entry of the thumbnail it is considered too old. Ripe Marrows make an excellent preserve."

This is almost the last fair word the marrow gets. Mind you, the Victorians' liking was for marrow to be boiled and stuffed, but mostly boiled and for long periods. The vegetable hardly looks or tastes its best with this treatment, which merely aggravates its wateriness. Nevertheless, does it really deserve to be called "this dreary vegetable," with "its slimy, pappy taste" (by T. A. Layton in *Choose Your Vegetables*) or "the Bunter of the kitchen garden" by Jane Grigson? I think not.

The golden rule, as all agree, is to follow the thumbnail rule and to pick a marrow when it is young, no longer than a foot. Once it grows larger, swelling up into a striped green balloon, it is best picked for the compost heap.

The juvenile vegetable marrows—known in the U.S. as zucchini—earn none of the opprobrium which their elders suffer. The names for this squash tell the story: "Zucchini" means a miniature *zucca,* Italian for gourd, and "courgette," the British name for this vegetable, is a diminutive of the French *courge,* meaning squash or gourd. Very small zucchini, no bigger than a finger (and particularly their flowers), are now part of high cuisine and deservedly so, though perhaps their appearance (rather than their flavor) is the main part of their attraction.

NUTRITION

One excellent quality the whole family possesses is that all members are low-calorie and a reasonable source of vitamins A and C; otherwise, they contain carbohydrate, calcium, and potassium.

VARIETIES

Standard zucchini varieties include Cocozelle, Seneca Gourmet, and Dark Green. Gold Rush has yellow skin but is zucchini-flavored and zucchini-shaped. Ronde de Nice is zucchini-colored and -flavored but baseball-shaped. Pattypan squash comes in yellow, pale green, and white varieties—all bruise easily and must be picked very young for good flavor. Old-fashioned Yellow Crookneck is still the tastiest yellow summer squash. The blocky, pale green, Middle-Eastern varieties, such as Ghada and Zahra, are becoming more and more popular.

CHOOSING AND STORING

Look for zucchini and summer squash with no yellow or brown patches. Whether the skin is green or yellow, pale or dark, the color should be vibrant. Smaller squash will be younger and therefore will have thinner, more tender skins.

In ethnic markets, particularly Latin American, you will sometimes see the blossoms or flowers on sale. These are delicate and easily droop and fade. If you grow zucchini or summer squash, the flowers can be picked and cooked within the hour. Pick the male flowers, borne on thin stems, and leave the female flowers on the plant so that their swollen stems can develop into more zucchini.

ZUCCHINI and SUMMER SQUASH *Cucurbita pepo*

COOKING

Zucchini and summer squash can be peeled or left unpeeled, then cut into cubes and fried in olive oil with garlic and fresh gingerroot. Or cut them into disks, dip in batter, and deep-fry. They are best, I believe—like yams, gourds, and sweet potatoes—when used in Indian and Asian recipes, for then their sweetness and delicacy of flavor can be offset by harsh or even aggressive spicing.

The smaller the zucchini, the less cooking it needs. The really tiny ones, no bigger than your thumb, merely need to be blanched or turned in butter, or both, before serving. Slightly larger zucchini can be sliced lengthwise, then fried quickly in olive oil or butter—a minute is quite long enough. Zucchini 6 inches long need first to be trimmed, then perhaps sliced into eighths lengthwise for stir-frying, or cut across into disks for frying.

Larger zucchini and summer squash can be poached or steamed. They can also be grated and stir-fried for a moment. The last method is very satisfactory, because they remain almost raw, yet lose about a third of their bulk in liquid that evaporates.

Grated zucchini can be salted and left in a colander to drain for an hour. Squeeze them dry, add chopped mint and chives, and then press them into ramekins and refrigerate for a couple of hours. Serve these ZUCCHINI MOLDS as a first course, turned out on individual plates with a few red salad leaves and sitting in a pool of either tomato coulis or SQUASH SAUCE (see page 135).

Zucchini are highly favored in Italy. Anna del Conte mentions them blanched and covered with a creamy béchamel topped with Parmesan; sautéed in butter and oil and flavored with oregano; or finished with tomato and basil. Zucchini are also stuffed: a recipe from Mantua uses onion, eggs, and ricotta and Parmesan cheeses, bound with some crumbled amaretti cookies.

Stuffed zucchini flowers have become a rather trendy dish; indeed, they look wonderful on the plate, but tend to taste so delicate they may not seem worth the trouble. Geraldene Holt, in *The Gourmet Garden*, quotes a 1912 recipe by Mrs. Yates' cook, Charlotte, for the surplus male flowers. The cook filled each flower with a mixture of cooked rice, ground chicken, and garden herbs, tied the petals with thread, and braised them in a light broth.

VEGETABLE MARROW STUFFED WITH BLACK BEANS AND RICE

⅔ cup dried black beans, soaked for an hour
3 tablespoons chopped fresh gingerroot
1 dried hot red chili, broken up
½ teaspoon asafetida (optional)
⅓ cup patna or other long-grain rice
sea salt and freshly ground black pepper
1 medium vegetable marrow or 4 medium zucchini
for the green herb sauce:
generous handfuls each of minced parsley, chives, basil,
tarragon, chervil, or dill
1 teaspoon red wine vinegar
1 tablespoon Dijon mustard
½ cup green olive oil
sea salt
a little sugar

Cook the drained black beans with the ginger and chili in boiling water for about 40 minutes, until almost done. Drain and mix with the asafetida, uncooked rice, and some seasoning.

Trim the stem off the vegetable marrow, cut a canoe shape in the top so that it forms a lid, then scoop out all the pith and seeds, leaving a lining of flesh. (Hollow-out zucchini and pre-bake, cut side down, about 5 minutes—to remove some of the water—before stuffing.)

Fill the marrow with the stuffing and replace the lid. Cover with foil and place in a baking pan, making sure the marrow lid is on top.

Bake in an oven preheated to 400°F for 45 minutes (about 25 minutes for zucchini), then let cool down a little, say 5–10 minutes, before unwrapping the foil. Slice across, serving two slices for each person (serve zucchini whole). Serve with a green herb sauce made by mixing the ingredients together.

RIGHT Vegetable marrow stuffed
with black beans and rice

SUMMER SQUASH WITH GREEN PEAS AND BEANS

1½ pounds summer squash
½ pound fresh green peas, shelled
½ pound fresh green beans, trimmed
2 tablespoons sunflower oil
3 onions, chopped
¾ cup dried shredded coconut
½ teaspoon cumin seeds
½ teaspoon asafetida (optional)
1 teaspoon hot chili powder
½ teaspoon turmeric
½ teaspoon sea salt
some cilantro leaves, chopped

Dice the squash into ½-inch cubes. Bring a little salted water to a boil and plunge in the squash, peas, and beans. Bring back to a boil, and simmer for 3 minutes. Drain the vegetables well.

Heat the oil in a large pan and throw in the onions, followed by all the flavorings and the salt. Cook briskly for a moment, then add the vegetables, stirring thoroughly so that all are coated with the spices. Cover and simmer for 12–15 minutes.

Serve sprinkled with some chopped cilantro.

STUFFED ZUCCHINI FLOWERS

4 small zucchini with flower attached
a small can of light beer
¼ cup flour
1 teaspoon salt
a dash of Tabasco sauce
oil for deep-frying
for the stuffing:
⅔ cup cooked saffron rice
6 tablespoons mixed minced parsley, chives, and dill
2 tablespoons fromage blanc
sea salt and freshly ground black pepper

Mix all the ingredients for the stuffing together and gently fill each flower, tucking the petals underneath to enclose the filling.

Make a batter by mixing enough of the beer into the flour to produce a smooth, runny batter. Season with salt, pepper, and Tabasco.

Heat some oil for deep-frying. Dip each zucchini into the batter and deep-fry for 3 minutes, until golden brown all over. Turn from time to time. Drain on paper towels. Serve with a tomato coulis.

SPAGHETTI SQUASH

Cucurbita pepo

Also known as vegetable spaghetti, this particular vegetable appeared in our gardens only in the 1960s. It gained a high profile by the publicity it received from an enthusiast on either side of the Atlantic. In London, *The Times* diarist Michael Leapman had a small allotment and would relate the vagaries of vegetable-growing in his column. The golden globe of a spaghetti squash, with its interior of strands that are a little sweet and fresh to the palate, was one of Leapman's triumphs, and many readers wrote in to speak of their love for the vegetable. Similarly, in Los Angeles, the vegetable was made popular by Frieda Caplan, of Frieda's Finest Produce Specialties, who distributed fruits and vegetables and was adventurous in extolling the virtues of rare ones. The efforts of these two innovators has not been in vain: the spaghetti squash is today a common sight in the supermarket, and many gardeners grow it with enthusiasm.

There is, after all, no other vegetable quite like it. Once the strands have been disgorged from the shell and are tossed in a sauce, few people would know that they are not spaghetti until they tasted a forkful.

NUTRITION

It is very low in calories, but it is an excellent source of folic acid, is high in fiber, and has small amounts of vitamin A, niacin, and potassium.

CHOOSING AND STORING

You can eat spaghetti squash fresh, but it will keep throughout the winter. If keeping for several weeks, hang it in a net bag from a hook, so that no part of the exterior touches a surface. However, spaghetti squash is at its best eaten sometime in the few weeks after it has been picked. Choose them about 8 – 10 inches long, weighing about 2 – 2½ pounds.

COOKING

Stick a skewer into the ends to pierce the skin, and either boil the spaghetti squash whole or bake in an oven for about 30 minutes. You can also slice the vegetable in half and steam it with the open surface face down. Once tender, get rid of the seeds and comb the strands out of the shell with a fork onto a serving dish. Pour a sauce over and toss thoroughly.

To experience the delicate and quietly invigorating flavor, try merely adding butter and freshly ground black pepper with a little chopped raw garlic. The Sicilian method for spaghetti with *ailio crudo* serves the garlic on a little separate dish so that you can add the amount desired. Served with a well-flavored vinaigrette or a tomato or pesto sauce, it makes a very good autumnal first course, refreshing the palate without filling the stomach.

The squash can be cooked whole, then cut in half (if left unsliced it will go on cooking) and left to cool for a few hours, or until the next day. Then its strands can be turned into a salad, as follows.

AUTUMN SALAD

1 red bell pepper, cored, seeded, and cut into strips
1 red onion, sliced thinly
1 marmande or other large tomato, sliced in chunks
a large handful of basil, chopped coarsely
1 tablespoon capers
2½ pounds spaghetti squash, cooked and cooled
for the vinaigrette:
3 tablespoons olive oil
juice of ½ lemon
1 teaspoon Dijon mustard
a pinch each of sea salt and freshly ground black pepper

Put the vegetables, basil, capers, and spaghetti squash into a large bowl and mix thoroughly. Mix the vinaigrette ingredients together just before serving, pour the vinaigrette over the salad, and toss.

CHAYOTE

Sechium edule

Also known as christophene, mirliton, and a host of other names, this is a native of Central America and the West Indies. The fruit is pear-shaped or roundish and deeply furrowed, and has a single large seed. The color varies from yellow to pale and dark green. It grows on a perennial vine, with heart-shaped, angled, or lobed leaves; as well as the fruits, the young shoots, leaves, and large, fleshy roots are all cooked and eaten in various Mexican and West Indian dishes: the root can weigh anything up to 20 pounds and tastes quite like sweet yam.

Buy chayote small and pale, so that you can eat the skin. They are bland in flavor but very juicy, thus highly refreshing; the seeds can be eaten, too. They keep well, stored in the cool and dark. The skin on darker ones can be peeled with a potato peeler, but if you are cooking them leave it on.

If using them raw they are good in any of the cucumber recipes (especially the ones with spices and peanuts) or simply sliced, blanched, and served with a mustardy sweet vinaigrette. If cooking, use in combinations with tomatoes, bell peppers, onions, and chilies, simmered with olive oil and garlic.

The older chayotes can be stuffed like bell peppers with mixtures of spicy vegetables and rice, then baked in the oven. Or they can be halved, each side scooped out and chopped with garlic, tomato, and anchovy, then filled with the mixture and baked with a little Parmesan cheese sprinkled over the top.

In Mexico, they are used in dessert dishes, in tarts, pies, and cakes. *Chayote rellenos* consists of chayote shells stuffed with spiced dried fruit.

OTHER SQUASH VARIETIES

WINTER SQUASHES

• Acorn: pointed and dark green in color, with orange flesh and a mild flavor.
• Buttercup: flattened Turban, dark green and gray. Sweet, dense orange flesh.
• Butternut: very sweet, dark yellow-orange flesh;

usually cylindrical with a bulb at the end; good for long storage.
• Sweet Dumpling: small and round, with green and cream stripes; the flesh is pale yellow, and sweetish in flavor.

SUMMER SQUASHES
• Crookneck: yellow, bulbous to oval with a swan neck; the flesh is pale cream with a mild flavor.
• Pattypan: yellow or green, round, flattened, and fluted with white flesh, very mild.

CUCUMBER

Cucumis sativus

Cucumber has a marvelously refreshing effect in hot climates. I remember my landlord giving me lunch at his farm when I lived on the island of Lesbos. The huge Greek meal of several courses finished with three or four large cucumbers, peeled and sliced lengthwise, to be eaten like celery sticks.

It is thought that the wild cucumber still grows in the foothills of the Himalayas, and its origins lie in Asia. Certainly, some of the best recipes derive from Indian and Asian cuisine, but cucumber was a favorite food of the Romans. The Emperor Tiberius doted on cucumbers and had them at his table every day of the year. They were grown on trays that could be wheeled into the sun. Cucumbers were often served cooked. Apicius boils them in pieces with taro in a sauce for roast crane and duck; they are also stewed with cumin, honey, celery seed, liquamen (see right), oil, and brains, then bound with egg, sprinkled with pepper, and served.

Cucumbers loom large in Roman cooking, but were valued particularly for their invigorating and refreshing aspect when raw. Apicius advises serving peeled cucumbers simply dressed with liquamen, an idea that is still common in Indonesia, China, and the Philippines.

The refreshing qualities of cucumber also appealed to the peoples of northern Europe. Charlemagne ordered cucumbers to be planted in the estates of his realm. We know them to have been common in England in the reign of Edward III, though they were lost soon after, when their cultivation was neglected during the long Wars of the Roses. They were reintroduced at the end of the sixteenth century, when Elinor Fettiplace gives a recipe for pickling both cucumbers and gherkins. At the same time they were less popular in France; the *Maison Rustique* asserts that cucumber juice corrupts the veins, and that they are better kept as meat for mules. The English writer John Evelyn (1620–1706), on the other hand, finds them cool and moist, and serves them in slices with oil mingled with lemon and orange. He also goes on to recommend a broth made from them, and tells us that young cucumbers can be boiled with white wine.

A recipe by Sarah Harrison, in *The Housekeeper's Pocket Book* (1739), stews sliced cucumbers, flours them, fries them, and then serves them, with a glass of claret poured over, under roast mutton or lamb. One cannot help thinking that cooking has progressed into simpler methods, for why boil first before flouring and frying? However, cooked cucumber can be unexpectedly good, teaming up well, as one might expect, with many fish dishes.

LIQUAMEN

Liquamen, the most popular condiment of Ancient Rome, was made by a sophisticated process from small fish, including anchovies, that were salted and rotted. The intense, salty, fishy essence that resulted was used much like soy sauce is today, sprinkled on all manner of savory dishes. We have its equivalent today in the Indonesian fish sauce called *nam pla* and various different names in the different countries that make it. The protein, minerals, and vitamins it contains turn the rice it flavors into a nourishing and sustaining meal.

NUTRITION
If you remove the peel from cucumbers they will lose all their Vitamin A. They are 95 percent water, but have some vitamin C, folic acid, and fiber. They are also high in potassium and sulfur.

CUCUMBER *Cucumis sativus*

ABOVE *Cucumber and peanut salad*

VARIETIES

The main distinction is one of shape, since the flavor of all cucumbers is much the same. There are short, dark green "ridge" varieties (said to be named after the ridged beds where they were grown); these have slightly pimply skins, and are known as Kirby or pickling cucumbers. Long, smooth-skinned, rather fat kinds for slicing are known as "slicers." The third kind are the long, skinny cucumbers variously known as "burpless," "English," or "Japanese," and said to be more digestible.

Gardeners distinguish between "outdoor" and "greenhouse" varieties, chosen according to the way in which they are grown. For both outdoor and indoor cultivation, there is the option of all-female plants which are virtually seedless.

GHERKINS

Cucumis anguria

A cousin to the cucumber, the true gherkin is native to the West Indies and parts of South and Central America. It was noted in Brazil in 1648, and was used in soups and pickles in the Caribbean. Until the nineteenth century gherkins were not cultivated, but were gathered from the wild.

Gherkins are synonymous with pickles, but the distinction between true gherkins and the small, immature ridge or Kirby cucumbers also used for pickling is somewhat blurred: the dill pickles that originated in Eastern Europe are often made from larger, softer "pickling cucumbers" of the *Cucumis sativus* species.

Gherkins and small cucumbers for pickling are not always easy to find on the market. Seedsmen offer a range of gherkins, and they are as easy to cultivate as the rest of the family. A plant or two will give you masses of fruits over one summer, enough for jars of pickles and plenty to eat raw. Gherkins have comparatively thick skins, and if you decide to eat them raw instead of pickling them, harvest them when small, no bigger than your little finger. The flavor is sensational if eaten straight after picking.

If you are bored with pickling gherkins, cook them whole, tossed in a little butter or olive oil with garlic. They need only a few minutes in the pan. Like boiled cucumbers, gherkins are absolutely delicious with fish; or add them hot to a first-course salad so that the leaves will wilt.

CHOOSING AND PREPARING

Buy cucumbers when they are very fresh—firm and bright green. If the cucumbers are waxed, they will have to be peeled (farmstand and greenmarket cucumbers are generally not waxed).

I like to eat cucumbers in their season—summer. I never buy those shrink-wrapped ones that taste of nothing. A cucumber picked straight from the garden has a real and distinctive flavor. Fresh cucumbers will keep happily in the salad drawer of a refrigerator for a week. But why keep fresh food at all? It should be eaten on the day you buy it or the day after.

If you want sliced cucumber for a salad or sandwiches, the big question is whether to salt the slices beforehand. I like to extract some of the water, so tend to slice the cucumber with its peel on, sprinkle a little salt over the pieces, and leave them in a colander for an hour. Then rinse the salt off under running water and dry the pieces before using in a salad.

Cucumber needs very little dressing and is best when simply prepared. The ideal dressing would be a few drops of sesame oil, a pinch of sugar, and a few turns of the pepper mill with a squeeze of lemon. If you want a designer effect on the salad (and don't mind losing a quarter of the vitamin A), run the prongs of a fork down the outside of the cucumber before slicing it, to give an attractive striped effect. At one of the first dinner parties I ever gave, when I was in my twenties, a guest looked at the cucumber and commented, "I see it died of a thousand cuts." Unusual then maybe, but not so much now.

However, quite the best cucumber salad dishes are those from Asia. All of these make marvelous lunch dishes with a few other salads, cooling, refreshing, and stimulating. Here are two cucumber and peanut salads, an excellent combination and a favorite one in the East. The first recipe comes from Julie Sahni and has become one of my staple summer dishes. The second, from Thailand, is inspired by Vatcharin Bhumichitr.

CUCUMBER AND PEANUT SALAD

for 2

1 large English cucumber
2 tablespoons roasted peanuts
1 tablespoon minced cilantro
1 tablespoon minced mint
1 teaspoon sugar
juice of ½ lemon
1 tablespoon sunflower or peanut oil
1 teaspoon mustard seeds
1 teaspoon cumin seeds
½ teaspoon asafetida
½ teaspoon turmeric
2 dried hot chilies, broken up
½ teaspoon sea salt

Cut the cucumber in half lengthwise and remove the seeds with a teaspoon unless they are very inconspicuous. Shred the flesh with the largest holes of the grater into a colander and squeeze out some of the moisture, or all that you can manage to get out.

Grind the peanuts (these can be salted or not, according to personal taste) into a powder. Place the shredded cucumber in a bowl and add the peanuts, herbs, sugar, and lemon juice.

Heat the oil in a pan, throw in all the rest of the ingredients, and heat until the seeds splatter (put a lid over the pan when this happens). Cook for a few seconds longer; the whole process should take no longer than a minute and a half.

Pour the contents of the pan over the cucumber and serve immediately. This is important: if the salad is left, the cucumber will exude liquid, which will ruin the appearance and flavor of the dish.

CUCUMBER *Cucumis sativus*

THAI CUCUMBER
AND PEANUT SALAD

3 tablespoons roasted peanuts
1 large English cucumber, shredded as above
1 garlic clove, minced
1 each small hot red and green chili, finely sliced
juice of 1 lemon
3 tablespoons light soy sauce
1 large tomato, peeled and sliced

Grind 2 tablespoons of the peanuts into a powder, reserving the rest for garnish. Squeeze the shredded cucumber before placing it in a bowl. Add the rest of the ingredients and toss thoroughly until well mixed. Serve at once, garnished with the reserved peanuts.

SIMPLE BOILED CUCUMBER

2 large English cucumbers
2 tablespoons butter
1¼ cups milk (soy is excellent)
1¼ cups water
sea salt and freshly ground black pepper
2 – 3 tablespoons minced parsley

Trim the cucumbers and slice in half, extract the seeds and slice the flesh in 2-inch chunks.

Melt the butter in the pan, throw in the cucumber pieces, and sauté for a moment or two. Add the milk, water, and seasoning, bring to a boil, and let simmer for 10 – 15 minutes. Drain, but keep the liquid for boiling new potatoes or add a little of it to a purée of potatoes instead of milk or cream.

Sprinkle the minced parsley over the cucumber and serve. Or, you can thicken the liquid that the cucumber has cooked in with a *beurre manié*, add the parsley, and serve the cucumber with this sauce. This simple side dish is good with fish and shellfish.

RIGHT A selection of winter and summer squashes, including acorn, chayote, and butternut, and gourds

THE SQUASH FAMILY *Cucurbitaceae*

146

GOURDS

These are the Old World cousins of the squashes. They originated in Africa, India, and farther east, but are now grown all over tropical and subtropical climes. The most famous is watermelon (*Citrillus lanatus*), a native of tropical Africa, and possibly also of India. Its red- to coral-colored or yellow flesh is wonderfully sweet and juicy; the oily and nutritious black seeds are consumed in some places (seedless varieties are also available). Other gourds can be divided into bitter and mild categories. The bitter ones are useful in cooking, especially in Indian and Chinese dishes, giving that hint of dissonance that stimulates the palate. This bitterness is due to quinine.

CHINESE BITTER MELON

Momordica charantia

This bitter gourd has many names, among them African cucumber and balsam pear; in India, it is known as karela. Its close relative, balsam apple (*M. muricata*), is slightly different. The plant is a vigorous vine that can climb up to 12 feet. The fruits have warty skins, "knobbly as a prehistoric crocodile," one writer imaginatively expressed it; they change color as they ripen, from silvery-white to pale and ever darker green. Fully mature they turn a brilliant orange-red. They are hugely important in both Indian and Chinese cuisine.

They are picked unripe for their bitterness. Joy Larkcom says there is a "hint of okra and eggplant" in the flavor (which I have never detected); she further claims that the bitterness "appears to bring out the flavor of other ingredients during cooking and is, in turn, neutralized by them." This is certainly so.

In China, the gourds are used in soup and stir-fries. They are picked while still pale green; they are cut in half, the pulp is removed, and the flesh is sliced and boiled for three minutes to remove bitterness before the final cooking. In India, they are picked at a later stage. Sometimes they are sliced and salted for an hour to allow some of the bitter juices to run out; they are also often stuffed with a spiced mixture.

NUTRITION

These gourds are high in dietary fiber and have a small amount of protein and carbohydrate. They are very high in potassium, and have small amounts of calcium and magnesium and a very little iron and zinc. When ripe they are very high in carotene and have fair amounts of vitamin C and folic acid.

KARELA CHAPATTI

1 pound bitter melon
2 tablespoons mustard oil
5 garlic cloves, chopped small
1 teaspoon hot chili powder
½ teaspoon ground cumin
½ teaspoon ground coriander
1 teaspoon amchoor (dried mango powder)
1½ teaspoons sea salt
1 teaspoon sugar
2½ tablespoons rice flour
2 tablespoons plain yogurt

Slice the bitter melon, with skin and seeds, and boil in salted water for 5 minutes. Drain. Heat half of the oil in a small frying pan and fry the garlic, chili powder, ground cumin, ground coriander, and amchoor for a minute. Add to the drained bitter melon, then mix in the salt, sugar, flour, and yogurt. Let stand for 30 minutes. Heat the rest of the oil in a pan, spread the mixture in it, and brown the underside, then place under a hot broiler to cook the top. When brown and done all through, leave to cool a little, then slice like a cake. Serve with rice and/or nan bread and other curries.

SMOOTH and ANGLED LUFFAS

Luffa cylindrica and *L. acutangula*

The luffas are also known as sponge gourds; both the smooth luffa (*Luffa cylindrica*) and the ribbed gourd (*L. acutangula*) are better known in the West as back scrubbers, and people often express surprise that they are eaten as vegetables. The plant is a spreading climber, which in its wild state grows rampant over shrubs and up trees; it is thought that it was taken into cultivation only a few hundred years ago. It is very likely that the dried skeleton still hanging on the plant suggested a host of domestic uses. The smooth luffa grows to about a foot long and is the sort more often used for back scrubbing, because it is easier to extract its fibrous skeleton. The angled luffa is the prettier vegetable: it is ridged and can grow up to 3 feet or more in length.

Luffas are eaten only when they are young; when mature they become very bitter. In China and Japan, the young fruits are dried and used in winter. If you grow them (from seed), use luffas as you would zucchini or cucumbers; they can be eaten unpeeled. You can cook them very simply, by slicing and frying in butter and oil for just three minutes. Or add them to a ratatouille-like mixture of bell peppers, tomatoes, and garlic, cooked in olive oil. You can also stuff and bake luffas (see *Indonesian Food and Cookery* by Sri Owen for some recipe ideas).

BOTTLE GOURD

Lagenaria siceraria

This gourd, also called cucuzzi, was a treasured plant in the Ancient World because if allowed to mature it develops a hard, woody shell—this is still used to make bottles, spoons, bowls, and musical instruments. The shape can be controlled while the plant is growing by binding the immature gourd in the way desired. Its use has been traced back to Mexican caves of 7000 BC and Egypt in 3500 BC.

Only the young gourds are eaten; when mature they become bitter, purgative, and poisonous. They come in various shades of pale green, yellow, and cream. They are called *lokhi* in India and *doodhi* in Africa. Cook in the same ways as luffas, above.

NUTRITION

The bottle gourds have only half the potassium of the bitter gourds, very little carotene, and much less vitamin C. Nutritionally, in fact, they are poorer cousins of the bitter gourds.

BOTTLE GOURD *Lagenaria siceraria*

Leguminosae or *Fabaceae*

THE

BEAN

FAMILY

FAVA BEAN *Vicia faba*

PEA *Pisum sativum*

HARICOT BEANS *Phaseolus vulgaris* and *P. coccineus*

LIMA BEAN *Phaseolus lunatus*

CHICK PEA or GARBANZO BEAN *Cicer arietinum*

LENTIL *Lens culinaris*

SOYBEAN *Glycine max*

ADZUKI BEAN *Phaseolus angularis*

MUNG BEAN *Phaseolus aureus*

ALFALFA *Medicago sativa*

It was the Romans who gave the name "legumen" to all edible seeds that form in pods. The great merit of these seeds to past generations was that they could be dried and stored through the winter, to be made into purées and porridges or ground into flour, but they also have great food value when consumed fresh.

As food plants, the bean family comes a close second to the grasses. It covers the immense range of beans, peas, and lentils, as well as clovers, vetches, and alfalfa. A side-benefit of growing leguminous crops lies in the residues of nitrates they leave in the soil, which benefit other crops grown in rotation. By planting varieties of this family every three years, gardeners and farmers can help avoid the chemical trap.

Many of the plants not only furnish food for humans and animals, but also provide edible oils, fibers, and raw materials for industry. Soybeans and peanuts yield oils. Tamarind and carob provide intense flavors. Gum arabic and gum tragacanth are used extensively in food production. Ornamental members of the family include acacia, mimosa, and wisteria.

FAVA BEAN

Vicia faba

The fava bean or broad bean is one of the oldest food plants and was one of the first to be domesticated. When picked in the wild state some thirty or forty thousand years ago in Central Asia, the seeds were no bigger than the little fingernail.

Legends and myths surround the bean, showing how complex and equivocal reactions of fear, respect, and admiration were engendered by this simple pod. The bean was both loved and despised in Ancient Egypt. Rameses III offered to the Nile god 11,998 jars of shelled beans, and, with barley, they were a constant item exported from Upper to Lower Egypt. But they were also a taboo food for some Egyptian priests, who believed that as the stems of the beans were hollow they were used by the souls of the departed as a passageway to the life after death. Pythagoras studied for at least twelve years with these priests, and brought such beliefs back with him to his school at Croton on the toe of Italy. From thence, the belief that the fava bean is associated with rebirth and new life filtered into our consciousness. In antiquity beans were often offered in sacrifice in the belief that they allowed communication with the invisible world. They also became an offering in marriage ceremonies to insure the birth of a male child.

However, aside from these mystical views of its sacred aspects, the fava bean quickly became a staple food for the masses throughout the whole of prehistory, paramount in the early civilizations, and almost up to the present. It has only been superseded in the last two hundred years by the potato.

The Romans made cakes of meal from dried beans if there was a poor grain harvest; indeed, flour can be made from all legumes for cooking. The prophet Ezekiel was commanded to mix a purée of beans with the grains from which he made his bread. God obviously knew how to eke out the food supply. The word "pulse" is from the Latin *puls*, meaning a porridge made from bean meal. Martial expresses the general love of beans in the lines, "If pale beans bubble for you in a red earthenware pot you can oft decline the dinners of sumptuous hosts" (*Epigrams*, Book XIII). The fava bean has much going for it, since it is both highly nutritious and hardy.

Unlike string beans and lima beans, favas grow best in cool weather. In mild-winter areas they may be sown in autumn for picking in mid-June, and from January to April for a succession of crops. The Goodman of Paris in 1393 advises, "do you plant them towards Christmas and in January and February and at the beginning of March; and plant them thus at divers times, so that if some be taken by the frost others be not." If the bean overwinters in the soil, some protection is needed against mice, which burrow down and eat this store of food.

Beans have also been grown since the Stone Age as a crop for livestock. Allowed to grow large and dry before being harvested, they are thus named the "horse bean." I recall as a young man eating almost my first *fasoulia* in Greece; noticing how huge the beans were, I asked what variety they could be. The "horse bean," I was told solemnly (by an elderly Hellenist) and was assured it was a quite different kind from *Vicia faba*—the fava bean. I am not sure I believed him, because the bean, though white and large, was the same shape and flavor as the fava bean. But he was right. The horse, sword, or Jack bean (*Canavalia ensiformis*) is still grown but mostly as a green manure or fodder crop. It is the other Old World bean, but always confused with *Vicia faba*. I wish I could get my hands on it and start growing it in my own garden. It made the best *fasoulia* I have ever tasted.

Ever since the Middle Ages the bean played its sacred role as the integral prize in the Twelfth Night cake, a custom that was common all over Europe.

The cakes were made with flour, eggs, raisins, and honey, flavored with ginger and pepper. Baked in the ashes, the round, flat cakes were made as large as the household required. One portion was set aside for God, another for the Holy Virgin, and three other portions for the Magi. These were all given to the poor. The rest of the cake was divided among the members of the household, and whoever had the bean in their portion became king for the day.

A custom also grew up to place a dried pea in the cake; whoever found that became queen for the day. Thomas Randolph (Ambassador to Elizabeth I) tells us that Lady Fleming was Queen of the Bean during the royal festivities in 1563. One imagines that the Virgin Queen herself did not take all that kindly to these customs, but perhaps she smiled upon them—if it was just for the day.

Castelvetro, writing a few years later, recommends eating young fava beans raw at the end of a meal, with a salty cheese from Crete or Sardinia, and always with pepper. They are still eaten raw in Greece, but as a *mezze*; the pods are flung on the table and you break them open yourself while downing the ouzo. Castelvetro also speaks of the merits of fava bean flour for cleaning impurities in the skin.

Fava beans were classless. They were one of the staple foods of the poor, able to withstand long, slow cooking and then drying, an excellent food supply for the winter. But the wealthy also enjoyed them, making rich and unctuous sauces—such as a velvety veal and chicken stock enriched with five egg yolks—to pour over the beans. Another favorite method of serving beans was to team them with bacon or ham.

FUL MEDAMES

Ful Medames is the brown fava bean that gives its name to the Egyptian dish in which it is the main ingredient. The word is thought to derive from *mudammas*, meaning buried. A dish was cooked by being buried in hot ashes and left overnight. *Ful* is simply the Arabic word for fava beans. Claudia Roden writes that it is "pre-Ottoman and pre-Islamic, claimed by the Copts and probably as old as the Pharaohs." It is eaten all over Egypt, both in the fields and in town, in Arab bread and garnished with tahina salad. See Roden's *A Book of Middle Eastern Food* for recipes, and note that you can also buy them in cans.

NUTRITION

Beans are a highly nutritious food, notably high in protein and a good source of the minerals calcium and iron, vitamin A, and vitamins B1 (thiamine) and B2 (riboflavin).

CHOOSING AND STORING

The fresh fava bean season is fairly short—just the summer months—so if you can, buy the pods small; the taste of the young fava bean is delicate and very fine. If the pods themselves are small enough, no longer than 4 inches, you can cook them whole. Even the tender leaves are edible: cook like spinach. Gardeners who pinch out the tops of the plants to deter aphids and stimulate bean development might try this tasty alternative to composting the leaves.

Try to cook fava beans as soon as they are picked, because the pods will grow limp within two days and the sugars in the beans turn to carbohydrate, changing the flavor and texture. If you have a garden, however small, I would recommend growing your own. Freshness is everything.

Having said that, the fava bean is the vegetable that suffers the least harm when frozen, provided the freezing is done when the crop is freshly gathered. Though still nowhere near having as much flavor as fresh, frozen beans can be used in all the recipes here. As a passionate consumer of food in season, I would never eat frozen beans outside the summer—which takes the point away from freezing them at all.

VARIETIES

Seedsmen's catalogues in Britain distinguish between green and white, round, and kidney-shaped beans, as well as those with longer and shorter pods. U.S. gardeners usually have fewer choices, but as far as possible they should choose the varieties that suit their climate—in some areas, for example, autumn sowing is a possibility; there is little difference in the final flavor whatever the chosen variety.

FAVA BEAN *Vicia faba*

The oldest variety, and still a favorite, is Green Windsor (and its variants Giant Windsor and Windsor Long Pod), cultivated first in Windsor, England, by Dutch gardeners. (Up to the end of the last century there still existed a garden near Eton called the Dutchman's garden.) Sutton Dwarf only grows up to 18 inches tall and therefore needs no staking. Both of these have shortish pods. Other varieties, which have long pods, are:

AQUADULCE is the favorite bean for autumn sowing.

LONG POD is tasty, but very sensitive to heat; for cool areas only.

FUL (or FOUL or FOOL) are sometimes sold as "green manure," but are very difficult to find.

EXPRESS is an early, fast-maturing bean which is also a heavy cropper.

PREPARING AND COOKING

If you are fortunate enough to be in possession of young beans, cook them whole. Simply trim the ends, rinse, and cook in boiling water for 4–5 minutes. The pods are unexpectedly filling, so you will find a pound in weight will happily satisfy six to eight people as a side dish. Another way with the young pods is to make a soup. Simply cook the pods, without the beans, in water or a light vegetable stock for 4 minutes, purée, and then push the thin purée through a sieve to eliminate the fibers. This soup will, of course, be richer and thicker if you include the beans as well as the pods. Finish the soup with a pat of butter or a swirl of sour cream.

When the beans become larger and more mature, the question is whether you have to peel the outer skin on the bean itself? Dorothy Hartley, in her *Food in England*, puts it precisely, quoting country people: "When the placenta (i.e. the little hook that fastens the bean to its pod) comes loose easily and leaves a white scar, the bean is still young enough for ordinary cooking, but when the scar becomes black, then the country people call them 'blackspotted beans' and reckon them indigestible food, though good enough for a hungry plough-boy—and indeed, some old country folks do not 'reckon you get the full flavor of a broad bean till the black spot is come and the grey skin is pretty tough'."

Most of the fava beans sold in the markets need no peeling, except at the end of the season. This seems a fiddly job to some, but the flavor of the bean is so special that it is worth it. The job is done with less hassle if the beans are boiled 2 minutes, left to cool, then peeled, rather than attempting to peel the new bean. The peeled beans are then finished by whichever particular cooking method is chosen.

Another way to remove the outer skins is to cook them unpeeled, then mash the beans and push through a strainer. This is an age-old method of making the bean meal or flour for bean cakes, breads, and croquettes. Andrew Boorde (1490–1549), the physician and traveler who was also Bishop of Chichester, comments "beene butter is use moche in Lent in dyvers countries—it is good for plowmen to put in their paunches." Hartley adds that this was "dried winter beans boiled to a mush in mutton broth and used as a thick spread upon coarse oatcake." A rather more refined version is to mix the ground beans with butter, yogurt, or sour cream, then flavor the mixture with garlic, parsley, or savory, and use it as a spread. You can also add a beaten egg and fry small cakes of the mixture as appetizers.

A Sardinian recipe—*faiscedda*—cooks the bean purée (flavored with nutmeg and cinnamon, thickened a little with bread crumbs, and held together with several eggs) in a pan as one large cake. It is fried on both sides and, when cooked through, sliced in wedges for serving.

The classic French flavoring for fava beans is the herb savory. If you use it, be circumspect because the herb can easily overpower the bean—not, one would think, an easy thing to do. I prefer to serve fava beans with parsley sauce. Nothing is simpler or more mundane, but the fusion of flavors is enormously satisfying. Be sure that the white sauce is rich in butter and very low in flour and that the parsley is chopped very small, so that it flecks the sauce like green threads.

RIGHT Fava bean, lentil, and red-currant salad (overleaf) with green beans in green peppercorn sauce
(see page 168)

FAVA BEAN, LENTIL, AND RED-CURRANT SALAD

for 10

This recipe makes a wonderful summer salad as part of a luncheon or party dish.

3 pounds young fava beans
1¼ cups brown lentils
a bunch of chives or scallions
a bunch of basil, chopped
1 garlic clove, minced
⅓ cup olive oil
1 tablespoon red wine vinegar
1 teaspoon Dijon mustard
a pinch each of sea salt and freshly ground black pepper
1 pint red currants

Shell the beans and cook them in boiling salted water for 4 minutes. Drain and reserve.

Boil the lentils in a large pot of boiling water for 10–12 minutes. Drain and reserve.

Put the beans and lentils into a large serving bowl while they are still warm, and stir well to mix. Chop the chives or scallions finely, and add to the bowl along with the chopped basil.

Make a vinaigrette by mixing the minced garlic, oil, vinegar, and mustard with salt and pepper to taste. Pour over the salad and toss well.

Lastly, take the stems from the red currants and mix those in too, carefully leaving a few to show, jewel-like, on the top.

BEAN TARTLETS WITH OEUFS MOLLETS

1 pound fava beans
a bunch of parsley, minced
a bunch of chives, minced
sea salt and freshly ground black pepper
4 baked tartlet pastry shells
4 eggs
1 tablespoon green peppercorns
in brine
⅔ cup sour cream

Shell the beans and boil them for 4 minutes.

Blend, using a little of the cooking water to make a smooth, thick purée. Stir in the minced parsley and chives and seasoning. Divide the bean purée among the tartlet shells.

Boil the eggs for 4 minutes. Immediately plunge into cold water and leave to cool. Tap each egg gently with the back of a spoon until the shell is finely cracked, then peel under running water. Dry the eggs (which should be thoroughly *mollet* or soft-boiled) and place one on top of each tartlet.

Finally, mix the drained green peppercorns with the sour cream, and spoon a generous amount of this mixture over each egg. Serve as a first course, with a little red lettuce garnish.

FAVA BEANS AND ZUCCHINI IN WHITE WINE

1½ pounds fava beans
4–5 zucchini
2 tablespoons butter
1 tablespoon oil
1 onion, thinly sliced
¾ cup dry white wine
salt and freshly ground black pepper
2–3 tablespoons chopped parsley

Shell the fava beans, and trim and slice the zucchini diagonally.

Melt the butter in a pan and add the oil. Throw in the onion, then add the beans and zucchini. Sauté for a moment or two, turning the pieces in the fat.

Add the wine and seasoning. Place a lid on the pan and let simmer for 5 minutes.

Pour into a serving dish and sprinkle with the chopped parsley. Serve immediately.

PEA

Pisum sativum

The pea was yet another vegetable that was domesticated very early in prehistory—possibly in India, for the name is Sanscrit. The original species would have been *Pisum arvense*, thought to be the original pea from which all others stem. We still grow and eat *P. arvense*, but know it in the kitchen as the split pea (it is also referred to as the field pea). Both this and *Pisum sativum* were eaten in Ancient Egypt—seed has been discovered in the tombs at Thebes.

However, though peas are mentioned several times by Roman writers like Columella and Pliny, they do not seem to have exerted much attraction for them. They are lumped in with the rest of the legumes, and one feels that peas must also have been used for porridge. As early as the fifth century BC, Greek plays mention "pease porridge, beautiful and brown." So it was certainly *Pisum arvense* that was grown extensively and became a staple part of the diet for the common people, cooked for long hours in soups and stews, dried in winter, and used to make pease pudding.

The green pea or garden pea that excites us took a much longer time to provoke a writer. A Frenchman at the court of Louis XIV in 1695 complains, "It is frightful to see persons sensual enough to purchase green peas at the price of 50 crowns per litron." The French court at this time was besotted by green peas. Madame de Maintenon wrote in a letter dated May 10, 1696, "this subject of peas continues to absorb all others. The anxiety to eat them, the pleasure of having eaten them, and the desire to eat them again, are the three great matters that have been discussed by our princes for four days past. Some ladies, even after having supped at the Royal table and well supped too, returning to their own homes, at the risk of suffering from indigestion, will again eat peas before going to bed. It is both a fashion and a madness."

More than a hundred years or so later the madness had not yet faded. Exorbitant prices were paid for the first green peas of the season. Brillat-Savarin notes that the first plate of green peas cost about 800 francs—equivalent to about $50 at today's rates.

Nor were peas valued for their simplicity—they appear to have been cooked in quite a complex manner. Boiled first for 20 minutes, they were then drained, mixed with butter and flour plus some pepper, salt, and sugar, and finally they were simmered for five more minutes. Then the dish was finished with cream and several egg yolks.

The *Cuisinier Gascon* (Amsterdam, 1740), on the other hand, gives a recipe for a *Macedoine à la Paysanne* that sounds very contemporary, except for the amount of butter. It consists of peas, fava beans and green beans (both diced to the size of a pea), and carrot slices, all cooked together in butter. The gourmet Grimod de la Reynière called peas "the gayest song of the month of May."

All this enthusiasm for the pea stimulated new types and hybrids (Thomas Jefferson grew thirty different varieties in his garden at Monticello), many of which were lost a hundred years later.

SNOW PEA

These peas produce thin, flat pods that are ready as soon as they reach full size. The whole pod is eaten before the seeds swell—hence the French name *mange-tout* or "eat-all." Also known as Chinese pea or Chinese pea pod, this type is associated with Chinese and Japanese cooking, but originated in the Mediterranean region. Gerard mentions the sugar pea in 1597, and it was known in France sixty years before the advent of the green pea that so delighted Louis XIV. Some years later a writer complains that it has disappeared, but it periodically reappears in the records and is today firmly established in supermarket displays and seedsmen's lists.

SUGARSNAP PEA

Similar to the snow pea (and possibly as old, though its modern popularity dates only to the introduction of the "sugarsnap" variety in the late 1970s), this edible-podded pea is eaten *after* the peas are swollen, when the pod looks rather like a short, slightly curved, flat green bean. The pods of the sugarsnap pea are deliciously sweet and crisp.

PETIT POIS or BABY PEA

Petits pois are the fruit of dwarf varieties specially bred to produce tiny but highly sweet peas. Rather than buy them canned or frozen, which is how they are marketed nowadays, you can grow them in your own garden. Boil in the pods, and then shell.

ASPARAGUS PEA
Lotus tetragonolobus

This is actually a type of vetch rather than a pea proper. The fruits are small ridged wings, which have to be gathered when they are tiny—no bigger than 1 inch—otherwise they are fibrous and inedible. Even when small they are not much liked, and for once I agree with the critics. The flavor is sweet and distinctly pea-like, but they have to be picked at exactly the right moment.

VARIETIES

Apart from the asparagus pea, and the cow pea or field pea family *Vigna unguiculata* subsp. *unguiculata* (black-eyed peas, crowder peas), the different types are all varieties of *Pisum sativum*, bred for slightly different characteristics: snow peas, intended for picking before the seeds swell; sugarsnap peas picked *after* swelling; petits pois, where the mature peas remain tiny; and a range of conventional types. Here gardeners can choose between a wealth of round and wrinkled or marrowfat varieties according to when they want to sow and harvest their crops, selecting ones with a dwarf or taller-growing habit to suit their space. Snow pea varieties include Dwarf Gray Sugar and Oregon Sugar Pod and the taller Sugar Snap. For petits pois, grow Waverex or Prescoville.

NUTRITION

Green peas and their pods are high in protein, carbohydrates, and vitamins B and E as well as calcium, phosphorus, and potassium.

RIGHT Runner and French beans

THE BEAN FAMILY *Leguminosae* or *Fabaceae*

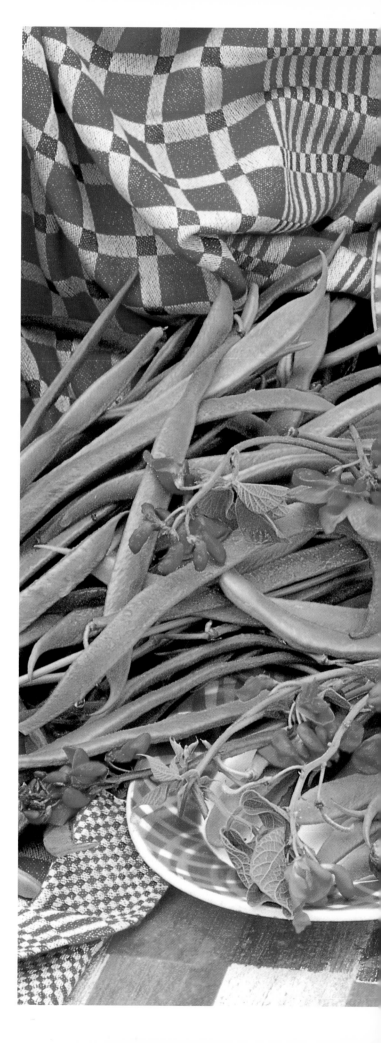

ABOVE *Fresh green pea soup*

CHOOSING

Fresh garden peas have a very limited season, alas, so make the most of them. It is tragic that every year one hears of children who, on seeing the fresh pods in the market, inquire what on earth they are, so convinced have they been that the green pea comes frozen in packages.

Look for pods that are a clear fresh green, not dull, and that have a bouncy shape, never drooping. Cook them on the day that you buy them. When the fresh green color has turned drab, the peas are older. They are still perfectly edible and delicious, but the sugar has turned to carbohydrate and they will have that slightly mealy consistency of the legume.

If you want to make your own dried peas, leave them on the plant until the pods become husk-like, then pick and shell the peas, spreading them out to dry on trays left in a cool, dark place.

COOKING

If possible, shell garden peas immediately before cooking. Shelling is a fulfilling task that most people enjoy, so share it among friends. Fresh peas need to be simmered in boiling water with a little salt and sugar for about 2 – 3 minutes. Drain and add a pat of butter. Some cooks like to add a few pods to the water plus a sprig of mint. It is a matter of taste: if you find these improve the flavor, use them.

Snow and sugarsnap peas are cooked very simply, either by steaming for 3 minutes, boiling for 1, or stir-frying for 2. They can also be eaten raw and are extraordinarily sweet and refreshing. You can also make an excellent soup out of them, which is best eaten iced. You would need a pound in weight to make enough for 2 – 3 people. Just trim the ends and cook in water or stock for 3 – 4 minutes, then cool and purée. Press through a strainer in case there are

---

THE BEAN FAMILY *Leguminosae* or *Fabaceae*

fibers, season, then add 1¼ cups buttermilk or thin sour cream, and refrigerate for 2 hours.

One of the classic methods of preparing peas, used by both Soyer and Dumas, is to cook them on a bed of lettuce, so they are steamed. Classic recipes also add white wine and copious amounts of butter and cream. It is a good method (see below) but, on the whole, peas need little added to them; they are magnificent in themselves.

FRESH GREEN PEA SOUP

For 6

2 pounds green peas in their pods
1½ quarts vegetable stock
a sprig of mint
½ teaspoon sea salt
½ teaspoon sugar
1¼ cups buttermilk or light cream
mint leaves for garnish

Shell the peas and cook the pods in half the stock for 5 minutes. Leave to cool, then purée and press through a strainer. Reserve the liquid.

Cook the peas in the rest of the stock, with the mint, salt and sugar, for 3 minutes. Leave to cool, then discard the sprig of mint, and purée. Combine this mixture with the pod liquid.

Taste for seasoning, then mix in the buttermilk or light cream. Refrigerate if serving the soup iced, and then decorate with the mint leaves. If serving the soup hot, reheat without boiling.

POIS ST. GERMAIN

2 heads of romaine lettuce
2–3 tiny carrots, sliced
1 onion, sliced
2–3 scallions with their green, chopped
2 glasses of dry white wine
2 pounds green peas, shelled
a pinch of sea salt
a pinch of sugar
2 tablespoons butter
chopped parsley for garnish

In a large saucepan, arrange the whole lettuce leaves so that they entirely cover the bottom, then add the carrots, onions, wine, and, finally, the peas. Add the salt, sugar, and butter. Place the saucepan over a low heat, fit a lid firmly on the top, and forget about it for 20 minutes, when all should be cooked and tender.

Pour into soup plates, garnish with parsley, and enjoy for lunch with good crusty bread. Quite my favorite way of cooking peas.

Note: An excellent purée of peas can be made by omitting the carrot and blending the above, adding 2 tablespoons of thick cream and plenty of freshly ground pepper at the last moment.

SOUFFLÉ DE POIS VERTS

2 pounds green peas, shelled
1¼ cups vegetable stock
4 tablespoons butter
3½ tablespoons flour
sea salt and freshly ground black pepper
1¼ cups milk
2 tablespoons grated Gruyère cheese
2 tablespoons grated Parmesan cheese
4 eggs, separated
1 tablespoon heavy cream

Preheat the oven to 425°F, and butter the bottom and side of a large soufflé dish.

Cook the peas in the stock; after 2 minutes take out half of them with a slotted spoon and reserve. Continue to cook the rest of the peas for 3 minutes longer, then season and purée. Reserve this purée to serve with the soufflé as the sauce.

Melt the butter in a pan, add the flour, and make a roux. Season, then add the milk and cheeses to make a thick, smooth sauce.

Remove from the heat and beat in the 4 egg yolks, then add the whole green peas.

Beat the egg whites until they are stiff, and fold them into the mixture. Pour the mixture into the soufflé dish. Bake in the center of the oven for 20 minutes, until golden brown and risen.

Serve at once with the pea sauce, reheated and enriched with the cream at the last moment.

PEA *Pisum sativum*

HARICOT BEANS

Phaseolus vulgaris and *P. coccineus*

This is a huge genus, packed with familiar names, but basically all are the same bean. Whether we call it kidney, French, or runner, whether it is oval, flat, or round, whether pink, purple, green, or black, whether the pods are smooth, short, straight, or curved, whether the whole pods are eaten fresh or the beans alone eaten dried, the haricot bean has proved to be astonishing in its variety.

Columbus was possibly the first European to have encountered the bean in Cuba, but it was rediscovered in the next few decades in Florida, in South America, and as far north as the mouth of the St. Lawrence river. This shows us how ancient its use as

food was (the bean has been discovered in Peru dating from 8000 BC and in North America from 5000 BC), for the bean had time to adapt itself to contrasting climates and habitats. The first settlers were hugely impressed by this food; "their ordinairie food is of pulse, whereof they have great store, differing in color and taste from ours," says John Verrazano in a letter written in 1524. In 1605, Champlain observed that when the Indians planted corn they put in each mound three or four Brazilian beans of different colors: the beans used the growing corn for support. Captain John Smith, in 1614, noticed that the Indians kept bags of beans stored away in a pit.

The European herbalists named them all kidney beans, believing they strengthened the kidneys. They based such a conclusion, of course, on the Doctrine of Signatures, where a kidney-shaped bean must do good to a kidney-shaped organ. The word "haricot" is

BELOW Yellow runner beans, French beans, and peas

THE BEAN FAMILY *Leguminosae* or *Fabaceae*

162

a corruption of the Aztec word *ayecott*. A *haricot de mouton*, a dish of mutton stew with turnips, onions, and potatoes, is now served also with haricot beans as if to fulfill the name. But this "haricot" comes from the French *harigoter*, meaning to cut up small, and one can also have a haricot of beef and game, all cooked and served without beans.

Once the new beans had reached Europe it did not take long before they were grown. They were eaten green to begin with and were most popular in Tuscany. The bean was known in France and England as the Roman bean, while Tuscans became *manga fagioli*, or "bean eaters." Runner beans were grown as decoration, clambering up poles made into arbors around places to picnic or banquet. Though the rich liked to eat them for their flavor, they also frowned upon them as the cause of flatulence, and for this reason, perhaps, horticulturalists did not grow many of the different varieties that were available.

It was not until the late nineteenth century that a vast number of different beans was grown commercially. Early beans were forced in the greenhouse; Cobbett notes that plants would come into flower ten weeks after germination. The types grown for drying did not catch on in Britain, but were grown extensively in France, Spain, and Italy. This has given rise to the idea that such beans need a warmer climate in order to flourish. This is not true as long as they are sown after the last frost. I grow both snap beans and flageolets in my own garden in England very successfully and, as we have seen, some types of haricot grow happily as far north as the area of the Great Lakes in Canada.

NUTRITION

All beans are rich in protein, carbohydrate, minerals, and vitamins. Dried beans have greater nutritional qualities than green beans, but less vitamin C. While all the beans have differing amounts of goodness, they are all rich in lysine, which is the essential amino acid that is lacking in grains.

All the dried beans are also high in the indigestible starches, stachyose and raffinose. These produce the wind in the gut that causes some people to avoid all dried beans completely. These two starches do not pass through the walls of the small intestine to become converted into blood sugar; instead, the intestinal bacteria break them down into carbon dioxide and hydrogen—an explosive mixture.

VARIETIES
GREEN BEANS

No one, to my knowledge, has discovered why the French bean, as its name implies, is popular in France and why the runner bean is never grown there. I believe the runner bean has more flavor, which makes French lack of enthusiasm for it even more puzzling. Because it is a climber, the runner bean is never grown commercially, for it is too difficult to harvest. This might explain its immense popularity in British cottage gardens.

Runner beans are far from hardy: plant them late, well after all risk of frost. They should be eaten young, before the beans inside have grown bigger than a tiny fingernail. They can then be cooked whole—simply trim the ends, as with the French beans. But if left to grow larger, they can be sliced. The British tend to slice them thin, on the diagonal, a habit that does nothing for flavor or appearance. Better, by far, if the bean has reached a size where the pod is fibrous, to leave it to dry out, because the dried beans can be used that season. They take only 10–12 minutes to cook and are full of flavor, apart from being prettily marked and looking attractive on the plate. Serve them with butter and a little chopped onion or shallot, or with Oriental sesame oil, lemon juice, and garlic. Runner beans also go well with a garlicky tomato coulis, with almond butter, or with a cream and green peppercorn sauce (see page 168).

French beans are variously known as snap bean, green bean, and string bean. They are always eaten young, as whole pods with immature seeds. Steam or boil them briefly, or serve them with any of the sauces suggested above for runner beans.

FRENCH BEANS: These have now been bred as compact bushes 12–18 inches high. They come in green, yellow, and purple pods, often stringless. The most popular varieties are Tendergreen, Venture, Jade, Jumbo (a Roma type), and Remus. Two climbing French beans are Blue Lake and Garrafal Oro, but there are

---

HARICOT BEANS *Phaseolus vulgaris* and *P. coccineus*

over forty listed in a seed catalogue against the large number of eighty-four dwarf varieties. Two yellow varieties are Roc dor (or Roc d'Or) and Kinghorn, while two varieties of purple beans are Royalty and Trionfo Violetto, a climber.

RUNNER BEANS *Phaseolus coccineus*: Most of these are climbing beans that will grow 8–10 feet high and need stick or trellis supports. Some favorite varieties are Red Knight, Streamline, Desirée, Butler, Ermergo, and White Dutch Runner.

BEANS FOR DRYING

Many of these beans straddle the divide between the green and dried categories, depending on when you harvest them. In most cases the fresh pods can be eaten whole (at least by the gardeners who grow them), and the shelled mature beans can be eaten fresh or dried. Some of the following varieties appear in seedsmen's catalogues; most can be found on grocers shelves, either canned or dried in packages. In late summer and autumn the season's crop can sometimes be found, semi-dried, in ethnic grocers or specialty food markets.

FLAGEOLET: Called thus because the French decided it resembled a flute, this bean stands supreme in its reputation as the essential gourmet bean. Either pale green or white, it can be bought in French markets, still in its dried pod, around September/October. These beans are so fresh they do not need soaking and will cook within 20–30 minutes. Once they are dried out and have been stored for a year or more, soak for an hour and give them another hour's boiling.

NAVY BEAN: A small white haricot, this has been specially bred for the baked bean industry. It can be used for home cooking, though, on the whole, I would tend to use the larger haricot varieties. Nevertheless, for authentic home-made baked beans, use this one.

RED KIDNEY BEAN: A popular bean for party food, as its color is dramatic. In the Sixties it caused some controversy when foolish people served salads for which the beans had been soaked and not cooked. The imagination boggles that the guests actually ate them. But some did and became ill with a toxin (hemaglutinin) present in the raw bean that can cause gastroenteritis. After soaking, the beans must be boiled vigorously for 10 minutes; this water is thrown away, and then the rest of the cooking begins.

BLACK BEAN or TURTLE BEAN: This is not the bean of Chinese black bean sauce, which resembles the adzuki bean. This black bean is much used in Caribbean cooking and in Mexico, in a soup and a sauce.

BORLOTTI BEAN: The most popular Italian bean, this can be a pale creamy-pink to beige and brown speckled like a bird's egg. Pinto beans are smaller but very similar, and are favored in Spain and the U.S., where they are grown.

BIANCO DE SPAGNA: Another firm Italian favorite, this is a large, white bean with a similar flavor to the borlotti. Canellini is another white bean, which is cooked with the bollito misto. It originated in Argentina, but has now become one of the most familiar beans in Italian cuisine.

COOKING DRIED BEANS

If the bean is picked when just dried from the plant, it needs no soaking and only a mere 15 minutes' cooking by boiling in water with *no* added salt. However, few of us can harvest our beans in this manner; the nearest we get to it is if we can buy white haricot or pale green flageolet beans from markets in September and October (as you can find them in France and Spain). Dried beans bought in farmers' markets through the winter months are that year's crop, and need at the most 30 minutes' cooking.

If buying dried beans in your local supermarket or healthfood store, always soak them. There is no need to soak them overnight. I favor blanching the beans with boiling water and leaving them for an hour, then draining and starting the cooking. Tom Stobart explains: "The objection to soaking is that it starts enzyme changes which would lead to germination; in warm weather, it may also start fermentation by micro-organisms. This is obviated by putting the beans into boiling water, blanching them for 2 minutes—which upsets the enzymes, kills the beans and most of the organisms—and then soaking them for 1 or 2 hours."

On the delicate subject of the indigestibility of beans, much has been written. I used to believe most firmly that changing the soaking water three times

before cooking helped, or that cooking with various anti-flatulent herbs, an old German remedy, would remove the hazard. But nothing really does the trick. If you love beans, as I do, you have to resign yourself to coping with a certain amount of wind.

I believe that knowing why the wind exists helps that necessary resignation to the inevitable. The reason is that some of the sugars in the bean's starch (the oligosaccharides) are left untouched by the enzymes in the digestive system, so they leave the upper intestine unchanged. Once in the lower intestine the bacteria go into action and break down the sugars into various gases. As Harold McGee points out, "the oligosaccharides are especially common in seeds because they are one form in which sugars can be stored for future use." They also tend to accumulate in the seeds' final stages of growth, which is why green beans give no trouble. Both cooking in water and sprouting the seeds will decrease the amount of oligosaccharides.

Beans need to be boiled for anything from 30 to 90 minutes; it all depends on the bean (flageolets need less) and how old they are. But the most common time is around an hour, after which they will be soft enough without collapsing into an unsightly mush. Always add salt at the end of the cooking or the skins will toughen.

For most recipes I would start the soaked beans in a little olive oil, with a sprig each of bay and rosemary and, perhaps, a sliced onion and a clove of garlic. Remember at the end of the cooking to remove the herbs. Beans and olive oil are natural companions, and most bean dishes, whether served hot or cold, will benefit from a little good-quality oil being liberally sprinkled over them.

All types of fresh and dried bean make superior soups. Here are my two favorites, which never fail to please. The second is my recipe to celebrate spring, a particularly rich, vibrant green soup with the strong lemony flavor of sorrel and the slight pepperiness of the watercress as foils to the flageolets. The first recipe is my version of the classic bean soup of Tuscany. Following that are two dried bean classics—baked beans and three-bean salad—plus a simple but delicious fresh green bean preparation.

TUSCAN BEAN SOUP

1 cup large dried haricot beans, soaked
3–4 tablespoons olive oil
1 head of garlic, peeled
2 tablespoons chopped oregano
2 medium potatoes, peeled and diced
11 cups water or vegetable stock
sea salt and freshly ground black pepper
a handful of parsley, minced

Drain the beans. Heat the olive oil in a large saucepan, throw in the whole garlic cloves (reserving two), and sauté for half a minute before adding the beans, the oregano, and potatoes. Continue to cook, stirring, for another half a minute, then add the water or stock, place a lid on the pan, and simmer for an hour, when the beans should be tender.

Season, then ladle half of the soup into a blender and purée. Return this purée to the saucepan. If the soup is too thick and chunky, add more water or stock. At this stage, vegetable stock is best as it will not dilute the flavor.

Chop the two reserved garlic cloves, mix with the minced parsley, and add after reheating the soup, just before serving.

SORREL, FLAGEOLET, AND WATERCRESS SOUP

⅔ cup dried flageolet beans, soaked for 1 hour
2 tablespoons olive oil
1 onion, thinly sliced
7½ cups vegetable stock
4 tablespoons butter
2 or 3 zucchini, thinly sliced
¼ pound sorrel leaves
a bunch of watercress
1¼ cups dry white wine
½ teaspoon sea salt
1¼ cups buttermilk or thin sour cream

Drain the beans. Heat 1 tablespoon of the olive oil in a large pan, throw in the sliced onion and the beans, and let them sweat for a few seconds, then add the vegetable stock. Bring to a boil and simmer for half an hour or until the beans are cooked. Let them cool, then purée half of the beans; return this purée to the pan and reserve.

Meanwhile, heat half the butter and the rest of the olive oil and sauté the zucchini for 10 minutes. Add these to the soup.

With the rest of the butter cook the sorrel leaves (take out the central spine if the leaves are big) for a few minutes until they turn into a dark khaki purée, then stir this into the soup.

Next, chop the washed watercress, including a generous amount of the stem, and place in a blender with ⅔ cup of the dry white wine. Blend this mixture to a smoothish purée. Add to the soup with the rest of the wine. Add the sea salt and taste. Heat gently again and, just before it reaches simmering point, add the buttermilk or sour cream. Stir and serve.

BAKED BEANS

1 cup dried navy beans, soaked
¼ cup olive oil
1 whole onion, sliced
3 garlic cloves, sliced
2 16-ounce cans crushed tomatoes
3 tablespoons dark brown sugar
⅔ cup red wine
2 tablespoons tomato paste
7½ cups water
1 tablespoon dried mustard powder, mixed to a paste
with a little water
sea salt and freshly ground black pepper

Preheat the oven to 325°F.

Drain the beans. Heat the olive oil in a large casserole dish, throw in the onion and garlic, and sauté for half a minute, then add the beans and cook for another minute, stirring all the time. Add the tomatoes, sugar, wine, tomato paste, and water and bring to simmering point. Place a lid on the casserole dish and bake in the oven for 3½–4 hours.

Take the beans from the oven, stir in the mustard paste, and check the seasoning.

THREE-BEAN SALAD

for 6 to 10

for the flageolets:
1 cup dried flageolet beans, soaked
3 tablespoons olive oil
3 garlic cloves, peeled
7½ cups vegetable stock
a handful of parsley
a bunch of watercress
3 tablespoons walnut or hazelnut oil
grated zest and juice of 1 lemon
sea salt and ground black pepper
2 leeks, very finely sliced
for the kidney beans:
1 cup dried red kidney beans, soaked and cooked
¼ cup olive oil
3 red bell peppers, cored, seeded, and sliced
1 hot red chili
3 garlic cloves
for the black beans:
1 cup dried black beans, soaked
3 tablespoons olive oil
¼ cup chopped fresh gingerroot
3 garlic cloves, peeled and sliced
a bunch of scallions, chopped
2 tablespoons sesame oil
grated zest and juice from 1 lemon

For the flageolets: Drain the beans; heat the olive oil in a saucepan, throw in the garlic and the beans, and sauté for half a minute. Add the vegetable stock, bring to a simmer, and cook for 30–45 minutes, or until the beans are tender.

Pour off about 1 cup of the liquid into a blender, and add the parsley, watercress, walnut or hazelnut oil, lemon zest and juice, and seasoning. Blend to a green sauce.

Drain the flageolets (save any liquid for soup) and add the green sauce and the finely sliced raw leeks. Stir and leave to absorb the flavor for 1 hour.

For the kidney beans: Drain the cooked beans and reserve. Heat the olive oil and add the bell peppers, chili, and garlic. Cook over a low heat for 10–15 minutes, then purée everything into a sauce.

HARICOT BEANS *Phaseolus vulgaris* and *P. coccineus*

Add some seasoning to taste, then pour the red pepper sauce over the kidney beans. Leave for at least an hour to allow the beans to absorb the flavors.

For the black beans: Drain the beans; heat the olive oil and throw in the ginger and garlic. Cook for half a minute before adding the beans. Cook for another minute, stirring the mixture, then add 7½ cups of water. Simmer the beans for an hour.

Drain, then add the chopped scallions, sesame oil, lemon zest and juice, and seasoning. Leave for an hour to absorb the flavors.

Serve the three-bean salad in a pattern of circles or triangles on a large, round serving dish. Of course, once the guests start serving themselves the pattern tends to blur, but it looks attractive at the beginning and the flavors contrast beautifully.

RUNNER BEANS IN GREEN PEPPERCORN SAUCE

1 pound small runner beans
(mixture of green and yellow if possible)
⅔ cup crème fraîche, fromage blanc, or sour cream
1 tablespoon green peppercorns in brine
a handful of basil, chopped

Trim ends from the beans; if large, slice them in two and make sure the sides are without fiber. Steam for 5 minutes, or boil for 3. Drain them well.

Meanwhile, mix the cream or fromage blanc with the peppercorns and stir in the chopped basil.

Leave for 10 minutes or so, then serve the beans with the sauce spooned over them, still slightly warm.

LIMA BEAN

Phaseolus lunatus

One of the largest beans we have, this originated in South America but is now grown all over the world. It is sometimes called butter bean. Lima beans prefer a warm climate, so are difficult to grow in cool-summer areas. Early European settlers in the New World confused this bean with another type of haricot, because lima beans come in many colors and patterns. The prettier forms marbled in red and pink are often slightly toxic (hydrocyanic acid), which is why we usually see only the pale green, plump, kidney-shaped beans that are grown commercially. The two varieties are the baby lima and the Fordhook. Lima beans are eaten fresh, straight from the pod like fava beans; they are also sold frozen, canned, and dried.

When dried, lima beans need an hour's soaking and will take up to 45 minutes' simmering until they are tender. They have a very pronounced flavor, quite different from the range of haricot beans, and make excellent dishes. They have one drawback: when cooked, the outside skin often peels away, making them look rather unsightly. One way of avoiding this is to turn the cooked beans into a purée that can be eaten with warm pita or garlic bread rather like hummus, as in the following recipe.

LIMA BEAN PURÉE

1 cup dried large lima beans, soaked
3 garlic cloves, minced
grated zest and juice of 1 lemon
⅓ cup olive oil
a handful of chopped mint
sea salt and freshly ground black pepper

Boil the beans in plenty of water for 45 minutes, or until tender. Place in a blender and add the lemon zest and juice, oil, and seasoning. Blend to a smooth, creamy purée. Stir in the mint and serve.

RIGHT Baked beans (recipe page 166)
and three-bean salad (page 167)

THE BEAN FAMILY *Leguminosae* or *Fabaceae*

CHICK PEA or GARBANZO BEAN

Cicer arietinum

Nicknamed "owl's head" in Egypt, this staple food in the ancient world is known to have been cultivated as early as 7000 BC. Both chick peas and lupin seeds were sold hot in the streets; Horace describes them as part of an "economical diet of onions, pulses, and pancakes." The Latin name, *cicero*, like the fava bean (*fabius*) and the lentil (*lentulus*), was used by several distinguished Roman families, which shows how popular it was. There were then many varieties, differing in size and color. Albertus Magnus, in the thirteenth century, mentions red, white, and black chick peas. You can probably still find many of these in the Middle East, though the type mainly available in the West is hazelnut-sized and golden-beige in color.

The chick pea has now become the chief leguminous crop of India, where it is called the Bengal gram. A pod will contain not more than 2 or 3 seeds. It is cultivated in all the Middle Eastern countries and still is a staple crop of Egypt and the eastern Mediterranean, where it is used in a number of dishes.

We buy chick peas dried in supermarkets, but it is well worth purchasing them in Mexico, Italy, southern France, and Spain, because the new crop needs very little cooking and has a far finer flavor than chick peas dried for a longer period. The alternative name of garbanzo bean has Hispanic origins.

Perhaps the most imaginative and delicious recipes using chick peas originate in India. Julie Sahni, in her *Classic Indian Vegetarian Cooking*, tells us that the most famous dishes come from the Punjab, where the chick peas are cooked, "either by braising them in tangy spicy cumin- and coriander-scented sauces or by boiling them and combining them with fresh herbs and seasonings, making delicious appetizers. In the south they are turned into a snack with an intriguing taste by adding jaggery (raw sugar) and coconut. Chick peas are also ground into a flour called gram or *besan*, which forms the basis of batters for fritters, dumplings and sweetmeats and, of course, spicy breads."

SPINACH AND CHICK PEA SOUP

Many Middle Eastern recipes using chick peas were brought to Spain by the Moors. I have enjoyed this Lenten dish many times in Spain; it is rather more than a soup and makes an excellent lunch.

⅓ cup olive oil
1 head garlic cloves, peeled
1 onion, sliced
1 heaped cup dried chick peas, soaked for an hour
1 pound spinach leaves, chopped
2 large potatoes, sliced
sea salt and freshly ground black pepper

Heat the olive oil in a large saucepan, throw in the garlic, onion, and drained chick peas, and cook in the oil for a few minutes before adding 2 quarts of water. Bring to a boil and simmer for 1 hour.

Add the spinach and potatoes and cook for 30 minutes longer. Season liberally and serve.

CHICK PEAS WITH YOGURT AND PITA

Fattet Hummus

As chick peas are still so redolent of Egyptian cuisine, I have included a slightly simplified version of Claudia Roden's recipe for a famous chick pea dish, favoring the Damascus version, though not completely.

2½ cups plain yogurt
¾ cup dried chick peas, soaked for an hour
⅓ cup olive oil
3 garlic cloves, minced
grated zest and juice of 1 lemon
sea salt and freshly ground black pepper
a large bunch of mint, minced
2 pita breads
3 tablespoons pine nuts, toasted

Pour the yogurt into a strainer so that it can drain. This takes an hour, or you can leave it overnight.

Boil the chick peas for an hour or until tender. Pour half into a blender with a little of their liquid, the oil, garlic, and lemon zest and juice. Blend to a smooth purée. Season, stir in the mint, and reserve.

Cut the pita breads in half and bake in a hot oven until crisp. Leave to cool, then break up into bits and throw into a large bowl. Pour some of the chick pea water over the bread so that it softens, then cover with the drained chick peas. Pour over the purée of chick peas, then cover that with the strained yogurt. Sprinkle the top with the toasted pine nuts and serve.

HUMMUS

¾ cup dried chick peas, soaked
2 garlic cloves, minced
grated zest and juice of 1 lemon
sea salt and freshly ground black pepper
¼–⅔ cup olive oil
a handful of mint, minced, or 3 tablespoons tahini

Boil the chick peas until they break easily on the point of a knife—about an hour, then drain, reserving the cooking liquid. Place the cooked chick peas in a blender with the garlic, lemon zest and juice, seasoning, and oil. Blend, then add enough of the cooking water to make a thick, creamy purée.

If you want fresh-tasting hummus, add the mint; if you would like one with a darker, more aromatic flavor, add the tahini. Or you could add neither: chick peas alone have a wonderful earthy resonance that is very satisfying.

LENTIL

Lens culinaris

Among the first plants to be domesticated, lentils were daily fare in the Ancient World. The crops are still grown in the Near East and the Mediterranean regions, hence the misleading assumption that lentils can only grow in a hot climate. This is not true; lentils can be grown as far north as Britain and in my opinion should be—they need a light, warm soil and warm growing conditions. The plant resembles a vetch, is small (rarely taller than 20 inches) and has short, broad pods. There are many varieties—brown, green, yellow, orange, and red. They are used extensively in Indian cooking, *masoor* being popular with the Muslim community, but in all over 50 varieties are grown there. One Parsee dish called *dhansak* requires a mixture of from three to nine different kinds of lentils for its effect.

Like other common vegetables, lentils have at times been scorned by the upper classes. Aristophanes, in his play *Plutus*, describes a man who has just acquired riches as not liking lentils any more. Apicius includes several recipes for lentils, one being a barley soup enriched with lentils, peas, and chick peas. But a sign of their popularity in ancient Rome is that the obelisk which stands today in front of St. Peter's made the voyage from Egypt buried within 2,880,000 Roman pounds of small, red lentils.

Now, of course, lentils are very much in fashion, despite having been spurned throughout history, beginning with the "mess of pottage" with which Jacob purchased Esau's birthright (this traditionally has always been considered to have been a lentil soup). Indeed, in Lebanon a dish of lentils, rice, and onions, called *migeddrab,* is also known as "Esau's dish of lentils." I must admit that I love all types of lentils, for their earthy flavors. There is no doubt that a meal with lentils as a part of it is one of the most rewarding and satisfying.

NUTRITION

Of all the dried pulses, with the exception of the soybean, lentils contain the most protein—25 percent. They are 54 percent carbohydrate, and contain vitamins A and B, iron, and calcium.

PREPARING AND COOKING

Lentils need no soaking: they can be cooked straight from the package; but do use copious amounts of water because they absorb an astonishing amount. Various types need different cooking times. Choose the kind of lentil for the particular dish, and gauge cooking times accordingly.

All lentils make wonderful soups, especially good when the days start to get colder. The recipes are all very simple; little need be added, just garlic or onion, salt, pepper, and a good quality oil, yet they are immensely satisfying. There is one, though, that has the addition of potatoes and greens (see below). All of these soups can be flavored with spices or left plain so that the earthy taste of the lentil comes through.

VARIETIES

SMALL YELLOW or ORANGE LENTILS: These give you the traditional Indian dhal or a purée for a lentil soup. They will cook down within 10–15 minutes into a mush. If you leave them to cool in what little water is left, they will absorb that, too. If you place the purée in a blender, it will become very smooth and creamy. This purée tastes very fine without any other addition, except salt and perhaps a little butter or oil, but it can also be highly flavored by all manner of Indian spices to make many types of dhal. You can also mix an egg into the dry purée, plus spices and herbs, chopped onion or garlic, and mold into cakes to fry as small patties or balls.

LARGE BROWN or GREEN LENTILS: These are much used in Indian recipes. They need 10 minutes' cooking. At this stage they have a certain resistance and bite to them and they are best used cold as lentil salads with the addition of oil and chopped herbs. If you give them another 5 minutes' cooking, they will have softened a little more and be suitable for all sorts of purposes, as an accompanying vegetable or as part of a main casserole or main dish. The great thing about these lentils is that they can continue to cook for up to an hour; though, by that time, they will be very soft, they will not finally disintegrate and each lentil remains separate.

PUY LENTILS: The French *lentilles vertes du Puy* are considered to be the best and are very much in gourmet fashion. Small, green, and delicate in flavor, they are, indeed, very good. They are also, because of their reputation, rather expensive. In all honesty, I do not think they are so far superior to any other small green lentil that they earn their expense. Nevertheless, it is a matter of personal choice. They will be cooked within 15 minutes and are generally eaten alone, hot or cold, to accentuate their individuality. Garnish them with fried, caramelized onion rings and dress with walnut or hazelnut oil and lemon juice.

POTATO AND LENTIL SOUP

for 6 to 8

1 tablespoon sesame oil
⅔ cup orange lentils
2 tablespoons olive oil
1 onion, chopped
3 garlic cloves, chopped
⅔ cup brown lentils
1 pound potatoes, peeled and chopped (3 cups)
¼ pound spinach, kale, or collard greens,
washed and chopped (about 2–3 cups)
sea salt and freshly ground black pepper

Heat the sesame oil in a pan and throw in the orange lentils. Stir over a heat for a second, then add 3½ cups of water, bring to a boil, and simmer for 10–15 minutes, until they are soft. Cool, then purée.

Meanwhile, in another pan, heat the olive oil, throw in the onion and garlic, and fry for a moment before adding the brown lentils and potatoes. Fry for another second or two, then add 1½ quarts of water. Bring to a boil and simmer for 20 minutes.

Halfway through the cooking time, add the chopped greens, stir them in, and replace the lid on the pan. When the greens are cooked, combine the two lentil mixtures, stir well and season. If the mixture is too thick, add more water or stock.

LENTIL BALLS WITH SPICY SAUCE

1¼ cups brown lentils, cooked for 20 minutes,
then drained and mashed coarsely
2 tablespoons gram flour (ground chick peas), sifted
2 garlic cloves, minced
1 tablespoon garam masala
½ teaspoon sea salt
a little flour
1 beaten egg
3 tablespoons toasted bread crumbs
for the sauce:
1 cup canned tomatoes
1 tablespoon Dijon mustard
1 tablespoon soy sauce
½ teaspoon Tabasco sauce

THE BEAN FAMILY *Leguminosae* or *Fabaceae*

Add the gram flour, garlic, garam masala, and salt to the mashed lentils, then shape the mixture into balls. Refrigerate for an hour.

Roll in flour, egg, and toasted bread crumbs, then deep- or shallow-fry in vegetable or peanut oil, so that the outside is crisp.

To make the sauce: blend the chopped tomatoes to a thin sauce. In a pan, bring this to a boil and reduce it by a third. Add the rest of the ingredients to taste.

PUY LENTILS WITH CREAM

This is an excellent dish whether hot or cold.

2 tablespoons olive oil
2 onions, chopped
1 heaped cup Puy lentils
1¼ cups heavy cream
sea salt and freshly ground black pepper
a generous handful of mint, chopped

Heat the oil in a pan, throw in the chopped onions, and cook for a moment, then add the lentils. Add 1½ quarts water, bring to a boil, and simmer for 20 minutes. Watch that the lentils do not soak up all the water (add more if you need to). Drain thoroughly and return to the pan. Pour in the cream, add seasoning and chopped mint, and serve.

SOYBEAN

Glycine max

It is ironic that a bean which is so high in protein and nutritional richness, which could feed the hungry world ten times over, is such a dull and tasteless creature. Of all the fascinating beans, this is the only one that lacks real character and flavor. There are over a thousand varieties of soy—which is not a bean at all; it belongs to the pea family—and in such a range there ought to be one or two that are delicious. The problem is finding them.

The true worth of the soybean, in my opinion, is in its by-products—soybean curd or tofu, soy sauce (including tamari), soybean paste or miso, soy flour, oil, and milk. The last I find highly refreshing to drink in the summer, sometimes mixed in equal quantities with yogurt, like a *lassi*. The oil is an excellent all-purpose polyunsaturated oil, while the flour can be added to breads, cakes, and pastries for extra food value. The flour has become valuable commercially, appearing in ice-cream and many other food products. Soybeans are also often sprouted (see page 177).

The soybeans stocked in wholefood markets are usually the round beige type, but there is also a small black variety. There is little difference in taste between the two. Both need soaking for around 10 hours in cold water, though if you pour boiling water over the beans, they need little more than an hour. A bean is soaked completely if it will split into two and the insides are flat rather than concave. If soaked for too long, goodness is lost in the water. Drain the soaking water from the beans and use new water for the cooking.

Another irony is that the soybean, unlike other legumes, has a substance called a "trypsin inhibitor," which blocks a trypsin enzyme essential for the digestion of protein. The key is for them to be thoroughly cooked, then the trypsin inhibitor is destroyed. If simmered on top of the stove, soybeans will need around 4 to 5 hours. One of the best methods is to cook them overnight in a crock pot. They can also be pressure-cooked for 25 minutes.

This is the science, but so far we are nowhere near the art. The main problem is that if the bean is left whole while cooking, it refuses with steadfast obstinacy to soak up the flavors around it. Hence, you have the insulated bland bean sitting in a sea of sauce. Breaking up the bean at the end of cooking helps. One whirl in the blender will crush the bean into several bits, or a little hard work with the potato masher will do the trick, too. Yet the bean bits still taste of nothing very much.

When the beans are pulped—blend the beans for a couple of moments until you have thick, grainy purée—they can at last be flavored. The beans can also be pulped after soaking, and the pulp cooked; in this case, the cooking time will be half that for the whole beans.

SOYBEAN *Glycine max*

ABOVE A selection of dried beans, peas, and lentils

The cooked pulp can be mixed with chopped vegetables, and spoonfuls of this mixture can be rolled in bread crumbs, or sesame, poppy, or mustard seeds, and then fried. If the mixture is too liquid, a tablespoon of soy flour will thicken it; or, if it needs binding, add a beaten egg. I would tend to use strong flavorings—shallots, onions, garlic, and herbs. Served with a miso sauce, these soybean croquettes can be far more delicious than they sound.

It is also possible to buy packets of dry-roasted soybeans, salted like peanuts. While the nuts have 27 percent protein, the beans have 20 percent more, so they are a very nutritious snack. Packets come in plain, salted, garlic, or barbecue flavor.

You can roast your own soybeans at home: spread the soaked, drained beans over an oiled baking sheet and place in an oven preheated to 350°F to roast for about 2½ hours, or until they are dark golden and crisp. Shake them twice, at the end of each hour. Toss the roasted soybeans in a flavored salt—celery, garlic, or sesame—or in your own flavoring made out of dried herbs and ground spices.

If the roasted soybeans are left unsalted, you can make *kinako*. Grind the roasted beans, or work them in a blender, until they are a powder. This flour has no gluten so it will not thicken, but it can be used to coat food before frying. It can also be mixed with butter or margarine, miso, or ground peanut or sesame, to make a paste for spreading on toast and crackers. In Japan, they sweeten *kinako* and use it to coat confectionery. It must be about the only example of chewy candies that are good for you.

The recipes that follow are for the whole soybean, an attempt at solving the challenge of the insipid flavor without pulping or crushing. The first recipe is an alternative to roasting the beans.

THE BEAN FAMILY *Leguminosae* or *Fabaceae*

SESAME SOYBEANS

1 cup dried soybeans
sunflower oil for frying
1 tablespoon sesame salt (that is, 1 part of sea salt to
5 parts toasted ground sesame seeds)

Soak the beans, drain them, then lay them out to dry on paper towels.

Heat ½ inch sunflower oil in a deep pan, throw in the beans, and fry them for 10 to 12 minutes. They are done when medium brown and crisp.

Let them drain on paper towels and, when cool, mix with the sesame salt. They will keep for months in an airtight container.

SOYBEAN FRITTERS

1 cup dried soybeans, cooked
1 cup brown rice, cooked
4 small onions, chopped
2 garlic cloves, minced
1 teaspoon each ground rosemary, dill seed,
marjoram, celery salt
a pinch of cayenne pepper or hot chili powder
1 egg
1½ tablespoons soy flour
sunflower oil for frying, plus a few drops of sesame oil

Mix the ingredients together well. Shallow-fry spoonfuls of this mixture in sunflower oil that has been flavored with a few drops of sesame oil. Cook until crisp on both sides, and drain on paper towels.

ADZUKI BEAN

Phaseolus angularis

This is one of the beans used for sprouting, but it can also be soaked and cooked. It is small and red, highly popular and cultivated widely in China and Japan. In the latter country it is boiled, mashed, and sweetened, then used extensively in cakes, candies, and red rice. The beans are even sold powdered.

Nutritionally they are rich, with 25 percent protein, and are a good source of vitamin C and many of the vitamin B complex.

MUNG BEAN

Phaseolus aureus

This is the tiny green bean most commonly used for sprouting. When we buy or eat bean sprouts in the West, we are usually eating the mung bean. The sprout is particularly rich in protein—35 percent—and also has B and C vitamins. B1 (thiamine) goes on doubling each day until day four. In China and India, the bean is soaked as well as sprouted. They do not need soaking and will cook quickly within 20 minutes. Mung beans are eaten in India in many of the *dhal* dishes. I include one here.

MUNG DHAL WITH YOGURT

3 tablespoons sunflower oil
1 teaspoon turmeric
½ teaspoon fenugreek seeds
½ teaspoon cumin seeds
½ teaspoon mustard seeds
½ teaspoon asafetida
2 fresh hot green chilies, chopped
¼ cup mung beans
⅔ cup plain yogurt
1 onion, minced
sea salt and freshly ground black pepper

Heat the sunflower oil in a large pan and throw in all the spices. Cook them until they begin to roast and expel their oils.

Add the asafetida and the green chilies and cook for another second or so, then add the mung beans. Stir thoroughly, then add 1½ quarts of water. Bring to a boil and simmer for about 20 minutes. Leave to cool slightly.

Drain off any excess liquid, though the beans should have soaked up all the liquid. Add the yogurt and onion and season. Serve warm.

MUNG BEAN *Phaseolus aureus*

ALFALFA

Medicago sativa

We are familiar with this member of the pea family only as a seed for sprouting, but I include it as it is a kind of miracle food. Also known as lucerne or buffalo herb, the plant has extraordinarily long roots, which can easily grow to some 40 feet beneath the ground. Sprouted alfalfa seeds have a high protein content (40 percent)—higher than beef or milk. They contain vitamins A, B, and C, with good amounts of D, E, G, K, and U. They also contain B12, calcium, iron, sodium, potassium, sulfur, phosphorus, silicon, aluminum, and magnesium. Deep-rooted plants like this, which can reach into the subsoil, gain minerals not available to shallower-growing plants. Alfalfa could solve developing countries' malnutrition problems, but although alfalfa powder is sent to these countries, it has not gained wide acceptance.

SPROUTING SEEDS

All manner of vegetable and cereal seeds can be sprouted, but members of the bean family are among the stalwarts. Mung bean sprouts, sold as bean sprouts, contain 37 percent protein, plenty of vitamin C, and many of the B complex vitamins. Adzuki beans are equally vitamin-rich, with 25 percent protein. Growing sprouts contain vitamin C (ascorbic acid is always concentrated in rapidly growing tissue). Other vitamins and minerals soon appear. After five or six days' germination, sprouts also contain vitamins from the B complex group, including B12 and vitamins E, G, K, and U.

Sprouts taste excellent and are undeserving of their minor place on our tables, relegated to the fringes of veganism or vegetarianism, or macrobiotic diets. Try experimenting, using sprouts as a major ingredient in sandwiches, where their crunchy texture can be appreciated. Mix with a sharp spread like anchovy, a yeast extract mixed in with slivers of onion, or avocado and arugula. They are delicious

LEFT top: Mung dhal with yogurt;
bottom: Sesame soybeans (both recipes page 175)

eaten just as they are, with a little sea salt, lemon juice, and maybe walnut oil. But they are so refreshing to the palate they really need no dressing at all.

Salads made from sprouts are a gift to dieters. Tasty and with plenty of crunch, they are filling, need minimal dressing, and provide many of the vitamins and trace elements necessary to the metabolism. Or stir-fry, which does not destroy sprouts' nutritional value. Throw them in at the last minute, with perhaps a few zucchini slices, to cook in sesame oil with garlic and ginger. They will only need half a minute's stir-frying, and should still have plenty of crunch.

Bean, alfalfa, radish, and many other sprouts can be bought ready-packaged at healthfood stores and supermarkets. Making your own is, of course, a lot cheaper. Warmth and water are needed to activate the seed's dormancy into growth. It is best to splurge initially on a bean-sprouter, available at healthfood stores. This consists of three perforated trays that drain into a bowl beneath. You sprinkle seeds in the trays and pour cold water through them each day. The idea is to keep the seeds moist. You can improvise a sprouter from a jar with a net covering, but do make sure you drain all the water, so the seeds never lie in a puddle. Seeds will sprout in darkness or light, but dislike direct sunlight and cold: the optimum temperature is 55–70°F. Most take between three and six days. Once the seeds have sprouted, keep them in a covered container in the cool or in the refrigerator for up to a week.

A word of warning. Always buy seeds intended for sprouting: healthfood stores generally have a range. Seeds from other sources intended for planting may have been treated with fungicides or insecticides.
- Alfalfa: High protein and vitamin content. Rinse once daily. Sprouts in about five days.
- Adzuki bean: High protein and vitamin content. Rinse once daily. Sprouts within four days.
- Lentil: Sprouts in about five days.
- Mung bean: Soak in water for 12 hours until the husk splits, then transfer to the sprouter. Sprouts in four days. Before using, rinse off husks in cold water.
- Soybean: Soak before sprouting, as for mung bean. Rinse four or five times daily. Sprouts in three to four days. Needs to be cooked before eating.

THE
POTATO
FAMILY

POTATO *Solanum tuberosum*
TOMATO *Lycopersicon esculentum*
EGGPLANT *Solanum melongena*
SWEET PEPPER *Capsicum annuum* Grossum Group
CHILI or HOT PEPPER *Capsicum annuum* Longum
Group and *C. frutescens*

What an astonishing change occurred in the Old World's diet after key members of this family were introduced from South America. Imagine the food of the twentieth century without the conspicuous bulk of the potato, the ubiquitous flavor of the tomato, or the fiery power of the chili pepper. Yet the change in most cases was far from abrupt.

The group's alternative botanical name is the nightshade family, and unfamiliar members were often treated with justifiable suspicion. Some powerful poisons run in the family's veins. The ancients were familiar with belladonna, henbane, and mandrake; a newcomer arrived on the scene with the discovery of nicotine, from tobacco. Even the everyday food plants such as tomato and potato contain toxic alkaloids in their leaves and stems. (No wonder some of our ancestors chose to grow them for decoration only.)

Today we still grow solanums and nicotianas as garden ornaments along with our petunias and daturas, as well as deriving visual delight from the bright fruits of tomatoes and peppers.

179

POTATO

Solanum tuberosum

The potato has become one of our major staple foods. It is the world's fourth largest crop, and 90 percent of this is grown in Europe. Its rise to this eminent status has, however, been a slow and checkered one, constantly dogged by a poor press and confused by many misunderstandings.

The potato is a native of southern Chile, growing high in the Andes around Lake Titicaca. The earliest sign of its consumption can be dated back to 3000 BC, and it became the Incas' staple food, but it remained a secret from the rest of the world until 1553, when Pedro de Leon wrote about it in the *Chronica del Peru*. The *conquistadores* took the potato back to Spain, but no one there was much interested in it. However, it was found to grow well in the northern province of Galicia, where the climate suited it, and so it began to be used by the Spanish as a food for the poor and the sick, and as army rations.

The introduction of the potato to the English-speaking world has been inextricably linked with Sir Walter Raleigh. It was he, I was always taught, who took the potato from Virginia to England in 1586. But the potato was unknown in the whole of North America and Mexico until the eighteenth century. What the English adventurers brought home was not from Virginia, and nor was Raleigh responsible for its presence on the ship. A large supply of tubers formed part of the provisions taken on board at Cartagena, in Colombia, by Sir Francis Drake as he sailed homeward after harassing the Spaniards in the Caribbean. On his way he called in at Virginia to collect the disgruntled settlers—among them Thomas Hariot, one of Raleigh's men, who is thought to have taken an interest in the unusual foodstuff. Back in England, the new potato is supposed to have been distributed to interested parties, including Raleigh, the herbalist John Gerard, and even the Queen. There are accounts of people mistakenly eating the leaves or fruits and throwing away the edible tubers, thus contributing to the low culinary esteem in which the potato was held. Some people assumed that what Drake brought

back must have been the sweet potato, since this is the kind that could be grown in the Caribbean where he provisioned his ship and the one that seems to have been more widely known. Whatever the precise nature of the tubers Drake imported, the spud must have arrived in England around that time. Both types of potato were evidently current in London by the 1590s. Within a decade of Drake's return, both were being discussed by Gerard in his *Herball*. Unfortunately Gerard fell into—and perpetuated—the error that since Drake's last landfall had been Virginia, that region was the source of the newer kind of potato.

Gerard and his contemporaries were obviously already familiar with the sweet potato, of which he had "planted divers roots (which I bought at the Exchange in London)" but which "perished and rotted" in the winter cold of England. Indeed, the sweet potato was "the common Potato" to which Gerard compared the newer "Virginian Potatoes." Gerard's opinion was a lot kinder than those expressed by many later writers. He described the new arrival as being similar in many ways to the sweet kind, "…equal in goodnesse and wholesomenesse to the same, being either rosted in the embers, or boiled and eaten with oile, vinegar and pepper, or dressed some other way by the hand of a skilfull Cooke."

The potato colonized the world by devious routes. As it originated in South America, you might expect it simply to have traveled northward—and perhaps to have arrived in Virginia for the first settlers to encounter. But, as we have seen, the potato touched Virginia only briefly, in the ship by which the settlers were leaving. As a serious crop it reached North America only in 1720, when Ulstermen settled in New Hampshire, bringing their Irish potatoes with them. There it was quickly renamed the Murphy, and by 1760 was being grown commercially. So how had it gotten to Ireland?

One story goes that potatoes were introduced when they were planted at Raleigh's property at Youghal, near Cork, in 1586. (If the provisions brought back by Drake had indeed consisted only of sweet potatoes, they would have proved short-lived, even in the mild winters of southern Ireland, but we know that by the early seventeenth century the white potato had become a staple food.) A more fanciful story is that potatoes formed part of the stores of the Spanish Armada and turned up in wrecks on the Irish coasts. Being miraculously hardy, the seed potato could easily have survived shipwreck and drowning; as the Spanish fighting forces (with the poor and the sick) were fed on potatoes, there would certainly have been plenty on board. Fanciful conjectures have a habit of turning out to be true, and I would put my money on that explanation. A more prosaic account is that it was introduced through trade with Flanders.

For by the last quarter of the sixteenth century, the potato had arrived in northern Europe. It took root in many places where cereals were difficult to grow, and was cultivated by poorer people to supplement their own diet or to feed to animals. Potatoes grown in Galicia were shipped to Genoa, and were eaten by the poor in northern Italy. From there the potato moved to Switzerland and on to Antwerp, where a specimen was painted for the first time. (Gerard used this illustration in his *Herball*, although the frontispiece portrait depicts him holding the sweet potato.) It was in Switzerland, in 1598, that a woman—God bless her—actually gave a recipe for roasted potatoes. Who, then, would be the first to suggest mashing and puréeing the divine spud with cream and butter?

No one yet: they were all too busy criticizing it. The potato has never been an overnight success. Experts were only too ready to decry it as tasteless while commending it as food for the poor. As early as 1663, the Royal Society recommended growing potatoes as a safeguard against possible famine, but few heeded. John Forster, apparently an ardent fan, published *England's Happiness Increased, or a rare and easie Remedy against all succeeding Dear Years: by a Plantation of the Roots called Potatoes*. But still the potato did not catch on, even among the people worst affected by the "dear years." Disturbed by a succession of cereal crop failures, in 1720 Frederick William I commanded the Prussian peasants to plant potatoes. There was widespread resistance to the new crop; the peasants pulled the plants up again, fearing that eating potatoes gave people leprosy. They were only reassured by seeing Frederick William himself eating potatoes on his palace balcony. (How were they served, one wonders—roasted, sautéed, or mashed? Alas, the observer does not tell us.)

Waverley Root, in his food dictionary, points out that people's reluctance to eat potatoes in the belief that they were harmful or poisonous had some justification. Solanine, which shows up as green patches on the potato (and which we cut out when we find it), is a poison capable of causing an unpleasant stomach upset. Root claims that the solanine in early potatoes—before they had been selectively bred—was of a higher strength and caused skin rashes that frightened people into believing they had leprosy.

Such bad press hampered the potato from becoming a large commercial crop. A botanist in 1719 writes grudgingly, "they are not without their admirers, so I will not pass them by in silence." Another botanist, Philip Miller of the Chelsea Physic Garden in London, writes in 1754: "they are despised by the rich and deemed only proper food for the meaner sort of persons." The French naturalist Raoul Combes writes in 1749, "Here is the worst of all vegetables…," adding with a sneer, "…nevertheless the people, which is the most numerous part of humanity, feed themselves with it." Brillat-Savarin appreciated the potato only as a protection against famine, dismissing it as "eminently tasteless." Diderot shared his opinion: "This root, no matter how you prepare it, is tasteless and floury." Nietzsche concluded that just as a diet composed mainly of rice led to opium, so one of potato must lead to alcohol.

In Scotland, the eating of potatoes was opposed by Presbyterian ministers, who considered them "an ungodly food because they are not mentioned in the Bible." In England, potatoes had become a field crop in the 1780s, but were mostly grown to feed cattle. But by 1832, the English authorities had recognized their nutritional worth and amended the Bread Act to allow potato flour to be used in the dough. In *The London Poor*, Henry Mayhew writes of the street trade in baked potatoes in the 1860s: "many gentlefolks buy them in the street and take them home for supper in their pockets; but the working class are the greatest purchasers. Many boys and girls lay out a half-penny on a baked potato." Mayhew's distinction between different types of potato sounds familiar to modern ears: "potatoes with a rough skin are selected from the others because they are the mealiest. A waxy potato shrivels in the baking."

Perhaps the change of heart in England had been helped by the official popularization of the potato in France during the late eighteenth century. A sponsored contest for "the best study of food substances capable of reducing the calamities of famine" had been won by Antoine Parmentier, a military pharmacist. Though we know Parmentier's name because it has been given to a soup, a hash, and an omelette, all containing potatoes, in his lifetime he was best known as a writer and for introducing a vaccine against smallpox in the army. Parmentier is said to have served a dinner at which all the courses—soup, entrée, entremets, salad, cake, crackers, and bread— were made of potatoes.

The potato was well on the road to its current dietary importance. It was planted wherever the climate suited it, and proved a good crop for land on which it was difficult to cultivate cereals or leafy vegetables. It is a paradox that the crop intended to eliminate hunger was the cause of some of the nineteenth century's worst famines. In the poor soil of Ireland, the potato had flourished when cereals had failed, and provided six times the nourishment. Every small cottage garden contained its plot of potatoes. William Cobbett referred to the potato as "Ireland's lazy root." One of the results, according to Charles Edward Trevelyan, permanent head of the British Treasury at the time of the famine, was that Irish women forgot how to cook. "There is scarcely a woman of the peasant class in the West of Ireland whose culinary art exceeds the boiling of a potato. Bread is scarcely ever seen and the oven is unknown." When blight destroyed the harvest in the 1840s, even the potato disappeared; up to a million Irish died of starvation or the diseases that followed.

The taste for the potato survived the lean years. Advances in understanding the nature of the diseases and improved cultivation techniques gradually assured more reliable potato harvests. Whether plainly boiled to supply bulk, transformed into a culinary masterpiece, or processed into chips and fries, the potato's place in the twentieth century is undisputed. In Europe and North America, most people probably eat potatoes on average once a day.

NUTRITION

Potatoes are 80 percent water and 2 percent protein, but are high in vitamin C and potassium. The nutrients tend to be in the skin and just beneath it. Potatoes also contain iron, phosphorus, calcium, sodium, sulfur, and vitamin B. No wonder they have become a staple food for the poor. The more a potato is stored throughout the winter and the more a potato is processed, the less nutrients it will have. So eat your potatoes as soon as you can after they are dug, and eat them without peeling if possible.

VARIETIES

There are perhaps 1,000 varieties of potato, of which 200 are available to gardeners. If you are a gardener you will take pleasure in growing the potatoes you enjoy but cannot purchase commercially. I love growing the waxy salad varieties: La Ratte, Pink Fir Apple, Charlotte, and Belle de Fontenay. Of these four, the first two have more flavor (but do remember that your soil and its particular combination of minerals is what gives a potato its own idiosyncratic taste). All of these potatoes are small and yellow-fleshed, perfect for summer salads or for boiling. One of the greatest potatoes I have ever discovered for baking is Golden Wonder; simply baked, it has a heavenly flavor. The crop is mainly grown in Scotland and Northern Ireland and goes straight into processing for chips. When I tried to get seed potatoes, to grow them in my own garden, I was told firmly that the flavor I was so enthusiastic about came from northern Celtic soil and could not be reproduced in my part of England. Perhaps. So far I have not had the opportunity to find seed potatoes to test the hypothesis.

Potatoes are divided up commercially into early, midseason, and late (for storage). One of the most famous British early potatoes is Jersey Royal, a small, kidney-shaped tuber that should be washed but not peeled, because the potato is always harvested before the skin has set. In Jersey, they proudly say that the potato cannot grow anywhere else, citing examples of attempts that always failed. The Jersey Royal appeared only a hundred years ago, when a Jersey farmer, Hugh de la Haye, cut a large potato with fifteen eyes and planted each eye. The result was a crop of these tiny potatoes. Their flavor was unique, and the crop was nurtured and valued for its early growth.

I was in Jersey one January when the seed potatoes were being planted. Every scrap of land is carefully utilized, even the smallest strip and often on the steepest slopes. The end product can hardly be bettered for flavor.

At a potato testing at Le Meridien Hotel in London's Piccadilly, attended by many food writers, there was general agreement on the superiority of potatoes that were grown organically. I have long thought that it is in the root vegetables that organic agriculture appears to show a marked improvement in flavor. Those standbys of the British housewife, the King Edward and Desirée, tasted dull and insipid even at Le Meridien; the organically grown potatoes were by far superior, having a full earthiness that was immensely satisfying.

At this event we tasted the rare but beautiful Purple Congo. These blue potatoes stay blue after cooking; the color does not leach out into the water. The Purple Congo spud is actually dark violet and distinctly reminiscent of Elizabeth Taylor's eyes. The other shock about the blue potato is that the flavor is not markedly different from the King Edward. Other blue potatoes are All Blue and Purple Peruvian.

CHOOSING

Markets typically offer only a few varieties of potatoes—Russets, red boilers (Early Rose, Red Norland, and others), and so-called California Whites, which are an "all-purpose" potato (and might be any of several varieties). Specialty stores and wholefood markets offer more choice, and it is helpful for the cook to know which varieties are good for which purposes—for salads, for mashing, for roasting, and for deep-frying or baking.

SALADS: Waxy varieties such as La rouge, LaSoda, Red Norland, Yellow Finn.

BOILING OR STEAMING: All of the above, plus Yukon Gold, Carole, Superior, Kennebec, White Rose.

SAUTÉING: All of the above two categories, as the potato has to be firm to keep the shape.

MASHING INTO A PURÉE: Russet Burbank, Shepody, Katahdin, Green Mountain, Butte, and similarly starchy types. Lindsey Bareham, in her excellent book *In Praise of the Potato,* comments that the *pommes purées* of Jöel Robuchon or Frédy Giradet is *not* the mash we know and love. They use La Ratte, a waxy potato, with cream and olive oil, and although this wonderful, golden, waxy spud gives a flavor resonant with "new potato" taste, the texture can never be as fluffy as a mash made with floury potatoes.

ROASTING: Almost any potato will roast satisfactorily, but the starchy ones, above, give slightly better results. Initial parboiling makes the exterior ragged and this, when roasted, soaks up the fat unevenly and crisps with the sea salt beautifully.

DEEP-FRYING: The starchy varieties suggested above, particularly Shepody.

BAKING: The starchy varieties are best, so use all those potatoes that are good for mashing.

STORING

New potatoes are best dug or bought little and often, as you need them (commercial outlets use the term "new" to mean small, red-skinned white boiling potatoes, regardless of their age). Avoid buying bags of

POTATO *Solanum tuberosum*

prewashed potatoes—they never keep as well. Late potatoes will store happily throughout the winter. If you have a garden, they can often be left in the earth and lifted late—before the first frosts—although there is some danger of re-sprouting if the weather is warm for several days. Store in the dark and the cool. They will slowly lose their nutritional richness and to some extent their flavor, too. Potatoes that begin to sprout in the early spring can still be eaten if they feel firm when gently squeezed. Simply take care to cut all the shoots out before cooking. The shoots are high in solanine, a poisonous alkaloid, which also makes the potato green, so cut out all green bits before using.

PREPARING

All new potatoes can be washed under running water and left unpeeled. Remember, the peel is an essential part of the nutriment. (One of the tragedies of the Irish is shown in a film of the 1920s where a family of farm workers is seen eating potatoes from a pile in the center of the table. The potatoes are hot and steaming, but each is peeled before being salted and eaten, so most of the food value is lost.) Older potatoes will probably need scrubbing to remove the earth and dirt. When you come to peel the potatoes, make sure you buy a peeler that is efficient enough to remove only a very thin layer of the outer skin. I find the swivel peeler is by far the best for this purpose.

For gratin dishes potatoes have to be cut in thin disks. Use a mandoline or a food processor, rinse the potatoes in cold water to remove some of the starch, drain well, and pat dry.

COOKING

BOILING: Put new potatoes into enough salted boiling water to cover and cook for 15–20 minutes. The timing depends on the size, variety, and how recently they were dug up. I have known very small potatoes, no bigger than quail eggs, just dug from my garden, to be cooked within 10 minutes. If you are using the potatoes for a salad, have the dressing ready in a bowl and add the drained hot potatoes to the dressing immediately. Hot into cold helps to fuse dressing and potato, and the potato absorbs more of the dressing.

BAKING: Pick out fairly large potatoes; the size of a mango is about right. Wash them by scrubbing under cold running water, then prick the outsides with a fork to prevent them from bursting inside your oven. Bake in the oven preheated to 325°F for 2–3 hours, or 375°F for 1 hour. Squeeze the crisp outside very gently: if it gives inside, they are done. Cut them in half and serve with butter, sour cream, grated cheese, or any favorite sauce. At this stage the insides can be scooped out and mixed with additions, then restuffed into the potato skin. The emptied skins can also be sliced, fried in olive oil, and eaten as an appetizer. Half a baked potato can be used as a container for other additions too, if some of the potato is removed: two poached or fried eggs with grated Parmesan cheese, anchovies, and sour cream, or chopped onion with grated Cheddar cheese. They offer a host of possibilities for the inventive cook, and make simple supper dishes as well as good party fare.

ROASTING: Peel the potatoes and cut them into pieces about the size of half an apricot or peach. Drop these into boiling water and let them cook for 3 minutes. Drain them thoroughly. Put them into the fat or oil surrounding roasting meat, fowl, or game, sprinkle them with a little salt, and roast for about an hour, turning them once so that they become golden brown.

STEAMING: An excellent way with new potatoes is to lay a bed of mint leaves at the bottom of a steamer and place the washed new potatoes on top. Steam for 15–20 minutes. If making a potato salad, this is a perfect way to cook the potatoes beforehand.

MASHING: Boil the potatoes until tender, then drain. Put the cooked potatoes back in the saucepan over a very low heat to drive off any excess moisture. Remove from the heat. Pour in a little milk and a few pats of butter. Then use a potato masher to combine everything, and season with salt and pepper (the last is important). How much milk and butter you use is up to personal taste: potatoes will soak up great quantities of fat, which is why in the past they were always considered fattening. But potatoes also need very little to turn them into a smooth purée. Instead of milk, you can use cream for a richer effect, fromage blanc for a very slight cheesy tang and a good texture

RIGHT Boiled Rose Finn Apple and blue potatoes

(perfect foil for a poached fish dish), or sour cream, which goes well with a thick gamy stew. Or, add lots of chopped parsley, dill, or cilantro, depending on what dish you wish your mash to accompany.

Never, but never, use a food processor to turn your potatoes into a purée. The potatoes go gray, gooey, and sticky and turn into wallpaper paste.

However, the best-quality mashed potatoes are also beaten after being mashed. This incorporates air and gives you a smoother, fluffier, lighter mash altogether. Use a fork, wire whisk, or electric mixer, but remember that beating only works if your additions are fairly light in themselves, hardly more complicated than milk and butter.

SAUTÉING: Peel the potatoes and boil for 15 minutes, then drain them thoroughly. Slice into disks of ¼-inch thickness or a little less. Heat some olive oil or sunflower oil (the first gives you flavor, the second a lighter, crispier potato), then throw in the pieces of potato. Fry until golden brown and crisp, turning them to ensure that they are done on both sides.

DEEP-FRYING: Responsible cookbooks warn you of its dangers. My mother once set the kitchen on fire, and I have to confess that I have only ever attempted deep-frying about twice in my life, using a wok. In my view it is not only dangerous, but wasteful; a normal domestic kitchen cannot re-use all that oil. It is also unhealthy, for the French fry absorbs vast amounts of fat, and I believe the end result is hardly worth the bother. The reader will conclude that the French fry is not a favorite food for me, any more than the commercial potato chip.

My advice is, if you must have fries, shallow-fry. Make sure the fries are cut not too thick. Rinse and dry thoroughly before cooking in hot olive oil or one of the polyunsaturated vegetable oils. Move the fries around the pan to make sure they are brown. They will cook within 10–12 minutes.

BAKING IN A BAG: A good method for smallish potatoes is to use a roasting bag, placing the potatoes in it with a little olive oil and some chopped mint and sea salt. Close the bag and give it a shake. Place in an oven preheated to 375°F and bake for 30 minutes.

FRYING IN A CLOSED SAUCEPAN: This method is excellent for new potatoes, and stems from a Richard Olney recipe, where the washed potatoes are placed in a pan that has a layer of olive oil in it. Then cloves from 2 heads of garlic are added (the cloves are *not* peeled). Add a little sea salt, then put the pan over a low heat, place the lid on, and leave. Just shake the pan occasionally. The potatoes are cooked within 40 minutes; the garlic is steamed.

I must point out that this recipe is only for garlic-lovers. We once ate this for lunch, then that night crossed to France, sharing our cabin with a friend. In the morning, she commented that the air was so thick with garlic fumes she could hardly breathe.

However, with or without garlic, the method is a perfect one, because the potatoes fry and steam at the same time. I have made it adding onions, shallots, and leeks, all delicious.

GRATINS: In this range of recipes, the potato is ennobled, raised to aristocratic eminence by being baked in the oven in shallow earthenware gratin dishes. These classic dishes are by far my own favorites. The potatoes need to be peeled, then sliced very thinly, either on a mandoline or in a food processor. Remove some of the starch from the slices by soaking in cold water, then pat dry. This is important, otherwise the slices will adhere together into a gluey stodge; what you want are layers of well-flavored individual slices encased in a creamy sauce. There are many versions of each of the classic recipes. I give my preferences here, but every good French cookbook will have its own. It is worth trying them all to find the recipes that suit you.

• For Gratin Dauphinois: Sprinkle a little salt, black pepper, and nutmeg between the layers of potato slices, then pour 2½ cups of cream over the top. Some cooks suggest par-boiling the slices in milk for 2 minutes to reduce the acidity of the potato, and thus prevent the cream from curdling. I have never found this necessary. Merely cook the gratin slowly, say for 2½ hours, at 325°F.

• For Gratin Lyonnais: Interleave potato slices with thickly sliced onion and pour over enough meat or vegetable stock (or cream) just to cover. Finish with Gruyère or Cantal cheese shredded over the top.

• For Gratin Crécy: Interleave potato slices with thickly sliced carrot, and use either stock or cream.

POTATOES SAUTÉED WITH ONION

I first learned to cook this robust dish in the 1950s when I was living in Vienna.

1½ pounds potatoes
3–4 tablespoons olive oil
2 large onions, sliced
sea salt
a large handful of chives, chopped

Peel the potatoes, boil them for 15 minutes, then drain and slice them into disks.

Heat the oil in a large frying pan and throw in the onions followed by the potatoes. Fry until both are golden and crisp, about 10–15 minutes

Serve sprinkled with sea salt and chives.

POTATO SALAD

2 pounds waxy new potatoes, unpeeled
2 red onions, thinly sliced
1 bunch of scallions, chopped
a large handful of parsley, chopped
2 tablespoons capers
1¼ cups aïoli mayonnaise
for the dressing:
⅓ cup olive oil
grated zest from 1 lemon
1 tablespoon lemon juice
1 garlic clove, minced
sea salt and freshly ground black pepper

Boil the potatoes in lightly salted water. While the potatoes are boiling, make the dressing by mixing the ingredients in a large bowl. Drop in the sliced red onions and let them marinate for a while.

When the potatoes are cooked, drain them, then slice into rounds and add to the dressing at once. (I never peel potatoes for a salad, because the peel adds so much flavor, but purists think the peel unsightly.)

When cool, add the chopped scallions, chopped parsley, and capers, then fold in the aïoli mayonnaise. Cover and refrigerate, but not for too long: the salad should be cool, not icy cold.

POTATOES WITH CELERY

2 pounds waxy potatoes
2 bunches of celery
3–4 tablespoons olive oil
2 tablespoons butter
1 tablespoon celery salt
1 tablespoon soy sauce
a handful of parsley, minced

Scrub the potatoes but do not peel them. Boil them for 12 minutes, then drain and dice into ½-inch chunks. Clean the celery and chop the central heart into ½-inch slices. Heat the oil and butter, throw in the vegetables, add the celery salt, and fry until the potato is crisp and brown. Finally, add the soy sauce and stir-fry for 3 more seconds, then sprinkle with the parsley and serve.

GRATED POTATO CAKES

2 pounds large potatoes
½ cup cream cheese
6 tablespoons flour
½ cup grated Parmesan cheese
½ cup shredded Gruyère cheese
1 onion, minced
sea salt and freshly ground black pepper
2 eggs
a handful of parsley, minced
⅔ cup light cream
vegetable oil for frying

Peel the potatoes and grate them. Place in a colander and rinse them under cold running water to get rid of the starch, turning them with your hand. Pat and squeeze them dry in a clean cloth.

Mash the cream cheese with the flour, cheeses, onion, seasoning, eggs, and parsley. Stir in the cream and the potato and mix thoroughly.

Heat some oil in a pan and drop spoonfuls of the mixture into it; the cakes should be about 2 inches wide (if too big, they will break). Cook 4 at a time, letting them become golden brown before turning them over and cooking the other side. Serve at once.

POTATO *Solanum tuberosum*

TOMATO

Lycopersicon esculentum

It is well-nigh impossible today to think of food without the tomato and its almost worldwide flavoring role. Who would have thought that its popularity could have grown so great, after the indifference and suspicion that followed its discovery? It took almost until the dawn of this century for the tomato to find acceptance. Its family, after all, contained the deadly nightshade, and at first people considered that this golden fruit must be either poisonous or an aphrodisiac. This explains its first name, *pomo d'oro*—"golden apple" or "love apple," for the earliest tomatoes to arrive in Europe were the yellow variety, only now creeping back into our seed catalogues.

Gerard's *Herball* is most unflattering: "the whole plant is of a ranke and stinking savour." Gerard links it with a derogatory remark about the Spanish, England's enemy at the end of the sixteenth century, who, we are told, eat these "apples" boiled with pepper, salt, and oil but "they yield very little nourishment to the body, and the same naught and corrupt." Rather than being eaten, tomatoes were used instead as decorative climbing plants. Perhaps some unfortunate person had eaten the leaves or the stem instead of the fruit and then had suffered abdominal pains—which is one of the mistakes that gave the potato its unhappy reputation.

The tomato originally grew in the Lower Andes, an area that now covers Ecuador, Peru, and Bolivia. The ancient Peruvians, it is thought, picked the small cherry-sized tomatoes in the wild and did not bother to cultivate them. But in its short season it was obviously enjoyed, because the tomato traveled northward as a weed long before the coming of Columbus (see page 124), and was very likely cultivated in Mexico. Its name is derived from the Spanish *tomate,* which, in turn, comes from the Aztec *tomatl.*

We do not know how the tomato reached Italy so soon—in 1522; since the Kingdom of Naples was under Spanish rule, it seems likely that all the foods from the New World were soon introduced to southern Italy. They crept into southern France, but most amazingly they were also soon known in Poland—their Polish name was *pomodory,* almost the same word as in Italian. In England, a few herbalists began to grow tomatoes in their private gardens as an ornamental curiosity. Olivier de Serres, agronomist under the French Henri IV, wrote, "they serve commonly to cover outhouses and arbors." It was not until the eighteenth century that two Italian Jesuit priests returned with the red tomato variety, which quickly ousted the yellow in popularity. The Italians and the Spanish were the first to enjoy tomatoes as a salad, a fact that caused some astonishment elsewhere. Philip Miller, in charge of the Chelsea Physic Garden in London, tells us, in 1752, that Italians and Spaniards ate tomatoes like cucumbers with pepper, oil, and salt, and some even ate tomatoes in sauces and as soups. Miller adds that the tomato gives "an agreeable acid to the soup" but he thinks that the nourishment they afford "must be bad." Poor tomato.

Reactions in North America were, if anything, worse. Long cooking before the tomatoes could possibly be palatable was earnestly advised. "Tomatoes will not lose their raw taste in less than three hours' cooking," Eliza Leslie wrote in 1848. The vinegar and spices added to tomato sauce were considered to be some antidote to any lingering poison. The sauce crept into English cooking at the beginning of the nineteenth century, for Pickwick is demanding chops with tomato sauce in 1836. The fact that the tomato survived at all must be due to the enthusiasm that amateur gardeners had for the vegetable (and still have, for that matter), so that rural cooking of the nineteenth century was full of tomato chutneys, pickles, and relishes.

Now tomatoes are a huge commercial crop. Canned, whole or crushed, made into juice, condensed into soup, used as flavoring for baked beans and numerous other convenience foods, they are one of the world's best-selling foods. Yet served as a raw salad vegetable, their quality has declined into a woolly, hard-skinned, tasteless ball of innocuous pap. Raw tomatoes are bitterly criticized, and have been for decades. Food producers and commercial growers are aware of public reaction, and continuous research goes on to find a tasty tomato with a reasonable shelf

life. There are some rays of hope. The little cherry tomato can be so acid that it sometimes seems like chemical warfare upon the palate, yet some varieties have both sweetness and flavor, though the average consumer finds it difficult to know, or remember, which ones. However, that intensity of flavor does not seem yet to appear in the larger summer tomatoes that are grown commercially.

The best tomatoes for sheer flavor grow in Mediterranean-type climates—such as those of California, Mexico, and southern Europe—in poor soil, often withstanding drought. In fact, tomatoes obviously like to struggle for their survival and their nourishment, and this alone gives them a concentration of flavor, even if the fruits are misshapen and small.

NUTRITION

The highest vitamin content is in the jelly that surrounds the seeds, so de-seeding tomatoes reduces the food value. They are high in fiber, potassium, and folic acid, which makes them a good fruit to eat throughout pregnancy.

VARIETIES

Tomatoes are the most widely grown home-garden vegetable. There are varieties adapted to all different climates, and classification is also done by size. Some seed catalogues use "early" and "late" descriptions.

ROUND or SALAD TOMATOES: the standard commercial crop, available all year in some form, but best when sun-ripened in summer. Relatively juicy, with high seed content. Celebrity, Bonny Best, Marglobe, and Rutgers are all reliable and flavorful. Oregon Spring and Early Cascade do well in short-season areas.

CHERRY TOMATOES: small-scale versions of the above, often with sweet, well-flavored fruit. Some plants are small enough for container-growing. Gardener's Delight is a favorite, as the name implies, both sweet and juicy. Sweet 100 is prolific and delicious. Currant is very small, like a wild tomato. Pixie and Tiny Tim are particularly compact plants.

PLUM TOMATOES: relatively fleshy, with fewer seeds and less juice. This is the Italian tomato that is generally canned. It needs good sun to ripen well. San Marzano is the variety to grow.

LARGE or BEEFSTEAK TOMATOES: outsize fleshy fruit with relatively few seeds; most need hot sun to ripen to full flavor. Oxheart Giant has huge pink fruit shaped like a heart. Marmande is my own favorite, irregularly shaped but with the finest flavor.

YELLOW TOMATOES: color variations on round types include Golden Boy, Lemon Boy, and the delicious cherry tomato called Sungold. Tigerella is striped in red and yellow.

CHOOSING AND STORING

The flavor is finest in fruit plucked from the plant after the sun has been on the leaves, but most of us now buy our tomatoes from the supermarket. A sign of freshness is a leafy-looking green calyx, not one that is withered and spidery. If not eating tomatoes right away, don't refrigerate them—at temperatures below 50°F, the flavor is diminished.

In the short summer season there are often gluts of tomatoes. Fortunately much can be made of the less-than-perfect tomato. Rather overripe ones are fine for sauces and soups (see Cooking, below), which, incidentally, freeze well. At the end of the season gardeners often strip plants and put any unripe tomatoes in a drawer or cupboard where they ripen slowly during the following weeks. Unripe green tomatoes also make excellent chutney and soup.

Among commercial products on the market, canned plum tomatoes are worth keeping in the pantry: out of season their sun-ripened flavor is preferable in sauces to the bland fresh fruit.

TOMATO JUICE: This will keep well as long as it is unopened. Once the pack, bottle, or can is opened, use within days.

TOMATO PASTE: Canned tomato paste must be used up once it is opened. It can be decanted into a jar, covered with olive oil, and kept in the refrigerator, but even with this precaution it will not keep much longer than a week. It is best to buy tomato paste in a tube. Store it in the refrigerator once opened, where it will keep for months.

DRIED TOMATOES: Commercial sun-dried tomatoes can be bought loose, often in cellophane bags, or packed in oil in jars. Store loose ones in airtight jars, and reconstitute by covering with boiling water and soaking for about 15 minutes. Keep the others in their oil, and when the tomatoes are all eaten use the oil for sauce, vinaigrette, or cooking.

DRYING TOMATOES: In the absence of warm sun or a fan-assisted fruit dryer, make your own dried tomatoes using a very low oven (the tomatoes do not cook, but simply dry out and contract as all the moisture evaporates). Cut the tomatoes in half (scrape away some seeds if they are very moist), sprinkle a little salt, sugar, and oregano on each one, lay them skin-side down on a baking sheet, and place in a very low oven to dry for a few hours. If you have a solid-fuel stove, you can put them in the bottom of the oven with it merely turned on. These tomatoes are best stored in olive oil or they will go moldy rapidly. The oil will develop a lovely flavor and it is very good in salad dressings.

PREPARING

Many recipes tell you to remove tomato skins and seeds before cooking. For one thing, both are indigestible. Indigestible means what it says in this case (it is not a euphemism for producing flatulence): the skins and seeds go right through the intestines unchanged and are excreted. There is nothing harmful about this for you or the tomato. However, both the skins and the seeds look unsightly in many recipes or spoil the texture. I never bother to seed the tomatoes as requested, but for most soups and sauces it is best to strain them. Skins and seeds are more obtrusive in some varieties and in some individual fruits than in others. Use your judgment about whether or not to remove them.

To remove skins, plunge the tomatoes into a bowl of boiling water, or pour boiling water over them, and leave for a minute or so. Puncture the tomato; the skin will split, and is then easily peeled away. Peeling would be necessary, for example, for a tomato and mozzarella salad where I would want the tomatoes to soak up the flavors of basil and oil, which only a skinless tomato will do.

For a well-flavored tomato soup, I would include not only the green calyx but if possible some green leaf, too. This is only possible if you grow your own tomatoes. It is from the greenery that the powerful tomato aroma emanates. Yes, I know I have said it is toxic, but in this tiny amount I have never known any vague disquiet after eating the soup, and it does make a difference to the final flavor.

Green tomatoes need not be skinned; they can be cut up for chutney as they are, and the soup below uses the entire thing.

COOKING

For soups and sauces, throw roughly chopped tomatoes into a dry pan, cover, place over a very low heat, and leave to cook in their own juice. They will be done within 10–15 minutes. Then purée and push through a sieve. The debris should be thrown away. This is a real homemade tomato purée and it tastes fantastic. To the tomatoes, before cooking, you can add cloves of garlic, basil, or a dash of olive oil, but nothing is really necessary: the tomatoes *au naturel* are excellent. About 1 pound of tomatoes will make roughly 1 cup of purée, so in order to make tomato soup for six people you would expect to need 6 pounds of tomatoes. Oddly enough, this is not the case: the more tomatoes you use, the greater the ratio of juice to tomato flesh. However, it also depends on how ripe the tomatoes are. It is best to use tomatoes that are over the hill and being sold off cheaply, because these are by far the juiciest. Using these I have been able to make enough soup for six people out of 4 pounds of tomatoes.

For a sauce, make your purée in the above manner, then reduce over a high heat to intensify the flavor. At the start of cooking add a little alcohol—wine or spirits, according to taste. One of the best tomato sauces I ever made had a slug of Scotch malt whisky added at the end of cooking. It diluted the sauce, yes, but oh, what flavor.

CANNED TOMATOES: In the winter making a good, well-flavored sauce from canned tomatoes would seem even easier, but canned tomatoes need to be lifted from their own banality, so I would add various other flavorings. Firstly, sweat some garlic and onion in olive oil, then add a pinch of oregano or marjoram, 2 diced boiled carrots, seasoning, a glass of red wine, and then the can of tomatoes. Cook for 5 minutes, then season and blend to a smooth sauce.

TOMATO PUDDING

Based on English summer pudding, this recipe was devised by Jennifer Patterson. Alas, since I have lost her book, I cannot say I am indebted to her for this particular version. However, the idea is to use a 1½-quart pudding basin or dome-shaped mold—these amounts will fill it about halfway.

1 small loaf of day-old bread, sliced
2½ pounds tomatoes
1 garlic clove, minced
a few basil leaves, chopped, plus more for garnish
1 teaspoon sugar
1 teaspoon sea salt
2 teaspoons unflavored gelatin

First line the pudding mold with slices of white bread, after cutting off the crusts. Fit the pieces neatly together so that the bottom and sides are covered, with the bread reaching about halfway or a little more up the sides. Cut out a piece to fit the top. Reserve.

Peel the tomatoes by pouring boiling water over them and leaving for 2 minutes. Remove the skins, then chop the flesh coarsely. (Do this in a shallow dish, or a similar utensil, so as not to lose any juice.)

Place the tomatoes in a pan with the garlic, chopped basil, sugar, and salt. Bring to a boil, then remove from the heat, and immediately dissolve the gelatin in the hot tomato mixture.

Pour the mixture into the bread-lined pudding mold. Make sure that as much as possible of the diced solid tomato is packed in: you need the pudding to be as firm as it can be. Place the bread "lid" on top. You may have plenty of juice left over; this doesn't matter. Pour it into a bowl to set, and serve with the pudding. Cover the bread lid with a plate of a size that will fit inside the mold and place a can of food on the plate. Leave for a day in a cool place.

Unmold and decorate with the spare jellied tomato sauce, chopped up, around the base and a few basil leaves scattered over the pudding itself.

RIGHT Red and yellow tomato chutneys (see overleaf) served with grilled eggplant slices

TOMATO MOLDS

for 6

a handful of basil leaves
2 pounds very ripe tomatoes
2 garlic cloves
1 teaspoon sea salt
1 teaspoon sugar
2 teaspoons unflavored gelatin
2 glasses of dry white wine

Reserve 6 basil leaves, and throw the rest into a saucepan with the tomatoes, the garlic, salt, and sugar. Place a tightly fitting lid on and leave over a low heat for 10–15 minutes. Leave to cool, then purée. Press through a sieve, throw away the debris, and reserve the sauce.

Dissolve the gelatin in the white wine and stir this into the tomato sauce.

Place a basil leaf at the bottom of each ramekin and fill with tomato sauce. Refrigerate for 6 hours. Unmold onto individual plates 5 minutes before serving by dipping the ramekins in hot water and easing the contents out with a knife. A sauce of yellow bell peppers goes well with this, but I regard arugula leaves as essential. Alternatives you might like to try are sour cream and green peppercorns, or a sauce of fresh green peas or leeks.

GREEN TOMATO CHUTNEY

2¼ pounds green tomatoes
2 heads of garlic, peeled and sliced
2½ cups cider vinegar
2 fresh hot green chilies, chopped
3 tablespoons grated fresh gingerroot
2 tablespoons brown sugar
1 teaspoon sea salt

Chop the green tomatoes coarsely and throw them into a preserving kettle with the rest of the ingredients. Bring to a boil and simmer, stirring now and again, until the chutney begins to thicken a little. Taste: it may need a little more sugar or salt. The chilies and ginger make this a fairly spicy chutney.

Leave to cool, then pack into sterilized jars. It will keep for months (process in a boiling-water bath for long storage), or it can be eaten at once.
Note: The same chutney can be made with red tomatoes, but because the fruit is ripe, you will not need the same amount of vinegar. Cut the amount by half, and use granulated sugar instead of brown. Also, the red chutney will disintegrate into something more like a rough purée.

GREEN TOMATO SOUP

This is an excellent way—other than making chutney—to use up a glut of green tomatoes.

2 tablespoons olive oil
2 pounds green tomatoes
2 garlic cloves, chopped
2 tablespoons sugar
1 teaspoon sea salt
1¼ cups buttermilk, or 3 tablespoons fromage blanc,
or ⅔ cup sour cream
basil leaves for garnish

Heat the oil in a saucepan. Roughly chop the tomatoes and throw them into the pan with the chopped garlic, sugar, and salt. Bring to a boil and simmer for just 1 minute, no longer.

Let the mixture cool, then purée in a strong food processor, adding the buttermilk, fromage blanc, or sour cream at the end.

To serve, float some chopped basil leaves on the surface of each bowl.

ABOVE *Green, yellow, and red tomatoes*

EGGPLANT

Solanum melongena

Though the eggplant or aubergine is an eminent member of the potato family, it was not discovered by Columbus in the New World. It comes from India, where it is believed to have been grown and eaten for more than four thousand years. It took some time to leave Southeast Asia, the ancient Mediterranean world was ignorant of its charms, and it was not until the thirteenth century that the great German scholar Albertus Magnus mentioned it.

It was the Moors of Andalusia who brought the plant to southern Europe from the Middle East. The derivation of the name "aubergine"—from the original Sanskrit through Arabic to Catalan and, finally, French—reflects this route. The vegetable was certainly cultivated in Sicily and southern Italy, where

Moorish influence was strong, but gained only a limited acceptance farther north. It appeared on the menu of a banquet given by Pope Pius V in 1570, but eggplants in general were considered unhealthy. Anna del Conte tells us that a fourteenth-century writer regarded them as "causing males to swerve from decent behavior."

One traditional dish remains part of the Italian repertoire—*melanzane fritte*, in which the eggplant is sliced, coated in batter, and deep-fried in olive oil. But it took almost to the present day for the eggplant to be generally accepted in Italy and elsewhere. Jean de la Quintinie, gardener to Louis XIV, first grew eggplants in France; Thomas Jefferson, who delighted in new foods, first grew them in America, but they remained a curiosity and did not really catch on in either country. It is only with the widening of food tastes all around the Western world in the last generation or so that eggplants have gained any of the popularity that they enjoy in Asia and the Middle East, where they are a central part of the cuisine. One reason for this could be that of all vegetables the eggplant most radically changes its flavor, texture, and appearance when cooked, and, secondly, that its flesh soaks up and fuses completely with added flavors. This is its prime quality and function in a whole range of Indian cooking. So wherever you find a cuisine that uses many and varied spices, you find eggplant.

In India and North America, you will often find white or creamy eggplants roughly the size and shape of an egg, so it is not difficult to see how the name eggplant came into being. There are, in fact, dozens of varieties of eggplant, from the dark purple sausage shape we know well, to oval and round ones in lilac shades, and others that are striped white and green. In fact, the common practice of Indian restaurants in the West of adding green peas to curries stems from their chefs' attempts to reproduce the look of a curry that contains little whole green eggplants the size of quail eggs, or even smaller.

NUTRITION

Eggplants are rich in vitamins B1, 2, and 3 and vitamin C. They also have small amounts of iron and calcium. The skin, as is the case with so many vegetables, is richer in nutrients than the flesh.

VARIETIES

Eggplants need warmth to grow: glass protection is usually called for in temperate climates, except in particularly sheltered sites and warm seasons.

There is relatively little difference in flavor between the varieties, and for once the size of the fruit has little to do with flavor and texture. Choice is a matter of personal preference—grow varieties that will do well in your conditions and that suit the dishes you plan to cook.

Among the purple-skinned types of eggplant, Dusky is early and productive. Orient Express is a popular long, skinny, "oriental" type. Ichiban is another. Neon has an unusual magenta-colored skin. Black Beauty is the old-fashioned standard, large eggplant. Easter Egg is small and creamy in color, about the size of a hen's egg.

STORING

Eggplants will keep in the salad drawer for two weeks or more if they are fresh. Inspect the calyx for color and perkiness; if dry and brown, the eggplant has already been kept too long. Eggplants should be firm to the touch and glossy in color; when old they get soft and a little limp and lose their sheen.

PREPARING

Eggplants must be cooked: they are unpalatable raw. They can be prepared in different ways depending on the finished dish. Some recipes counsel putting cut eggplants in acidulated water to prevent discoloring, but since the flesh changes color when cooked I think this is unnecessary. Many older recipes also advise you to sprinkle the flesh with salt and leave it to drain to remove bitterness. However, this is no longer a problem with most cultivars available in the West (I steam eggplants for just a few minutes, without salting, and there is not the slightest trace of bitterness).

The real value of salting is to counteract the tendency of eggplants to take up great quantities of oil. This is due, so Harold McGee tells us, "to the very spongy texture of its tissue: a high proportion of its volume consists of intercellular air pockets." He goes on to say that there comes a point when the heat of the pan and the concentration of oil induces a "collapse of structure" and the eggplant slices expel their oil. This is, frankly, a sorry and unpalatable mess. We do not want eggplant slices either full of oil or after expelling their oil, so the secret is to get rid of those "intercellular air pockets."

One way of doing this is by slicing the eggplant, salting the slices, leaving them out in the air for an hour or more, then rinsing the salt away, and patting the slices dry. The eggplant slices can then be floured, dipped in egg and bread crumbs or dipped in batter, and fried. Or they can be fried on both sides without such additions. Fry them in olive oil for a few minutes over a high heat until they are brown and crisp. For a purée the whole eggplant can be pricked and then baked in an oven preheated to 375°F for 30 minutes; after cooling, the interior flesh is taken out and the skin thrown away. Alternatively, a whole eggplant can be boiled for 15 minutes or steamed for 20

minutes. The quickest method I know is to cut the eggplant in slices and to steam them for 10 minutes.

If the eggplant has been boiled, baked, or steamed, the air pockets will all have vanished, so the flesh will not soak up enormous amounts of oil. However, adding oil to the eggplant flesh is a little like making mayonnaise: the flesh still seems to soak up an astonishing amount. Watch this tendency. It is impossible to give quantities, because eggplants differ in size and the flesh is of various consistencies. So taste the results continually.

Whole eggplants can be halved, salted, and left for an hour before being cooked. Or, they can be sliced lengthwise quite thickly, salted, left, rinsed, drained, and then grilled, sandwiched between a turning grid that chars the vegetable attractively.

COOKING

Eggplants have many uses, in a great variety of dishes. Claudia Roden lists 33 recipes in her classic *Book of Middle Eastern Food*, from eggplant meatballs to stuffed eggplants, and sweet and sour salads. First, they turn up as appetizers—purées made with yogurt, olive oil, and lemon juice, served with olives, sweet peppers, and pita bread.

Eggplants have entered legend. Not only do we have the famous *Imam Bayildi*—"the Imam fainted"—but Claudia Roden gives us another, Sultan's Delight. Both recipes are not particularly spectacular in themselves. The truth is that the eggplant puréed, with the addition of other flavorings or vegetables, is remarkably seductive. We are inclined to forget how astonishingly delicious this vegetable can be. So here are a few suggestions for various eggplant dishes in which it is puréed, and can be eaten hot or cold.

For the first, steam the sliced eggplants for 10 minutes. Heat a few tablespoons of olive oil with 2 minced garlic cloves, several skinned tomatoes, 2 sliced zucchini, and the steamed slices of eggplant. Cook for 10 minutes, then add a tablespoon of soy sauce and some crushed basil leaves.

Alternatively, steam the sliced eggplants for 10 minutes, then heat a few tablespoons of olive oil with 2 cloves of garlic and ½ teaspoon each of coriander, cumin and mustard seeds, 2 chopped onions, and 1 teaspoon turmeric. Throw in the eggplant and cook for another 10 minutes.

In both these cases the eggplant will disintegrate into a purée, leaving the strips of purple skin, but absorbing the flavors. Both dishes can be eaten as they are, hot, warm, or cool, or as a sauce with pasta.

Eggs can be broken and dropped into small indentations in both purées and cooked for a few moments, just to set the egg whites.

A third option is to bake or boil 2 eggplants. When cooked, scrape all the flesh into a blender, and add the juice of 1 lemon, 1 minced garlic clove, 2 spoonfuls of plain yogurt, and 4 tablespoons of olive oil. Blend to a thick cream. This is a basic purée to be used as an appetizer. But additions can be made to it. Chopped hot red or green chilies will make it fiery; chopped tomatoes, a spoonful of tomato paste, and a teaspoon of paprika will give the eggplant a tomato subtext; while a dash of oriental sesame oil and tahini plus toasted sesame seeds give you a nutty and highly delicious hummus-like purée which is characteristic of the Middle East.

CAPONATA

1 medium to large eggplant
3 tablespoons olive oil
1 onion, thinly sliced
1 cup canned crushed tomatoes
¼ cup red wine vinegar
1 tablespoon sugar
2 tablespoons capers
10 pitted black olives
10 pitted green olives
sea salt and freshly ground black pepper

Slice the eggplant lengthwise, then dice these slices into cubes; salt the cubes and leave in a colander for 1 hour. Wash under cold running water and pat dry with a clean towel.

Heat the olive oil in a pan, throw in the onion and eggplant, and fry until the eggplant is crisp and brown, stirring occasionally.

While this is happening, in another saucepan heat the crushed tomatoes, wine vinegar, and sugar. Let the sauce simmer for a few minutes, then add the capers, black and green olives, and seasoning.

Turn the eggplant and onion mixture into a serving dish and pour over the tomato and olive sauce. *Do not* cook the eggplant in the sauce, or the eggplant cubes will disintegrate.

Note: In the original Sicilian recipe, celery or artichokes are cooked with the eggplant and everything is eaten in the sweet-and-sour sauce. Chocolate is also sometimes added to the sauce, with toasted almonds. As there is no celery worth eating in the summer months, when the best eggplants are available, I have not added it to the recipe above. But you can add any other vegetable you wish to the cubed eggplant and onion as long as they remain separate and do not disintegrate into a mush when cooked in the oil. I suggest baby zucchini, leeks, carrots, and turnips.

EGGPLANT SESAME

3 medium eggplants
1 garlic clove, minced
juice of ½ lemon
1 tablespoon toasted sesame oil
6 tablespoons olive oil
sea salt and freshly ground black pepper
¼ cup sesame seeds

Prick the eggplants and place them in an oven preheated to 350°F. Cook for 40–45 minutes, then feel them: if soft, they are done.

Leave to cool, then scrape all the flesh out and place in a blender. Add the garlic, lemon juice, and sesame oil. Blend, then with the machine on low add the olive oil slowly, on the same principle as when making mayonnaise, but at a slightly faster rate. When the oil is absorbed and the eggplant has become creamy, season with salt and pepper.

In a deep frying pan heat the sesame seeds until they begin to pop and turn golden brown. When these have cooled, add 3 tablespoons to the eggplant and mix them in.

Turn into a serving bowl and sprinkle the last tablespoon of seeds over the top. Eat with hot pita bread or crudités.

SWEET PEPPER

Capsicum annuum Grossum Group

This is a shrubby annual plant that bears fruit within a couple of months. The glossy fruits are roughly bell-shaped (hence bell peppers) and hollow: their botanical name derives from the Latin *capsa* meaning case or box. At first normally green, the fruit turns yellow and then red if left to ripen on the bush (this is not true of purple and white peppers, which are that color from first formation).

Compare this description with that of another kind of pepper. The peppercorns we grind up and use to season dishes on the table come from a vine (*Piper nigrum*) that can grow to 30 feet. This begins to fruit after three years, and will continue for 20 more, and bears its tiny green berries on long, spray-like stems. One would think no two plants could be more dissimilar. However, when Columbus anchored off the Caribbean island he named Hispaniola (now Haiti and the Dominican Republic), he was convinced he had found the Spice Islands off the coast of India. Therefore, any vegetable that was fiery and used as a seasoning must be a pepper.

When the ships returned to Europe they carried with them "peppers of many kinds and colors...more pungent than that from Caucasus," as Peter Martyr wrote when he observed the triumphal arrival of Columbus at the Spanish Court in April, 1493. However, it would appear that Peter Martyr was not convinced these new vegetables were really pepper, though he adds "it is just as much esteemed."

On the second Columbian voyage to the New World it was noted that the main staple in the natives' diet was a bread made with sweet potato, eaten with a hot and peppery seasoning that was also used extensively with fish and any small birds the natives caught. The same seasoning was found in the highlands of Mexico at the court of Montezuma. When Cortes and his Spanish army reached this civilization they were impressed by the great range of dishes, which included turkey served with a sauce made from tomatoes, hot chilies, and ground squash seeds, and fish with sauces of hot yellow and red chili.

SWEET PEPPER *Capsicum annuum* Grossum Group

By then the Spaniards had christened the new vegetable (whatever the size, color, shape, or degree of fieriness) *pimiento*, after their word for black peppers—*pimienta*. If that is not confusing enough, another berry, which does resemble the peppercorn—allspice—was also named *pimiento*.

Thus the whole of the large capsicum family is now called peppers, though the small fiery one that started the misunderstanding took on the Aztec name, chili or chile. The Spanish took that word back to Europe with them, and very quickly it spread to the rest of the world.

The Spanish found that both the sweet peppers and the chilies grew well in southern Spain and in their new possessions in Sicily and southern Italy. Very soon sweet peppers spread around the Mediterranean. Their appearance was keenly appreciated: "a crimson and scarlet mixt: the fruit about three inches long and shines more than the best pollisht corall," says Lignon in his *History of Barbadoes, 1647–53*.

Today, familiar with the vivid colors—red, orange, yellow, purple, and black—that peppers display, we might imagine that some are recent and have been selectively bred. However, Peter Martyr's description belies such a thought. The Columbian pepper harvest that reached Spain included peppers of all colors, each with a different name. There was even a white pepper—both within and without. Another was violet without and white within.

No other vegetable among the Columbian discoveries was accepted so readily as the sweet peppers and their fiery nephew, the chili. (Some chilies belong to the *Capsicum annuum* species, others are kinds of *C. frutescens*—see page 206.) They became absorbed into southern European and Asian cuisines within the next half century, so much so that many of the best pepper dishes are Mediterranean in origin.

Paprika is made from dried sweet peppers. The type used is generally the European sweet pepper, which is large and mild. Hungary is the main producer of paprika; the more fiery the color, the greater the quality. In Spain they also grind sweet peppers, and there they call it *pimentón*. This is virtually the same as paprika, and, again, the more vivid the color, the better it is.

NUTRITION

Sweet peppers are high in vitamins B1, B2, and C, and are also rich in fiber, potassium, and folic acid. They are an excellent salad food if eaten raw.

CHOOSING AND STORING

The outside should feel hard and crisp; patches of softness or wrinkling show that the fruit is no longer fresh. The color should be glossy and vivid. If peppers are in prime condition when bought, they will keep for a few days. But they quickly fade and soften, so use them within three days.

VARIETIES

It is well worth growing your own peppers, outdoors in warmer areas, or in a greenhouse elsewhere. Peppers eaten just after picking have a quality and flavor that is sensational, both sweeter and more pungent and peppery than any bought from a market.

ACE: Green bell shape: a vigorous early variety.

LONG RED MACARONI: Deep red; mild and sweet.

SWEET BANANA: Exactly as the name suggests—sweet and mild.

CANAPE: Early, small-fruited pepper that does well in short seasons.

PREPARING AND COOKING

For all recipes peppers need to be cored and seeded. Simply cut off the top with the stem (for stuffed peppers you will need this top as the lid), then with a sharp knife gouge out the core with its seeds. Most peppers will also need the pithy lining cut away too, which is easily done if the pepper is sliced in half.

For certain dishes peppers need to be peeled. The outer skin, though thin, is tart and slightly bitter. This gives a pleasant stimulus to salads, but once cooked the outer skin becomes acrid and mars the sweetness of the pepper.

The easiest method of peeling is to use a potato peeler, preferably the swivel type where no pressure is needed. However, some dishes call for a smoky flavor in the peppers, which you can best achieve by blistering the skin over hot charcoal, then leaving them to cool before scraping off the skin. This can be tedious. You can also hold peppers over a gas flame with a pair of tongs, which will similarly give you a slight smoky flavor. Closing the charred peppers in a plastic bag to sweat for a few minutes before peeling helps the skins come off more easily.

But how to decide for any particular recipe whether the peppers should be peeled or not? Or by what method? This subtle problem can only be decided by trial and error. Try a favorite recipe with the peppers peeled, char-grilled, or left completely raw. It is a matter of personal taste.

Sweet peppers have been used for centuries in Provençal cooking. About twenty years ago there was a great vogue for one particular dish—ratatouille, a mixture of peppers, eggplant, onion, zucchini, and tomatoes stewed softly in olive oil. Unfortunately, this dish used to be overcooked, so that an unappetizing oily brown sludge would appear. Be sure when adding peppers to other vegetables to stop the cooking process before the individual vegetables disintegrate. (See my recipe below.)

When chopped and sautéed over a low heat in oil, peppers will cook in about 10 minutes. If stuffed and baked in the oven they will take about 30 minutes. I confess I am not an enthusiast of stuffed peppers (see Claudia Roden's book for the classic recipes), because I dislike the flavor of peppers when they have been cooked that long. Also, long baking makes the outside indigestible and the interior too soft to be enjoyable. If you want peppers and rice, I suggest you cook them separately and quickly, within 10 minutes.

The first pepper recipe I give here is an old favorite, one of the very first dishes I learned to cook in the 1950s. It makes an excellent dish for a summer lunch with a salad.

PIPÉRADE

3 tablespoons olive oil
1½ pounds mixed bell peppers, cored, seeded, and sliced
2 large onions, sliced
a pinch of oregano
1½ pounds tomatoes, peeled, or 1 cup chopped canned tomatoes
sea salt and freshly ground black pepper
4 eggs, beaten

Heat the oil in a frying pan and throw in the peppers and onions with a pinch of oregano. Cook, stirring occasionally, for 5 to 8 minutes, then add the tomatoes, turn up the heat, and cook for a further 3 minutes. (If the tomatoes are fresh this is all the cooking they will need. The mixture should be sloppy. If the tomatoes are canned there may be too much liquid, so raise the heat for a moment or two so that most of this evaporates.) Season. Now pour in the eggs and mix thoroughly as you would for scrambled eggs; the mixture should just set. Take from the heat immediately, and serve with good crusty bread.

RATATOUILLE

3–4 tablespoons olive oil
3 mixed bell peppers, cored, seeded, and sliced
1 onion, sliced
3 small zucchini, cut into chunks
1 small eggplant, diced, salted and left for 1 hour, then rinsed and dried
sea salt and freshly ground black pepper

Heat the oil and cook the vegetables at the same time, stirring occasionally. Cook for 12–15 minutes, no longer, so that the vegetables are softened and browned, but still in their individual pieces. Add seasoning at the end, because salting makes the juices run. Eat warm, with good crusty bread.

BROILED PEPPERS AND ANCHOVY

1 large red and 1 large yellow bell pepper
1 can of anchovies
1 small red onion, cut into rings
5 black olives, pitted
1 tablespoon olive oil
1 tablespoon capers (optional)
juice of ½ lemon
freshly ground black pepper

Peel the peppers with a potato peeler, then cut them in half and scoop out the seeds and core. Slice them in strips and lay on a large, round baking dish, keeping red and yellow colors separate in four quarters.

SWEET PEPPER *Capsicum annuum* Grossum Group

Lay the anchovies in two vertical and two horizontal lines. Lay a few onion rings in each square, with an olive half in the center. Dribble a little oil over the whole, and sprinkle with a few capers.

Place under a preheated broiler, close to the heat, for about 2 minutes. The peppers and onions should blacken a little, but not necessarily lose their rawness and crisp texture.

Give the dish a good squeeze of lemon juice, plus a few turns of the pepper mill, and serve.

THREE COLORED PEPPER PURÉES

Peppers come in the most vibrant colors—red, orange, and yellow. There are also black peppers; however, if you cook with them, the black turns green. You can, of course, make a purée from green peppers, but I much prefer to use the red, orange, and yellow—adjacent colors on the spectrum—for a more stunning effect. The purées are simple to make. Follow the method given here for the red peppers for the other colors.

2 tablespoons good olive oil
2 red bell peppers, cored, seeded, and sliced
2 garlic cloves, peeled
a pinch of sea salt

Heat the olive oil in a saucepan and throw in the peppers, garlic, and salt. Let everything sauté very gently beneath a close-fitting lid so that the peppers steam in their own juices. Cook for 12 – 15 minutes, then remove from the heat and let the peppers cool.

Blend to a thick purée. The oil will form an emulsion with the peppers.

Do the same with orange and yellow bell peppers. Keep in separate bowls. Use as a coulis around molds or for a first course where the food is in the middle of the plate. Pour into circles or triangles of color. For the last, use a piece of cardboard to keep the colors separate while you pour them on the plate. They are thick enough to stay where you put them.

RIGHT A parsnip mold (page 232) served
with the three colored pepper purées

CHILI or HOT PEPPER

Capsicum annuum Longum Group
and *C. frutescens*

After salt, the chili or hot pepper is now the most popular seasoning in the world. There are dozens of different chilies, which come in various shapes from small bells and round puffs to long, thin, tapering cones, all having varying degrees of fieriness. The chili was an instant and worldwide success almost as soon as it was discovered, such was the European desire for a spice akin to pepper.

Because of the Portuguese trading posts around the coast of Africa to the Indian Ocean and beyond, fifty years after the chili had been discovered it was known and sold in barter from Africa to Nagasaki. From then on the chili began to flavor cuisines from Gambia to Bangkok. In every region where it could be grown it was used—dried, ground, and whole—appearing in diverse dishes, giving a scorching zest to the staple diet.

The heat is due to a substance called capsaicin, which is in the pith rather than in the seeds, which many cooks discard. To get the maximum heat from chilies, insure that the pith is cooked; to reduce the hotness, take care to eliminate it. Nor are red chilies hotter than green ones. Red simply means ripeness and a greater sugar content.

New scientific research by Dr. John Prescott of C.S.I.R.O., the Australian national research organization, has discovered that capsaicin acts as a flavor-enhancer to other foods. It is thought that capsaicin triggers the release of endorphins, the body's natural painkillers, which creates a sense of general well-being and thus makes the pleasure of eating more intense. That is not all that capsaicin is thought to do (see the later notes on nutrition).

It is difficult to tell how much capsaicin is in a chili—size is no guide, because more of the substance is likely to be in the small bell-shaped chilies than in the larger thinner ones. If the plant has to struggle for survival, the amount of capsaicin will increase. So poor soil, hot sunshine, and inadequate watering will create a chili small but powerfully hot, while a plant grown in my own plastic tunnel in temperate England in rich soil and watered liberally will only be moderately hot. Capsaicin reaches its peak in the matured ripened chili, but here the heat is offset a little by the sweetness of the flesh.

The beneficial effects of capsaicin might help to explain the popularity of Tabasco sauce, which contains chilies, salt, and vinegar. The recipe for Tabasco was devised by Edmund McIlhenny for his own use in the 1850s. He was a New Orleans banker who had been given a handful of dried hot peppers by a friend on his return in 1848 from the war in Mexico. Edmund planted the seeds in his father-in-law's plantation, Avery Island, in southern Louisiana. The plants flourished, and there he made his sauce and gave bottles away to a few friends.

After the war, with the Southern states defeated and the economy in ruins, Edmund saw no future in banking. But the chili had taken over Avery Island, and by 1869, 350 bottles of Tabasco Pepper Sauce had been dispatched to selected wholesalers. The product never looked back.

Tabasco is an Indian word meaning "land where the soil is humid," and certainly Louisiana—with its bayous and swamps, its trees hung with Spanish moss like the swagging at Miss Haversham's wedding feast—is a place where in the summer you steam lightly. The seeds are planted and harvested in August—the pickers all carry a *baton rouge* the exact color of the ripe chili, so there can be no mistake in plucking them still unripe. The chilies are then mashed, placed in oak barrels with salt, and left to mature for three years. A wooden top with holes is covered with a layer of salt. This allows the gas to escape when the chilies are fermenting, but the salt insulates the contents from any bacteria.

The factory is thick with fumes, and the air sharp and acrid. The chili stings and catches the throat, seeming almost to scrape the lining of the windpipe. On a visit I made with other food writers, many of us coughed constantly, even though we had covered our mouths and noses with scarves and cardigans. But the workers we spoke to had adjusted to this peppery intake and swore they never had coughs or colds, or any form of sinusitis or hay fever.

After three years' fermentation the mashed chilies are tipped into hundred-gallon vats, and white vinegar twice the strength of table vinegar is added. The contents of the vat are kept moving for 28 days, and finally the juice is strained and poured off.

NUTRITION

For such a small, fiery fruit, chilies are surprisingly high in vitamins A and C. Capsaicin has beneficial effects on our digestive system, its ingestion stimulating the saliva, gastric juice, and the peristaltic movements of the intestines. It is thus good for constipation, because capsaicin irritates the intestinal lining and increases its movement, cutting down the time the meal takes to pass through. It is good for the circulation and is a healing element for stomach and intestinal ulcers. It is also an antiseptic, actually used on adhesive bandages.

A little chili used discreetly every day, like garlic, in at least one dish would undoubtedly have a beneficial effect on anyone's diet.

STORING

Chilies can be bought fresh, dried, canned, and pickled. They are useful to have in the pantry in all these guises. Fresh green chilies will, like sweet peppers, get limp and wrinkled after about a week and must be used or thrown away. They keep for a little longer if stored in the salad drawer of the refrigerator. Red chilies, on the other hand, will, if not used within a week or two, dry out and can be kept for many months, as long as they have dried out hanging up within an airflow.

Dried red chilies can be bought and stored in a clean jar; they will keep forever. I have a Victorian spice tin that belonged to my grandmother, still with some tiny red chilies in it, possibly used by her about 1900—who knows? I keep them for sentiment as a curio. I don't advise anyone to cook with such ancient spices. But I know that some dried red chilies in my kitchen (I tend to buy them in bulk) I must have had for five years or so.

Dried chilies can also be purchased flaked or ground to a powder, or in the form of Tabasco and a list of other hot sauces. Cayenne pepper was named after the capital of French Guiana, which lay on the Cayenne River. However, chilies are not grown in this area any more, and cayenne pepper can now be made from chilies grown anywhere in the world, from Louisiana to India and the Far East. There is very little difference between cayenne pepper and chili powder, though commercial chili powders may have colorings and other spices such as cumin added to the ground chilies.

Both cayenne pepper and chili powder will lose their pungency far quicker than a dried red chili. Buy these in small amounts, keep them in a cool, dry, and dark place, and do not expect them to taste as fiery after a year or two as they once did.

VARIETIES

Chilies do best in warm climates, but they can be grown outdoors in all but the coldest areas. They are easy to grow once they have germinated, and are prolific in fruiting. One small plant a few feet high could give you over a hundred chilies. None need be wasted, for those not used fresh can be threaded and hung to dry. Like sweet peppers, most chilies start out green and ripen to red.

SERRANO is small, green, and very hot.

JALAPEÑO is one of the most popular chilies in the U.S. In Mexico, the jalapeño is smoked and becomes a *chipotle*. It is often pickled, and used in salsas as well as many other dishes.

ETHIOPIAN is a long, thin chili that gets hotter as it ripens from green to red.

POBLANO is a large, dark green chili that is quite mild. It can be roasted or grilled whole. In Spain, they serve plates of them in the tapas bars. They are delicious, but astonishingly inconsistent: there will be one among twenty that is scorching hot, while the rest are sweet and spicy. It is like playing Russian roulette with your palate, but well worth it.

CASCABEL can be bought dried. Small, plum-shaped, with a nutty flavor, these are also roasted whole, and are used to make *salsa de chile cascabel*.

HABAÑERO is a small green, yellow, or red chili from Mexico that belongs to a separate species (*Capsicum sinense*). It is the hottest of all. The Caribbean Scotch Bonnet pepper is considered to be the same.

CHILI or HOT PEPPER *Capsicum annuum* Longum Group and *C. frutescens*

PREPARING

Take care when handling chilies as capsaicin is a skin irritant, especially painful if any gets into scratches or cuts—or worst of all, and most common, transferred to the eyes by rubbing into the eyelids. Infinitesimal amounts nestle beneath the fingernails and can irritate delicate skin even some hours after handling. It must be stressed that capsaicin, though beneficial, has this aggressive aspect; it is a general irritant and is used as an active component in anti-mugging sprays. When preparing chilies, to ensure utmost safety, either use rubber gloves or handle the chili with a knife and fork and wash the implements afterward. The chili can be easily dissected using a sharp knife and sliced, diced small, or (pith and seeds removed) left in a chunk.

COOKING

Chilies are often diced small and sweated in oil with other spices at the start of creating a dish, so that the fieriness will permeate throughout. However, with some Asian and Indian recipes, one chili can be added whole and left to permeate the dish and give another aspect of heat. I am fond of this method; it is subtle, and the heat has a quite different quality. There are other recipes where the chili is added last. Chopped and diced small, it is fried with a mixture of spices and then stirred in at the last moment. Several lentil dishes use this method, where the bland pulses suddenly acquire a small pool of fire. Those nervous of the heat can avoid the spicy bits if they wish.

ROUILLE

This is the fiery mayonnaise of Provence, eaten atop croûtons in bouillabaisse. But it has a hundred uses—with crudités, for example, and with globe artichokes and asparagus. It is one of the great sauces. Add 1 teaspoon of harissa (below) to a mayonnaise made with 1 cup olive oil. Or follow this recipe.

1 large dried hot red chili
1 garlic clove, unpeeled
1 cup olive oil
2 egg yolks
a pinch of sea salt

Blanch the chili and the garlic and leave for an hour. Peel the garlic, slice the chili, and place both in a blender with a little of the olive oil—enough to turn the chili and garlic into a paste.

In a separate bowl, add the oil drop by drop to the egg yolks. As they emulsify, continue to pour until all the oil has been absorbed. Lastly, add the chili paste and the salt. Beat thoroughly.

Some cooks suggest adding a drop of tomato paste for color; it doesn't do the flavor too much harm either, but it is then not a classic rouille.

Another short-cut rouille: Add to 1 cup aïoli mayonnaise 1 teaspoon Tabasco sauce and 1 teaspoon of hot red Hungarian paprika or Spanish *pimentón*.

HARISSA

This is the fiery-hot North-African sauce traditionally served with couscous.

4 ounces dried hot red chilies
6 garlic cloves, unpeeled
1 teaspoon ground coriander
1 teaspoon caraway seeds
1 tablespoon dried mint
a handful of cilantro leaves, chopped
2 tablespoons olive oil
1 teaspoon sea salt

Soak the chilies in enough warm water to cover for an hour. Blanch the garlic in a small pan of boiling water and, when cool, peel the cloves.

Place the chilies with their soaking water in a blender with the garlic, ground coriander, caraway, and mint. Blend to a purée. Add the cilantro leaves, oil, and salt and blend again.

The sauce keeps happily in the refrigerator for weeks if covered in oil.

*RIGHT Broiled peppers and anchovy (page 203)
and rouille served with crudités*

THE
PARSLEY
FAMILY

CARROT *Daucus carota*

CELERY *Apium graveolens* var. *dulce*

ALEXANDERS *Smyrnium olusatrum*

CELERIAC or CELERY ROOT *Apium graveolens*
var. *rapaceum*

FENNEL *Foeniculum vulgare* var. *azoricum*

PARSNIP *Pastinaca sativa*

SKIRRET *Sium sisarum*

PARSLEY *Petroselinum crispum*

PARSLEY ROOT or HAMBURG PARSLEY
Petroselinum crispum var. *tuberosum*

ROCK SAMPHIRE *Crithmum maritimum*

This family includes about 250 plant genera across the temperate regions of the world. Many are aromatic herbs (anise, dill, caraway, chervil, lovage, angelica, and cumin) with feathery leaves, but all have the flowers arranged in a conspicuous flat cluster (which is sometimes slightly dome-shaped) at the top of their stems—this inflorescence is the umbel that gives its name to the family.

*Many species of umbelliferae are poisonous: the family includes poison hemlock (*Conium maculatum*), water hemlock (*Cicuta maculata*), and fool's*

211

parsley (Aethusa cynapium). But other species are household names that we happily consume all the time. The aromatic leaves are consumed in parsley; the tap root is edible in carrot and parsnip (and, in its swollen form, in celeriac), while the succulent stems are the attraction in celery and fennel.

CARROT

Daucus carota

One might think that carrots, like cabbage, radish, and garlic, have a long and detailed history, but what little was written about them is both obscure and conflicting. Surely this phallic root with such a luscious color would have been much admired, praised, and celebrated in antiquity? But the truth is that the carrot as we know it is a much later addition to the table, while the wild carrot that the ancients knew was, and is, small, pale, and tough. The yellow, lilac, or purple carrot came from Afghanistan, and is unlikely to have traveled to classical Greece until Alexander brought it back from Persia; I suspect that this root, though purple, must also have been small and irregular in shape. The orange-red carrot, grown large, would have been nature's gift to the Greek phallic cult; even the small purple carrot might have had its devotees, yet neither is ever mentioned. In the whole of Athenaeus, although much is written about other vegetables, the carrot (and its cousin, the parsnip) is never alluded to.

The cultivated form of the purple carrot could have appeared in Asia Minor in the eighth century BC. It is thought to have been recognized as part of the gardens of Babylon, but it is placed among the scented herbs of King Merodach-Baladan (d. 694 BC). Pliny mentions a Syrian plant called *daucon* in Greece and *gallicam* in Italy. It could be a carrot or a parsnip; he describes it as "slender and bitter," which makes it quite unlike our present carrot with its high sugar content. Columella mentions carrots briefly, while Apicius suggests that they be eaten raw with salt, oil, and vinegar and gives one modest recipe for cooking them in cumin sauce with a little oil.

By the second century AD, Galen comments that the wild carrot is less fit to be eaten than the domestic. So we now know that the carrot was being cultivated then. But was it our carrot? Surely, if so, its color would have been remarked upon? No; Galen must be talking of the purple variety. Even if the Romans seemed apathetic, you would think that, as the Dark Ages closed over Europe and the peasantry were reduced to grubbing for roots, the sweetness of the carrot would make it precious. But it is ignored. Surely this is proof that today's carrot, which we know and love, was not yet formed and that what was left at the end of the Roman civilization was something unremarkable, not far removed from the wild carrot itself. Yet the carrot responds to cultivation and speedily improves. To breed our red carrot, you would need the yellow variety to be crossed with the purple and this did not seem to occur for centuries, though both were indigenous to Afghanistan.

Albertus Magnus (1200–80), the great German scholar, who was particularly precise and detailed, mentions the carrot's cousin the parsnip but fails to record the carrot, which suggests that the vegetable may have been used in its wild state, still uncultivated in the thirteenth century. Both purple and yellow carrot seeds were brought by the Moors to Spain, and because of the Spanish conquests in Flanders the vegetable was grown in the Netherlands by the late fifteenth century. From there it reached England, and the feathery tops became a great success as decoration on hats and clothes in Elizabeth's court.

Perhaps we can narrow down the date of one step toward the true cultivation of today's carrot, for the first mention of it in a way we can recognize comes in the instructions that the Goodman of Paris compiled for his sixteen-year-old wife. He tells her that the carrots are purchased in the market in bundles, and though red they always include one white one. Now the Goodman is particular about his kitchen garden and grows beets, leeks, cabbage, parsley, peas, spinach, lettuce, pumpkin, turnip, radish, and parsnip among the vegetables. But the carrots have to be bought at market and they are not yet uniform in color. The Goodman's book was written in 1392; Albertus Magnus had written his work around 1260, by which time the Moors had already introduced sugar cane, rice, cotton, and the citrus fruits into Spain.

Recipes for carrot, and quite often for orange, are legion in Moorish cooking, and they, in turn, were influenced by the Persians. Margaret Shaida (*The Legendary Cuisine of Persia*, 1992) claims it was the early, dark purple carrot that the Persians cooked with, and it was this carrot that Alexander the Great took back to Greece after he had conquered the Persian Empire. If so, as she admits, it never really made an impact on either Greece or Rome.

However, when the carrot reached England it was still thought of as either a pot-herb or a medicinal aid. Gerard mentions a yellow variety but tells us that the purple carrots were still the most popular, even though they lost their color when cooked and turned brown. One suspects that this was the reason the Romans were less than enthusiastic, since they had an aesthetic eye for what looked good upon the table. By the early seventeenth century in Italy, Castelvetro was preparing salads from pink and yellow carrots, with pepper as the most important seasoning. But it was in Holland in the seventeenth and eighteenth centuries that carrots were bred in orange and red varieties. They were bred for sweetness as well as color (though the sweetness must have taken time, for Ude, in 1824, recommends blanching carrots "to take off the tart taste"). Though white and purple varieties were still popular in France at the beginning of the nineteenth century, Dumas recommends the best carrot as being palish white or yellow; as his *Dictionary* was published in 1873, this shows a quite late disdain for the red carrot. Dumas gives a recipe for carrot soup, but one feels it was unappealingly pale. Yet this was the century when carrots came into their own in France, associated with the spa, Vichy, where raw carrots were given daily as part of the cure, or Crécy, where the chalk soil is supposed to be good for carrot cultivation. In fact, carrots like a light loamy soil, which encourages a long straight root.

NUTRITION

Carrots are rich in carotene and vitamin A, and contain significant amounts of B3, C, and E. They also contain sodium, calcium, phosphorus, potassium, fiber, and folic acid. All the nutrients are stored close to the surface, so it is best to wash or scrub carrots, but not to peel them.

Research ties regular consumption of beta-carotene vegetables and fruits with a defence against lung cancer. The myth about helping night sight—R.A.F. pilots in the Second World War were encouraged to eat carrots—has elements of truth in it, because vitamin A is essential for the correct functioning of the eyes. Carrot juice is also used to prevent eye, throat, tonsil, and sinus infections.

CHOOSING

The most delicious carrots are the young ones, about the size of the little finger. Most people would choose to eat them raw, but if cooked they need only to be blanched in a little boiling water for a minute.

Try to pick carrots loose or, better still, in bundles, with their feathery tops looking fresh and green, but not packaged in plastic bags. Feel them for firmness. Old, tired carrots are best avoided altogether; their nutritional richness declines seriously, so they have little to offer. This is not to say that the mature, largish carrot, newly dug or bought fresh, is not a marvelous vegetable, scrubbed lightly, then used for a myriad of different dishes. Grated raw, the flavor is fine, sprinkled with celery salt and with lemon juice added at the end. Or use in any of the following ways.

PREPARING AND COOKING

Wash and trim the carrots but do not peel. Their cooking times depend on their size and how they are cut. Whole carrots need about 20 minutes boiling or baking. You can bake them like potatoes in Gratin Dauphinois (see page 186), sliced thinly, or in stock with garlic. You can roast them, chopped in chunks, around a piece of meat or game bird.

An excellent simple carrot soup can be made from stock and half a dozen carrots, boiled and then blended. The classic Crécy soup includes onion, butter, potato, egg yolks, and cream, but I have never found such additions necessary or even worthwhile. You might, though, like to experiment with adding orange zest to the carrots when they begin cooking and some orange juice at the end.

CARROT Daucus carota

Another simple recipe is all the variations on carrot salad, where the vegetables are shredded and mixed with oil and vinegar and perhaps other ingredients and flavorings. Again, you could add orange juice—or even rosewater in honor of the carrots' early Persian past. Such salads go well with toasted pine nuts, or toasted mustard seeds. The carrot, after all, is also much used in Indian cooking, and there are many raw salads with mixtures of spices that are both exciting and satisfying.

One of the classic ways of cooking carrots is to add butter to a little of the poaching water and to finish with some sugar so that the vegetables absorb the liquid and end up glazed. It is pretty to look at and highly satisfying. I have rarely known carrots cooked in this way to be left. This method goes by various names. In the late 1800s it was referred to as THE FLEMISH WAY. The carrots are simmered in about 2 tablespoons of butter, a wineglass of water, salt, and pepper and then finished with a pinch of sugar, a dash of chopped parsley, two egg yolks, and a little cream. Elizabeth David has a less rich version called CAROTTES VICHY, where the carrots are cooked with 2 tablespoons of butter, salt, and two lumps of sugar, then finished with more butter and parsley.

My own version dispenses with the parsley altogether and uses the same amount (2 tablespoons) of butter (to, say, 1 pound of carrots sliced diagonally) and ⅔ cup of water. When the water and butter are absorbed, add a little more butter and a heaped teaspoon of brown sugar. Shake the pan for 2 minutes over the heat so that the carrots become glazed and do not stick. Instead of adding sugar at the last moment, try adding marsala, Madeira, or a sweet sherry. Carrots also go well with a little finely sliced gingerroot, added before the sugar or wine.

Do not always shred carrots when making salads. Slice them paper-thin with a mandoline or in a food processor, then dress in the Indian manner: fry a selection of seeds—mustard, cardamom, cumin, and coriander—in sesame or mustard oil, then pour them over the raw carrots with the addition of lime and lemon juice, salt, and pepper.

The idea of using carrots as a savory is as recent as the last century, for carrots were used since ancient Persia in sweet dishes. Now, Margaret Shaida tells us, carrot "is conserved and preserved in jams and syrups, partnered with orange peel and almonds."

In the Second World War carrots were used extensively in jams, desserts, and cakes. It seems to be only in the latter that we still use them. This recipe for carrot cake is far and away the best I've ever tasted. It was published in Michael Bateman's column in the *Independent on Sunday* in Britain; he thinks he got it from the book *Laurel's Kitchen*. I have added the alcohol and the orange zest and juice, though lime will do. It is extravagant with honey, but that is the secret of its extreme deliciousness.

CARROT CAKE

1¼ cups honey
grated zest and juice of 1 orange
1 wineglass of dark rum
½ cup water
1 packed cup finely grated carrots
½ cup butter
¾ cup raisins
½ cup chopped dates
1 teaspoon ground cinnamon
½ teaspoon grated nutmeg
½ teaspoon ground cloves
1⅔ cups wholewheat flour
a pinch of sea salt
2 teaspoons baking soda
1 cup shelled walnuts
for the topping:
5 ounces (⅔ cup) cream cheese
⅔ cup crème fraîche
2 tablespoons softened butter
3 tablespoons confectioners' sugar
1 teaspoon vanilla extract

In a saucepan, heat the honey, orange zest and juice, dark rum, and water with the grated carrots, butter, raisins, dates, and the ground cinnamon, nutmeg, and cloves. Boil for 5 minutes, then remove from the heat and leave to cool until lukewarm.

In a bowl, mix the flour with the salt, then add the baking soda and, finally, the walnuts. Make a well

ABOVE *Carrot cake*

in the middle, and pour in the carrot mixture. Mix together well to make a batter.

Preheat the oven to 350°F. Pour the batter into a greased 10-inch cake pan and bake for about 1 hour. The cake is done when you insert a skewer and it comes out clean. Leave it in its pan for 10 minutes before unmolding onto a wire cake rack.

For the topping: cream the cheese with the crème fraîche, mix in the softened butter, and beat in the confectioners' sugar and the vanilla. Spread the topping over the cake when it has cooled.

CARROT PUFFS

This is an eighteenth-century recipe, quoted by Dorothy Hartley, which I adjusted and placed in my first cookbook: "Scrape and boil them and mash them very fine, add to every pint of the pulp about ½ pint of bread crumb, some eggs, four whites to the pint, a nutmeg grated, some orange flower water, sugar to taste, a little sack, and mix it with thick cream. They must be fried in rendered suet very hot."

That is an eighteenth-century English recipe; the following one is a modern version. These puffs are far more delicious than they sound.

Boil 1 pound sliced carrots; drain, then mash them. Add the juice from 1 orange, the yolks of 2 eggs, and enough bread crumbs to bind the mixture. Then fold in the beaten whites of the eggs.

Heat a little olive oil in a pan, and when it is hot enough, mold the mixture with your fingers into round puffs the size of a ping-pong ball. Drop these into the oil and fry, turning them, until they are brown and crisp on the outside. (They should be crunchy on the outside and light in the center.)

Pile them in a dish and serve them at once.

CARROT *Daucus carota*

CARROT APPETIZER

This carrot relish is derived from one of Julie Sahni's recipes in her *Classic Indian Vegetarian Cooking*.

3 tablespoons mustard oil
1 tablespoon mustard seeds
1 dried hot red chili, broken up
½ teaspoon turmeric
½ teaspoon asafetida
1 pound carrots, cut into sticks
½ teaspoon salt
½ teaspoon sugar
2 tablespoons lemon juice

Heat the oil and cook the seeds, chili, turmeric, and asafetida. Add the carrot sticks, the salt, and sugar. Stir-fry for 2 minutes longer, then add the lemon juice and cook for another minute.

CARROT AND RED PEPPER TERRINE

1 pound carrots
2 tablespoons olive oil
3 large red bell peppers, cored, seeded, and sliced
1 dried hot red chili, crushed
½ cup ricotta cheese
1 cup shredded sharp Cheddar cheese
3 eggs, beaten
1 tablespoon Dijon mustard
½ teaspoon asafetida
1 teaspoon sea salt

Trim and dice the carrots, so they are about the size of a thumbnail. Heat 1 tablespoon olive oil in a pan, throw in the carrots, and sweat for 5–10 minutes. Remove and reserve.

Heat the remaining olive oil in the pan, and cook the sliced bell peppers and crushed chili, covered, over a low flame for 20 minutes.

Leave to cool, then add the ricotta cheese, eggs, mustard, asafetida, and salt.

Line a terrine dish with well-buttered foil, leaving enough foil overhanging to use as handles. Pour in the terrine mixture, cover with buttered parchment paper, and set in a bain-marie. Bake in a preheated 425°F oven for 50–60 minutes, or until risen.

Let cool for 1 hour before unmolding, and refrigerate before serving. Serve on a bed of arugula or delicate salad leaves, accompanied by a sauce such as: pesto, or the celery sauce on page 220, or a bitter orange sauce (made in winter, when Seville oranges are in season), or a laver sauce. This last is made from a sea vegetable related to Japanese nori, sometimes available ready-cooked (and of excellent quality) in cans. Simply empty it into a pan, mix with a little butter or orange juice, and reheat.

CELERY

Apium graveolens var. *dulce*

I have eaten wild celery (*Apium graveolens*) in both Greece and Sicily, and you will find smallage, which is a cultivated wild variety, piled high in the markets of Italy and France. There they consider smallage by far the best type of celery to cook with, flavoring soups and stews with that very distinct aromatic savoriness. "It is an agreeable pursuit to roam the pleasant, wild countryside, picking plants here and there...should you find lovage or mountain celery— to be picked green, fresh and fragrant." The fourteenth-century herbal, *The Four Seasons of the House of Cerruti,* goes on to warn that the smell makes the head feel heavy and that it heats the blood.

Wild celery is certainly much more pungent in smell and taste, but also naturally a great deal more fibrous. The stalks are thin and very green, but it is a pleasure on a walk to pluck the stalks and suck the juice from them. I have never noticed a heaviness in the head as a result, but the plant is a diuretic.

The wild plant grows in marshy salt-impregnated ground near the seashore. It is a tough little plant, extending from Sweden to Egypt, from Britain to Asia, and has even been found in New Zealand and Tierra del Fuego. The ancients used it medicinally and for flavoring, yet also considered it a plant of funereal disposition. One type of celery is mentioned as standing as the doorkeeper to heaven; it was woven into garlands to adorn mummies in Egypt. Sturtevant reviews the evidence from the Ancient World and concludes there is not one shred of evidence for thinking that celery was used as food then or later. Yet Athenaeus mentions celery—obviously the wild kind, for he says it is similar to marshwort and likes to grow in water. We have a complaint by an Attic playwright, Epicharmus, that devouring grubs wind their way "in and out among the leaves of basil, lettuce and fragrant celery," which certainly implies the plant was cultivated in a Greek garden. If celery was this wild variety called smallage, and if it was extensively used in the kitchen, its seeds were certainly prized as much as its stalks. Pliny writes of the pleasure given by "celery stalks swimming in broth." These must have been young shoots, which would have been tender.

Apicius cooks it with green beans, leeks, rue, oil, and liquamen (see page 143); he reduces it to a purée with lovage, oregano, onion, and wine; he uses it to stuff a suckling pig, and in a vegetable stew with bulbs. He also suggests it makes a good laxative.

Luigi Alamanni, who wrote *La Coltivazione* (1546), six books in praise of the rustic life, mentions celery in passing, but praises the quality of Alexanders for the sweetness of the roots (see overleaf). However, sixty years later Castelvetro gives detailed directions on how to grow celery and how to blanch it in early autumn. This is obviously still smallage, for though he says the plants need to be planted out seven inches apart "for they grow quite large heads," today's celery would need twice that space. Castelvetro is an exception in that he recommends eating celery—although many horticulturalists speak of its cultivation and of the wild plant being transferred to gardens, it is, they stress, not for food but for medicinal use: celery was thought to purify the blood, and only its seeds were to be used as a flavoring. Cultivated smallage in France is called *céleri à couper* (celery for cutting and not necessarily for digging up, also called *petit céleri*) and is used in soups, stews, and broths.

The celery we now know did not appear until the eighteenth century. Obviously breeding it was a struggle, for John Ray mentions that in English gardens the cultivated form often degenerates back into smallage. By 1778, two sorts of celery are noted in England, one with hollow stalks and the other with the stalks solid. In Sweden, the richer classes preserved their celery in the cellars for winter use.

Whether smallage or cultivated celery, the distinct flavor had its passionate adherents. Used for centuries in soups and broths, by the beginning of the nineteenth century celery as we know it now was a firm favorite among vegetables in the kitchen.

Ude (cook to Louis XVI and then the English aristocracy), in 1824, gives three recipes—a purée, stewed celery with white sauce, and celery *à l'espagnole*, made with that Spanish sauce that had so recently swept France with its addictive popularity. The sauce is made with a great quantity of Serrano ham. One recipe for Spanish sauce required "twelve ducks, a ham, 2 bottles of old Madeira and 6 pounds

BELOW Harvesting celery

of fine truffles." It was Louis XV's cook, Menon, who made Spanish sauce a success in France; he always put a double amount of ham into it, which dominated every other ingredient.

Mrs. Beeton, a little later in the century, gives two recipes for celery sauce, the first flavored with spices (2 blades of mace might be overpowering) and herbs and finished with cream and lemon, the second without the herbs and cream. Mrs. Beeton also gives celery salad (which mixes the raw vegetable with either Stilton or Cheddar, both "masked" with mayonnaise), a celery soup, and three recipes for stewed celery. She ends with one for Celery Vinegar where ¼ ounce of celery seed is pounded in a mortar, covered with 1 pint of cold boiled vinegar, then left for 2 weeks to infuse, and finally strained. "This is frequently used in salads," she says.

From then on, celery was widely cultivated and was used extensively in the kitchen. In the 1930s no English banquet would have been complete without braised celery as one of the vegetables. Celery soup was also a favorite at dinner parties. From the same period Arabella Boxer quotes a celery sauce to be served with game. Sadly, we seem to have lost the art of making soup from celery (see below), though, unfortunately, canned celery soup seems to be always with us, like the ghost of cuisine past.

ALEXANDERS
Smyrnium olusatrum

So called because it is supposed to have originated in Macedonia, the kingdom of Alexander the Great, Alexanders also spread itself over Eastern Europe and Asia Minor. It was eaten with enjoyment in the Ancient World: the raw root was used as a salad, much as we now use fennel.

For centuries it enjoyed much popularity. It was mentioned by Theophrastus in 322 BC, and then by Pliny and Columella. The Romans brought it to Britain as one of their pot herbs, and it remained part of the kitchen garden until the eighteenth century. It appears in Charlemagne's list of vegetables to be grown on the estates of his ninth-century empire. Gerard, in 1597, says it "groweth in most places of

England." It still does, in colonies near the sea. A biennial, it is easy to recognize by its greenish-yellow umbelliferous flowerhead.

The whole plant is edible, though both leaves and stems become impossibly tough by midsummer, when mature. When young, the stems are delicious steamed or boiled. In *Wild Food*, Roger Phillips counsels peeling them like rhubarb, and even on youngish plants the knuckly leaf-joints may have to be cut off. In the U.S., in the nineteenth century, Alexanders was blanched by mounding soil up the stems, then was cooked and eaten like cardoon.

The Greek name *smyrnium* derives from myrrh and refers to its scented, myrrh-like taste. The flavor is stronger than that of celery, highly aromatic, and has a tinge of aniseed. Other names are "black lovage" (its black seeds were sold by apothecaries under the name "Macedonian parsley") and "horse parsley."

This is an important food plant that we now seem almost to have lost in cultivation. A few seedsmen list Alexanders under herbs, but enterprising gardeners could gather a few of the plentiful wild seeds to sow in their own gardens.

NUTRITION

With a vegetable as delicious as celery it is somewhat of a surprise to discover that there is little food value in the plant. But celery does raise the alkali levels in the body, so it is excellent for people who suffer from ailments like gout and rheumatism. It is also helpful for high blood pressure. Celery is a perfect food for dieters because it has no calories to speak of, and a few sticks chewed before or between meals can adequately take the edge off the appetite.

VARIETIES

Gardeners can grow "dirty celery" (see below) but most seed is for the "self-blanching" types that are available in supermarkets all year. Gardeners can also buy smallage seeds as "cutting celery" from some of the seedsmen who cater to minority tastes.

RIGHT Celery and celeriac

CHOOSING, PREPARING, AND COOKING

I cannot pretend to any liking for the celery that is sold in supermarkets; the taste is so inferior, it seems to me no pleasure at all to eat. The green celery grown in California and Spain, which is also enjoyed in Italy, is all water and no taste, to my palate. I want what they call "dirty celery" where I live, that is, celery that has been earthed up to be properly blanched.

This celery has the right nutty bite and is good for cooking as well as eating raw. The season is from November to February, too short for this wonderful vegetable. Failing "dirty celery," the self-blanching celery sometimes found in farmers' markets (not grown commercially) has more taste than supermarket celery, and is worth looking for.

To prepare celery, break off the outer stalks that are too fibrous or damaged to eat raw, and scrub the dirt off with a brush under running water. Keep trimmings and leaves for flavoring stocks and so on. Have a large pitcher filled with cold water, and as you clean the stalks put them in that. Shave the rough bits of celery off the core or heart (this has the best flavor) and leave it attached to the inner stalks. Eat raw dipped into sesame salt or use for cooking.

In the 1950s and '60s celery enjoyed a great vogue as an appetizer to be served with cocktails at parties. They were called "celery boats" and only the stalks with deep troughs were chosen. These were filled with a mixture of blue cheese and butter, or cream cheese and walnuts, and either left whole, in which case the guest waved a baton of stuffed celery around, or else sliced into bite-sized pieces.

CELERY SOUP

2 bunches of celery, trimmed
2 tablespoons butter
½ teaspoon white pepper
½ teaspoon celery salt
7½ cups vegetable stock
1½ cups light cream or thin sour cream
2–3 tablespoons minced cilantro

Wash the celery thoroughly, cutting off and throwing away all damaged parts, then slice the rest across.

Melt the butter in a large pan and sweat the celery with the pepper and celery salt. Add the stock and simmer for 20 minutes.

Leave to cool and then blend to a purée. There should be no fibers if only the inner stalks have been used and they have been cooked enough. But if there are fibers, press the soup through a coarse sieve.

Reheat gently, adding the light cream or sour cream, then sprinkle the cilantro on the surface of the soup before serving.

For *CELERY SAUCE* use the same method but add no stock. Let the chopped celery cook in the butter in a covered pan over a low heat for half an hour, then leave to cool and purée, adding a small wineglass of dry sherry and a tablespoon of heavy cream.

BRAISED CELERY WITH MUSHROOMS

2 bunches of celery
2 tablespoons butter
1 tablespoon olive oil
¼ pound mushrooms, sliced (1½ cups)
½ teaspoon asafetida
⅔ cup white wine
sea salt and freshly ground black pepper
1 teaspoon flour

Discard the damaged outer stalks of celery, then cut the leafy top half of the stalks away, leaving the bottom half and the heart. Slice each bunch in half and wash thoroughly, turning the heart upside down and rinsing under running water.

Melt the butter in a shallow baking dish and add the olive oil, mushrooms, and asafetida. Stir in the white wine and let it all bubble and cook for a moment. Season, then lay the 4 celery halves, flat-side down, in the sauce.

Braise in a preheated 375°F oven for 30 minutes. Take out of the oven and thicken the sauce with the flour (first mixed with a little cold water).

CELERIAC or
CELERY ROOT

Apium graveolens var. *rapaceum*

"There is another kind of celery called Capitatum, which is grown in the gardens of St. Agatha, Theano, and other places in Apulia, granted from nature and unseen and unnamed by the Ancients. Its bulb is spherical, nearly the size of a man's head. It is very sweet and odorous...." So writes Baptista Porta, a Neapolitan, in his *Villae*, published in Frankfurt in 1592. Porta goes on to say that if the soil is not rich the plant will degenerate and differ little from the usual smallage.

Where did such a close cousin of celery derive from, with its massive rounded roots (*rapaceum* means "turnip-like")? Porta was writing from the kingdom of Naples, which covered southern Italy. Apulia (now Puglia) was dotted with ports that had a thriving trade with Asia Minor and the Eastern Mediterranean. A little earlier, around 1573–5, a traveler in the East named Rauwolf had spoken of *eppich*, a root that was a delicacy eaten with salt and pepper, which he had tasted at Tripoli and Aleppo. Smallage had far too small and undistinguished a root to be treated as a delicacy; besides, it is too bitter to be eaten raw, so Rauwolf's observation is thought to be the first mention of celeriac or celery root. But it is not until 1729 that the plant is described in England by Stephen Switzer, a writer and seedsman in Westminster Hall; he admitted that he had never seen it, but he had been furnished with a supply of seeds for the plant from Alexandria.

Alas, though Switzer wrote a pamphlet, "Growing foreign vegetables," given away with the seeds, celeriac did not catch on in England, though it made some headway in both France and Germany. Certainly in France it gave its name to one particular dish, *celeriac rémoulade*, which I always think is overrated. There are better things to do with raw shredded vegetables than cover them in mayonnaise. Another classic way of treating celeriac is to purée it and mix this with the same amount of puréed potato. Many writers are ecstatic about this dish, but why, I ask myself, dissipate the fine flavor of celeriac with that of potato so that you have neither? The flavor of celeriac is too fine and subtle for such insensitive treatment.

It must have been Elizabeth David, in *French Provincial Cooking,* who first alerted the British to the existence of this vegetable. She it was, too, who first suggested the mixture of potato and celeriac, but on the same page she gives a simple and delicious recipe for celeriac stewed in butter (see below).

NUTRITION

Astonishingly, unlike celery, celeriac is a storehouse of energy, because the growing plant is high in carbohydrate and minerals, it has vitamin C and some B vitamins, and is very rich in iron.

PREPARING AND COOKING

Select smaller bulbs of celeriac, about the size of a tennis ball or a little larger, and buy them when the green leaf is vivid in color and has not faded. Larger celeriac bulbs tend to be woolly in the center, and most of it then has to be thrown away. Choose smooth-skinned bulbs for less waste. Peel the knobbly outer skin away and use the celeriac at once. If left, the flesh will oxidize and brown and look unsightly; if you do have to leave them for a few minutes, pop them in water acidulated with lemon juice.

One of the simplest methods of cooking celeriac is to cut them into chunks the size of a roasting potato, slip them into the roasting pan with the meat juices, and let them roast for half an hour. If made into a purée like rutabaga they tend to be a little watery, which is why, I surmise, the idea of mixing them with mashed potato came about. But they can be substituted for potato in all the gratins (see page 186).

Cream has always been an acceptable foil, though too rich, I suspect, for our tastes today. I tend to use celeriac in ways in which it does not combine with cream or mayonnaise. Once cut or sliced, celeriac cooks very quickly, far more quickly than celery. Mrs. David's timing for the following recipe—10 minutes—is, in my opinion, a mite too long, but such things depend so much on the heat of the burner and are impossible to prescribe precisely.

CELERIAC or CELERY ROOT *Apium graveolens* var. *rapaceum*

CELERIAC STEWED IN BUTTER

2 medium heads of celeriac
2 tablespoons butter
2 tablespoons olive oil
sea salt and freshly ground black pepper
1 teaspoon Dijon mustard
a few drops of wine vinegar
a little minced parsley

Peel the celeriac and slice thinly on a mandoline or in a food processor.

Heat the butter and olive oil in a wok or frying pan and throw in the celeriac slices. Cook them, moving them around, over quite a fierce heat for about 5 minutes, then add seasoning, the mustard, and wine vinegar. Stir-fry for 2 minutes longer, when they should be just browned at the edges.

Serve sprinkled with the parsley.

CELERIAC AND HALUMI SALAD

½ pound Greek halumi cheese
2 medium heads of celeriac
2 tablespoons olive oil
2 – 3 garlic cloves
1 dried hot red chili, crushed
sea salt and freshly ground black pepper
2 or 3 stalks of celery heart
lemon or lime juice
chopped cilantro or finely sliced scallions

Drain the halumi cheese and cut the slab into ½-inch cubes. Throw into a frying pan that is *without fat* and dry-fry until each cube begins to melt a little, turning them over so that each side browns. This will take a little longer than you think—about 5 minutes. When done, tip into a bowl and reserve.

Peel and trim the celeriac, then dice into cubes about the same size as the cheese. Heat the olive oil in a frying pan, add the garlic and chili, and throw in the celeriac. Season with salt and pepper and cook until the celeriac is just shaded with gold.

Tip into the bowl with the halumi. Slice the celery and add. Squeeze lemon or lime juice over all, mix thoroughly, and sprinkle with either cilantro or scallions. This makes an excellent first course served on a bed of salad leaves.

WARM CELERIAC SALAD

2 medium heads of celeriac
2 garlic cloves, minced
3 tablespoons walnut oil
1 teaspoon wine vinegar
1 teaspoon Dijon mustard
½ teaspoon sugar
sea salt and freshly ground black pepper
a little chopped parsley and scallion

Peel and trim the celeriac, then slice across in ¼-inch chunks. Slice these down into large French-fry size. Steam these for 5 minutes.

In the meantime, make the vinaigrette by mixing all the rest of the ingredients. Toss the warm celeriac pieces in the vinaigrette and serve immediately, either as a first course on a bed of salad leaves or as a salad after the main course.

STUFFED CELERIAC WITH MUSHROMS AND GINGER

2 medium heads of celeriac
2 or 3 tablespoons olive oil
3 tablespoons grated fresh gingerroot
1 fresh hot red or green chili, finely sliced
¼ pound mushrooms, sliced (1½ cups)
¼ pound oyster mushrooms, sliced
1 red or orange bell pepper, cored, seeded, and sliced very thinly
1 wineglass of Madeira, marsala, or sweet sherry
sea salt and freshly ground black pepper
a little cilantro or scallion, finely sliced

Peel and trim the celeriac, cut in half, and square off the base of each half so it sits firmly, cut-side up. Hollow out a circular portion in each half, about

RIGHT Celeriac and halumi salad

½ inch deep and 2 inches in diameter (though this depends on the size of the original head). Chop the pieces taken out and reserve.

Heat the oil in a pan and brown the 4 scooped-out halves, then remove and place them in a baking dish. Bake at 375°F for 30 minutes.

In the meantime, throw the ginger and chili into the oil, followed by the chopped celeriac and the mushrooms. Toss until they are almost cooked, about 4 minutes. Then add the sliced bell pepper and cook for 2 minutes longer. Pour in the Madeira and season. Mix thoroughly, then take off the heat.

Spoon this mixture into the 4 celeriac containers, garnish with the cilantro or scallion, and set on a bed of leaves. Serve warm, though it is also unexpectedly good when cold.

FENNEL

Foeniculum vulgare var. *azoricum*

Florence fennel, sweet fennel, or *finocchio dulce* is the white bulb that we eat raw or cooked; in Italy, in the past, it was also served as a dessert, with the fruit and cheese. There is no difference in flavor between the bulb, the leaves, and the seeds—all taste very pleasantly of aniseed in varying degrees of strength. There is also little difference between the plant we use as the herb and the one whose bulb we eat. So it is often difficult to distinguish in the past which fennel was eaten.

Like many gardeners before me, I once attempted to grow the bulb fennel and found it turned into the herb fennel. No one had told me that the bulb has to be harvested very early in its growth; the stalks must not grow more than a foot high, for the bulb is in fact the expanding leaf stems, and once they grow above ground there is no bulb to speak of. The plant is also difficult to grow in Britain's climate; it needs warmth and rain to begin with, and while we have plenty of the latter, unfortunately we seldom have the former at the same time.

Fennel as an herb was certainly one of the first to be cultivated in the early Assyrian and Babylonian gar-

dens (others were cumin, sesame, mint, basil, coriander, anise, thyme, asafetida, bay, arugula, saffron, and sage). All of these and more were later grown by the Greeks and Romans. As a seasoning, fennel was one of the most popular herbs in the Ancient World. The new stems of fennel were considered a great delicacy and were earthed up or blanched to make them tender. Columella gives a recipe for preserving stems and shoots—among them cabbage sprouts and fennel—in brine and vinegar. He also uses fennel seed with toasted sesame, anise, and cumin mixed with puréed dried fig and wrapped in fig leaves and then stored in jars to preserve it.

Pliny regards fennel as very useful "for seasoning a great many dishes." He also makes the curious observation that snakes are very fond of the plant. Archestratus (the fourth-century BC Greek gourmet) tells us that fennel was placed in the brine with olives when curing. Indeed, it appears in nearly every herb mixture.

Fennel seeds were immensely popular from the earliest times, used both medicinally and as flavoring. They were constantly mentioned in Anglo-Saxon medical recipes and were a favorite plant of Charlemagne. Fennel shoots, fennel water, and fennel seed are all mentioned in an ancient record of Spanish agriculture of AD 961. John Evelyn, in *Acetaria,* talks of the "sweetest fennel of Bolognia" which is aromatic, hot, and dry. He says it "expels wind, sharpens the sight, and recreates the brain; especially the tender Umbella and Seed-pods." Evelyn recommends eating the stems peeled and dressed like celery and tells us that the Italians eat the blanched stem, which they call *cartucci,* all winter long. But did they know and consume the bulb? Did the Romans themselves grow it? Sturtevant considers *finocchio* in the form of sweet fennel to be a late development, and points to Stephen Switzer's mention of it in 1729 as having just been introduced to England, but it was still rare in 1765. It appears a little later, in a catalogue of 1778, as Azorian Dwarf or finocchio, and again in 1783 as Sweet Azorian fennel, which surely implies that it was cultivated in the Azores and its seeds exported. However, it remained a rare vegetable, though the herb fennel, its seeds and leaves were used extensively as a sauce for fish.

Finocchio really only became a regular sight in greengrocers within the last thirty years, though it has been used in Italy ever since it first appeared. Vincenzo Corrado gives eleven recipes for the bulb in his *Il Cuoco Galante*, published in Naples in 1778. Cooked in oil with anchovies, cooked in milk with cinnamon and grated nutmeg, cooked in capon stock, served with a shrimp coulis, there seems no end to Corrado's invention. He must have loved the vegetable, and no wonder: it is amazingly refreshing, both raw and cooked.

The seeds are now used commercially in a multiplicity of ways, to flavor candy, gum, and liqueurs as well as being used in savory and sweet dishes in the domestic kitchen. In India, the seeds feature in the flavoring of many dishes. Toasted seeds are often offered after the meal as part of a *digestif*.

NUTRITION

Fennel contains oil and protein, and is high in vitamins A and E, calcium, and potassium. Fennel and ginger make a good digestive tea. Fennel is low in calories and high in water content.

PREPARING AND COOKING

Buy the smaller bulbs as there is less wastage. If there are only large bulbs available, you can always boil the discarded tough outer skins for stock and soups, while the feathery leaves can be chopped and added as a fresh herb to sauces or stuffings.

Once the bulb has been trimmed of these outer tough leaves, it can be sliced whichever way you like—across in rings or downward. I prefer the latter and simply serve the sliced bulb with oil and lemon as a separate salad. In a mixed salad it is a treat to discover a slice of the anise-flavored root. It also looks good as part of a mixed selection of crudités. The sliced bulb is so attractive that to serve it raw any other way, for example shredded, seems to me one of the great culinary crimes.

If you wish to use the leaves in fish cooking, they should be soaked in water first and then wrapped around the fish before the fish is baked or char-

LEFT Fennel niçoise (overleaf)

grilled. It is a good thing to fill the cleaned fish with the chopped leaves and stems to flavor it further.

The cooked bulb goes well with Parmesan, tomato, olives, and garlic, and it also makes a marvelously refreshing soup.

FENNEL SOUP

4 bulbs of fennel, trimmed and chopped
2 tablespoons butter
1 large onion, sliced
1 tablespoon fennel seed
2 quarts vegetable stock
sea salt and freshly ground black pepper
1¼ cups light cream or thin sour cream

Reserve the green fronds of the fennel for garnish. Heat the butter and throw in the onion, fennel seed, and sliced fennel. Cook for a moment or two, then add the vegetable stock and simmer for 20 minutes. Season to taste. Leave to cool, then blend to a purée.

Reheat gently, adding the cream or sour cream. Before serving, garnish with the chopped leaves.

FENNEL FRITTERS

This makes a tasty and unusual appetizer or snack.

2 bulbs of fennel, trimmed
oil for frying, preferably olive oil
for the batter:
1 egg
¾ cup all-purpose flour
a pinch of sea salt
⅓ cup water or milk, or ⅓ cup of each

First make the batter: stir the egg into the flour and salt, then add the water or milk. (If you use milk, the batter will be thicker and heavier; with just water, the batter is more like a Japanese tempura batter.) This batter can be used at once.

Slice the fennel lengthwise into ½-inch pieces, dip them in the batter, and fry in hot oil, turning once, until golden brown. Drain on paper towels for a moment, then serve at once.

FENNEL *Foeniculum vulgare* var. *azoricum*

FENNEL IN A WHITE WINE SAUCE

2 or 3 bulbs of fennel, trimmed and quartered
1 wineglass of dry white wine
1 tablespoon butter
1 teaspoon flour
sea salt and freshly ground black pepper

Reserve the green leaves, and poach the quartered fennel in a little water, no more than 1 inch deep, for about 5 minutes. Remove the fennel and reduce the water by half. Add the white wine and bring back to a boil. Season. Mix the butter and flour into a *beurre manié* and stir in to thicken the sauce.

Pour the sauce over the fennel quarters, sprinkle the chopped green herb over, and serve.

VARIATION

Place the fennel in its thickened sauce in a baking dish and sprinkle ¼ cup of grated Parmesan cheese over the top. Bake just until the cheese has melted and the sauce is bubbling.

FENNEL NIÇOISE

2–3 tablespoons olive oil
1 can of anchovies
5 garlic cloves, sliced
3 or 4 bulbs of fennel, trimmed and quartered
5 large tomatoes, skinned and chopped
12–16 pitted black olives
freshly ground black pepper

Heat the olive oil in a pan and throw in the anchovies and garlic, then the quartered fennel. Turn the vegetables and cook for a moment, then add the chopped tomatoes and the olives. Put a lid on the pan and leave to simmer for 15 minutes, when the fennel should be cooked. Season with black pepper.

PARSNIP

Pastinaca sativa

The wild parsnip was introduced to Europe from the Caucasus; it grew also in North America, and Darwin found it in South America, growing around Buenos Aires. The root of the wild plant is aromatic, white, and sweet, which is why it was so popular from the earliest times—although in the early records the parsnip is confused with the carrot, and one is never too sure which root is meant. Like all plants in the wild there is a great variety of types and sizes. At some point a fleshier-rooted form must have appeared.

The Emperor Tiberius had such a fondness for parsnips that he had them brought every year from Gelduba upon the Rhine, where they are said to have grown to perfection. Rome brought the cultivated parsnip to Britain and Gaul, along with carrots, turnips, radishes, and skirrets. Pliny observed that both radishes and skirrets grew better in Britain, and so, one imagines, did all these root vegetables. Certainly the parsnip was a feature in the crops grown by all the Anglo-Saxon farmers after the end of the Roman Empire.

The parsnip had many uses, not only as another root to be stewed in the one-pot meal. It was valued for its sugar content—crushed and the liquid drawn off, it was then boiled and used as honey. The whole root, like the wild parsnip, could also be used for fermented drinks, and a wine or beer was made from it. It was also used to make jam or marmalade and in puddings and tarts.

Before the potato was introduced to the Old World (and certainly long before it found acceptance in culinary circles), parsnip was the main starchy vegetable to be served with the meal, being roasted in the pan beside the meat or beneath it. John Evelyn's buttered parsnips were dusted with ginger for added sweetness. A popular Elizabethan dish was fritters of skirret and parsnip in butter sprinkled with sugar. But Evelyn, ever resourceful, also suggests boiling the parsnip and serving it cold as a winter salad with oil and vinegar. He adds that it is more nourishing than the turnip. Hannah Glasse gives a recipe for salt cod with hard-boiled eggs melted in butter and "parsnips boiled beat and fine with butter and cream."

Why are the French so dedicated in their dislike of the parsnip—*panais*? Did they not use it in the past? The Goodman of Paris sowed parsnip seed in his garden, yet the parsnip in France is used in *pot-au-feu* and little else. You will certainly never be served roasted parsnips, for they always prefer turnips.

SKIRRET
Sium sisarum

Skirret produces clusters of roots similar in flavor to parsnips. An ancient plant, native to China, it was known in Europe in Roman times, and continued to be grown and eaten until superseded in recent centuries by other improved root crops such as carrots and parsnips. The sixteenth-century name, "sister," was applied to the carrot as well as to skirrets; in France it was sometimes known as *carotte blanche*. Calling it "sisarum," Evelyn describes it in his *Acetaria* as seldom eaten raw, but "being boiled, stewed, roasted under the embers, baked in pies, whole, sliced or in pulp, is very acceptable to all palates." He also commends it for not provoking wind. The fleshy tubers no bigger than a little finger are sweet and floury but perhaps something of a chore to clean. Seed is available for the home gardener, but the vegetable—well known up to about a hundred years ago—is almost never seen in stores today.

NUTRITION

Parsnips are quite high in vitamin A, some of the B vitamins, and vitamin C. They also have calcium, phosphorus, and potassium, as well as plenty of other minerals. Of course, if they are boiled to a pulp, a lot of this nutrition is lost, but with circumspect cooking methods at least half is retained.

CHOOSING AND COOKING

Once parsnips have had a frost the starch in the roots turns to sugar, hence parsnips should always be eaten in midwinter. Gardeners can leave them in the ground and dig them when needed. Try to choose small parsnips; the larger ones tend to have a woody center that has to be cut out. This feature is prominent in the wild parsnips. Small parsnips also need little or no peeling, but just trimming.

For roasting they need to be parboiled for 2 minutes—no more. But I prefer not to cook parsnips whole; cut them up into chunks about 3 inches long, either halving or quartering the thick end, depending on how big the parsnip is.

After the parboiling, drain them well, then put the parsnip chunks into the roasting pan around the bird or meat. They will be done in 30 minutes. I must confess, though, to liking my parsnips and roasted spuds well done—that is, turned a deep golden brown and highly crispy—so I have often left parsnips to roast for up to an hour. They come out crisp on the outside with a little sweet gooey softness in the center. Very satisfactory.

I must say that I am no devotee of the plain boiled parsnip, even with lots of butter or cream. But glazed parsnips are quite another dish, and these have been neglected in the repertoire of cuisine, ever since medieval and Tudor cooking where sweetened parsnips featured as a favorite aspect of many meat dishes. The mainstream of parsnip cooking appears to be rural English (the Scots and Irish both prefer rutabaga and potatoes), where there are dishes many and various. Parsnips here are often, one suspects, a main dish baked with a little bacon, or boiled with some pickled pork. There are numerous recipes for parsnip cakes, fritters, soup, and wine. In her *English Cookery Book* published in 1943, farmer's wife Lucie G. Nicoll tells us: "The recipes are a selection of the best from many thousands I have encountered in twenty-five years of managing a farm household." She goes on to talk of how many generations back some of these recipes go, for all were handed down. On the overleaf I list a few—excellent, basic, and tasty.

I have not included Mrs. Nicoll's recipe for parsnip soup, because in *Good Things* Jane Grigson gives, in my opinion, the best recipe of all, in which she adds curry powder at the beginning of cooking. Because of its sweetness, I think parsnip needs spices to offset and counter the sugar. All the other recipes that mix it with leeks, for example, in a kind of variation of

Vichyssoise, are too sweet for my taste. Instead of curry powder, you could use ginger, hot chili, and lime, which works very well—as in the recipe for parsnip molds you will find overleaf.

PARSNIP CAKES

Boil 3 or 4 parsnips in salted water until quite soft. When cool, mash them with a beaten egg and a few bread crumbs, and season with pepper and salt. Make into small patties, roll in egg and crumbs, and fry to a golden brown. Sufficient for 4 or 5 people.

PARSNIP FRITTERS (1)

Serve these with chops. First, boil parsnips in salted water till tender, then cut into rings ½ inch thick. Dip in frying batter, deep-fry in hot oil, sprinkle with salt, and serve very hot.

PARSNIP FRITTERS (2)

Cut some parsnips into small pieces, then boil until they are soft. Mash them with a fork, then add a little chopped parsley, onion, and any scraps of cold meat, also a few drops of relish. Mix all together and form into fritters. Coat in crumbs and deep-fry until they are a golden brown.

GLAZED PARSNIPS WITH MARMALADE

1½ pounds small parsnips, trimmed
2 tablespoons butter
1 heaped tablespoon sugar
sea salt and freshly ground black pepper
1 heaped tablespoon bitter marmalade

Quarter the parsnips and slice into 3-inch chunks (no need to peel). Blanch them in boiling salted water for 3 minutes. Drain well.

RIGHT clockwise from left: Parsnip fritters, carrot and red pepper terrine (page 216), parsnip cakes

Melt the butter and the sugar in a baking dish and place the parsnips in this, turning them over so that they are well covered. Season and add the marmalade. Place the dish in an oven preheated to 375°F and bake for 20–30 minutes, or until they have browned and look well glazed. Excellent with game or ham.

PARSNIP MOLDS

1 pound parsnips, peeled, trimmed, and cut into chunks
2 tablespoons butter
3 tablespoons grated fresh gingerroot
1 fresh hot green or red chili, chopped small
1 egg
1 cup heavy cream
sea salt and freshly ground black pepper

Boil the parsnips in a little salted water for 5 minutes, then drain well and reserve.

Melt the butter, add the ginger and chili, and cook over a low heat for a few minutes.

Blend the parsnip, butter, spices, egg, cream, and seasoning together and pour into individual ramekins. Cook in an oven preheated to 375°F for 20–30 minutes, or until the center has risen.

Leave to cool in the ramekins, then unmold and serve with a tomato or red bell pepper coulis and garnished with a few salad leaves.

PARSLEY

Petroselinum crispum

Where would the cuisines of the world be without this ubiquitous herb? Not only does it give its name to the family, but—with its gastronomic companion, garlic—it is among the very oldest flavorings stemming from the Mediterranean area. In addition, its general use in cooking makes necessary its appearance in these pages.

Parsley and rue often bordered Greek gardens. The victors in the Isthmian games would be crowned with chaplets of parsley, possibly because it was said that Hercules crowned himself with the herb after killing the Nemean lion (he choked it in his arms). In battle, the warriors in Homer fed their horses with it, while wreaths would also be made from it to be laid upon the tombs of the dead. All this reverence and esteem clung to the herb, so that by the seventeenth century Culpeper thinks parsley very comfortable to the stomach and good for wind, and Aubrey (aware of its ancient symbolism) mentions that only the tops of the leaves may be admitted to the table, for it is more proper to be used in forcemeat stuffings for fowl. He approves of it in medicinal drops, however. The ancients were rather more enthusiastic than Aubrey gives them credit for. Dioscorides gave parsley its name; Pliny said that sauces and salads should never be without it; and Horace decorates his dining room with roses and parsley.

The Romans knew five different kinds of parsley, but possibly they are not the same kinds we know today. The most familiar to us is the curly kind or moss-curled parsley (this is the one to use for deep-frying in whole sprigs, see below). It grows better in the northern climes than in the Mediterranean, because it will survive colder temperatures and lack of sun. It is a great pity that this type has been demoted to the role of garnish and is often left ignominiously at the side of the plate uneaten.

The least known variety is Neapolitan or Giant Italian parsley, which is grown as much for its stems as it is for its leaf. It grows in southern Italy and was little known outside that area until this century. The stems of the plant are hollow, and they are blanched and eaten like celery. Pliny refers to a Macedonian parsley or black parsley of which the stalks could be eaten, and it is thought that the Neapolitan parsley could well be the same one. The other three parsleys look a little similar: the plain-leaf, the fern-leaf, and parsley root or Hamburg parsley. The flavors of all five types are broadly similar, but with slight differences—yet not different enough to suggest one type against another should be used in any particular dish.

PARSLEY ROOT
or HAMBURG PARSLEY
Petroselinum crispum var. *tuberosum*

Parsley root had a great vogue in the eighteenth century. Miller, in his *Gardener's Dictionary* of 1771, says: "This is now pretty commonly sold in the London markets, the roots being six times as large as the common parsley. This sort was many years cultivated in Holland before the English gardeners could be prevailed upon to sow it. I brought the seeds of it from thence in 1727, but they refused to accept it, so that I cultivated it several years before it was known in the markets."

Now the only chance of eating it is to grow it in your own garden. Once dug up the root looks very like parsnip, but tastes more like celeriac, yet sweeter and more aromatic.

If you are lucky enough to grow parsley root in your garden, then clean the root and treat it like parsnip. Chopped into chunks and boiled in a little water with a pinch of salt, it will cook within about 4 minutes. Drain and toss with a little butter.

MEDICINAL

The leaves of parsley are dried to make parsley tea, and the seeds of the plant are used for the extraction of its oil, Apiol. Parsley has a carminative, tonic, and aperient action; it is also a diuretic; and a poultice of the fresh leaves has been used to relieve stings and bites from poisonous insects. The chewing of parsley leaves is suggested to cleanse the breath and to keep the skin healthy.

NUTRITION

The leaves are tremendously high in carotene and potassium, calcium, and vitamin C. They also have small amounts of vitamin E, riboflavin, and thiamin.

CHOOSING AND STORING

Parsley has a short shelf life, and it is best to use it quickly after purchasing or picking. Plunge the stems in a glass of water, keep it in a shady part of the kitchen, and use within three days. Parsley sold in airtight plastic bags seems to keep fairly well in the salad drawer of the refrigerator, but not for more than two days. Even then you might still find a soggy strand lurking among the foliage. Parsley is also sold chopped and frozen and this is an excellent standby to keep in the freezer, if you intend to use parsley for a sauce or to add to a hot dish. This is a good way of freezing your own glut of parsley if you are unable to keep it growing through the winter.

COOKING

We tend to think of cooking with parsley only in terms of chopping it and using it in sauces or adding it to stews or vegetable dishes. To my mind, for example, fava beans in parsley sauce is one combination made in heaven. But sprigs of curled parsley can be deep-fried. DEEP-FRIED PARSLEY may sound unlikely, but try it—the result, I promise, will astonish you. The sprigs need only about 5 seconds in hot oil, when they will turn dark green and frizzly. Take them out and blot on paper towels, then eat at once. They are so good that they are best served as appetizers. Take this idea one step further by dipping the sprigs into a light and seasoned tempura batter before deep-frying: they will need a little longer to cook, say 12 seconds. You can serve these with other tempura vegetables, if you like, or as an accompaniment with fish. The more densely curled the parsley is, the better it is for cooking. Never try to cook flat-leaf parsley or parsley root—it will just go limp, then shrink to a blackened speck.

When using chopped parsley in a sauce, make the sauce first and add the parsley only at the last minute so that it simply heats through. Parsley must never be cooked, just heated—except when fried as above.

PARSLEY *Petroselinum crispum*

ROCK SAMPHIRE

Crithmum maritimum

This plant, much loved in antiquity and highly popular until the eighteenth century, can be found only in the wild. It grows on rocky coastlines from the Crimea to Ireland; certainly it is still flourishing all around the coasts of Britain and France. The samphire that is a popular wild food (also called glasswort or salicornia) is marsh samphire and is a completely different plant (see page 58). The popularity of rock samphire (sometimes called sea fennel) in the nineteenth century was so great that demand outstripped supply, so marsh and golden samphire were substituted for it in the London markets. Customers found this both annoying and disappointing, hence both samphires declined in popularity. Also, as the urban sprawl continued to encroach upon the countryside, people turned toward cultivation in their back yards and allotments and forgot about gathering wild foods from the countryside. It takes only one generation for such knowledge, passed on for thousands of years, to be forgotten forever.

Golden samphire (*Inula crithmoides*) also grows in salt marshes and on sea cliffs, but it is rare, plentiful only on the Isle of Sheppey, which is conveniently near for the London markets. The young branches of golden samphire were mixed in with rock samphire. Green writes in deep resentment in his *Universal Herbal* (1832): "It is a villainous imposition because this plant has none of the warm aromatic taste of the true samphire."

Pliny wrote that Theseus had a meal with samphire before leaving to fight the Minotaur. Both the Greeks and the Romans used samphire in salads, sometimes lightly steamed, and they also took it in wine to clear the complexion and give a happy expression. The name derives from Saint Peter, though the French originally called it *perce-pierre*—"rock piercer."

It has, according to Gerard, "many fat and thicke leaves somewhat like those of the lesser Purslane, of a spicie taste, with a certain softnesse." Lady Fettiplace, in her book (1604), gives a recipe for pickling samphire, along with other pickling recipes for items as various as purslane and broom buds.

It was John Evelyn's favorite vegetable. He talks of its ability to sharpen the appetite, preferable to other herbs and salads. Evelyn cultivated it with seeds from France. He observed that the cultivated kind did not pickle as well, because it had a more tender leaf and stem, but for salads there was nothing better. Here is Evelyn's recipe for pickling samphire:

"Let it be gathered about Michaelmas or in the spring and put two or three hours into a brine of water and salt, then into a clean tinned brass pot with three parts of strong white wine vinegar and one part of water and salt or as much as will cover the sampier, keeping the vapour from issuing out by pushing down the pot lid, and so hang it over the fire for half an hour only. Being taken off let it remain cover'd till it be cold and then put it up into small barrels or jars with the liquor and some fresh vinegar, water and salt, and thus it will keep very green. If you be near the sea that water will supply the place of brine. This is the Dover Receit."

What kept the color bright green was the copper salts (certainly toxic) produced by the vinegar reacting with the brass of the pot.

Shakespeare mentions "half way down/Hangs ore that gathers samphire, dreadful trade." Dorothy Hartley confesses to being puzzled by this quotation, for Shakespeare—being sound on food—would be bound to know that samphire also grows on shingle. But gathering samphire from the face of steep cliffs was well known. Robert Turner wrote in 1664 about samphire-gatherers on the cliffs of the Isle of Wight, where it is incredibly dangerous to gather, "yet many adventure it, though they buy their sauce with the price of their lives." The Lord of the Manor of Freshwater charged a yearly rent from the cliff-gatherers, who would find gull eggs and samphire on the green shelves in the 600-foot cliffs. The Islanders made a sauce out of samphire and butter, but most was pickled—much of it kept for themselves; the rest they sent to London. But this was not the only island to export its samphire. Thomas Cogan, in *The Haven of Health* (1584), says that on the Isle of Man they also pickled samphire in casks of brine. In the nineteenth century, wholesalers would pay as much as four shillings a bushel for it.

Though scarcity in both coastal and inland areas caused the popularity of rock samphire to decline at the end of the nineteenth century, not everyone forgot it. Dorothy Hartley writes engagingly as ever of the effect of samphire upon some people:

"Samphire grows on rough shingle; there is a lot on the pebble ridge at Bideford. You can smell it before you find it. Among all the delicate subtle scents of the country, samphire holds unique place. People who dislike it say it smells of sulphur, but others sniff it ecstatically, and seem to make themselves slightly drunk on the aroma. Then, surprisingly, someone who dislikes it the first time will try again, and find they like it extremely well! It's the most complete puzzle—I have never yet met anyone who was neutral to it. There is something 'magic' about samphire.

"You can sometimes buy it in country markets, but the liking for it is so uncontrolled that you find some families—miles away from the sea—getting it sent to them, as a delicacy, while the rest of the community look on in bewilderment. Try it; for if you like it you will have added a very pungent, enjoyable, and health-giving item to your diet."

She goes on to quote a recipe of 1650 for Samphire Hash. This was pickled cucumbers, capers, samphire, lemon, pepper, and nutmeg boiled in strong stock with a little vinegar and thickened with egg yolk. It was used as a sauce for mutton, and was garnished with more samphire and barberries.

It was a great thrill one Christmas to find rock samphire growing on the Mediterranean island of

ABOVE Rock samphire growing on a cliff face

Gozo. Samphire flourishes on those high rocky cliffs; great shrubs of it go unnoticed and unharvested by tourists and Gozitans alike. Recently I found it growing in profusion all over the rocks at Antibes, again entirely ignored by both tourists (there, one supposes, to have their palates stimulated) and French gourmets. I picked a huge bunch and later that evening we had a feast. How sad it is that we have forgotten how to feed ourselves from the wild.

Samphire flourishes all through the summer months. If you spot it on isolated beaches or rocky coasts in Britain or northern Europe, pick the leaves and steam for five minutes or poach in boiling water for three, then serve with a garlicky vinaigrette or a lemon butter sauce.

ROCK SAMPHIRE *Crithmum maritimum*

A
MISCELLANY
OF
VEGETABLES

Gramineae

CORN *Zea mays*

Malvaceae

OKRA *Hibiscus esculentus*

Convolvulaceae

SWEET POTATO *Ipomoea batatas*

Araceae

TARO *Colocasia esculenta*

Dioscoreaceae

YAM *Dioscorea* spp.

Lauraceae

AVOCADO *Persea americana*

The miscellany of vegetables in this chapter do not belong to one botanical family but are the single representatives of a series of different families. They are native to tropical, subtropical, or warm temperate regions. Apart from taro and yams, which are normally imported, all of the others can be and are grown by home gardeners, according to climate and other cultivation requirements.

THE GRASS FAMILY

Gramineae

Grasses were the first food plants to be cultivated by human kind, probably by accident. Wild grasses flourish on poor soil, among stones or in gravel; they like a dry and a wet season (humidity is too lush for them); they need to germinate quickly in spring rain and to have their life cycle concluded with mature seeds ready to fall before the ground thoroughly dries in the height of summer. They, therefore, colonized the bare ground and rubbish heaps provided by early peoples. Because they had evolved large food reserves in their seeds, these were found to be good to eat.

Economically they are the most important group of flowering plants because of these nutritious grains. Grasses also provide food for all herbivorous animals, including the domesticated ones, and shelter for many other creatures that were eaten. Sugar cane has been grown since the earliest times and is still a highly important economic crop due to the world's insatiable desire for sweetness. There are, among the Gramineae, two vegetables, one of which since 1492 has assumed a major part in the world economy—maize or corn. The other vegetable is bamboo, which I have omitted from this book because it is still only readily available in canned form in the West.

CORN

Zea mays

The first record of corn, or maize, is in the sacred book of the Quicke Indians of Guatemala in the eighth century. Here the story is told of the discovery of white and yellow maize, which the gods ate so that man became strong. Here, too, is the first reference to corn being the Indians' first mother and father, the source of life. It was so much esteemed that in the palace gardens of the Incas there were decorations of gold and silver maize with all the grains, stems, spikes, and leaves depicted in fine detail.

Columbus first saw corn in Cuba in November, 1492, noting "a kind of grain called *maiz*, of which was made a very well-tasted flour." The early explorers soon discovered that corn came in various colors—red, white, yellow, blue, and even black—but blue corn was the most valued. They were also impressed by the Indians' agriculture. Diego Columbus once estimated that a corn, bean, and squash plantation he walked through was 18 miles long. In Peru, it was noticed that in each hole three grains of maize were sown, along with a fish head to provide slow-release fertilizer. Thomas Hariot, reporting on the first English settlement in Virginia, talks of corn as a grain of "marvelous great increase." He observed that the corn was sown early, with three dead fish laid over the heaped-up mound; beans were planted later and would twine around the corn stem. The first settlers learned not only how to grow corn but when to pick it and how to cook it—discovering how much more delicious corn is when picked and cooked immediately, before the sugar turns to starch. They learned how to cook corn, beans, and peas together "by boyling them all to pieces into a broth," and also noted that "sometimes they bruse or pound them in a mortar and thereof make loaves or lumps of dowishe bread." Sometimes this bread contained dried huckleberries. It is interesting to note how much traditional American cooking owes to the Indians, even the names: succotash (*misickquatash*), pone bread and blueberry muffins, hominy or grits (*rocka hominy*), and samp (*nasaump*)—a kind of meal pottage made of unparched corn, which for years the settlers ate as both breakfast and supper with milk and butter added. It was also called hasty pudding. The corn mush could be left to cool in a loaf pan, then sliced, dipped in egg yolk and crumbs, and fried in bacon fat.

Sturtevant says, "the culture of corn was general in the New World at the time of the discovery; it reigned from Brazil to Canada, from Chile to California; it was grown extensively in fields; and it had produced many varieties—always an indication of antiquity of culture. It furnished food in its grain, and, from its stalks, sugar to the Peruvians, honey to the Mexicans and a kind of wine or beer to all the natives of the tropics."

It was a different story in Europe. Taken to Spain by Columbus, corn took some time—until 1610—to move to Sicily and from there to the rest of Italy. However, by 1650 Italy had taken to it in a big way. They, too, made a porridge out of the grains (they had originally used millet, spelt, or chick pea flour). They, too, let the porridge cool before slicing and frying or grilling it; in northern Italy, *polenta* is still eaten with enthusiasm.

But where the poor lived off corn and nothing else, they inevitably became ill. The symptoms of *mal de rosa*, as Philip V's doctor, Gaspar Casal, called it, included a reddening and roughness of the skin across the arms and face, accompanied by general lassitude, headaches, diarrhea, and insanity. The poor of Andalusia first showed the symptoms, then northern Italy, followed by France, Hungary, and Romania. It was noticed that the spread of pellagra occurred wherever corn was cultivated. If corn was only part of the diet, with vegetables, eggs, and fish, health was retained. It was where corn comprised all of the diet that pellagra inevitably followed. Yet millions of people in Mexico and the American South ate little else, and pellagra was unknown there—that is, up to the beginning of this century. By 1912, there were thousands of cases of pellagra in the Southern cotton-growing areas. What was different in Mexico or in the early 1900s in the American South?

First, the Indians would eat their corn with beans, squash, and a pinch of wood ash in the pot. The last, it was believed, softened the skins of the corn kernels

ABOVE Corn for polenta

and made them easier to grind and digest. Ash in lime, or alkali as we now know it, releases the niacin and lysine in the corn which would otherwise have been unavailable to the human body. Also, beans and squash complement corn nutritionally and turn it into a staple food.

In 1905, a cereal mill called the Beall Degerminator started producing factory-refined corn. It removed the germ that contained the oil so that the mush or porridge which the poor now ate was nutritionally inadequate. It took many years for this to be discovered; the story is in *The Food Factor* by Barbara Griggs.

If you are intrigued by the story of corn, read Margaret Visser's fascinating *Much Depends on Dinner*. Here you will learn that you cannot buy anything in the North American supermarket that has been untouched by corn. Meat and milk are largely corn, because livestock and poultry are fattened on corn-stems and corn; frozen meat and fish have a corn-starch coating, the golden coloring of soft drinks and puddings is corn, and so on, while corn oil, corn syrup, and cornstarch all permeate other foods.

NUTRITION

The fresher the corn is, the more nutritious; it is then a good supply of vitamins A, B, and C, and is high in phosphorus, potassium, and sulfur. It is a good source of starch in the diet, but the protein is of lower nutritional value than that of other cereals. The yellower the corn, the more carotene it contains.

VARIETIES

Five different types of maize or Indian corn known to the Native Americans are still grown today. Pop and flint corn have high protein content and a hard, waxy starch. Dent corn, with a soft starch that produces a dent in the kernel, is grown for animal feed. Flour corn is grown now by the Indians in South and Central America only for their own use; it is low in protein, has a waxy starch, and is easily ground by hand. Both flour and flint corn may have variegated kernels.

Sweet corn, the fifth type, is a variety that stores more sugar than starch, which is why it tastes so good eaten fresh from the cob without the processing that the coarser corns require.

Native to subtropical Central America, corn needs just the right combination of moisture and warmth to swell and ripen the grain, but breeders have produced a range of different types of hybrid corn, adapted to growing conditions from the subtropics to high mountain deserts. These include corn engineered to stay sweet a long time after picking.

CHOOSING

If you grow corn, you will know that there is nothing like the picking and cooking of the first ripe ear. The sweetness of the kernels sings on the palate, and you know that Mark Twain was right when he said a cauldron of boiling water should be set up in the midst of the corn field so that the ears can be thrown straight in as they are picked and shucked. (Butter, preferably unpasteurized, is the only accompaniment for such a feast, with a little sea salt and a hefty grind of the pepper mill.)

BELOW Polenta served with pigeon breasts in a red-currant sauce

A MISCELLANY OF VEGETABLES

To tell if an ear is ripe, keep a sharp eye on its size. Watch the silky threads, too, for signs of turning from light gold to brown. When an ear has grown 7–8 inches long and feels full and slightly bumpy, gently part the outside husky covering and see whether the kernels are round and fat. If they look golden and glossy and give a little when pressed, they are ripe. If small and creamy in color, leave the ear to grow. Another test is to pierce a kernel with a fingernail: pick the ear if a milky juice appears.

If the silk is dark brown when corn has reached the market, do not worry; the kernel will still be sweet, particularly if this is a supersweet hybrid (this is generally all that is available in supermarkets).

In the last few years fresh baby corn has become available, although not widely obtainable. It is grown in California, and imported from Mexico. It will keep happily for a week in the refrigerator. But again, all vegetables are best used as soon as possible, and packaged ones are no exception.

COOKING

Corn needs to be shucked (husks and silken threads stripped off). Slice away the base and boil for 6–10 minutes. Do not use salt in the water, and test the kernels by sticking the point of a knife in after the 6 minutes. When cooked, drain well in a colander and serve with melted butter, sea salt, and freshly ground black pepper. I always remember the delight of my small son when, aged five, he discovered that corn was eaten in a gorgeously messy fashion—picked up and gnawed, while butter became smeared over fingers and cheeks. This, of course, is partly why it is such a popular and satisfying food. It is eating at the trough and socially permissible. Of course, it was not always so. *Hints on Etiquette,* published in 1844 in America, lays down the law: "It is not elegant to gnaw Indian corn. The kernels should be scored with a knife, scraped off into the plate, and then eaten with a fork. Ladies should be particularly careful how they manage so ticklish a dainty, lest the exhibition rub off a little desirable romance."

In many parts of the world corn is street food, and the ears are roasted over charcoal. Certainly this is one excellent method of cooking it in the summer when the grill is alight. Ears will cook quietly at the side when other foods occupy the center. They need about 10 minutes' cooking over very hot coals, but if pushed to one side they can keep warm or cook very slowly for up to an hour.

You can also roll the ears in a flavored olive oil and broil them, turning to cook on all sides, but they need a watchful eye because they can easily burn. They can also be wrapped in foil and baked in an oven at 375°F for 20–25 minutes.

Raw or cooked, the kernels can be sliced from the cob and used for other dishes. This might seem a chore, but it takes very little time. If you are tempted to use canned or frozen corn, do make sure there is no added sugar in these products, which makes the kernels unbearably sweet.

Baby corn is perfect for many stir-fry dishes, used whole, sliced in half lengthwise, or cut in smaller pieces across. These have a delicate flavor. If you want to cook them plainly, they only need 1 minute's boiling before they are ready.

CORN PUDDING

This recipe, from the *American Heritage Cookbook,* has been handed down in the family of General Daniel Morgan, a Revolutionary War hero.

> *⅔ cup all-purpose flour*
> *3 eggs, beaten*
> *2 tablespoons butter, melted*
> *1¼ cups light cream*
> *1 teaspoon sea salt*
> *corn kernels cut from 3 cooked ears, or 1 heaped cup*
> *thawed frozen or drained canned corn kernels*

Mix the flour with the eggs to a smooth paste, then add the butter, cream, and salt. Beat vigorously and, finally, add the corn. Let the batter stand for an hour. Preheat the oven to 375°F. Pour the batter into a buttered baking dish, set in a pan of hot water, and bake for 30–40 minutes, or until the pudding has puffed up and is golden. A knife inserted in the middle should come out clean, but as with soufflés I rather prefer the center to be moist and runny.

CORN *Zea mays*

CORN OYSTERS

for 10–12

corn kernels cut from 2 cooked ears, or ¾ cup thawed
frozen or drained canned corn kernels
¼ cup cornmeal
3½ tablespoons all-purpose flour
2 eggs, beaten
½ teaspoon sea salt
freshly ground black pepper
sunflower oil for frying

In a bowl, mix the kernels with the cornmeal, flour, and eggs, then add the seasoning.

Heat the oil in a pan and fry spoonfuls of the mixture until brown on both sides.

FRIED BABY CORN WITH OKRA AND GARLIC

2 tablespoons olive oil for frying
¼ pound fresh baby corn, sliced in half lengthwise
½ pound okra, sliced lengthwise
5 garlic cloves, sliced
1 tablespoon chopped cilantro
½ lemon
sea salt

Heat the oil in a pan and throw in the corn, okra, and garlic. Fry briskly for 3 minutes or so, until the vegetables are tinged with brown. Serve on a platter sprinkled with the cilantro, lemon juice, and salt.

SUCCOTASH

⅔ cup dried navy beans, soaked and boiled until tender
corn kernels cut from 2 cooked ears, or ¾ cup thawed
frozen or drained canned corn kernels
2 tablespoons butter
2 tablespoons heavy cream
sea salt and freshly ground black pepper
a generous handful of chopped parsley and chives

Drain the navy beans and add the corn kernels, butter, and heavy cream. Simmer for a few minutes, then season and stir in the chopped fresh herbs. Serve the succotash at once.

POLENTA

1 teaspoon sea salt
1¼ cups cornmeal
½ cup grated Parmesan cheese
2 tablespoons butter

Bring 2½ cups water and the salt to a boil. Add the cornmeal to another 1¼ cups of cold water in a bowl and add to the boiling water, stirring all the time. Once it has boiled again, lower the heat and simmer for 10 minutes, stirring frequently.

Pour into a buttered loaf pan, let cool, and refrigerate for an hour or two.

Cut into ½-inch slices and place in a shallow baking dish. Sprinkle with the Parmesan, dot with the butter, and broil until golden.

THE MALLOW FAMILY

Malvaceae

This comprises a large group of flowering plants, herbs, shrubs, and trees. They include such familiar flowers as hollyhocks and hibiscus. Economically, cotton is the most important family member, but a close second in this century has to be the nuts which are an ingredient of cola drinks. Kola nuts, from *Cola nitida*, are high in caffeine and the glucoside kolanin, which is used extensively for flavoring drinks. The one vegetable of the mallow family—okra—is now a fairly common sight to us.

OKRA

Hibiscus esculentus

Okra is also known as "ladies' fingers." The multi-sided green or, rarely, purple seed pods from this annual plant may be long and slender—hence the nickname —or are sometimes shorter and more rounded in shape. Though we might associate this vegetable immediately with the American South, it originated in tropical Africa. The name okra comes from the Twi language of the Gold Coast, now Ghana, which called okra *nkurama*, while gumbo comes from the Angolan word, *ngombo* or *kingombo*, which became attached to the Creole dish in which okra is an ingredient.

Though the evidence for its existence in Ancient Egypt is slight, it was almost certainly there. A fruit called *banu*, which is fairly close to the Arabic *bamia*, is mentioned in a papyrus. Okra is now extensively cultivated in Egypt, elsewhere in Africa, and in India. From Africa it was also taken west to Brazil some time before 1658. The Spanish Moors knew okra well; we have an account of a resident in Seville who visited Egypt in 1216, and describes okra being eaten when young and tender.

The most striking quality in okra is its mucilaginous seeds. If the vegetable is cooked with liquid, the contents ooze out into a gummy thickening. In the American South this was employed in soups and stews, particularly in Creole gumbo (which can alternatively be thickened with filé powder, the dried pounded leaves of the sassafras tree, also mucilaginous). Unlike okra, filé powder cannot be cooked, even simmered, or else it makes the gumbo stringy. Gumbos can be made from various mixtures, including fish, shellfish, frogs' legs, turtle meat, chicken, or even ham, shrimp, tomatoes, and oysters; it is, in fact, not unlike the original ingredients of the *paella* or French *potage bonne femme*. Whatever is at hand is turned into a one-pot meal. A visitor to New Orleans in 1805 spoke of the quantity of shrimp eaten and added, "also a dish called gumbo. This last is made of every eatable substance and especially of those shrimp that can be caught at any time."

But there was another gumbo—called Gumbo Z'herbes—which originated in the African Congo and was introduced to New Orleans by the black slaves on the plantations. Gumbo Z'herbes was made with any green leaves, herbs, and seasonings at hand; in Louisiana, the ingredients changed to the herbs and

BELOW Okra at market

OKRA *Hibiscus esculentus*

greens sold in the French Market in New Orleans by the local Cherokee and Choctaw Indians. The Gumbo Z'herbes was traditionally served on Maundy Thursday (the Thursday before Good Friday).

NUTRITION

Okra contains generous amounts of calcium, magnesium, potassium, and phosphate; it is high in vitamin C and carotene, with traces of thiamin, riboflavin, and vitamin B6. Few of the nutrients are lost when okra is fried briskly in olive oil; more are destroyed by slower simmering in a gumbo.

CHOOSING

In temperate climates you can grow varieties of okra in a greenhouse or in favored warm spots. Pick the pods when they are 2–3 inches long.

Okra is cultivated in large quantities in the southern states of the U.S. for the canning industry. Pods are picked every few days to insure that only the smaller ones go to market: older ones tend to be tough and fibrous. I would not recommend using canned okra; it is already cooked. At a pinch it could be added to stews at the last moment. (The okra or *bhindi* curries you find in many Indian restaurants often look as if they have come out of a can and just been spiced and sauced in the kitchen.)

Fresh okra is a real treat. Choose small pods that are bright green and firm; they should be just springy when gently squeezed. Once they begin to soften, or show any brown patches, they are too old and should be dismissed. If you have to keep them for a few days, put them in the cool drawer of a refrigerator. Really fresh okra will keep there for up to a week.

PREPARING AND COOKING

Rinse okra under a tap and drain it well; you do not have to prepare it in any other way. Most food writers tell you to snip off the stem, but there is no need. It is perfectly edible. And if you do, there is a chance you may snip into the top and expose the seeds and pith. This *can* be a mistake, but it depends totally on how you are going to cook it, and whether you need

RIGHT Seafood-okra gumbo (overleaf)

the mucilaginous quality or not. On the whole, I am against vegetables that make a slimy jelly, so I am not mad about gumbo. But I do love okra.

If you want to try the taste of okra plain, simply throw it into a hot pan with a little olive oil (and a chopped clove of garlic, if you wish) and fry for a few minutes. There is nothing mucilaginous about okra cooked in this way. If you add a chopped hot chili to the oil, this makes an excellent dish of appetizers for serving to friends with cocktails. Frying also allows you to gauge whether you want the okra fairly soft or crisp on the outside. Just cook a little longer if you want the latter, which is what I prefer. You might think that it is exposing the seeds, coupled with heat, that causes the gummy juices to be exuded. But no, for you can cut the okra pods in half down the center and fry both halves; this makes the okra look very pretty once it is served.

The first time I cooked okra was in the 1950s when there was very little literature about it and none I had seen. I treated it like any other vegetable, throwing the pods into a little salted water and poaching them for about 5 minutes. At the end of this time I looked into the pan and found something fit for a horror film, a kind of mess of slime, as if rotting vegetation and frog spawn had fused. I threw it away and did not try okra again for many years. I missed a lot.

Okra needs only one or two minutes' frying. The mucilage will only seep out if you add liquid and cook longer than a few minutes. For most dishes you do not need longer.

OKRA WITH BELL PEPPERS

2 tablespoons olive oil
1 fresh hot red chili, chopped
3 garlic cloves, sliced
1 red bell pepper, seeded, cored, and sliced
1 orange bell pepper, seeded, cored, and sliced
2 or 3 tomatoes, skinned and chopped
1 pound okra
sea salt and freshly ground black pepper

Heat the olive oil, throw in the chili and garlic, and cook for a moment, then add the bell peppers. Fry them for about 5 minutes, then add the tomatoes and the okra and stir to mix. Cook for 3–4 minutes longer. Add seasoning to taste and serve.

SEAFOOD-OKRA GUMBO

for 6 to 8

I include this gumbo (from the *American Heritage Cookbook*) because these soup-stews are so closely identified with okra.

1 pound raw large shrimp in the shell
4 tablespoons butter
1 pound okra, sliced
2 onions, minced
1½ tablespoons flour
½ pound tomatoes, chopped
12 shucked oysters in their liquid
2 teaspoons sea salt
1 garlic clove, minced
a pinch of cayenne, or ¼ dried hot red chili
(or more to taste)
½ pound lump crab meat
Tabasco sauce
Worcestershire sauce
boiled rice

Peel the shrimp and sauté in half the butter for several minutes or until they turn a bright coral color.

Heat the remaining butter in a large saucepan, add the okra, and cook, stirring frequently, until tender. Stir in the onion and cook for several minutes, then stir in the flour until smooth. Add the tomatoes and stir in well, then cook the mixture for several minutes longer, still stirring.

Add enough water to the oyster liquid to make 2 quarts of liquid. Stir this into the okra mixture and add the salt, garlic, and cayenne or the chili. Leave to simmer for 1 hour. Add the shrimp, stir them in, and simmer for 5 minutes longer.

A few minutes before serving, add the oysters and cook over a low heat until the edges begin to curl. Then add the crab meat and Tabasco and Worcestershire sauces to taste and heat through. Serve the gumbo in soup plates over boiled rice.

OKRA WITH ONIONS AND EGGS

This is a Parsee dish I have adapted from one of Madhur Jaffrey's recipes.

2 tablespoons mustard oil
3–4 garlic cloves, chopped
2–3 onions, sliced
1 fresh hot green chili, minced
(pith and seeds removed for a milder taste)
1 pound okra
1 teaspoon turmeric
3–4 eggs, beaten
sea salt and freshly ground black pepper

Heat the oil and throw in the garlic, onions, chili, and okra. Sprinkle over the turmeric and cook, stirring frequently, for about 4 minutes.

Add the eggs and seasoning and let them set over the vegetables. An excellent supper dish or snack.

THE MORNING GLORY FAMILY
Convolvulaceae

This family of flowering plants includes 1,400 species widely cultivated for their colorful, funnel-shaped flowers. In my garden in Greece, the blue morning glories had an intensity of color that they seem never to have elsewhere. Plants of the family tend to be twining climbers, woody vines, and herbs. Gardeners are all too aware of bindweed, which races to stifle your favorite seedlings. The family includes one important food plant—the sweet potato.

SWEET POTATO

Ipomoea batatas

This was the first potato to be taken to Europe from the New World. Columbus encountered it in Haiti in 1492, and in 1514 Peter Martyr mentions *batatas* as being cultivated in Honduras, giving the names of nine varieties. For years there has been confusion as to which potato was originally taken to Europe, and which potato Raleigh planted in his gardens at Youghal in southern Ireland. In the portrait from the frontispiece of his *Herball* (1597), John Gerard holds the leaf and flower of the potato plant: the flower is unmistakably of the morning-glory type.

By 1526, Oviedo tells us, sweet potatoes were carried to Avila in Castile, where the Spaniards took to them with much enthusiasm. They came in three different kinds—red, yellow, and white. Within a few years they were in general cultivation in Spain, Portugal, and probably also Italy. They had also been taken from the Americas to China and the Philippines, where they were cultivated.

The sweet potato had been grown in the warmer parts of the Americas for centuries and had become a staple plant. We do not know for how long, because details of neolithic cultivation are inevitably lost to us, but the sweet potato had certainly crossed the Pacific Ocean and become established in Tahiti, the Fiji islands, and New Zealand. Unlike the coconut or the bottle gourd, the sweet potato cannot float for a long time and so be dispersed naturally by the oceans; it had to have been taken to its destination. It might have reached Polynesia when Indians in frail crafts fled the Spanish invaders, or it could have come earlier from some Indian armada of explorers, sliced and dried like taro as part of their provisions.

It is surely due to the sweet tooth of the Renaissance elite that the sweet potato became an instant success; unabashed, they added more sweetening—sugar and dried fruits—and spices to the vegetable when they cooked it, as in the pies made for Renaissance princes. Richard Hakluyt ate some sweet potatoes in 1589 and writes: "These potatoes be the most delicate rootes that may be eaten, and doe farre exceed our parseneps or carets."

Gerard writes, "The Potato roots are among the Spaniards, Italians, Indians [he was still under the impression that Columbus had discovered India], and many other nations, ordinaire and common meat; which no doubt are of mighty and nourishing parts, and doe strengthen and comfort nature; whose nutriment is as it were a mean between flesh and fruit, but somewhat windie; yet being rosted in the embers they lose much of their windinesse, especially being eaten sopped in wine.

"Of these roots may be made conserves no lesse toothsome, wholesome, and dainty, than of the flesh of Quinces; and likewise those comfortable and delicate meats called in shops, Morselli, Placentulae, and divers other such like.

"These roots may serve as a ground or foundation whereon the cunning Confectioner or Sugar-Baker may worke and frame many comfortable delicat Conserves and restorative sweet-meats.

"They are used to be eaten rosted in the ashes. Some when they be so rosted infuse and sop them in wine: and others to give them the greater prace in eating, do boile them with prunes and so eat them: likewise others dresse them (being first rosted) with oile, vinegar, and salt, every man according to his owne taste and liking. Notwithstanding howsoever they be dressed, they comfort, nourish, and strengthen the body."

Because Gerard distinguished the white potato from the sweet as the potato from Virginia, historians and botanists were confused for some time. The white potato from Peru failed to find acceptance in Europe for over 200 years, unlike the sweet. Marnette's *The Perfect Cook* (1656) includes a recipe for potato pie, obviously using sweet potato as it includes cinnamon, nutmeg, mace, grapes, and dates. It took another hundred years for the white potato to be named; in the *Oxford English Dictionary* of 1775 "sweet potato" makes its first appearance. To add to the confusion, in the U.S. and the Caribbean, the sweet potato is often called a yam, because it reminded the slaves of the vegetable they had known in Africa.

The sweet potato has an unusually high yield, four times that of rice. It tolerates poor soils and is resistant to drought, making it an important secondary crop throughout subtropical countries. However, even in the warmer climate of southern Europe it did not catch on, any more than the white potato had done. Today in Europe the sweet potato is still bought mainly by those peoples who have emigrated there from countries where it is an established part of the diet. What a lot the rest of us are missing.

NUTRITION

Sweet potatoes show markedly antioxidant properties; they lower blood cholesterol and oppose the free radicals which can ravage body cells. The darker the orange of the potato flesh, the greater the concentration of beta-carotene. The vegetable is also rich in vitamins C and E.

VARIETIES

There are hundreds of varieties spread around the world. They come in ovoid or tapering root shapes. The skin can be smooth or ribbed, pink, red, purple, brown, or yellow. The flesh, too, comes in a variety of shades from white to cream, golden, and sometimes almost a deep tangerine—the color of a pumpkin. The paler the color of the flesh, the drier and more floury it will be, so darker colors will tend to be more sweet and moist.

CHOOSING AND STORING

Feel the tubers for firmness. Check that the color looks fresh, and discard any with soft patches. Store them in a cool, dark place for a week or a little more.

COOKING

Sweet potatoes can be used for any dish or method of cooking that white potatoes are used for. But remember they are sweet, so they can be used for pies and desserts as well. If you have not tried sweet potatoes, start with simple recipes like roasting and deep-frying and see how you like the result.

Baking, for example: All the potatoes need is to be washed, pricked, and then placed on the top rack of an oven preheated to 400°F to bake for an hour. The crisp skins are delicious.

Or slice them thinly in a food processor or with a mandoline and deep-fry to make chips. These are an excellent appetizer to serve with cocktails.

RIGHT clockwise from left: Baked sweet potatoes, mashed sweet potatoes as a casserole topping, and spicy sweet potatoes (see overleaf)

Or shred them, mix them with a little chick pea flour, and fry like latkes. Or boil them, mash into a purée, and use them as a topping for a vegetable casserole. Or add an egg to the mashed potato and fry the mixture as fritters.

Julie Sahni gives a recipe for Sweet Potato Puffed Bread in her *Classic Indian Vegetarian Cooking*—a flavored poori, in fact, that sounds delicious. (My pooris never puff up so I have not tried it.) But see the African recipe below (Sweet Potato Puffs) for something similar.

In India, the sweet potato is often used in vegetable curries. These are the recipes I find most satisfying, where the sweetness of the vegetable combines beautifully with the pungent spices. Here are two examples inspired by this tradition.

SWEET POTATO PUFFS

2 or 3 sweet potatoes
¾ cup all-purpose flour
1 teaspoon baking powder
1 teaspoon sea salt
½ teaspoon ground cinnamon
½ teaspoon freshly grated nutmeg
2 eggs, beaten
sunflower oil for deep-frying

Boil the potatoes for 20 minutes, then peel and mash. Chill for an hour.

Mix together the flour, baking powder, salt, and spices. Mix the eggs with the mashed potatoes, and combine the flour and spices with the potato mixture. Beat until a stiff dough forms.

Knead the dough, then roll it out on a floured surface to about ¼-inch thickness. Cut out 3-inch disks. Deep-fry in hot oil. (Use a wok because it takes less oil than a deep-fryer.)

When they are puffed up and brown, drain on paper towels. Serve the puffs sprinkled with sugar, or instead of bread for lunch.

SPICY SWEET POTATOES

2 or 3 sweet potatoes (about 2 pounds)
2 tablespoons peanut or mustard oil
1 tablespoon mustard seeds
2 fresh hot green chilies, chopped
1 tablespoon garam masala
1 teaspoon sea salt
2 tablespoons chopped cilantro

Boil the potatoes whole in salted water for about 15 minutes. Drain and let them cool. Peel them (the skins will slip off easily) and slice them across into disks about ¼ inch thick.

Heat the oil and throw in the mustard seeds. Let them heat until they are hopping in the pan, then add the chilies and pieces of potato. Fry until the underside gets a little crisp.

Add the garam masala and salt, turning the potatoes over so that they are covered with the spices. Cook until they become crisp. Sprinkle with some cilantro and serve.

SPICY CRUMBED POTATOES

2 teaspoons hot chili powder
1 teaspoon turmeric
1 teaspoon garam masala
1 teaspoon sea salt
2 eggs, beaten
2 sweet potatoes, boiled and peeled (as above)
peanut or mustard oil for frying
⅓ cup toasted bread crumbs

Mix the spices and salt with the beaten egg. Slice the sweet potatoes thickly (as in the previous recipe), put them in a bowl, and pour the egg mixture over them. Leave for an hour.

Heat oil in a frying pan. Dip each piece of potato into the bread crumbs to cover both sides, and fry until crisp and brown.

THE ARUM FAMILY

Araceae

Nearly all this large family of climbing shrubs, herbs, and marsh plants lives in the tropics. Probably stemming from the palm family, it includes ornamental plants—philodendron, monstera, arum lily, and that spotted-leaf houseplant, dieffenbachia. The edible member of the family is taro; besides its tuberous root, the stems, shoots, and leaves became a staple food in the Pacific very early on in history.

TARO

Colocasia esculenta

These edible tubers have been eaten for certainly all of nine thousand years—for so long that, like the onion, the original wild plant has entirely disappeared. But the colocasia genus is both huge and diverse, with varieties adapted to many different growing conditions. Common names, too, have proliferated for the same or similar vegetables: *eddo* and *dasheen* are Caribbean names. All of the plant is eaten—the immature coiled leaves and the young shoots. It is thought to have originated in India, from where it traveled west, east, and south; it became the staple traveling food—taro tubers were sliced, dried, and smoked. Taro was also boiled and ground into a starchy paste called *poi,* which is fermented. Most westerners find *poi* disagreeable, likening it to sour wallpaper glue.

Today, the humid tropical lowlands of America and those of Southeast Asia have an agriculture and diet largely based on the starchy tubers, roots, and rhizomes (taro, sweet potato, yam, and arrowroot) that were first introduced from Asia. Paradoxically, a rice-growing culture has intruded and taken over from the original yam and taro cultivation in those countries of Southeast Asia that first regarded taro and its look-alikes (for they are all of different families) as a staple food.

It is puzzling that taro achieved this status, because toxic crystals of calcium oxalate lie just beneath its skin. These produce an allergic reaction, so the vegetable must be peeled under running water (or wear gloves). The toxin is rendered harmless by cooking.

Taro's early success as the staple food of one third of the world has to be explained by its ease of cultivation and its huge harvest. An experiment in 1844, in South Carolina, proved that one acre of rich, damp soil produced one thousand bushels of taro by the second year. Some enthusiasts have spoken of its distinct artichoke-heart and chestnut flavor, but I have to confess that the first taro I ate, on the island of Katatonga in the South Pacific, was extremely disappointing. This had been cooked in a pit called an *umu,* dug two feet deep into the earth or sand. This hole is filled with logs and a fire is lit which is then covered with stones. When the stones are hot the taro roots, wrapped in banana leaves, are laid in the pit on top of the meat and poultry and covered in more leaves and palm fronds. The *umu* is left for twelve hours.

I found the food overcooked and the taro very doughy and insipid. The one success of this feast—called *umukai*—was the taro leaves: they had been cooked to a purée and then mixed with minced onion and coconut milk. The islanders likened the taro leaves to spinach, but the dish was less aggressive and tasted more like Swiss chard stem.

NUTRITION

Taro is rich in thiamin (vitamin B1) and other B vitamins as well as vitamin C, potassium, and iron. Low in protein but a rich source of starch, the starch grains are easily digested, making them particularly suitable for children and invalids.

VARIETIES

Taro varieties come in all sizes, from large to small, and they are often called eddoes or dasheen. They are all barrel-shaped, dark brown, and rather shaggy on the outside. There are also very small, smooth taros shaped like a kidney and with a pinkish bud, which is its attachment to the larger, hairier taro. These are much less widely available than the larger taro. They are much favored by the Chinese and Japanese.

TARO *Colocasia esculenta*

251

STORING AND PREPARING

Store them like potatoes, in the dark and the cool, but it is not advisable to keep them for more than a couple of weeks. They should be firm to the touch. Once peeled, keep them in salted water to prevent discoloring unless you are going to cook with them at once. Use gloves when peeling to protect against any possible skin reactions.

COOKING

I prefer to boil them in their skins; once tender, the skin peels off easily. However, cooking with the skin on sometimes causes discoloring—some varieties turn gray or a dingy lilac, changing from the original raw creaminess. This does not affect flavor and hardly matters when the taro is being used in combination with other vegetables or coated with a sauce. Taro absorbs liquid as readily as legumes, so use this quality to advantage by flavoring the liquid you are cooking the taro in: use a good stock, for example, or garlic and tomato, milk and combinations of spices. Taro must also be served hot; if allowed to cool, it becomes sticky or dry and unpalatable.

Taro can be steamed or boiled; it can be chopped and added to stews where it will absorb a rich cacophony of flavors; or it can be added to vegetable soups to contribute thickness and bulk.

If steamed or boiled, taro is quite sweet and nutty, a kind of mixture of potato and water chestnut. If small and unpeeled the taro will need about 25 minutes steaming, then the skins will slip off. Boiled, the small taro need 12–15 minutes. Larger taro will need twice that amount of time, either steamed or boiled. Since it soaks up an enormous amount of fat or juice, roasting taro can be a nightmare, as it has to be continually basted as it cooks. However, deep-fried taro works wonderfully, as it crisps quickly and keeps its interior flavor and texture.

BELOW Callaloo soup

STIR-FRIED TARO WITH SHRIMP

2 tablespoons sesame oil
2 tablespoons mustard oil
2 garlic cloves, sliced
1 fresh hot red chili, chopped
3 tablespoons grated fresh gingerroot
3 small taros, peeled and thinly sliced
4 large raw shrimp, peeled
1 small glass Shaoxing wine or dry sherry
1 teaspoon each sugar and sea salt
a few thin scallions, trimmed

Heat the oils in a wok and add the garlic, chili, and ginger. Stir-fry for a moment, then add the taro. Fry for a minute or so until the oil is almost absorbed.

Throw in the shrimp and stir-fry for another minute. Add the wine, sugar, and salt and stir-fry for another minute. Serve garnished with the scallions.

TARO VEGETABLE STEW

3 tablespoons olive oil
3 garlic cloves, sliced
1 large onion, sliced
½ teaspoon asafetida
1 tablespoon oregano
2 fresh hot red chilies, whole
1 large taro, peeled and diced
1 16-ounce can crushed tomatoes
1 vegetable bouillon cube, crumbled
¼ pound small carrots, trimmed
¼ pound small leeks, trimmed
¾ cup peas (frozen will do)
sea salt and freshly ground black pepper

Heat the oil in a large saucepan and throw in the garlic, onion, asafetida, oregano, and whole chilies. Sauté for a moment before adding the taro, tomatoes and their juice, 2½ cups of water, and the bouillon cube. Bring to a boil and simmer for 15 minutes. Check that there is still some liquid; if low, add another ½ cup water. Add the carrots and leeks and simmer for another 10 minutes, then add the peas. Simmer for 3 minutes longer. Season.

TARO AND MUSHROOM FRITTERS

1 pound taro, peeled and diced
½ pound mushrooms, cleaned
1 garlic clove, minced
1 tablespoon soy sauce
1 egg, beaten
vegetable oil for frying

Boil the diced taro in plenty of water for 15 minutes, then add the mushrooms and let them steam on the top for another 15 minutes. Remove from the heat and let the vegetables cool, then drain.

Purée the mushrooms, and mash the taro with the minced garlic and soy sauce. Mix in the puréed mushrooms and beaten egg.

Fry spoonfuls of the mixture in a little oil until both sides are brown and crisp.

ELEPHANT EAR

These are the shoots that are forced from taro corms; they are, in fact, the tightly coiled leaves of the mature plant. They are a great delicacy in Asia, much as we esteem asparagus. They can be cooked in the same way—briefly poached in salted water, then drained and eaten with melted butter or hollandaise.

Alternatively, they can be lightly cooked in a spicy curried sauce. Jane Grigson gives a Nepalese recipe in her *Exotic Fruits and Vegetables*.

CALLALOO

These are the leaves of the taro plant, which are poisonous if eaten raw. In the Pacific islands, they are thoroughly boiled and then often used to wrap vegetables or meat and cooked again in an *umu*—cooking pit. Callaloo has also given its name to a Caribbean soup of salt pork, bacon, crab, shrimp, onions, and okra flavored with garlic, hot chili, lime, and coconut milk. For this the leaves are shredded and cooked with the meat and not until that is cooked until tender is the fish added. The term callaloo is also sometimes used for amaranth leaves in ethnic markets.

TARO *Colocasia esculenta*

THE YAM FAMILY

Dioscoreaceae

The yam family of vines and shrubs is indigenous to tropical and warm temperate regions. They all tend to have large roots or a network of tubers like those of a potato. Very early in history, many of them were grown for their edibility, including the Chinese yam or cinnamon vine (*Dioscorea batatas*). Others have been cultivated as ornamentals for the garden—for example, the European black bryony, which has yellow flowers and poisonous red berries. A new function has lately appeared for the yam family: *Dioscorea* provides a principal raw material that is used in the manufacture of birth-control pills.

YAM

Dioscorea spp.

Each major culture throughout the world survives on a staple food. The yam, a root that can grow to a huge size, was the staple food of Africa, and must have been one of the earliest foods to sustain the herbivore diet of primate and hominid, before that of humankind itself. As a whole we were unimaginative about the food and preparation of our diet in those six million years before the advent of fire. But sticks and flints abound to scrape, grate, and slice roots, and techniques like fermentation—burying foods so they would half-rot, so as to become more digestible—have, I am certain, a timeless pedigree.

There are 600 species of yam; they come in all shapes, sizes, and colors. Every country, almost every district, and certainly every island has its own particular favorite yam that it cultivates, harvests, and cooks. In some Pacific islands yams are venerated as nature's pantry, for they can be left in the ground to grow to an enormous size. On the Pacific island of Ponape the yams are described as "four-man" and

LEFT Yams, taro, elephant ear, and callaloo leaves

"eight-man"—or whatever the manpower needed to lift the tuber from the ground.

All of the yams were Old World plants, except one variety indigenous to America, the cush-cush or Indian yam (*Dioscorea trifida*). There is also the white yam (*Dioscorea alata*), cultivated in Africa and Asia, and the Malacca yam (*Dioscorea atropurpurea*), which is eaten in Thailand.

A source of confusion is that in the U.S. sweet potatoes are often called yams. They are nothing of the kind, of course, but when African slaves were taken to labor on Southern plantations they mistook the sweet potatoes that grew in that part of the world for the yams they had known in Africa. The two look and taste very similar, though yams do not have the sugar or vitamin C content of sweet potatoes.

Yams usually look like shaggy, brownish-black tubers. The largest we normally encounter are the size and shape of a monster zucchini, but the fingered yam (*Dioscorea olata*) looks a little like a brown mitten, and the sweet yam (*Dioscorea esculenta*) looks like a large baking potato covered with a few roots. In the East, you might find the Chinese yam (*Dioscorea batatas*), which is shaped like a club, and which has flowers that smell of cinnamon.

CHOOSING AND STORING

Yams must be hard, without cracks or any soft parts. They often seem of formidable size: 2 feet long and with a circumference of 6 inches. They store well, so it is difficult to tell how long they have been in the market. But if you buy your yams in ethnic markets, where there is a constant demand for them, what is for sale is bound to be in prime condition. Sometimes, the yams will be cut open to show how moist and creamy the interior is. If not, scrape a yam with your fingernail to see how juicy it is. You can buy yams by the piece, according to the weight you need. Yams can be stored back home at room temperature for a few weeks.

NUTRITION

Yams are nearly all starch, but they are rich in potassium, folic acid, and zinc, and vitamins B1 and 2. Potatoes have twice the vitamin C content of yams.

PREPARING

Wash the yams under a running tap, then peel thickly to remove both the skin and the layer beneath. All yams contain dioscorine, which is poisonous (though cooking completely destroys it); this lies near the peel. Cut the yam into whatever size pieces you want. If not cooking at once, keep in salted water, because yam discolors easily.

COOKING

In the countries where yams are a staple food, they are generally boiled and mashed, or peeled and roasted, or left unpeeled and roasted over an open fire or char-grill. They form the starch of the meal and are nearly always eaten with fiery sauces and spicy foods. Yam fries well, either in sticks or disks. It can also be grated and mixed with flour, yeast, and salt for breadmaking. Plainly boiled yam should be served with plenty of butter or chili sauce. Pounded yam is boiled yam beaten with a wooden spoon to let the air in and then molded into a dough, with added salt to taste. It is served, rather like biscuits, with spicy stews and soups.

A tube-shaped yam of about 3-inch circumference can be peeled, then cut into disks about ¼ inch thick, parboiled for 3 minutes, then fried in olive oil with garlic. These can then be used like artichoke bottoms with other ingredients, well-spiced, piled on top, as in the recipes for kohlrabi (see page 104). You can use yams in any of the recipes as a substitute for potatoes, sweet potatoes, or taro.

SPICY YAM SOUP

2 tablespoons mustard oil
2 tablespoons peanut oil
2 fresh hot green chilies, chopped
2 fresh hot red chilies, chopped
6 garlic cloves, chopped
2 large onions, chopped
¼ cup chopped fresh gingerroot
2 pounds yam, peeled and chopped
2 vegetable bouillon cubes, crumbled
sea salt and freshly ground black pepper
⅔ cup sour cream or buttermilk

Heat the oils in a large saucepan and throw in all the flavoring ingredients down to (and including) the ginger. Sauté for several minutes, stirring all the time. Throw in the yam, cook for another minute or two, then add 7½ cups water and the vegetable bouillon cubes. Bring to a boil and cook for 30 minutes. Season and stir in the sour cream or buttermilk.

YAM AND BELL PEPPER SALAD

*2 pounds yam, peeled and cut
into 1-inch chunks
1 each green, red, and orange bell peppers,
cored and seeded
2 red onions, sliced
12–15 pitted black olives
basil, chives, parsley, or dill, for garnish
for the vinaigrette:
1 tablespoon red wine vinegar
1 fresh hot green chili, minced
1 tablespoon Dijon mustard
⅓ cup extra virgin olive oil
1 teaspoon sea salt*

Boil the yam pieces in salted water for about 20 minutes, then drain well. Let cool.

Slice the bell peppers and place in a large bowl with the onions, then add the yams and olives.

Make the vinaigrette, pour over the salad, and toss. Leave to marinate for an hour or so.

Toss again and pile the salad on a serving dish. Garnish with any chopped fresh herbs in season.

FIERY YAM FRITTERS

*1 pound yam, peeled and chopped
2 tablespoons mustard oil
5 fresh hot chilies, chopped
5 garlic cloves, minced
1 tablespoon mustard seeds
1 tablespoon cumin
½ teaspoon asafetida
sea salt
1 egg, beaten
oil for frying*

Cook the yam pieces in boiling water for 20 – 30 minutes, then drain well and mash.

Heat the mustard oil in a pan and throw in the chilies, garlic, mustard seeds, and cumin. Cook for a moment until the chilies and garlic have browned, then sprinkle on the asafetida.

Add to the mashed yam, sprinkle with salt and mix thoroughly with the egg.

Mold into small patties and fry in hot oil until browned on each side. Excellent with a green salad.

THE LAUREL FAMILY
Lauraceae

The laurel family of flowering plants is characterized by its aromatic leaves and woody stems. Many reach great height as trees and are used for lumber, medicinal extracts, and some of the essential oils used in perfumery. Camphor, cinnamon, and cassia all come from different members of this family, which includes the bay tree (*Laurus nobilis*), a native of the Mediterranean region. The avocado is perhaps the major food plant in this family.

AVOCADO
Persea americana

Botanically the avocado counts as a fruit, like the tomato, so should not appear in this book at all. However, we eat it as a vegetable. It also contains more protein than any other fruit, and up to 25 percent fat, so it really qualifies for inclusion here.

Avocados are native to the New World, found first in Mexico. The name avocado comes from the Aztec word for it—*ahuacatl*—which is a shortened version of "testicle tree." Avocados have had a reputation for being aphrodisiac, on and off, before and since they were discovered by Columbus. A mature avocado tree, seen in the flesh, as it were, is an impressive sight, often 60 – 80 feet tall, with spreadeagled branches like a fine oak tree, but with those glossy oval leaves and pendulous fruit. A splendid example I saw in Israel reminded me more of an illuminated manuscript, a depiction of the Tree of Life; I almost expected a serpent coiled around the trunk and a nude Cranach-shaped Eve poised to offer me a fruit.

It was Oviedo, historian to Charles V, who in his report to the Emperor in 1526 first described the flesh as being similar to butter. A few hundred years later one of its names was "midshipman's butter," because avocados were taken on board ships as part of the provisions and given to junior officers. But in sixteenth-century Europe the avocado did not find favor as sweet peppers had. Though the English did plant a tree in the Botanical Gardens, Bangalore, in 1819, most of Europe ignored the avocado until the middle of this century. The problem was partly one of propagation. You do not necessarily get good fruit from a plant that has been grown from seed. Avocado trees must be propagated by budding and grafting from reliable parent trees, a fact that was only realized at the beginning of this century. This knowledge allowed the production of superior stock and the establishment of orchards producing fruit of uniform appearance, size, and quality—a necessity when commercial production is involved.

Much work in selective breeding had been done by American botanists at the end of the nineteenth century. They worked with the three distinct types: the Mexican avocado, with a thick skin, small fruits, anise-scented leaves, and a high oil content; the Guatemalan avocado, which has medium to large fruits with a thickish skin and a lower oil content; and the West Indian avocado, which will grow well only in the tropics but whose fruits will reach the size of a melon. These three spawned nearly 500 varieties.

In the market now you will find four varieties of avocado that have sold commercially—Pinkerton, Fuerte, Bacon, and Hass. The last is the small, knobbly, black avocado that gave the fruit the nickname "alligator pear." Pinkerton and Fuerte are pear-shaped and ripen early in the year. Bacon has smooth, rather thin skin and is available from late fall to early spring. The avocado is notable for staying on the tree fully grown, but not finally ripening for nine to ten

months. The Hass avocado can stay on the tree from October until the following June.

Avocados are now grown all over the world in tropical and sub-tropical countries, though they are not partial to windy conditions or too dry a climate. They thrive in Florida, California, Hawaii, Latin America, the South Pacific, Australia, South Africa, and the Canary Islands, as well as Israel and many of the Mediterranean countries.

Today Israel exports something near to 100,000 tons of avocados. The first seeds were planted in Palestine in 1895, but it was not until 1956 that Israel began to farm the fruit commercially. Growing avocados requires huge initial outlay as there is no fruit for the first six or seven years, but then trees can go on bearing for up to 80 years. In Mexico, it is not uncommon to have trees that are over 150 years old.

The tree produces its fruit once every two years. It flowers every other year because the fruit stays on the tree for so long. The avocado begins to ripen 24 hours after it is picked. It will then take four to ten days at a temperature of around 42°F to reach perfection, and be ready for eating.

The avocado butter tradition continues in all the countries where avocados are cheap and plentiful. Spread on bread or tortillas, it makes a cheap and nutritious snack, especially popular with children.

Jane Grigson tells us that the avocado had crept into very grand English grocers in the 1930s before the Second World War. But I remember it first in the 1950s. I had my first avocado in about 1955, at a restaurant where it was served peeled and fanned out on the plate with a vinaigrette sauce. This method of serving was entirely unknown then, and did not become trendy for another thirty years. I ate my first avocado soon after James Bond ate his, for in Ian Fleming's first Bond book, *Casino Royale* (1953), Bond chooses to conclude the meal with half an avocado, while his girlfriend eats the strawberries.

NUTRITION

Avocado contains some dietary fiber, a large amount of potassium, and some carotene and vitamins E, C, and B6 as well as thiamin and riboflavin. Its protein content is as high as its carbohydrate content. The fat it contains is mostly monounsaturated. The calorie content is lower than many people think.

CHOOSING AND STORING

Avocados are displayed either unripe, i.e. hard, or ripe, when they are soft and sometimes sold cheaper. The unripe ones will ripen within 4–10 days at room temperature; once that has happened the avocado will keep in the refrigerator for a few more days.

If you choose to buy a ripe avocado, first inspect it for any patches of brown or black coloration and refuse one that is not green and does not give slightly to gentle pressure. The Hass avocado (the black knobbly one) does not show any discoloration, so its softness is the only sign of ripeness. But serious errors can be made with Hass, as the skin is so thick it does not always give enough when gently squeezed. I have returned home to find, on slicing the fruit in half, that some of it is black and inedible.

PREPARING

Cut a ripe avocado in half, dig out the pit with a teaspoon, and fill the central cavity with a garlicky vinaigrette. That is the simplest, and a quite delicious, method of enjoying this fruit. But the cavity can also be used to hold shrimp, crab, or even lobster. It can also hold various salad ingredients in a tomato and chili sauce—like chopped cucumber and scallion. One can be highly imaginative and also vary the type of sauce: diced potato and sour cream is heavenly. In fact, ripe avocado flesh can be so enhanced that it becomes one of those ambrosial delights when any ingredient or flavoring that is a little sharp and acidic is added.

Avocados can also be peeled and sliced either across or lengthwise. Once this is done they must be sprinkled with lemon juice, because the flesh oxidizes quickly and starts to go black. Grind a little coarse sea salt over just before serving. It is the above

BELOW Various types of avocado

AVOCADO *Persea americana*

method of serving avocado at a party as an appetizer that I came across in Israel. It is simple but good.

Avocado flesh can also be diced and added to a vinaigrette for a green salad—the avocado pieces will coat the leaves. If you add chopped hard-boiled egg, onions, capers, and garlic croûtons, this becomes a delicious summer salad-meal. Diced avocado added to an onion and potato salad is also excellent, as are young spinach leaves and diced avocado, or apple, avocado, walnuts, and watercress. The choices are almost infinite; because avocado has 25 percent protein, these salads are sustaining and nutritious.

Purées can easily be made from the flesh once it is ripe. In this state it is a staple ingredient in a host of different sandwiches. Particularly good mixtures include avocado and arugula; avocado, onion, and dill pickle; avocado and the paprika cheese Liptauer; or avocado and any hot Indian chutney.

In Israel they scoop the flesh out of several ripe avocados, add salt, pepper, and lemon juice, mash thoroughly together, and keep in an airtight jar in the refrigerator for use as a spread. As long as there is no air in the jar, it will keep for a few days without discoloring. Avocado purée can also be mixed in with mayonnaise and used as a dip for crudités.

Soups are simplicity to make, as are sauces. The soups should be iced, and the sauces go well with fish or vegetable dishes.

COOKING

Strictly this is inappropriate, because avocados must never be cooked. But they can be served hot. The timing and the temperature are important: if the avocado begins to cook, it becomes bitter and unpleasant.

However, avocado halves can be filled with a hot sauce and placed in a hot oven for about three minutes, then served. This just gives the avocado enough time to become hot, but *not* to start cooking.

Alternatively, lay slices of avocado on hot toast, then cover with strips of mozzarella and place under a hot broiler so the cheese melts. This is particularly good as the avocado is barely warm, but one achieves a pleasing complexity of texture as well as temperature. For sparkle, first spread a tiny smear of harissa or a hot chili sauce on the toast.

ICED AVOCADO SOUP

for 6

1 large English cucumber, chopped
3 green bell peppers, cored and seeded
1 garlic clove, minced
a large handful of fresh parsley, chopped
3 ripe avocados, pitted and peeled
sea salt and white pepper
5 cups soy milk
1¼ cups buttermilk or sour cream

Blend the cucumber, bell peppers, garlic, and parsley to a thick purée in a food processor. Add the avocado flesh and blend again. Season, and add the soy milk gradually with the machine running.

Finally, stir in the buttermilk, or sour cream. The soup should have the consistency of heavy cream.

Chill in the refrigerator for a couple of hours before serving.

CHILI AVOCADO CREAM

3 tablespoons olive oil
2 fresh hot green chilies, chopped (seeds and pith removed for a milder taste)
3 ripe avocados, pitted and peeled
sea salt
⅔ cup heavy cream

Heat the olive oil in a small pan and fry the green chilies for a moment until they just brown a little, then transfer them to a blender and purée. Add the avocado flesh, salt, and cream. Blend to a thick purée.

Use as a sauce for large shrimp or poached fish, or as a dip for crudités.

GUACAMOLE

This traditional Mexican dip, to be eaten with tortilla chips, achieves the best results if you do not use a blender or food processor, and mix by hand instead.

3 ripe avocados, pitted and peeled
1 or 2 fresh hot green chilies, finely diced
3 or 4 ripe tomatoes, skinned and finely diced
grated zest and juice of 1 lime
1 garlic clove, minced
⅔ cup olive oil
2 tablespoons chopped cilantro

In a large bowl, mash the avocado flesh coarsely and add to it the chilies, tomatoes, lime zest and juice, and the garlic. Mix thoroughly.

Add the olive oil slowly, beating it into the mixture. Finally, stir in the cilantro.

STIR-FRIED AVOCADO SALAD

2 tablespoons sesame oil
2 tablespoons mustard oil
2 garlic cloves, sliced
2 fresh hot green chilies, finely diced
¼ pound baby carrots, trimmed but left whole
¼ pound baby leeks, trimmed but left whole
¼ pound broccoli florets, trimmed and separated
6 tablespoons dry sherry or vermouth
1 tablespoon soy sauce
1 teaspoon sugar
2 ripe avocados, pitted and peeled
5 crisp lettuce leaves
2 tablespoons chopped cilantro

In a wok, heat the two oils and throw in the garlic and the chili. Fry for a moment before adding the vegetables. Stir-fry the carrots, leeks, and broccoli for about a minute, then add the sherry or vermouth, soy sauce, and sugar. Stir-fry for another minute, then remove from the heat.

Slice the peeled avocado lengthwise and carefully mix in with the vegetables, so that the pieces are covered with the sauce but do not break up.

Arrange the leaves of lettuce over a platter and gently tip the wok so that the contents pile up in the center. Sprinkle with the cilantro. Serve at once, while still warm, or eat when cooled. An excellent summer lunch dish.

HOT STUFFED AVOCADO

2 tablespoons olive oil
1 fresh hot green chili, diced
1 garlic clove, chopped
¼ pound potatoes, peeled, boiled, and diced (1¾ cups)
1 can of anchovies
freshly ground black pepper
⅔ cup sour cream
2 ripe avocados, halved and pitted
½ cup grated Parmesan cheese

Preheat the oven to 375°F.

Heat the olive oil in a pan and add the chili and garlic. Fry for a moment or two, then add the diced potato and the anchovies in their oil. Move the potato around so that it is covered with the spices and the anchovy. Let it brown a little, then add black pepper. Stir in the sour cream. Remove from the heat.

Place the two halved avocados on a baking sheet and fill the cavities with the stuffing, making sure you cover all the exposed avocado flesh. Sprinkle evenly with the grated Parmesan.

Slip the baking sheet into the preheated oven to bake for 3 minutes and serve at once.

AVOCADO *Persea americana*

261

MUSHROOMS

AND

TRUFFLES

Mushrooms

CULTIVATED MUSHROOM *Agaricus bisporus*

MEADOW or FIELD MUSHROOM

Agaricus campestris

PARASOL MUSHROOM *Lepiota procera*

OYSTER MUSHROOM *Pleurotus ostreatus*

CÈPE OR PORCINI *Boletus edulis*

CHANTERELLE *Cantharellus cibarius*

GIANT PUFFBALL *Calvatia gigantea*

MOREL *Morchella esculenta*

Truffles

BLACK or PÉRIGORD TRUFFLE

Tuber melanosporum

SUMMER TRUFFLE *Tuber aestivum*

WHITE or PIEDMONT TRUFFLE *Tuber magnatum*

Mushrooms and their allies belong to a fundamentally different group from the other vegetables in this book, all of which are produced by chlorophyll-based "higher plants" that flower and fruit in their myriad ways. Modern biologists classify the fungi—which lack chlorophyll and reproduce by means of spores, not seeds—in a separate kingdom of their own, on a par with the plant and animal kingdoms.

263

MUSHROOMS

It is not surprising that a certain magical aura surrounds mushrooms and other fungi. Not only are some hallucinogenic and others poisonous, but they all appear suddenly as if from nowhere. The first writer to mention fungi is Theophrastus (c.300 BC), who describes truffles as having "neither root, stem, branch, bud, leaf, flower, nor fruit." If that is not enough, he goes on to say that neither do they have "bark, pith, fibers, nor veins." Pliny sounds more enthusiastic: "Among the most wonderful of all things is the fact that anything can spring up and live without a root." But suspicions were never entirely erased. Mushrooms were thought to be engendered by thunder and to grow where lightning struck the ground. Other explanations for the appearance of mushrooms included the supposed venom of toads, and some "evil ferment of the earth."

However, there is little doubt that various mushrooms were much enjoyed as food in Ancient Rome. Special silver vessels (*boletaria*) were designed for cooking them, and their delights were celebrated in verses and epigrams. In the last half of the second century BC, when the Sumptuary Laws came in to curb the excessive use of meat and fish at banquets, mushrooms and other edible fungi became a favorite gastronomic delicacy.

The ideas about the generation of mushrooms formed in the classical world remained throughout the Middle Ages, until, in 1679, Malpighi decided that fungi have their own "seed" and that "they can sprout from the growth of fragments of themselves." A little later, in 1707, J. P. de Tournefort discovered mycelium. "According to appearance these white threads are none other than the developed seeds, or germs of mushrooms." It was Tournefort who began the cultivation of mushrooms of the *Agaricus* genus, which includes meadow and horse mushrooms and their close relatives. His paper presented to the French Academy described the method. Ridge beds were prepared in the open from turned stable manure encased with soil and inoculated with pieces of moldy horse manure. Tournefort believed that stable manure

always carried invisible mushroom "seeds," which in a few days would reveal themselves as delicate white filaments and have "*une odeur admirable de champignon.*"

The idea crossed the Channel to London, where Philip Miller reproduces the method in his *Gardener's Dictionary* (1731). He advises that if there is a dearth of mushroom spawn, you should go out in August and September and then open the ground around mushrooms to find "white knobs which are the off-sets or young mushrooms." Stable yards would generally have a shady corner given over to the hoped-for growth of mushrooms, and the land-owning aristocracy had mushroom beds built in darkened outhouses. The whole process was an uncertain business, however, and it took until the end of the nineteenth century, when pure-culture spawn was developed in 1894, for mushroom-growing to begin to develop into a commercial industry.

In France, the disused underground limestone quarries in the Paris region became the center of mushroom cultivation in the mid-nineteenth century—hence the name *champignons de Paris*. With the patenting of the method using pure-culture spawn, France had a monopoly that enabled it to become the leading mushroom-producer for almost twenty years.

It seems somewhat astonishing that the West had not learned from the Far East long before this, for the *shiitake* mushroom (*Lentinus edodes*), which grows on the bark of logs, had been cultivated for two thousand years both in Japan and in China. In the second century BC mushroom cultivation is described in *The Pharmacopoeia of the Heavenly Husbandman*. The straw mushroom (*Volvariella volvacea*) is also widely cultivated in Southeast Asia.

Evidence of the use of mushrooms as food has been noted all around the globe, from the *Polyporus mylittae* eaten by Australian aborigines, the large *Poria cocos* made into bread by Native Americans, and the "globular, bright yellow fungus" (*Cyttaria darwinii*) noted by Darwin in 1834 growing at Tierra del Fuego, which was eaten by the natives. These and scores of other edible fungi are not cultivated, but are gathered in season in the wild. For all the sophistication of contemporary science, which has helped us understand the complex processes by which fungi grow, and the conditions and specific hosts they require, most of the prime edible species continue to resist various attempts to cultivate them. At a time when produce from all around the world appears constantly and consistently on supermarket shelves, wild mushrooms retain a degree of their ancient mystique. This is due partly to the intrinsic unpredictability of their fruiting, which depends very much on suitable weather conditions, but also not least to the fact that collectors like to preserve an aura of secrecy around their hunting grounds.

There are many thousands of different fungi—new ones are continually being discovered; and they have always had an equivocal relationship with humankind. They play a vital role as agents of decay, as one of the elements that help to maintain the earth's biosphere; they have been a source of drugs and are used commercially today in medicines. They can attack plants and decimate harvests (a fungus is responsible for the dreaded potato blight), but they also play a part in insuring the maintenance of soil fertility by breaking down organic residues.

Among those important in foodstuffs—which include the yeasts responsible for fermentation and the molds that produce cheeses—we vegetable consumers are most concerned with the "higher fungi." These are the species in which the fruiting body of the mushroom—the reproductive part of the organism, which distributes the spores (carried under the cap on the gills of the familiar "mushroom-shaped" kinds)—is large and succulent enough to be tasty, but at the same time lacking any substances that are harmful to humans.

Only a few mushrooms are poisonous or hallucinogenic; many more are tasteless or impossibly tough, and hardly worth gathering for cooking. But a few dozen are of such enormous gastronomic worth that an autumn mushroom hunt in your local woods and fields could almost be considered a necessity.

A handful of species can be cultivated and are routinely available in markets. They all have their counterparts and close relatives in the wild. The purchased one's have the virtues of availability and consistency, but their flavor sometimes verges on blandness. A reliable tactic is to use the cultivated mushrooms in bulk for texture, and to augment them with a few precious wild mushrooms—even reconstituted dried ones—for added flavor.

NUTRITION

Mushrooms contain vegetable protein, vitamins B1 to 6, phosphorus, potassium, sulfur, and folic acid.

CHOOSING

Whether your source is a supermarket, a market stall, or the fields and woodlands, select young, firm, fresh specimens with no bruising or discoloration.

It is worth investing in a couple of good field guides to help identify mushrooms picked in the wild, but never eat fungi you have gathered yourself without having their identification confirmed by an expert. In some countries pharmacists or public health officials are authorized to do this and will offer checked mushrooms for sale on market stalls.

Avoid gathering mushrooms at busy roadsides or on old mining or industrial sites, because mushrooms tend to concentrate any toxic substances such as heavy metals that occur in their vicinity.

STORING

Don't allow mushrooms to steam and sweat in a plastic bag on the way home, whether they are wild or cultivated ones: they travel best in a basket, lightly wrapped or covered. Once home, most varieties will keep in the fridge for a few days at most. Mushrooms do not freeze well in their natural state. If you have a glut—especially of wild mushrooms, which are far too precious to waste—it is best to preserve them in some way such as by drying, pickling, preserving in oil, or cooking and then freezing.

A good holding-pattern for a large haul of fresh mushrooms of any kind is to clean them and sauté them in butter and/or oil as soon as possible: even if not eaten right away, they keep better for a day or so in this state and can also be frozen.

Dried mushrooms are increasingly available, at a price. Choice slices of favorite species such as porcini, in small packages, are the most expensive, but you can buy small quantities by weight in many stores. Since their merit lies in taste rather than texture, it is

not vital to have pristine slices: the cheaper oddments taste just as good. It is worthwhile drying even scraps of any wild mushrooms that you find for this reason.

Reconstitute dried mushrooms by pouring boiling water over them and leaving them for half an hour. Use the soaking water whenever possible (for the same recipe, or save it for stock or soup); it contains a great deal of the flavor. But do strain it carefully to eliminate any grit.

DRYING YOUR OWN MUSHROOMS

Slice the mushrooms, especially fleshy ones like closed-cap meadow mushrooms and cèpes, into pieces no more than ½ inch thick. One method is to place clean newspaper over the top of a solid-fuel stove and leave the mushrooms laid out on this overnight. However, any dry heat will do—in an airing cupboard, on a wire tray over a radiator, or in a *very* low oven with the door left slightly ajar. When completely dry and shriveled, pack the mushrooms in airtight jars and make sure the lids are screwed on tightly. Dried mushrooms will keep for years.

They can be added to soups and stews as they are, but generally it is best to reconstitute them by soaking (see the method above).

PREPARING

Wipe or dust off dirt particles with a soft brush rather than washing mushrooms (you need to avoid increasing their water content). There is no need to peel most types. Cut off any stem bases that are earthy. Follow any specific instructions for individual mushroom species: some have tough stems that are best discarded, but in common mushrooms, cèpes, and chanterelles the stems are as delicious as the caps. Also note any special preparation needed to make a particular kind of mushroom palatable. Some wild kinds must be cooked because they are toxic raw; others are digestible only after blanching (and the water must be thrown away).

LEFT Cultivated mushrooms, crimini, meadow, and oyster mushrooms

COOKING

To savor the special flavors, simply frying in butter and olive oil is unbeatable. Pepper and salt are necessary; parsley, garlic, shallots, cream, and other additions are optional.

Mushrooms are largely water, which makes them tend to shrink during cooking and to exude lots of liquid—sauté briskly to avoid the risk of them stewing in their liquid and becoming tough. You can pour off the juices that seep out at the start of cooking, then add them back to the pan to evaporate when the mushrooms are sizzling merrily, or add the juices to an accompanying sauce.

Recipes involving mushrooms as fillings, sauces, and so on are virtually interchangeable, which is just as well when the occurrence of the wild varieties is so unpredictable. A small number of wild mushrooms—or a few dried ones from the pantry—can be relied on to perk up the impact of a dish in which the bulk is supplied by blander cultivated kinds.

THE CULTIVATED MUSHROOM

Agaricus bisporus

This is the mushroom that has been cultivated in Europe and America for some 150 years. It is occasionally found growing wild, and a number of close relatives—other, wild *Agaricus* species—are very similar in appearance, including the meadow or field mushroom. All are the familiar umbrella shape, white-fleshed, with pinky-beige gills when young, maturing to deep brownish-black.

In markets these come as button mushrooms or large mushrooms for stuffing. They are merely the same mushroom at different stages of growth and degrees of openness. The whole fruit-body is edible, apart from any earthy stem base.

There is no difference in flavor between the different types. All will shrink when cooked as they have a high water content. They can, alternatively, be eaten raw, or can be left to marinate in a vinaigrette and served as a salad—in my view, one of the tastiest methods of dealing with cultivated mushrooms.

The larger flat ones can be broiled or baked, gill-side upward, with a little garlic butter or oil on top. They can also be stuffed. These large mushrooms make excellent soups and sauces, too.

CRIMINI MUSHROOM: This is a form of *Agaricus bisporus* with a thicker stem, a pleasant mahogany-colored cap exterior, and richer flavor. Portobello mushrooms are the opened, mature verson of the crimini. This mushroom cooks well and if sliced through in half, stem as well, will keep its shape and look enticing in stir-fried Chinese dishes.

MEADOW or FIELD MUSHROOM

Agaricus campestris

These wild cousins of the cultivated mushroom have a wonderful flavor and aroma. Found in meadows and fields, they open to large, flat caps with very black gills when mature.

These also lose a considerable amount of moisture and so shrink when cooked. They are best fried in oil or butter with a little garlic. So excellent are they like this I could not endure to use them in any more complicated manner.

PARASOL MUSHROOM

Lepiota procera

This wild mushroom is shaped exactly like a pointed parasol or umbrella when fully grown. The cap surface is buff-colored or gray-brown with darker shaggy scales and the gills beneath are white.

The closed young parasol is completely egg-shaped. The stem grows very long and often becomes too fibrous to eat. I have seen parasols growing near me with caps a foot in diameter. Sometimes fully opened parasols have become desiccated and tough,

but before they reach this stage they are very good to eat. They can be fried, whole or sliced, in oil or butter, or dried and stored.

OYSTER MUSHROOM

Pleurotus ostreatus

This is one of the most delicious mushrooms, first noted and drawn in 1601 by the botanist Clusius as part of a collection of 86 watercolors of various mushrooms found in Austria and Hungary. Now cultivated, it is widely available (though on the expensive side). The mushrooms grow in clumps on wood. The cap, stem, and gills are all the same color—a pale buff-gray, sometimes faintly tinged with blue or pink. A yellow species is also often available on sale.

I like to tear oyster mushrooms in strips (the stems are tough, particularly in larger specimens, and must be thrown away) and to add them to stir-fry dishes. But if you are feeling extravagant, cook them as a dish by themselves, fried in sesame and olive oil, with garlic and baby corn. With good crusty bread to mop up the juices and a green salad, this makes a marvelous meal.

CÈPE or PORCINI

Boletus edulis

Known as *porcini* in Italian and *cèpe* in French, this is one of the best wild mushrooms. It grows on the ground in woods all over Europe, and is widely distributed across North America. With a rounded cap atop a stout stem, it is easily identified, as all the boletes have a mass of sponge-like tubes beneath the cap rather than gills. Fresh cèpes can be found in the fall in specialty produce markets, but much of the European crop is dried and sold commercially. Dried porcini from Italy tend to be expensive, but you need very little to achieve wonderful results. As with

RIGHT Various types of wild mushroom

oyster mushrooms, the flavor is so good it is a mistake to swamp fresh cèpes with other ingredients and flavors. They are best simply fried in butter and olive oil, with the addition of a little parsley. Jane Grigson, in *The Mushroom Feast*, gives a host of inviting recipes. Both cap and stem are delicious—only the earthy stem base needs to be trimmed away. However, except with very young cèpes, where the tubes are still firm and creamy white in color, it is often best to scrape away the spongy mass of tubes beneath the flesh of the cap: they can become unappetizingly soggy when cooked.

CHANTERELLE

Cantharellus cibarius

This is a funnel-shaped wild mushroom that is easily recognized because the gills (actually gill-like wrinkles rather than true gills) run from the underside of the cap straight into the stem, like the ribs of fan vaulting. It appears on the ground in woodland areas. The color is striking—ranging from a pale cream to deep egg-yolk yellow. The entire mushroom is edible—just discard the base of the stem. Use a soft brush to dislodge specks of dirt from between the gills and from folds in the cap. The flavor is excellent, fried in butter with chopped shallots and a little tarragon or parsley. Chanterelles can also be bought dried or dried at home, and are easily reconstituted with boiling water in the usual way.

GIANT PUFFBALL

Calvatia gigantea

By far my own favorite, this creamy-white, spherical fungus can grow larger than a football. Eventually it matures to a brown sponge-like ball that puffs out its billions of snuff-colored spores. Harvest puffballs while they are still pure white, from the size of a large grapefruit upward. The outside has a velvety texture, and the whole fruit-body should feel fairly

firm: if it feels spongy the puffball will already have gone too far. The critical test comes when you cut it open: if it is completely creamy white inside, you can eat it; if it has turned yellow deepening to a sandy buff, you should discard it.

If you catch a puffball in its prime, what a treat you have in store. Slice it like a large loaf, into pieces about ½ inch thick, and fry in olive oil and butter, with a little garlic. The pieces will shrink, but not that much; fry until just tinged with gold. I once served puffball like this as appetizers at a party and foxed everyone as to what they were.

A puffball will keep for several days even after half of it has been sliced away, if covered in with plastic wrap and kept in the refrigerator. Watch it carefully for signs of coloring: as soon as it begins to turn yellow, it becomes inedible.

MOREL

Morchella esculenta

This and other morel species are among the great edible fungi—in Scandinavia they call them the "truffles of the north." Morels are seen in the spring—March to May—and tend to grow on loose sandy soil overlying chalk. They also like burnt areas, so they can be an unexpected fruit from forest fires.

Morels are roughly conical in shape, with a deeply crinkly, sponge-like exterior. They are hollow inside, and all this convoluted shaping means that earwigs and other insects lie in their recesses. Thorough cleaning is vital. Cut the morels in two and wash quickly under a running tap, inspecting the crinkly tops and interior crevices for any persistent insect life. (Brief washing is acceptable for morels—an exception to the general rule.) Morels can be dried by threading and hanging up in a warm kitchen for a couple of days, then storing in an airtight container. To reconstitute, either soak in water for half an hour or add directly to cooking, if the dish has liquid or a sauce and will continue to cook for ten minutes.

RIGHT Wild mushroom salad (overleaf)

Recipes for morels are often quite rich; they are teamed with cream and egg yolk, sherry, and buttery pastry. Fine, if your digestion will endure it. But I prefer all my fungi done in the simplest manner; their flavors are so striking and so satisfying, they need very little added. If you feel like experimenting, try some of the morel recipes in Jane Grigson's *Mushroom Feast*, that wonderful source book on the cooking of all mushrooms.

WILD MUSHROOM SALAD

This is an excellent method of enjoying the harvest from a mushroom hunt. Choose young cèpes, chanterelles, meadow mushrooms, and parasols. Wipe them clean, discard the stem bases, and cut in half or slice thickly if large. Blanch them in boiling water and leave for 30 minutes.

Drain and dry well with paper towels, then pack the mushrooms into a glass jar and cover with extra-virgin olive oil flavored with the grated zest from a lemon and 2 smashed garlic cloves. Leave the jar in the refrigerator for one or two days.

Fill a platter with the leaves from a head of romaine lettuce, take out the fungi with a slotted spoon, and lay them on the lettuce. Sprinkle with balsamic vinegar and sea salt. (Use the olive oil that is left over for a vinaigrette.)

MUSHROOM PÂTÉ

This is best made with meadow mushrooms. If these are not available, use the flat, open cultivated kind, with a little more dried porcini or any other dried wild variety to pep up the flavor.

6 tablespoons butter
1 fresh hot red chili, seeded and minced (optional)
1 bay leaf
1 pound meadow mushrooms, chopped small
2 ounces reconstituted dried porcini,
chopped small
2 tablespoons soy sauce
2 cups fresh white bread crumbs
sea salt and freshly ground black pepper

Melt the butter in a pan and add the chili, if using, and the bay leaf, followed by the mushrooms and porcini with their soaking water. Season and put a lid on the pan. Leave to cook slowly over a gentle heat for 15–18 minutes.

Remove from the heat, and add the soy sauce, bread crumbs, and seasoning. Mix together thoroughly and leave to cool to room temperature.

Pour into a mold, smooth the surface, and cover with plastic wrap. Place something heavy (like cans of food) on top. Chill for 24 hours.

This gives you a fairly chunky texture. If you desire a smoother pâté, then purée the cooked mushrooms with their liquid in a blender before adding the bread crumbs.

PORCINI SAUCE

This sauce is wonderful served on fresh pasta, polenta, or rice.

2 ounces dried porcini
4 tablespoons butter
¼ pound cultivated mushrooms, diced (1¾ cups)
sea salt and freshly ground black pepper
3 tablespoons flour
⅔ cup white wine
1 teaspoon soy sauce
1¼ cups vegetable stock

Reconstitute the porcini by pouring enough boiling water over them to cover, and leaving them to soak for 30 minutes.

Melt half of the butter in a pan, throw in the cultivated mushrooms, and stir over a medium heat for 2 minutes. Add the porcini with their soaking water and sprinkle with a pinch of sea salt. Put the lid on the pan and let them sweat for 5 minutes. Leave to cool and then purée in a blender.

Make a roux with the remaining butter and the flour, season, and add the rest of the ingredients. Bring to a boil and allow the sauce to thicken, then add the porcini and mushroom purée, mixing it in thoroughly.

Reheat when you need the sauce.

MUSHROOM RISOTTO

You can use cultivated mushrooms for this dish, but it is best
if made with a mixture of meadow and oyster mushrooms.

4 tablespoons butter
3 tablespoons olive oil
2–3 shallots, diced
¼ pound mushrooms, chopped
⅔ cup arborio rice
a pinch of saffron strands
⅔ cup white wine
sea salt and freshly ground black pepper
1¼ cups vegetable stock
½ cup grated Parmesan cheese

Melt half the butter with the olive oil in a saucepan, add the shallots and the mushrooms, and let them cook gently for a few minutes.

Add the rice and saffron; mix thoroughly, letting the rice soak up the juices, then add the wine, seasoning, and the vegetable stock. Bring to a boil, then simmer with the lid on the pan for 8 minutes.

Remove from the heat and let stand for 5 minutes. Melt the remaining butter and stir it in with the Parmesan before serving.

FILO MUSHROOM PARCELS

Filo pastry is obliging, as long as you work quickly, and can be made into any shape you care for—a coin-purse, where the tip is pinched together, a triangular *samosa* shape, or a roll like *dolmades*.

> *2 sheets of filo pastry*
> *1 garlic clove, minced*
> *2 tablespoons olive oil*
> *1 egg, beaten*
> *1 tablespoon sesame seeds*
> for the filling:
> *2 tablespoons butter*
> *2 ounces dried porcini, reconstituted and diced*
> *½ pound cultivated mushrooms, diced*
> *1 bunch of scallions, chopped*
> *1 wineglass of red wine*
> *a pinch of ground coriander*
> *1 bay leaf*
> *sea salt and and freshly ground black pepper*
> *⅔ cup sour cream*

Preheat the oven to 400°F. Thaw the filo pastry if it is frozen.

Make the filling: melt the butter in a pan and throw in both kinds of mushrooms and the scallions with the wine, coriander, bay leaf, and seasoning. Leave, covered, on a low heat for 10 minutes, then take the lid from the pan and raise the heat to evaporate all the liquid: this should take about 2 minutes. Leave to cool, and mix in the sour cream.

Unfold the filo pastry. Mix the garlic with the olive oil and paint the sheets with the mixture. Cut the sheets into 8- × 4-inch strips.

Place a tablespoon of the mushroom mixture at the end of a strip, leaving ½ inch clear at either end, then roll up the pastry strip, tucking in the sides as you go. Continue making parcels in this way.

Place the parcels on a baking sheet, the end of the roll underneath. When all are on the baking sheet, paint each one with beaten egg and sprinkle the sesame seeds over the top.

Bake in the oven for 10 minutes or until they have puffed up a little and turned golden brown.

TRUFFLES

These are the stuff of legends. Before I had ever even heard the name, I smelled the astonishing, pervasive aroma. In the early 1950s a friend drove back from France with a truffle in a matchbox, which was in her handbag. Not only the matchbox, and the handbag too, but also the whole interior of the car smelled of the most enticing, appetizing fare—an intensity of smell that I breathed in as if it were life-saving oxygen. I inquired what it was and began to learn about truffles. It seemed to me a miracle and deeply maddening that this intensely aromatic fungus lay hidden, undetected by us, just beneath the earth. I remember that she cooked me a simple risotto with this precious object, made up of merely a little butter and chopped shallot, then some white wine, rice, and slices of the truffle. It was heaven.

Like all good things, the truffle has a long and honorable history. Theophrastus describes it as a vegetable, descended from lightning and capable of reproducing itself by seed. Plutarch ponders on its source as being a chemical reaction involving soil, water, heat, and lightning. Others believed that the truffle grew out of the sting from a fly on the root of a tree. The Romans thought that the best truffles came from Africa. Juvenal writes: "Lybians, unyoke your oxen, keep your grain, but send us your truffles." He also advises Romans to prepare them with their own hands, for truffles are far too precious to leave to the servants.

It was John Ray, in the seventeenth century, who classified the truffle as a mushroom. Later, in 1851, Edmond Tulasne (described as the founder of modern mycology) uncovered the fact that the truffle's mycelium surrounds the roots of a host tree and forms what is now known as a mycorrhizal association. (This symbiotic relationship occurs with various other mushrooms, including cèpes and chanterelles.) It was realized that truffles always grow near oaks—deciduous oaks in some areas, evergreen and cork oaks in others (in Spain, for example, where I have collected and eaten them). Since truffle and tree form a symbiotic relationship, truffles cannot be grown independently of the host.

In recent years in France, crops of oaks have been planted in soil that has been impregnated with truffle mycorrhiza, and truffles are being produced within five years.

BLACK or PÉRIGORD TRUFFLE

Tuber melanosporum

Périgord truffles are ebony-black (though the immature fungus is a deep, dark red) and knobbly, and can have a diameter anything from 1 inch to 6 inches. Truffles should be succulent, but firm. At the beginning of this century, when truffles were reasonable in cost, they were sometimes baked whole in the oven, like a potato. But like everything else, truffles vary in quality. The worst ones are innocuous and insipid, while the very best are so astonishing in their flavor that the moment you eat them remains quite unforgettable. Waverley Root tells of his experience when

BELOW Black truffle

he felt that all they had was "a faint licorice flavor"; later he saw truffles "as large as tangerines, almost black with a suggestion of purple, attractively pebbled and glistening as though they had just been oiled." When he finally eats one he is rendered almost speechless: "My mouth was flooded with what was probably the most delicious taste I have ever encountered in my entire life, simultaneously rich, subtle, and indescribable."

So do not judge black truffles by those inedible bits in canned foie gras: wait until you have a chance to buy fresh ones in a market or go on a truffle hunt and find them for yourself. In 1892, 2,000 tons of truffles were harvested, but the numbers had already declined by the beginning of the First World War—only 300 tons were collected from Périgord. Now, France produces only 25 to 150 tons annually. The season for harvesting them runs from November to March. The scent of the truffle contains the highest pheromone content of any plant (the reason why that aroma seduces one's sensibilities). The sexual stimulus is what excites the sow and the dog to dig for the object. Sows can only be used up to about seven months old, because after that they become far too strong for their handler, and the sow cannot be held back and will then eat the truffle. Terrier dogs have to be trained early on by smearing a truffle on their snouts; when they have dug down to the truffle—generally a foot or so beneath the surface—they are very quickly rewarded with a favorite food and the truffle goes into the bag.

SUMMER TRUFFLE

Tuber aestivum

This is the type of truffle that grows in Britain. It is looked for in late summer in chalk beech woods, just under the surface and occasionally just showing through. The last British truffle hunter, Alfred Collins, retired in 1930. He searched in the Winterslow area of Wiltshire, where truffles had been harvested for 300 years, with the help of two trained dogs. On a good day he could collect 25 pounds. In

story of mine published in *The London Magazine*. He invited me to tea at his seventeenth-century villa—la Pietra. The tea turned out to consist of very dry martinis and paper-thin white truffle sandwiches: an amazing combination of excellent Italian bread, unpasteurized butter, and slivers of white truffle.

My next most memorable white truffle experience was thirty-five years later, when Anton Edelmann, of the Savoy Hotel in London, cooked me a white truffle risotto, for which the truffle was as large as an apple and we shaved slivers from it ourselves.

COOKING

When cooking truffles, the rule is to keep it simple. If you are fortunate enough to find a fresh truffle, slice it, add it to a few beaten eggs, and make an omelette, or use it in a simple risotto as above, or sauté it in olive oil with onion and garlic to make a sauce for pasta.

Sometimes people pickle the white truffles in brandy and then add a few drops of the brandy in their cooking. I have tried this and found that the brandy quickly lost or killed the flavor of the truffle, but I may have used inferior truffles.

Other recipes team truffles with bacon and cook them *en croûte,* or add them to a stuffing to use for game or fowl. This seems to me to be dangerously near gilding the lily. I would prefer my truffle diced, cooked with a little garlic in some olive oil, and eaten on toast. No dish could be greater.

1920, he put the price up to two shillings and sixpence a pound—about twenty cents. His father once found a truffle weighing 2 pounds and he dutifully sent it to Queen Victoria, who replied that she would send him her portrait. Later, a single gold sovereign arrived with her image stamped upon it.

WHITE or PIEDMONT TRUFFLE

Tuber magnatum

This is the famous white truffle of Bologna and northern Italy. It is larger than the black, and many people prefer its flavor. I tasted it in the late 1950s when I was in Florence and contacted Harold Acton. I had met him once in London and he had admired a short

SOME FLAVORINGS FOR VEGETABLE COOKING

AMCHOOR

Amchoor (sometimes spelled amchur) is so wonderfully delicious I am astonished that it is not better known outside Indian cuisine. It is made from unripe mangoes dried in the sun and then finely ground to a powder. With a flavor that is of an intense, almost dark, fruitiness, it is commonly used in northern Indian vegetarian cooking as a souring agent in the same way as tamarind. Generally it is added as a dressing, after the cooking. It is also useful in marinades where it acts as a tenderizing agent: 1 teaspoon of amchoor is equivalent to 3 tablespoons of lemon or lime juice. It is available in ethnic markets, but if you can't get hold of it an appropriate amount of lime juice will give a little of its effect.

ASAFETIDA

In its original state, asafetida is a large bulbous root that grows in the Middle East—mine comes from Afghanistan. It is dried and ground to a powder for use as a flavoring. It is a very ancient spice indeed, and was much loved in the ancient world.

Its aroma is redolent of garlic that merges into an intense savoriness which can be incredibly powerful—akin to body odors. Some people find it utterly repulsive but others adore it. In fact, the world seems to be split into two camps—asafetida lovers and haters. I am of the former persuasion and believe this spice to be a huge boon to vegetarian cooking, because, in my opinion, it can lift dishes into the gourmet class.

It does, however, lose some of its strength the longer it is stored. The last batch I bought was very fresh and had the kind of smell that could clear not just a room but a football stadium. So this note is a warning: smell before buying and if you don't like the smell leave it alone. Also, if it is very fresh you will probably only need a pinch rather than a half teaspoon.

SPECIALIST SUPPLIERS

There are a lot of good companies, many of them selling seed specifically adapted to particular regions—deep South, far North, Western mountains, prairie Midwest, etc. All are listed in:
The Garden Seed Inventory, published by the non-profit Seed Savers Exchange. It lists "all non-hybrid vegetable seeds available in the U.S."—well over 6,000 varieties—and gives the mail-order sources (245 altogether) from which they can be purchased. The current edition is the 4th, available for $24.00 softcover, $30.00 hardcover, plus $4.00 shipping, from Seed Savers Exchange, 3076 North Winn Rd., Decorah, IA 52101. Phone and fax: (319) 382-5872.

ACKNOWLEDGMENTS

The Publishers would like to thank the following for supplying vegetables for photography:

Bedfordshire Growers Ltd
Charles Bransden Ltd
Clarissa Dickson-Wright
English Village Nurseries Ltd
Garson Farm
Kew Gardens
Lisdoonan Herbs
Plaxtons of Woodmansey
The Potato Marketing Board
Members of the Roehampton Garden Society
Ryton Organic Gardens
Sapphire Produce
Peter Stovold of John W. Stovold & Sons
Thames Valley Market & Salads Ltd

PICTURE ACKNOWLEDGMENTS

10 The Image Bank (Cesar Lucas); 11 The Image Bank (Steve Satushek); 27 Tony Stone Images (Michael Busselle); 31 Sutton Seeds; 36 Agence Top (Pierre Hussenot); 59 Jacqui Hurst; 68 Mise au Point (Arnaud Descat); 83 Photos Horticulture; 100 Photos Horticulture; 102 Photos Horticulture; 109 Holt Studios International (Nigel Cattlin); 114 Jacqui Hurst; 121 Robert Harding Picture Library (Nigel Blythe); 129 Eric Crichton; 149 Anthony Blake Photo Library; 183 Zefa Pictures; 217 Denis Hughes-Gilby; 235 Photos Horticulture; 239 Travelpress (Silvio Fiore); 243 Anthony Blake Photo Library; 276 Jerrican (Viard); 277 Agence Top (Jean Noel Reichel).

BIBLIOGRAPHY & LIST OF SOURCES

THE ANCIENT WORLD

Apicius, *The Roman Cookery Book*. Trans. Barbara Flower and Elisabeth Rosenbaum (Harrap 1958). For years critics complained of the proliferation of spices in the cuisine, which they thought would be bound to conflict, but few of these critics had ever tried the recipes. Then it was pointed out that there were no more spices in Apicius than in Indian cuisine. People who have followed the recipes are enthusiastic about the results.

Athenaeus, *The Deipnosophists*. 15 vols. Trans. Charles Burton Gulick (7 vols. Loeb Classical Library; London, Heinemann 1961). The original title also means "The Learned Banquet." Completed after AD 192, it is written in the symposium form, set at a banquet where philosophy, literature, law, medicine, and food are discussed. This is our main source of information on what was eaten in the ancient world. Athenaeus cites 1,250 authors, gives the titles of more than 1,000 plays, and quotes more than 10,000 lines of verse.

Cato and Varro, *On Agriculture*. 1 volume. Trans. W. D. Hooper and H. B. Ash. (Loeb Classical Library; Heinemann 1954). Cato (254–149 BC) was brought up on a farm. *On Agriculture* was written around 160 BC and deals with vine-, olive-, and fruit-growing.

Columella, *De Re Rustic*. 3 vols. Trans. Harrison B. Ash (Harvard University Press 1955). A Spaniard who served as a tribune in the Roman army in Syria about AD 60, Columella composed a treatise on farming, its livestock, fishponds, bees, and gardens. He was concerned with the decline of Italian agriculture caused by absentee landlords, the growth of enclosures, and dependence on imported food.

Dioscorides (first century AD), *Materia Medica*. Trans. M. Wellman (1907–14) now out of print. A Greek who became a physician in the Roman army, his work gives a list of drugs that are natural remedies from vegetable, animal, and mineral sources. It became the standard textbook on pharmacy for many centuries.

Herodotus, *The Persian Wars*. 4 vols. Trans. A. D. Godley. Herodotus (490–425 BC) describes the struggle between Greece and Asia from the time of the 6th century to Xerxes' retreat from Greece (478 BC). Throughout there are many observations on food and customs.

Hippocrates, *Hippocratic Corpus*. 6 vols., on medicine, disease, and diet. Hippocrates was a Greek physician born on the island of Cos about 460 BC. In this work there is much about the effect of certain foods upon the health of the body.

Horace, *Odes and Epodes*. 1 vol. Trans. C. E. Bennett. Roman poet (65–8 BC).

Horace, *Satires, Epistles, Ars Poetica*. Trans. H. R. Fairclough.

Martial, *Epigrams*. 2 vols, Trans. W. C. A. Ker (Loeb Classical Library; Heinemann 1943). The book includes a collection of elegant couplets designed to accompany gifts of food and drink, or gifts taken home from banquets.

Ovid, *Collected Works*. 6 vols. and many translators. There is much evidence that Ovid, Roman poet (43 BC–AD 17), loathed the killing of animals for food and, like Seneca, Plutarch, and others, was vegetarian. (See *The Heretic's Feast*, Colin Spencer, Univ. Press of New England, 1995.)

Palladius, author in the 4th century AD of a Latin treatise on agriculture. All translations now out of print.

Pliny, *Natural History*. 10 vols. Trans. H. Rackham, W. H. S. Jones and D. E. Eicholz (Loeb Classical Library; Heinemann 1963). A huge and comprehensive work on botany, zoology, and the medicinal properties of plants and certain foods. A fount of information.

Xenophon, 7 vols. (428–354 BC) Greek historian and disciple of Socrates. *Memorabilia, Apologia and Symposium*, while two others recount his experiences in the Persian wars, where his observation of food as part of the culture is acute.

THE MEDIEVAL WORLD

Albertus Magnus (1200–1280, canonized 1931): the teacher of St. Thomas Aquinas and the most prolific writer of his century, he was the only scholar of his age to be called "the Great." He translated Aristotle and expounded on him but did not endorse him. He wrote seven books on vegetables, *De Vegetabilibus,* and twenty-six books on animals, *De Animalbus.* These Latin works have been translated into German but not into English.

The Four Seasons of the House of Cerruti. Trans. Judith Spencer (Facts on File Publications, New York 1983). A set of 200 illuminations on herbs, fruits, crops, wild and domesticated food, with accompanying text. A vivid portrait of life in the Po Valley at the end of the fourteenth century, the text carries the tradition of Arabic medicine into Christian Europe.

The Goodman of Paris, trans. Eileen Power (Routledge 1928) *Le Ménagier de Paris*. A treatise on moral and domestic economy by a citizen of Paris that was first published in 1846, but it was written in 1393. It was a book written by a wealthy man for the instruction of his young wife. He was at least sixty and she was fifteen when she married him. He tells her how to look after wine, preserve fruits and vegetables, how to prepare water scented with sage, camomile, rosemary, or marjoram in which to wash the hands at table, how to cultivate countless vegetables, and how to cook them.

THE AGE OF DISCOVERY

Castelvetro, Giacomo, *The Fruits, Herbs and Vegetables of Italy*. Trans. Gillian Riley (Viking 1989). Beautifully illustrated, this is a fascinating text. Castelvetro found it difficult to understand the English dislike of vegetables and tried to introduce a better understanding of their cultivation and cooking.

Culpeper, Nicholas (1616–1654): a writer on astrology and medicine. *Culpeper's Complete Herbal* (Meyerbooks 1987).

Dìaz, Bernal (1492–1581): a Spanish soldier who took part in the conquest of Mexico. He wrote at the end of his life *A True History of the Conquest of New Spain*, a highly readable account which has become a sourcebook of rich information of the foods and diet of the New World.

Evelyn, John (l620–1706) *Acetaria—a discourse of Sallets* (Prospect Books 1982). A great enthusiast for the enjoyment of vegetables, his text contains much information that is applicable today and gives details of other vegetables we have almost forgotten.

Elinor Fettiplace's Receipt Book, ed. Hilary Spurling (Viking/Salamander 1986). An excellent sourcebook for understanding the cooking of the landed gentry in the Jacobean age.

Gerard, John (1545–1612): published his *Herbal* in 1597. There are many editions, one of the most recent published by Bracken Books in 1985.

Marquette, Jacques (1637–1675): French Jesuit missionary and explorer. Among his many other journeys, he was the first to travel down the Mississippi river and to report its course.

Martyr, Peter (1457–1526): Chaplain to Ferdinand and Isabella and historian to the Spanish conquests. His collection of 812 letters is valuable source material for the New World.

Muffet, also Moufet and Moffet, Thomas (1553–1604): physician and author.

Murrell, John (c.1630): writer on cookery who improved his knowledge of his art by foreign travel. Published *Two Books of Cookerie* (1638).

Tusser, Thomas (1524–1580): agricultural writer and poet, published *Hundred Good Pointes of Husbandrie* (1557).

WRITERS OF THE PAST

Acton, Eliza, *Modern Cookery* (1859). When first published it included a detailed subtitle which said that the book was for private families in which the principles of Baron Liebig have been applied—it was also 650 pages long. An abridged version, *The Best of Eliza Acton* (1974), edited by Elizabeth Ray, is available from Penguin Books.

Adam's Luxury and Eve's Cookery (Prospect Books 1983). First published in 1754, one half is a treatise on kitchen gardening, which still has useful hints for today, while the other half is a collection of recipes.

Aubrey, John (1626–1697): antiquary and writer, renowned for his acid, vivid, and intimate portraits of his contemporaries. *Brief Lives* (2 vols. 1898, edited Charles Clark.)

Beeton, Mrs., *Every Day Cookery*. There have been many editions of this book in the last 150 years which have adulterated the original text in a misguided effort to bring it up to date. It began as recipes and housekeeping ideas sent in by readers of Samuel Beeton's *The Englishwoman's Domestic Magazine*, a monthly started in 1852. His young wife then compiled these into a book under her name. The original edition and others from the nineteenth century are invaluable in providing a picture of the Victorian domestic scene.

Boulestin, Marcel, *Simple French Cookery for English Homes* (Heinemann 1924). Elizabeth David praised Boulestin for his taste in the manner by which he brought French cooking to England.

Dallas, E. S., *Kettner's Book of the Table, a Manual of Cookery, Practical, Theoretical, Historical* (Centaur Press 1968). First published in 1877, this is a scholarly encyclopaedia of gastronomy, which blends historical research and literary allusions with wit and anecdotes, telling us much about the taste and cuisine of the 1870s.

Glasse, Hannah, *The Art of Cookery Made Plain and Easy* (1747, Prospect Books 1983, a facsimile of the first edition). The best-known English cookbook of the eighteenth century, enjoying continuous popularity from the time of its first publication.

Grieve, Mrs. M., *A Modern Herbal* (Penguin Books). First published in 1931, with an introduction by Mrs. Leyel of Culpeper's, this is a marvelous collection of arcane knowledge, remedies, and recipes. A sourcebook for all herbalists and wild-food lovers, which gives some understanding of how the majority of humankind gathered food and healed themselves since time immemorial.

The Ladies Companion (1753) was a cookbook owned by Martha Washington.

Layton, T. A., *Choose Your Vegetables* (Duckworth 1963). A good guide, as lively as when it was written, packed with useful information on gardening and cooking.

Leyel, Mrs. C. F., *The Gentle Art of Cookery* (Chatto & Windus 1974). First published in 1925. Mrs. Leyel's cooking is dominated by a discriminating flair for good things. She was much admired by both Elizabeth David and Jane Grigson. Mrs. Leyel was also the founder of Culpeper's and the British Society of Herbalists.

McMahon, Bernard, *The American Gardener's Calender, adapted to the Climates and Seasons of the United States* (Philadelphia, 1806).

Miller, Philip (1691–1771): gardener to Chelsea Botanical Gardens, he discovered the method of flowering bulbous plants in bottles filled with water. Published *The Gardener's and Florist's Dictionary* (1724) and *Gardener's Kalender* (1732).

Mortimer, John (1656–1736), *The Whole art of Husbandrie* (1701, sixth edition published in 1761). A popular work.

Ray, John (1627–1705): thought of as the father of natural history in Britain, he published several volumes culminating in his *Historia Plantarum* from 1686–1704.

Sturtevant, E. L., *Edible Plants of the World* (Dover 1972). Written in the late nineteenth century, this is a scholarly comprehensive book on the edible food plants of the world. A lifetime's work that explores the origins and history of cultivated plants.

Turner, William (died 1568): Dean of Wells, physician and botanist, he published his *Herbal* in 1564, which marks the start of scientific botany in England.

CONTEMPORARY COOKBOOKS

Bareham, Lindsey. *In Praise of the Potato* (Overlook Press 1990)

Bhumichitr, Vatcharin. *Thai Vegetarian Cooking* (Crown 1991)

Boxer, Arabella. *Book of English Food* (Hodder & Stoughton 1991)

Conte, Anna del. *Secrets from an Italian Kitchen* (Corgi Books 1993)

Cost, Bruce. *Bruce Cost's Asian Ingredients* (William Morrow N.Y. 1988)

David, Elizabeth. *French Country Cooking* (Elizabeth David Classics, Knopf 1980)

Dimbleby, Josceline. *The Practically Vegetarian Cookbook* (Random House 1994)

Gray, Patience. *Honey from a Weed* (Prospect Books 1986)

Grigson, Jane. *Jane Grigson's Vegetable Book* (Michael Joseph 1978)

Holt, Geraldene. *The Gourmet Garden* (Pavilion)

Hom, Ken *Chinese Cookery* (BBC Publications 1984)

Olney, Richard. *Simple French Food* (Macmillan 1992)

Owen, Sri. *Indonesian and Thai Cookery* (Piatkus 1988)

Roden, Claudia. *A New Book of Middle Eastern Food* (Knopf 1974)

Sahni, Julie. *Classic Indian Vegetarian Cooking* (Morrow 1985)

Shaida, Margaret. *The Legendary Cuisine of Persia* (Penguin 1994)

So, Yan-kit. *Classic Food of China* (Macmillan 1992)

Spry, Constance & Hume, Rosemary. *The Constance Spry Cookery Book* (Weidenfeld & Nicolson 1971)

Willan, Anne. *French Regional Cooking* (Hutchinson 1981)

A GOOD READ

Griggs, Barbara. *The Food Factor* (Viking 1988)

Hartley, Dorothy. *Food in England* (Macdonald 1964)

Larkcom, Joy. *Oriental Vegetables* (Kodansha 1991)

Mabey, Richard. *Food for Free* (HarperCollins 1972)

McGee, Harold. *On Food and Cooking* (Simon & Schuster 1984)

Phillips, Roger. *Wild Food* (Pan Books 1983)

Root, Waverley. *Food* (Simon & Schuster)

Stobart, Tom. *The Cook's Encyclopaedia* (Batsford 1980)

Toussaint-Samat, Maguelonne. *History of Food*. Trans. Anthea Bell (Blackwell 1992)

Visser, Margaret. *Much Depends on Dinner* (Simon & Schuster 1988)